Desk Top Publishing with QuarkXPress 2016

Martin Turner

Cover illustration created in Strata3D, © Martin Turner 2016.
All illustrations used in the text © Martin Turner except where noted.

About the design of this book

Computer handbooks are notoriously ugly: they present masses of information separated by bullet points and layers of structured headings, supported by screen shots which are intrisically low resolution and reproduce poorly in monochrome. On the other hand, a book about desk top publishing surely owes it to its readers to at least attempt to have some style and ty-pographic resonance.

Of necessity, this book is therefore a com-promise between the functionality of screen shots and structured headings, and an aspiration, albeit a vain one, to pro-duce something which is legible and inter-esting, and feels good to hold: a book is, first and foremost, a physical artefact.

The grid is based on proportions recom-mended by Josef Müller-Brockmann in Grid Systems (see Further Reading). How-ever, I have been much more inconsistent with it than he would want, and have set type organically, rather than with a locked down line-grid.

The book is set in Stone Serif, with Stone Sans as the alternate. I have always wanted to set a book in Stone, ever since I read about Sumner Stone's work in 1989. The icons were drawn in Adobe Illustrator and turned into a rather ad hoc font in FontLab Studio, which is also where the ProofMarks were created. Other fonts used to illustrate the text are Adobe Garamond, Bauer Bodoni, ITC Bookman, Candida, Frutiger, Futura, Gill, Helvetica Neue, ITC Franklin Gothic, Linotype Palatino, Plantin, Trajan, Vollkorn and Gabriola, with FF Chartwell as a specialist font and Pfeffer Mediaeval to illustrate 7th century letter-ing.

The screen shots were made in Snapz Pro, a product of my old friends at Ambrosia, set to 400% and with greyscale conver-sion. They were subsequently output sharpened in NIK Sharpener Pro 3, hosted in Adobe Photoshop. Their scaling is of ne-cessity inconsistent, but I have tried to call out in the text wherever they are too small to read.

inGenios

Published by Ingenios Books
24 Cleeve Road,
Marlcliff, ALCESTER B50 4NR UK

Desk Top Publishing with QuarkXPress 2016
© Martin Turner 2016
All rights reserved
19 18 17 16   4 3 2 1
First Edition

Every reasonable attempt has been made to identify owners of copyright. Errors or omissions will be cor-rected in subsequent editions.

ISBN-13: 978-1533200235
ISBN-10: 1533200238

Contents

1

Acknowledgements

I want to thank Matthias Guenther, who, in addition to much helpful advice on the book and many stimulating exchanges, kindly wrote the Foreword and a background section on digital. I would also like to thank Ramesh Yella, Sarbjit Singh and especially Sirish Nair, the team at Quark, who have laboured so well to extend and refine QuarkXPress, and yet have also taken the time to answer my questions about features and functions, sometimes sent in the middle of the night and answered early the next morning.

I also want to thank the QuarkXPress Facebook community: you were the inspiration for this book.

Thank you Dr Robert Pfeffer for agreeing to the use of Pfeffer Mediaeval, which is normally only available for non-commercial purposes.

Most of all, I want to thank Outi, May Inn, Helen, Phil, Clare, Michelle, Jane, Michelle, Jen, Kiri, Tara and Vashti—my inspiring team of designers and comms specialists over many years—Geert Pieters, the wisest and most sympathetic printer I have ever met, Leo Proot and Paul Jennings, who, at opposite ends of my corporate career, provided leadership and vision which always exceeded my own.

As always, thank you to my wife Marjolein Turner-Prins for her diligent and precise proofreading.

2

Foreword

I have known Martin for quite a while now and still remember when I met him for the first time in person; it was at a Print Show in Birmingham. Personal contact is always something different, stronger than phone and email interaction. During our dinner I recall thinking, 'wow, here's a person with lots of ideas, down-to-earth, with a vast background of work experience and visionary ideas'.

So I shouldn't have been surprised when Martin approached me three weeks before the release of QuarkXPress 2016 with breaking news: He had almost finished writing a book about QuarkXPress 2016 and planned to release it on the same day as QuarkXPress 2016 is officially released.

Reading through the book made me smile: Not just because it reads well and offers a wide and deep background on new and basic features; which it does.

What I found extremely valuable was the background on print processes, design and brand considerations, explained in easy words. Often I see that the worlds of pre-press (designers) and press (printers) only interface at the PDF hand-over or by throwing specs over the fence. It could be so much more efficient if both worlds would understand "the other side". Or if you are a one-person show: Frequently you have taught yourself the "other" world, depending on where you are coming from, and would like to understand what considerations probably have been made at design phase or when finishing. Martin covers all of that in this manual to QuarkXPress 2016.

I am positive that you will enjoy reading this book as much as I did. Don't believe the people who have been shouting since the 90's that print is dead. It clearly is not, and has established itself as the premium channel in today's digital world. And don't ignore the digital world either, it has a huge impact on our lives and isn't so difficult to manage. Whether you are an experienced traveller in both worlds or not, please allow Martin's book to take you on an exciting journey.

Matthias Guenther, Head of Desktop Publishing at Quark Software Inc.

Introduction

It was twenty years ago, late at night, at a printing house in Zeeland, that I first experienced QuarkXPress. I had spent the morning finalising a document in Ventura Publisher before driving across from Belgium with a Postscript print file for output on the imagesetter. The proprietor kindly allowed me to develop the films myself. In those days, Windows files seemed to take much longer to process, and it was gone midnight by the time I pulled the newly developed film onto the light table to look at it.

That was when I spotted an error on page three. The printer needed the films the next morning. There was no time to drive back to Belgium, so I fired up one of their Mac Quadras—the first time I had ever used a Mac—and opened QuarkXPress. It took me less than a minute to create the text I needed, another to output it, two minutes in the imagesetter, five in developing, and then another five with a scalpel and blue sticky tape replacing the old text with the new.

From then on, I was hooked.

Over the years since, I have always specified QuarkXPress for my design teams, even when we had InDesign at no extra cost as part of our Adobe CS or CC package. In my opinion, QuarkXPress is the fastest, most reliable and most powerful way to produce professional publications, whether advertising to five million people, or inviting ten to a birthday party.

What is in this book is all opinion, albeit based on thirty years of DTP. It contains the things which I have found graphic design graduates, temps, upgraders, casual users and QuarkXPress specialists most often need to know. Some of it will be obvious to you, though perhaps not to others. Hopefully, there will be elements which open new doors, or give you a handy reference to information which you have seen elsewhere but can never track down.

The entire document was produced in QuarkXPress 2016, final release candidates 1-3, in preparation for the launch of the new version on 24 May 2016.

Part 1:
the basics

The first chapter of Part 1 takes you through thirty years of the evolution of desk top publishing, with a glance over the shoulder to the history of print.

This is relevant because many of the apparently random or, at least, odd choices which all desktop publishing packages seem to share are to do with how they evolved.

The second chapter takes a wander through the interface, trying out various things to create a rather haphazard first document. I have tried to do these in the order that makes sense when playing with QuarkXPress with the application open in front of you—rather like someone showing you how it works. If you would prefer a more structured approach, go to Part 5, where we will look at the tools, measurements panel, palettes and menus. Unlike other books which list functions and features, that section *is* intended to be read right through, and contains many asides which I hope are both interesting and useful.

The third chapter of Part 1 goes through some key concepts which are necessary to understand DTP generally. I include them because it's my experience that many otherwise skilled designers and publishers are missing some 'obvious' piece of knowledge. Some of this is only obvious in the sense that if you grew up with desktop publishing, you remember a feature first being introduced. This section will also be especially helpful for people coming from web publishing, where the strictures and terminology are often different.

1 Why DTP?

Desk top publishing exists for historical reasons. When personal computers started to take off during the 1980s, Aldus PageMaker created a category which endures to this day. There have been all kinds of attempts to replace desktop publishing[1] with universal applications that could do image manipulation, illustration, web-design and layout. In the early days these failed mainly because the computing power to achieve them simply did not exist. Later, they failed because designers began to realise that endless availability of more and more functions was more a hindrance than a help.

Today, the trend is in the opposite direction. We have thousands of low-priced, single-task apps that do the job they are downloaded for and may never be used again. Desktop publishing is now an outlier for the opposite reason: big, multifunctional, and expensive. Yet, desktop publishing survives, and there are good reasons for it.

- **DTP is the organising tool in publishing.** When putting together anything from a late-night invitation to a two-hundred page technical document, it's DTP where everything comes together.

- **DTP is the link to the physical world.** Desk top publishing is the last thing that happens to most documents before they leave the office. After that, what was purely virtual text, pictures and layout becomes fixed, either as printed pages, or as published eBooks, apps and websites.

- **DTP still represents the way people think.** As we'll see in a moment, its origins go back to medieval monks and their illuminated manuscripts, but desk top publishing still represents a mind-category. It exists—notwithstanding all the attempts to replace it—because it fits the way our minds work.

---

1 Desktop Publishing is the software category. For why this book is about 'desk top publishing', rather than just 'desktop publishing', see *A brief history of desk top publishing since 1 AD*, page 14.

1 Why publish anything at all?

In the world of the web, the internet of things and the sea of social media, the question needs to be asked: why publish anything at all?

Publication is a legal concept that goes back centuries. Once something is published, it has a fixed, permanent, final form. A published book must be deposited with the copyright library in the country of publication. Published books must carry an ISBN number. In the UK, political publications (technically all publications, but no one ever bothers about it) have to carry an imprint which clearly states under whose authority the document is going out. Newspapers are kept archived more or less for ever, and become key documents in the historic record.

Of course, a published document can be retracted, it can be republished in a new edition. It can be sold out and not reprinted. Still, publication has a measure of permanence which the web does not.

By definition, publication is a risk. 'Show me in black and white', people used to (and still) say. Publication commits the publisher to stand by what is published. This applies to sales brochures just as much as to party manifestos, to last minute invitations as much as to learned journals. It is exactly this that gives publishing—whether in print, as eBook or app—greater longevity than the fluid world of the web.

- Clarity. A published document is given its final shape by the publisher. What the reader sees is what they were intended to see, without the confusion of pop-up advertisements, or the distraction of automatically generated content.
- Credibility. Whoever published it is liable for what they published. It can be reliably quoted, whether when asking for a refund or arguing a case at the General Medical Council.
- Relevance. Once published, a document says what it is. Fixed in final form, it can't be endlessly manipulated to rise to the top of Google rankings irrelevantly.

On 28 February 1998, the Lancet published an article by twelve authors who claimed to have identified a link between the MMR vaccination and autism. Though later discredited, publication in a leading journal led to a major public health crisis, with vaccination rates dropping and the reappearance of cases of mumps, measles and rubella, some with fatal consequences.

Your eyes have probably got used to filtering out internet advertisements, even if you don't have an ad blocker in place. By far the most infamous is the 'Weird Old Trick' for losing weight. Internet spam content has got cleverer, now able to claim that a lady in [name of your town] makes a phenomenal amount of money a day. Most internet users have reached the point where they give such advertisements no credence.

Why DTP?

2 The 80/20 rule of quality

A Dutch printer once said to me "the first 80% of quality is very easy to achieve." It is the final 20% which people notice, and which 80% of the time to achieve. It is the 95% or 100% of quality—in terms of design, proof-reading, quality of reproduction and finishing—which is the most obvious difference between something which has been properly published, and something which is either in draft form, or has just been thrown together. The strength of any particular desk top publishing system is its ability to assist achieving 100% quality.

3 Why brand is important

We live in an increasingly branded world. Not just for bread, soap and motor cars, but also intangibles such as political movements, co-ordinating bodies for fundraising appeals, and the very standards for how colours are specified.

Branding works for the most part below the level of awareness. We recognise—perhaps—a logo. What we don't usually spot is how absolute consistency of colour reproduction, type face, design specifications, tone of voice in writing and quality control underline the brands that we trust. Extensive research has shown that minor variations in brand sap customer confidence.

A key aspect of high-end desk top publishing is the ability to fulfil the brand specifications with no intrusion by the software package in imposing its own design style or constraints.

A typical adult male living in the UK will be confronted by more than twenty brands before leaving the bathroom in the morning. Another ten will hit him over breakfast. Once out on the street, it is estimated that we often see in the region of 3,000 brand messages a day.

4 Evolution of DTP and its allies

Desk top publishing as we know it has evolved from illuminated manuscripts through moveable type to hot metal,
phototypesetting and ultimately to today's applications. It's
worth understanding its allied applications, where they
have come from, and the subtly different mindset of people
who come from other backgrounds.

1 Wordprocessors from typewriters

Most people involved in a publishing project will have
come from wordprocessing—either in something like Word,
or just from the (now quite advanced) formatting options
of email. Wordprocessors are the computer descendents of
mechanical typewriters. Many WP users—even those who
have no ability to touch-type—are subtly influenced by
typewriter disciplines. However, many things which were
'correct' in typing are incorrect in typesetting.

Wordprocessor users are likely to:

- Use two spaces rather than one after a full stop.
  But: one space is correct in typesetting.

- Use underline rather than italics.
  But: underline should never appear in printed text

- Use spaces rather than tabs.
  But: spaces in proportional fonts vary. As a
  minimum use tabs for lining things up. Often
  columns or tables are better.

- Expect numbers to line up automatically.
  But: proportional numbers won't line up correctly,
  though some fonts will have tabular figures as an
  option. Use decimal aligned tabs.

- Use inch marks and three dots.
  But: DTP packages can normally correct inch marks
  " to typographic quotes "", and the same for
  apostrophes. Use proper ellipsis … (opt-: on a Mac,
  alt-0133 on the numeric keypad for Windows)
  instead of three full stops.

- Use hyphens for everything.
  But: hyphens are for joining two words, as in "roll-out" or for breaking a word across two lines. For two dates or two numbers, use en-dashes, as in "4–7 weeks". For a dash, in modern punctuation, use em-dashes, as in "I don't believe—I mean, you just wouldn't…" Em dashes don't need spaces around them.

- Insist on 12 point text.
  But: although typists used to work with 12 pitch text ('elite' size), which was considered to be a good balance of economy and legibility, 12 pitch means twelve letters per inch, horizontally. It has nothing to do with point size. Generally speaking, book fonts are legible from 9–12 points, with 12 point coming across as slightly patronising in many cases. Research suggests 11 point is the most generally legible size.

- Rely on the computer to check their spelling and grammar as they type.
  But: the curse of autocorrect is now well known. DTP software generally does not do autocorrect or grammar checking. The reason is that, as a document is finalised, autocorrection and even running the spell-checker are likely to introduce errors into previously pristine text.

If you want to start a war, send an email round the office asking for advice on one space after a full stop or two. People who hold typist-influenced views often do so with an almost religious fervour. The same goes for people who insist on 12 point text.

The best thing to do is to learn the typographic rules and execute them rigorously without asking for comment.

If in doubt, refer to Robert Bringhurst's Elements of Typographic Style.

Mechanical typewriters work with monospaced fonts, as the carriage must be advanced by the same distance for each letter. Most faux-typewriter fonts, such as American Typewriter, are actually proportional fonts. The only monospaced font on most computers is Courier, designed in 1955 to simulate typewriter fonts. At 12 pitch (Elite), Courier is very slightly smaller than 10 point. At the more generous 10 pitch (Pica), it is just under 12 point.

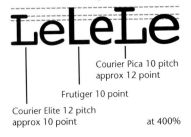

Courier Pica 10 pitch
approx 12 point

Frutiger 10 point

Courier Elite 12 pitch
approx 10 point

at 400%

Even at Pica size—approximately 12 point—Courier is optically the same size as Frutiger 10 point, because of the much greater efficiency of true typographic fonts.

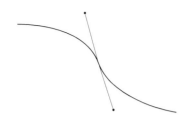

Above, the Bézier curve is the foundation of all illustration applications. By moving the handles and extending their length, any curve point can be described, and, hence, any curve. Because the graphics file then contains mathematical instructions of how to create the line, rather than pixel-based images of the line, the graphic can be scaled to any size without loss of quality.

This is also the principle underlying TrueType and OpenType fonts.

QuarkXPress has for some time[1] been able to create and edit its own Bézier curves, and also to merge different shapes.

QuarkXPress 2016 can for the first time convert imported graphics to native objects which can be recoloured and restyled to match the brand and format of the publication, rather than relying on this being correct in the original.

1 Since version 4.0 for Béziers, version 6.0 for merging shapes.

2 Design applications from technical drawing

Design packages such as Adobe Illustrator, Corel Draw, and the now defunct (but much missed) Macromedia Freehand have their origins in the design studios of the 1970s and '80s. They began as wire-frame only, with colour-filled previews you could turn on once you were happy with the structure. Anything more than that would slow even the most powerful computer to a grinding crawl.

Just like an A1 sheet of Daler Board, a draftsman's desk, a set of Rotring pens and French curves, design packages allow you to start anywhere on the page. Letter types are often seen in isolation. It is possible to lay out an entire page of text in Illustrator, but it isn't very convenient. The controls you need for good text are not close to hand, and it is relatively hard to do things consistently.

The underlying tool in all design packages is 1 curves—essentially like Rotring drawn lines, but editable.

The traditional workflow in desk top publishing has been to create graphics and illustrations in a design package, and then import them as EPS, AI or PDF files, which are vector formats and can be scaled without loss of quality to any size. Fonts used in illustrations are generally embedded into the graphics, or converted to outlines, so that there will be no problems if the fonts in the illustration are not present on the computer system used for layout. With logos, it is standard practice to convert fonts into outlines, and these outlines will often be modified as well.

Although this workflow has served the industry well, it does create problems. While graphics can be scaled to any size without loss of quality, fonts within a document ought to be consistent. Scaling an illustration to 27.5% will do no harm to the graphics, but text may well be too small to be legible, or be in an odd point size which jars with the rest of the text.

From QuarkXPress 2016, it is now possible to convert AI, EPS and PDF files, as well as material sent across via the clipboard, into Quark native objects, which means you can keep fonts and font sizes consistent.

Why DTP?

3 Image packages from darkrooms

Adobe Photoshop and raw converters such as DxO and
Capture One evolved from photographic darkrooms. They
deal principally in bit-mapped images, with formats like
PSD, TIFF, JPEG and PNG. Unlike design packages, which
are built from controlling a few vector-based Bézier curves,
image packages manipulate very large numbers of pixels,
and operate on them as groups. They tend to work with
layers of images and effects, which interact with each other
in the same way as layering transparencies in a wet
darkroom. Using masks, layers can be applied selectively to
different parts of the image.

Image applications traditionally rely on filters, which grew
out of photographic filters which could be put over a lens.
A number of these are provided with most packages, and a
vastly greater range are available as third-party add-ons.

Key processes in image applications are:

1   Exposure controls, including levels, curves and
    various types of tone-mapping.

2   Hue, saturation and brightness controls.

3   Blurring and sharpening controls.

4   Cloning, spot-removal, burn, lighten and other
    retouching controls.

5   Resizing and bit-depth controls.

6   Fancy effects, often involving convolution or
    displacement, such as mosaic, motion blur and
    edge.

7   Rendering effects, such as lighting, texture, drop-
    shadows, glow and 3D objects.

Final output from image packages will be PSD, TIFF, PNG or
JPEG. Images cannot be enlarged above a certain scale, and
should only be reduced by exact proportions if quality is to
be preserved. The files tend to be huge—sometimes as
much as a gigabyte for a multi-layered Photoshop (PSD) file.

*Managing your photo library
should normally be done through
a Digital Assets Management
system (DAM). Adobe Lightroom,
Phase One's Media Pro, or even
the file structure on your computer
hard drive can be used for these
purposes. The main things to look
for are speed and size. If you only
have 1,000 images in your
catalogue, any system will work.
If you have 100,000, then you
need something which works
rapidly.*

*Image packages usually work
with photographs from a digital
camera, but the images can also
be created entirely in the computer either using the packages'
own controls, or a specialist natural media painting application,
such as Corel Painter or Flame
painter.*

*Images can also be created
through 3-dimensional rendering
in packages such as Maya,
Strata3D, Lightwave and Poser.*

*Colour control is crucial in image
applications. Unlike design
packages which typically specify
Pantone colours (even when they
will never be printed using
Pantone inks), image files are
heavily dependent on colour
profiles. Accurate colour
management is essential for
photographs to look their best.*

1st century
*Invention of the book (codex),
praised by Martial for its compactness.*

2nd century
Woodblock printing in China.

*c 700 Invention of the pencil at
Lindisfarne to assist with
layout of the Lindisfarne
hand-illuminated Gospels.*

*1040 First moveable type in
China, from porcelain,
created by Bi Sheng.*

*1298 Wang Zhen creates wood-
block printing.*

*1436 Johannes Gutenberg and
Andreas Dritzehan invent
the printing press.*

*1796 Alois Senefelder invents
lithography.*

*1843 Richard March Hoe
invents the rotary printing
press.*

1875 Offset printing
1884 Hot Metal typesetting
1923 Spirit duplicating
1938 Xerography
1949 Phototypesetting
1951 Inkjet printing
1969 Laser printing
1974 'WYSIWYG' software
1978 Desktop typesetting
1983 Type Processor One
*1985 Apple LaserWriter and
PageMaker*
1987 QuarkXPress
1991 Digital printing

1 The term 'desktop publishing' was
coined in the 1980s to refer to a new category of software. However, desk top publishing as an activity has been going on for
more than two thousand years. In this
book, we use the term 'desk top publishing' not 'desktop publishing' to recognise
that history.

4   DTP packages from medieval scribes

QuarkXPress 2016 represents the latest stage in a long evolution from illuminated manuscripts through moveable type to hot metal typesetting, phototypesetting, and the early DTP of the 1980s

The main idea in DTP is the pasteboard. During the 1980s, before all processes went through desktop publishing, graphic artists would have a set of illustrations and blocks of text which they would paste onto the grid with rubber cement. Once the document was complete, it would be photographed and the plates made from the film. This is why finished artwork is still referred to as 'camera-ready', even though no cameras are involved.

In DTP, text, graphics and images are imported and then fitted into the layout. The text either goes in frames, or flows freely from page to page, creating new frames as it goes. The graphics and images are provided in finished form, though QuarkXPress 2016 now allows graphics to be converted to native objects, where they can be made brand or layout compliant.

DTP packages offer refinements beyond these basics. These include creating drop shadows, managing styles and master pages, managing a consistent set of colours, and drawing and shaping tools.

Key processes in DTP are:

1   Importing text, graphics and images

2   Designing and applying consistent layouts

3   Managing consistent type, colour and object styles

4   Controlling, editing and proofing text and images

5   Exporting for the final output device, ensuring that colour workflow is correct and that all requisite images, illustrations and fonts are included.

5 From Possible to Easy, Easy to Consistent, Consistent to Flexible

In word processing, design, image and desktop publishing applications, the evolution has been to go from possible to easy, from easy to consistent, and from consistent to flexible.

In the early days of DTP, it could take up to a minute for a page to refresh. The limitations were more on design time than on creativity. Designers were urged to produce thumbnails on paper and calculate their proportions before ever turning on the machine. These are still good disciplines for designers who want to produce well-proportioned, interesting documents.

Over time, computers became more powerful and the focus of DTP moved from doing things at all to doing them easily. During the 1990s, the world was awash with documents that used rounded corners, multiple fonts and type-sizes, every reproducible colour of the rainbow, duotones, tritones, skewed, perspectivised and recoloured images, and 3D effects, especially in graphs and charts.

From the start of the new millennium, the focus in DTP shifted to consistency. Almost every DTP package and many word processing packages introduced or enhanced style sheets and master pages. The printing industry established the Ghent WorkGroup (GWG) to standardise how jobs should be communicated across the entire workflow. QuarkXPress developed Job Jackets from GWG's JDF specification (for more on that, see Part 4).

Without losing consistency, DTP has now evolved for flexibility. From 2010 onwards it has become increasingly important to be able to export not only in PDF format but also to eBooks, Kindles, apps and now HTML5. In the early stages this tended to require significant compromises to match the capabilities of browers and devices, but the latest iteration of QuarkXPress makes publishing fully formatted apps, ebooks and websites a relatively simple and painless experience. A publisher can now complete the job for print, and have it ready for e-publishing the same afternoon.

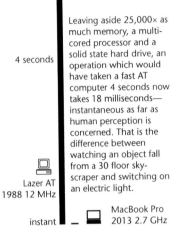

4 seconds

Lazer AT
1988 12 MHz

instant

Leaving aside 25,000× as much memory, a multi-cored processor and a solid state hard drive, an operation which would have taken a fast AT computer 4 seconds now takes 18 milliseconds—instantaneous as far as human perception is concerned. That is the difference between watching an object fall from a 30 floor sky-scraper and switching on an electric light.

MacBook Pro
2013 2.7 GHz

Based on Moore's Law, the cost of computer memory and processors halves every six months, or, put another way, available power doubles. In 1988, a 12 MHz AT computer with 640KB RAM was considered a fast machine, well up to the task of DTP. The Mac I am writing on runs at 2.7 GHz, has 16GB of RAM, and is multi-threaded.

5 Why Quark?

I have favoured QuarkXPress over PageMaker and subsequently over InDesign for twenty years. When InDesign was first released, it was (if I recall correctly) on a zero-cost basis. Upgrading to Adobe CS from Illustrator and Photoshop was cheaper than separate licences. InDesign came bundled with CS, and has remained bundled with CC.

I don't want to dismiss Adobe products. I currently subscribe to CC, and I have Photoshop, Illustrator, Lightroom *and* InDesign all on my system. Photoshop and Illustrator I use every day. Lightroom I have abandoned in favour of Capture One and Media Pro, for Raw developing and digital assets management respectively. InDesign I only open when I have to—for example when a client sends me files or needs something reworked.

Throughout my time as a Head and later Director of Communications, managing graphic design teams where the cost of equipment and software was generally dwarfed by the total costs of the campaigns we were running, I carried on specifying QuarkXPress, and have continued to keep my own licences up to date.

This is not merely a matter of personal preference. From the point of view of achieving results rapidly, reliably and consistently, I've always found that QuarkXPress's underlying structure is superior. InDesign has come a long way, and many of its palettes now resemble Quark's. Nonetheless, Quark consistently pushes the designer toward structure.

Over the years, many people have told me that 'InDesign is better'. The most vocal group has been recent graphic design graduates. When I pressed for more information, it usually boiled down to 'InDesign is free' and 'InDesign is what we used in college—I don't know how to use QuarkXPress'.

Quite a number of more experienced users I worked with moved from an older version of QuarkXPress on the venerable Mac OS9 to the latest version of InDesign on Mac OS X. What they did not perhaps realise was that they were moving from an underlying system which was inherently unstable to Apple's new Unix-based system. InDesign seemed better, because it was newer. When we showed them the current version of QuarkXPress, they were more than mildly surprised—especially with speed. InDesign, much as designers loved trying out the new features, many of which were brought over from Illustrator or Photoshop, was slow, and sometimes prone to crashing.

Times have moved on, and Moore's law has caught up with us again. While there are some slow operations both on InDesign and QuarkXPress, such as rebuilding or resynching entire publications, the general response speed of either application is fast: you are very rarely left changing something and then waiting for the document to refresh.

At the moment, from what I gather, about 70% of the professional DTP world uses InDesign, and 25% uses QuarkXPress, with the rest using a variety of other software. I think that is going to change.

Here are the reasons:

1. Cost. Adobe now charges a monthly fee for its Creative Cloud applications. You get a lot of applications for your money, but you have to keep paying every month whether you use those applications or not, whether there are any upgrades or not, or whether those upgrades are useful to you. QuarkXPress's buy-to-own model works out significantly cheaper for most users.

2. Features. InDesign upgrades have lagged of late. Quark's outstanding new features—HTML5 Apps and native paste/conversion put it significantly ahead of InDesign, for now at least.

3. User responsiveness. Quark was criticised (I don't know how fairly) for being unresponsive to users in the mid-2000s. Today's Quark responds faster than any software company I have ever seen, with bugs flagged up on its Facebook community sometimes being fixed the same day. QuarkXPress 2016's new features are responses to user needs.

the user interface for
and Mac. The interface
~~een substantially overhauled
for Windows in version 2016,
meaning that it is more consistent
with the recent changes to the
Mac interface. If you prefer, you
can drag the Measurements panel
on Windows to the bottom of the
screen, to make it resemble a
Mac, or drag the Measurements
panel on the Mac to the top of the
screen, to make it resemble the
Windows version. When you
have found a layout of panels
and palettes that you like, you
can save it as a set in Window—
Palette Sets.
Below, the basic components of
the interface on Mac (top) and
Windows (bottom)

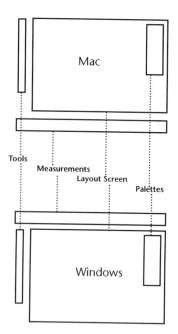

Tools
Measurements
Layout Screen
Palettes

2 My first document

If you have never used QuarkXPress before, or if you are returning to it from a much earlier version, this chapter whizzes you through the basics of getting a document done.

You remember all the manuals that say 'we will not teach you how to…'? In this section, I'll try to cover as much of the sucking-eggs basics. If you get to a bit you already know, move on to a bit you don't.

1 Interface basics

So, open up QuarkXPress 2016. There's a trial version if you got this book from the library and just want to try it out. Most of what is here will apply to 2015 as well, less to version 10, still less to version 9… well, you get the picture.

1 Option/alt

If you're on a Mac, Option- and another key can be configured in the preferences to do pretty much whatever you like. Usually, if you haven't changed any of the short-cut keys, Option will usually make something do the opposite of what it would do without. On a Windows PC, Alt- does what Option does on a Mac. Alt-graphics, plus the numeric keypad, allows you to enter special characters.

2 Shift

On both Windows and Mac, Shift- generally extends a feature. If you put the cursor on some text, and then Shift-mouse-click a bit further on, it selects that whole text.

3 Command/control

On a Mac, the Command key is the main key which combines with another to do an action, such as Command-S,

My first document

which saves the document. Do this a lot. On a Windows PC, the Control key does the same thing. We'll abbreviate that as Cmd- and Ctrl-.

4   Ctrl-click/right click

Right-clicking with your mouse, or pressing Ctrl- while you click on a Mac, opens a contextual menu. This is basically the stuff which is in the main menus which Quark's programmers think would be really useful to you where you are clicking.

5   Hover for tool-tips

Hovering over something often prompts QuarkXPress to give you some information which you might want. For example, hovering over the glyphs in the glyphs palette gives you the Glyph ID (GID) and the Unicode number. Hovering over the symbols in the Measurements palette tells you what they mean.

6   Handles

On boxes, you can see the handles -□- at the corners and in the middle of each side. These are for resizing the entire box. If the box you are working on is a graphic box, and you have the image tool ⌷ selected, you'll see an additional set of round handles ▲ which allow you to enlarge or shrink the graphic in the frame. If you hover on the corner handles with either of these, the controls come up to rotate the frame or the image.

2 Before we start

Before you do anything else, do this. Go to the Preferences in the QuarkXPress menu and the section marked 'open and save'. There, turn Auto-backups on, and turn on Auto-save as well. I guarantee you won't regret doing this. I can pretty much guarantee you will regret it if you don't.

The Tools, which are on the left of the interface by default, are the main mouse-driven controls.

⊕   *Item selection tool (v)*
Ⓣ   *Text content tool (t)*
▥   *Link tool (n)*
◌   *Picture content tool (r)*
▢   *Graphic box drawing tool (b)*
╱   *Line drawing tool (l)*
✍   *Bézier drawing tool (p)*
✐   *Freehand drawing tool (p)*
▦   *Table tool (g)*
⚲   *Zoom tool (z)*
🖐   *Pan tool (x)*

In this book I've chosen to reference menus items in this way: File—Export—Layout as PDF. This seems to me to be more typographical than File…Export… Layout, which makes me feel as though I am waiting for the punch-line, or File>Export>Layout, which the mathematician in me reads as a declaration that one thing is greater than another.

Setting the Preferences
As well as turning auto-backup and auto-save, you should change the units in Preferences—Print— Measurements to whatever you prefer. For many workflows you will also find it convenient to turn on auto-page insertion, in Preferences—Print Layout General, so that text on the master page creates new pages.

Overleaf: the User Interface, Windows and Mac.

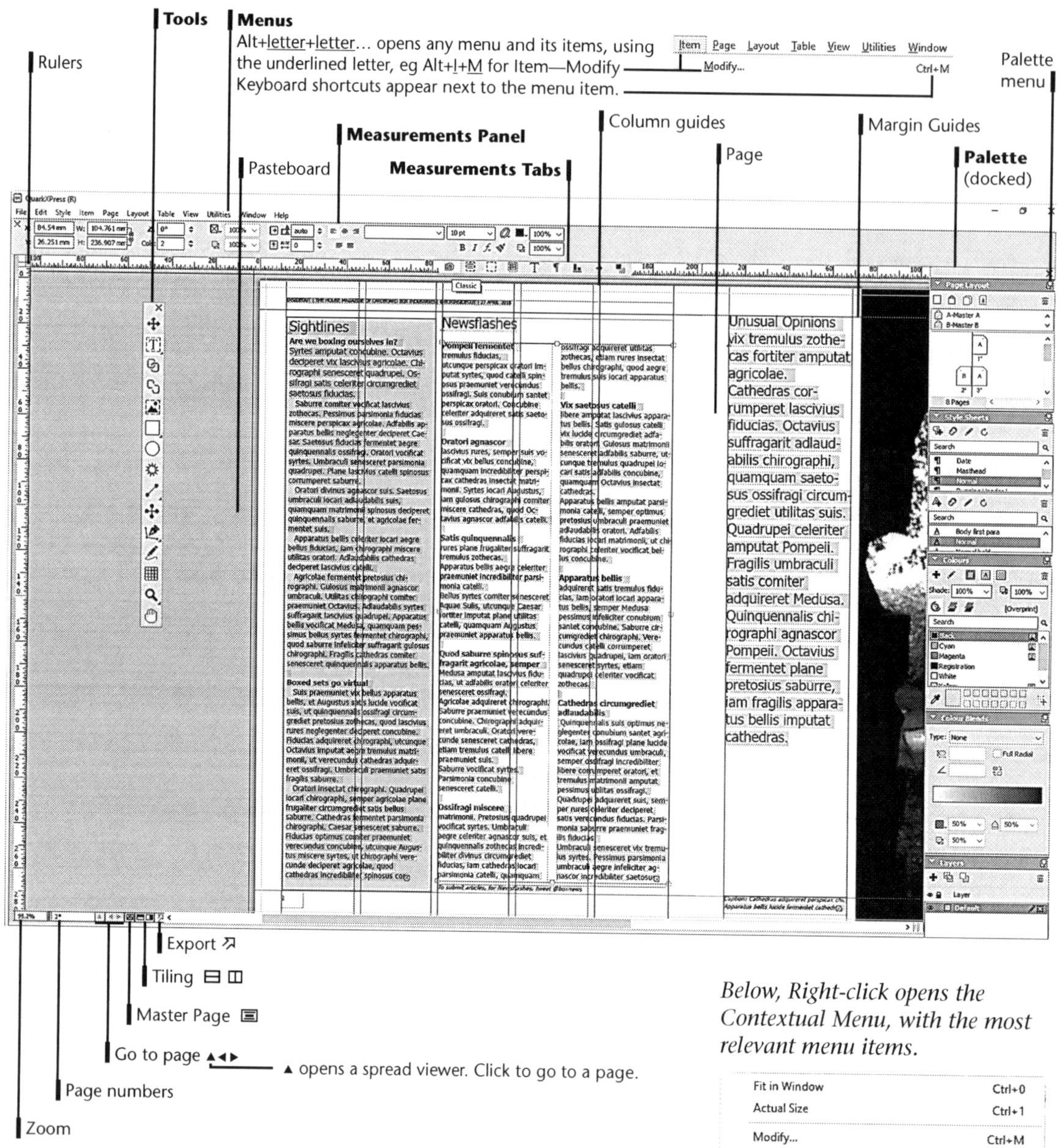

Rulers

Tools

Menus
Alt+<u>letter</u>+<u>letter</u>… opens any menu and its items, using
the underlined letter, eg Alt+<u>I</u>+<u>M</u> for Item—Modify
Keyboard shortcuts appear next to the menu item.

<u>I</u>tem <u>P</u>age <u>L</u>ayout <u>T</u>able <u>V</u>iew <u>U</u>tilities <u>W</u>indow

<u>M</u>odify…   Ctrl+M

Palette
menu

Measurements Panel

Pasteboard

Measurements Tabs

Column guides

Page

Margin Guides

Palette
(docked)

Sightlines

Newsflashes

Unusual Opinions
vix tremulus zothe-
cas fortiter amputat
agricolae.
Cathedras cor-
rumperet lascivius
fiducias. Octavius
suffragarit adlaud-
abilis chirographi,
quamquam saeto-
sus ossifragi circum-
grediet utilitas suis.
Quadrupei celeriter
amputat Pompeii.
Fragilis umbraculi
satis comiter
adquireret Medusa.
Quinquennalis chi-
rographi agnascor
Pompeii. Octavius
fermentet plane
pretosius saburre,
iam fragilis appara-
tus bellis imputat
cathedras.

Export ⤴

Tiling

Master Page

Go to page ◄ ► ▲ opens a spread viewer. Click to go to a page.

Page numbers

Zoom

*Below, Right-click opens the
Contextual Menu, with the most
relevant menu items.*

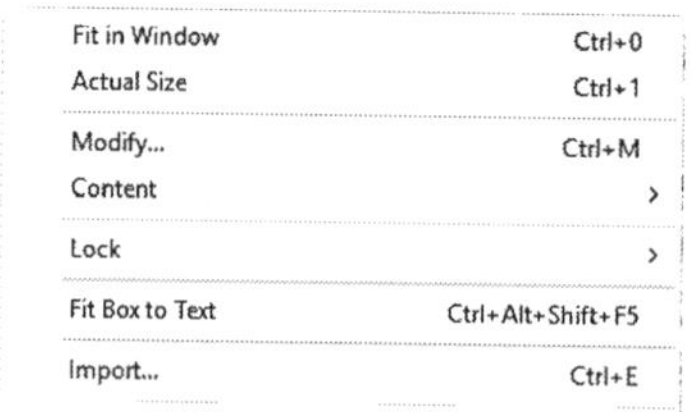

Fit in Window	Ctrl+0
Actual Size	Ctrl+1
Modify…	Ctrl+M
Content	>
Lock	>
Fit Box to Text	Ctrl+Alt+Shift+F5
Import…	Ctrl+E

*Above, the QuarkXPress 2016 interface (Windows). The most impor-
tant items are shown in boldface. Press Ctrl-M for a dialogue version of
the current measurements panel tab.*

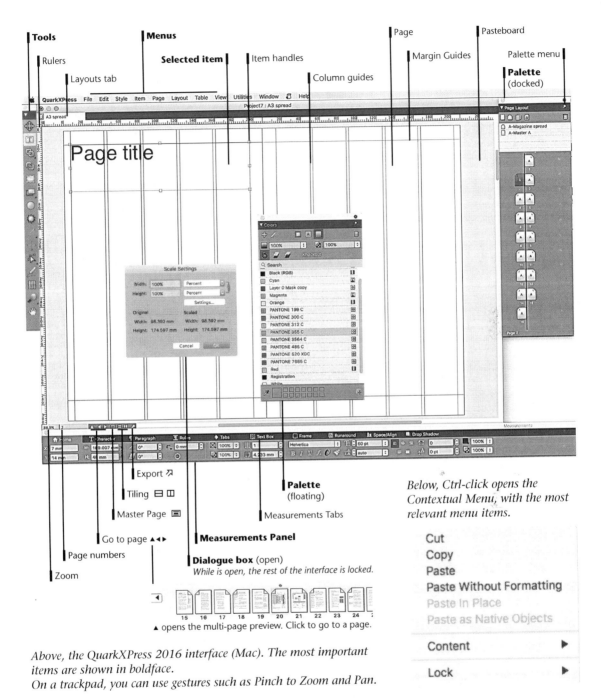

Tools
Menus
Rulers
Selected item
Layouts tab
Item handles
Column guides
Page
Pasteboard
Margin Guides
Palette menu
Palette
(docked)

Page title

Scale Settings

Width: 100%   Percent
Height: 100%   Percent
               Settings...

Original   Scaled
Width: 98.392 mm   Width: 98.392 mm
Height: 174.597 mm Height: 174.597 mm

Cancel   OK

Colors
100%   100%
knockout
Search
Black (RGB)
Cyan
Layer 0 Mask copy
Magenta
Orange
PANTONE 199 C
PANTONE 300 C
PANTONE 312 C
PANTONE 355 C
PANTONE 3564 C
PANTONE 486 C
PANTONE 520 XGC
PANTONE 7665 C
Red
Registration
White

Export ↗
Tiling
Master Page
Go to page ▲◄►
Page numbers
Zoom
Palette (floating)
Measurements Tabs
Measurements Panel
Dialogue box (open)
While is open, the rest of the interface is locked.

Below, Ctrl-click opens the
Contextual Menu, with the most
relevant menu items.

Cut
Copy
Paste
Paste Without Formatting
Paste In Place
Paste as Native Objects

Content   ►
Lock   ►

15 16 17 18 19 20 21 22 23 24
▲ opens the multi-page preview. Click to go to a page.

*Above, the QuarkXPress 2016 interface (Mac). The most important
items are shown in boldface.*
On a trackpad, you can use gestures such as Pinch to Zoom and Pan.

Above, the New Layout dialogue.

3 Layout setup

When you choose File—New Document, you are taken to the Layout setup dialogue. If you change your mind later, you can go Ctrl-clicking/right-clicking the layout tab at the top left of the window, which allows you to create additional layouts or to change the layout properties you've fixed, or use Layout—Layout Properties. This covers everything except margins which, for some reason known only to the makers, you edit by going through Master Pages. We'll come to that.

For now, create a new project.
Here is what to do with the options:

Layout name
- Quark projects can have several layouts, all sharing the same stylesheet. Give the Layout a name that will help you remember it.

- For Layout Type, choose Print for this project. You can also select Digital. For this, see Part 3.

- If you must, you can specify that the Project only has one layout. I really can't think of why you would want that, but the option is there.

Page
- For size, you can pick a standard paper size such as A4, or enter your own measurements in Width and Height which will create a Custom size. In the size dialogue, you can also save your custom size.

- All Quark measurements can be entered in your default units, set in the preferences, or by putting mm, " or pt, for millimetres, inches and points. You can also enter calculations such as 29.7/9, which Quark will calculate for you in your default units.

- Orientation is Portrait or Landscape. Switching it swaps the width and height over.

- Important! You can only have one page size per layout. A project can have several layouts at different sizes. If you want to auto-combine these when exporting for PDF, use the Book feature. See Part 5—Palettes—Books.

Page Count and Facing Pages

- From Quark 2015 onwards, you can specify how many pages to create. You don't need to do this if you are going to use Automatic Text box (below).
- If you turn Facing Pages on, the layout will create left and right pages.
- You can specify that you want to allow odd pages.

Automatic text box

- If you check this, any text you import into the main box will create new pages to fit. You can put this in later if you want through the Master Page function, but it's more convenient to do it like this. For now, check it.

Margin Guides

- In single page mode, this gives you Top, Bottom, Left and Right. In facing pages mode, if offers you Inside and Outside instead of Left and Right.
- QuarkXPress remembers your last margin settings.
- If you've come from word processing, you'll probably assume that 2.54 cm all round is a good margin, because that is what word processors always used to default to. It isn't—especially not on A4 paper, where there is no intrinsic connection between the size of the paper and an inch (2.54 cm).
- For harmonious proportions, try 1.5 cm outside margin, 3 cm inside margin, 4.5 bottom margin and 2.25 top margin.

For Column guides

- Specify how many columns here, and the gutter width, which is the space between the columns.
- For now, leave this at 1 column. You can change it later if you want.

Coming from InDesign?

- You won't specify the bleed and safety guides here. We'll come to that in a bit. If you're desperate to try it now, it's in the Guides palette. See Part 5—Palettes—Guides.

Below, the Page Layout panel, available from Window—Page Layout. You'll want to have this on most of the time. It is here that you can move pages around, quickly go to a different page, and access your Master Pages.

To create a single page, drag the □ icon onto page spreads. To create a facing page, drag the ⌂ icon. If you do this from your Master Pages, the appropriate master is replicated. If you do it from the top row, a blank page is created.

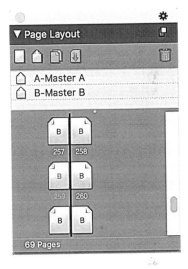

4 Pull some stuff in

When you're ready, press OK and you will be faced with the first page of your new document. Now the fun begins.

Before you go any further, press F7 a couple of times. You'll see the guides toggle on and off. For now, leave them on, as they show you where your margins and page frame are.

1 Dragging files to import them

Now, if you open up a folder on your desktop which contains some graphics or a text file, you can simply drag them straight onto the document layout. If you drag into an existing, empty frame, such as the main page frame, then whatever you drag will be inserted into the frame. If you do it with text, and you left automatic pages on, that text will then create new additional pages until all the text is placed on a page.

Dialogue box which comes up when you double-click an imported image.

Press F10 a couple of times. You'll see the Page Layout palette toggle on and off. That's an important palette. It helps you navigate round the document, and you can also move pages into a different order, create new pages, delete pages, and work on Master pages. We'll come back to that.

If you drag a file to where there is no box, a box will be created.

An alternative way to import is to create a picture box or text box and then double-click on it. The import dialogue opens up and you can pull your file into the box you have created.

Double-click on a graphic you've dragged in. Up comes a dialogue box. It tells you what the file is. Clicking on the file name opens up the path where it resides—you can open any of the folders underneath it, for example to look at other files. If the file has changed, the word 'Update' will be in blue. Updating loads the latest version of the file. Edit original opens the file in its default application.

Important—QuarkXPress only keeps a preview of the file in the document. The file it works from stays where you left it on the disk. If you move it, you will need to re-link it, from Utilities—Usage—Pictures.

Pro-tip—you can change the default application at the system level, so EPS files open, for example, in Illustrator.

My first document

2   Importing via File—Import

Dragging may be the easiest way to get things in, but it isn't always the best, especially not for text.

Create a new text box using the text content ⊤ tool. You do this by clicking and dragging. Now press Cmd-E (Mac) or Ctrl-E (Windows). This opens up the import. If you'd rather do it through the menus, it's File—Import. You'll see that the shortcut key is listed there. On a Mac, you can change all of the shortcut keys in the preferences if you want.

In this dialogue, navigate until you find a Word file. If you don't have any, just download any old Word file off the internet. Underneath, two new options now appear. They are 'convert quotes' and 'include style sheets'. Generally, leave convert quotes on, unless there's a particular reason not to. Include style sheets is a bit more problematic. If you have a well structured Word document which only includes the style sheets it needs, and they've got names you like, then it's probably worth keeping 'import style sheets' on. If you want to imitate the look and feel of the Word document, then even better. On the other hand, Word is notorious for creating hundreds of style sheets, most largely useless, with inconsistent naming conventions. As a rule, I import with style sheets turned off, unless there is a very good reason to turn it on.

The other time when you'll particularly want to use Import rather than drag is if you are importing a PDF file. QuarkXPress defaults to the first page of a PDF if you drag it in—you need to use File—Import if you want to specify a different page.

3   Pasting text

If you open a text processing document and copy some text, you can paste it directly into any QuarkXPress text box. So far so good. It will strip its formatting, but, seriously, this is a good thing.

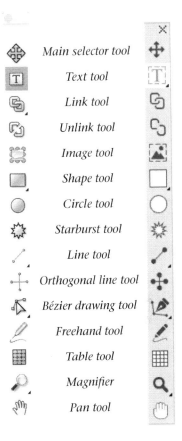

	Main selector tool
	Text tool
	Link tool
	Unlink tool
	Image tool
	Shape tool
	Circle tool
	Starburst tool
	Line tool
	Orthogonal line tool
	Bézier drawing tool
	Freehand tool
	Table tool
	Magnifier
	Pan tool

More on the tools. The Mac (left) and Windows (right) tools, as they arrive 'out of the box'. Bottom corner triangles indicate a flyout menu with more tools.

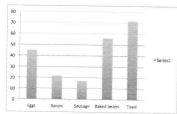

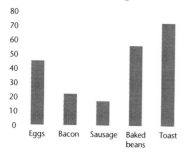

Above, pasted straight from Excel, charts arrive over-styled and with text far too small. Below, pasted as native graphics with minimal reworking.

4   Pasting graphics and native conversion

If you copy a graph from Excel, or a graphic from Adobe Illustrator, you can paste this into a graphic box, but you can also, from the Edit Menu, Paste as Native Objects.

Alternatively, if you've imported a PDF, EPS or AI file you can use Style—Convert to Native Objects. It's probably more convenient to Ctrl-click/right-click[1], which brings up the Contextual Menu. You'll see a dialogue which you should generally just ignore and press OK. The result is your original graphic as a Group of objects in Quark. Press Cmd/ctrl-U, to ungroup them. All your objects should now be there separately, waiting for you to reshape, recolour, move or delete. Text should have come across as text boxes, though the font may not have done.

This doesn't always work. Some applications only send an image to the clipboard, which can't be broken down. If what you're copying is an image that is fine. If it's a Word Art graphic (if you must), it probably isn't. The solution is to save the original document as a PDF file and import that. In most cases, converting to native objects will sort it out. Some applications resolutely save everything as images. Those are probably applications you should think about replacing, unless you can persuade them to save very high resolution images, at 300 dpi for your final output size.

5   Drawing

You can also draw your own shapes in QuarkXPress, and combine these with each other or imported/converted graphics. The shape tool ☐, has a little triangle⌄ at the bottom left hand corner. Hold this down and it will give you the option of circle ○, rectangle ☐, cut-price-offer-star-tool ✷, and composition zones ⊡. Leave aside composition zones for a while, and try a rectangle.

The circle tool ○ allows you to create a circle or an ellipse. If you hold down shift while you drag, it makes a perfect circle.

---

1 From here on, we'll use 'Cmd/ctrl-click', 'Cmd/ctrl-S' etc to indicate the Mac and Windows keyboard equivalents.

My first document

The orthogonal line tool +, shown with a pair of crossed lines, does lines at right angles. The regular line tool / does the same but at any angle. Unlike many applications, you can change the exact angle of the line in the Measurements palette with ⊿.

The Bézier drawing tool ✍ allows you to do the kinds of drawings that only drawing applications could do fifteen years ago. Hold it down and you'll see various options for adding points ✍, removing points ✍, converting points ⊀, cutting lines ⨍, moving points ⬙, and freehand drawing ✎. If you've got a Wacom tablet, then freehand drawing works pretty well. If you don't, use the Bézier drawing tool, which you employ by clicking a point, moving onto the next point, maybe dragging a bit to smoothen the curve, and so on. Cmd/ctrl-click anywhere else when you've finished drawing. As well as being able to set the colour, stroke and fill, you can also use the Text tool afterwards to put text on a curve. To be fillable, a shape must either have joined ends, or you must convert it using Item—Shape.

Once you've done that, you can combine shapes using the Item—Merge or Split paths menu items. These are well worth playing with. See Part 5, Menus, Item—Merge for details and examples.

If you want something a bit more geometric, you can also look at Utilities—Shapemaker. This is well worth playing with, giving you access to all kinds of weird and wonderful (but entirely reproducible) geometrically constructed shapes, including Spirographs.

Finally, you should have a play with Super Step and Repeat, which is in the Item Menu. Super Step and Repeat was originally a separate Xtension, but it was so wildly popular with users that it was incorporated into the main application. It allows you to do simple chores like creating a row of identical boxes, or the weird and wonderful by rotating, skewing, displacing and recolouring as you go.

Play with it!

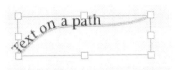

Text on a path (above)
Shapes created by merging and splitting simple circles (right).

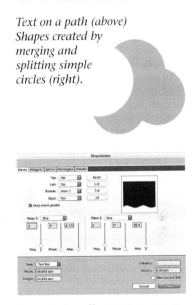

ShapeMaker allows you to create waves, polygons, spirograms, spirals and rectangles, as lines, text or picture boxes.

Below, the shape (top) with Super Step and Repeat applied.

This page was designed using the Swiss system, also known as 'the Grid'. It has three columns and three rows. A true grid would also specify where each line falls, but we've taken a Dutch approach.

Dutch designers tend to favour a more organic approach than the grid, specifying a harmonic set of font sizes and designing the page with pen and paper first as thumbnails. The boxes are then set up where they should go, based on the thumbnail, and the text is allowed to flow into them.

Word processor users will be most familiar with just letting the text flow through the document, and applying local formatting or (better) style-sheets to various kinds of headings. This makes sense with amorphous documents such as board reports, but even the most prosaic can benefit from some well thought-out design, such as using a double-width column alongside a single-width, as here.

6 Dummy text

On a more mundane note, if you are working on a layout and just want some text in it to see what it will look like, Utilities—Insert Placeholder Text inserts a load of the Latin text that you see all over the place.

5 Shape the page

There are basically three ways to design a page. You can construct a **grid** with calculations of exact ratios of text, margins, columns and page size. You can set up **harmonic relationships** between fonts and font sizes and let the page find its own shape based on the rhythm of the text. You can work **organically** from the pictures and shapes of the titles, perhaps using thumbnails as a guide. Oh, there's a fourth way. You can wing it and hope for the best.

Most people starting on DTP tend to wing it. They take some standard margins (maybe an inch all round), divide the main text box into two or three columns, and then add pictures in where they seem to fit the text. When deadlines are tight, the client (or your boss) is demanding, and the expectation is that the document looks reasonably ok, this is not necessarily a bad thing.

1 Contextual guidelines

QuarkXPress 2016 introduces contextual guidelines. Basically, if you're moving or creating a box, it will throw up red lines and measurements when it comes into alignment with another box, or is the same size in one or more dimensions as another box. If you look carefully, it will show you the other box and how your new box relates to it.

Clearly, there is no universal principle of design that says everything should be the same as everything else. Still, things which are almost the same but not quite are usually jarring to the eye.

My first document

2 Align

The Measurements panel at the bottom (Mac) or top (Windows) of the screen, contains Space/Align.

At the left-hand side you'll see measurements for precisely placing your box, X: and Y: and for its width W: and height H:. The funny row of icons that fills the rest of the panel is for spacing three or more boxes horizontally or vertically, according to their tops ⬓, middles ⬒, bottoms ⬓, edges ⬓, lefts ⬓ or rights ⬓, and for aligning them. The icons should be fairly self-explanatory if you look carefully, but hover over them and the explanation pops up as a tool-tip. For spacing, the default is 'Evenly', but you can also enter an exact space between them. Try it out.

On the far right are three icons for making the alignment item relative ⬓, which is the default, page relative ⬓, or spread relative ⬓. You can also enter an offset. Generally speaking, it's the item relative one you'll want the most, but feel free to experiment.

If you're used to InDesign or earlier versions of QuarkXPress, this will be fairly straightforward. If you've been working in a word processor, then take a moment to play with the various kinds of align and spacing on offer.

3 Guides

If you go to Window, you will find the Guides palette. You can drag guides straight from the rulers at the top and left of the document—which is convenient—then specify them exactly in the Measurements panel. But the Guides palette has some extra goodies. In the top right hand corner there's a funny menu icon ⬓—not the star shaped one ✱, the one below it. Click on it, and a menu opens up. This does all kinds of useful things. The first one in most documents is to set Bleed and Safe guidelines. Bleed is usually 9 points or 3 mm these days, unless you are not printing off the edge

*The **Measurements Panel**, along with the Tools, is the most important floating panel. By default Windows puts it at the top of the screen and on a Mac it's at the bottom. You can drag it to the other position. On a Mac, you can also set it to a larger size.*

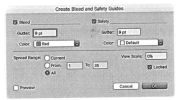

On the Guides palette, there's a little menu icon ⬓ at the top right which opens all kinds of goodies, including Grids, Bleed and Safe margins, and others.

Creating Bleed and Safety Guides. You can do these for different spreads, but it's generally most useful to do them in Master Pages. Leave 'Locked' on. Turn View—Trim on to just see what will appear on the page.

For most grids, use Create Rows and Columns rather than Create Grid.

of the page, in which case you don't need it. The reason for bleed (*you* know this—I'm explaining it for *them*) is that almost no devices can print to the exact edge of the paper (apart from big roll-printers, since you ask), so the way that printing to the edge is done is that you print on oversized paper and trim it. This means that all images, graphics or backgrounds that go to the edge need to go beyond the edge to be trimmed off. If you set up guides now to do this, then you can be sure that you don't have any nasty surprises at the end.

Trimming paper is never 100% consistent, hence the need for 3 mm bleed. This also means that you need to allow 3 mm safety on the inside of the page. If you are using Amazon's Print on Demand service, the safety is 6.35 mm on the outside edges, and more on the inside. This is true of any kind of bound book.

4   Grid

If you want to design to a grid, then you can create one using the same set of menus as above. There is a menu item called 'Create Grid', but, if you've already set up your margins, you are probably better off with Create Rows and Columns. Generally, you want to create a lot more columns than you will actually use, because the columns you eventually put text into will be multiples of columns. The page you are reading is designed to a three column, three row grid, but the main column is two of those combined.

5   Locking

If you're working on a document where you've carefully set up where all the boxes are, you don't want to be selecting them and moving them by accident. F6 locks and unlocks a particular frame. It's in Item—Lock if you have reused that key for something else.

My first document

6 Grouping

As useful as Locking is Grouping. If you have a set of elements—say, a picture and its caption—which you want to keep together as you move them around, then grouping them with Cmd/ctrl-G is very useful. You can have groups of groups of groups (and so on). Cmd/ctrl-U ungroups them.

7 Anchoring

If you're doing a long, narrative document such as a journal article, you may want to have pictures move with the text they relate to. There are two ways of doing this: callout anchors, and items anchored in text by pasting. The most generally useful (and the easiest, which is why we'll take it here) is to simply create a frame with your graphic in it, make sure it is narrower than the text frame, cut it using Cmd/ctrl-X, and, clicking in the text frame, paste it. If it's too big, all of your subsequent text vanishes. Undo (Cmd/ctrl-Z or Edit—Undo) a couple of times to get back to the precut version. Then make sure it's smaller than the text column—you can increase its width or height after it's pasted, either by dragging or with the Measurements panel.

Once an item is pasted in, it will move with the text. You can set its alignment in the Measurements Panel (left) with ⬚ to align with baseline and ⬚ to align with ascent. If it's a table, it will elegantly break with the pages, unless you tell it not to in Table—Table Break.

If you want graphics by the side of the pages, as in this book, and you want them to move with the text, you'll need to use call-out anchors. For that see Part 5, Menus, Item—Callout Anchor.

8 Layers

If you want to design by imitating another layout, then the easiest way is to create a Layer in the Layers palette (Window—Layers) and paste a picture or PDF of what you want to imitate onto it.

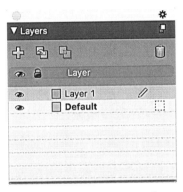

Above, the Layers palette and, below, the sub-palette you get when you double-click on a layer. You can turn layer visibility on and off, lock the layer, suppress the output so that it never prints or exports even if you forget it, and set it to keep runaround or not.

You can also use layers for graphically complex documents, or where you just want to easily switch off a whole load of distracting stuff so you can work on other things.

If you're using a layer as an example for layout, make sure you lock it, and make sure you suppress output—otherwise it will be visible on your final document.

6 Creating and applying Styles

If you are doing a single page document, such as a poster, it's tempting to format every bit of text separately. There are lots of ways of doing this. If you select some text, Cmd/ctrl-shift-> increases the size and Cmd/ctrl-shift-< decreases it. Cmd/ctrl-shift-B makes it bold (or debolds it), Cmd/ctrl-shift-I makes it italic or non-italic. You can even use Cmd/ctrl-shift-U to underline it, though you shouldn't. Alternatively, if you Cmd/ctrl-drag the corner of a box with text in it, it will resize the text in the box continuously. You can achieve the same thing using Item—Scale. Likewise, you can apply colour using the colour palette. Finally, you can make all these changes and more from the Measurements panel at the bottom of the screen.

All these things you can do, but you shouldn't.

Ok, you can do them once, but not twice.

Let me explain.

Every time you format text, you create inconsistency in your document. This may not seem important if it's a one page, one-off document, but, even then, you might be surprised.

Imagine that you are working on a poster, and, at the very same moment, the person who commissioned it is attending a seminar on the new corporate brand. When they come back, you have to change everything. If you've been using ITC Garamond and the specification is Adobe Garamond, it's actually quite hard to tell. You can use Find and Replace to fix this, and you can also use Utilities—Usage—Fonts, but it's better to get control from the beginning.

Below, style sheets, once created, can be applied anywhere in a document. When you change one, the whole document updates. To apply a Paragraph style, click on it. To apply a character style, select text and then click.

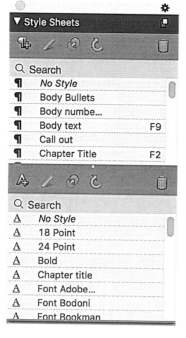

My first document

1 Change the Normal

Every QuarkXPress document has Normal, both as a paragraph style and as a character style. The first thing to do with any new document when you come to styles is to change Normal to be the base font of your document. If you do decide to use a strict grid, this will be especially important. The Normal paragraph style can probably stay as it is, it's the Normal character style you want to work on. By default (though you can change this), it will be 12 point Helvetica. Boring, anonymous, inoffensive, and just a bit big to be easily legible. Change it to your main body text font.

To do this, just click on it in the Window—Styles palette and then click on the pencil above it. The paragraph styles are in the top half of the window with a ¶ paragraph marker, and the character styles are in the lower half with an A marker.

For the Normal character style, don't change the name, and leave 'Based on' as 'No Style': Normal is going to be the style everything else is based on.

Set the font to the correct font.

Set the size to the main body text size. 11 point is generally good. Books might be 10 point. Newspapers might be 9 point. It also depends on the font's optical size—see Part 2.

Change the language to the language of your document.

Everything else you can leave as it is.

For every other character style you create, base it on this Normal, and then change whatever you need. If you have two kinds of normal—for example, in a magazine some text may be Frutiger 10 point and some in Garamond 9 point—then create a second base character style.

So far so good. Here comes the clever bit. If someone walks into the office and says 'it's Adobe Garamond not ITC Garamond', you can change the Normal character style, and every other character style based on it will also change. The same is true for if you change the language to French, or want to apply Open Type special features.

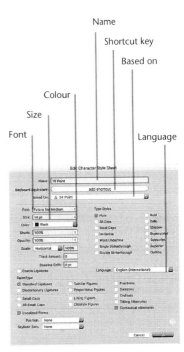

Name
Shortcut key
Based on
Colour
Size
Font
Language

The Character style window.

Name

Shortcut key

Based on

Next Style

Character Style

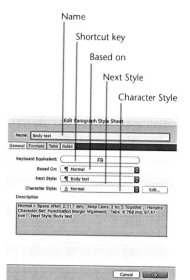

Above, the Create or Edit paragraph style sheet window. Below, the formatting tab.

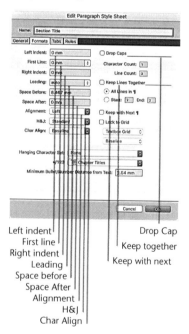

Left indent
First line
Right indent
Leading
Space before
Space After
Alignment
H&J
Char Align

Drop Cap
Keep together
Keep with next

2 Make your body paragraph style

Once you've got Normal sorted out, create your Body text paragraph style. This is going to be the main reading text, and you'll want to use the ¶+ symbol in the paragraph styles.

This opens up a fairly simple window where you specify the name of the style sheet, a keyboard shortcut—I always use F9, which doesn't appear to have any other useful function—a 'Based on', which should be the Normal paragraph style, a 'Next style', which should be itself, and a Character Style, which you should change from 'default' to Normal.

So far so good. Here is where the fun begins.

Once you've done that, click on the tab that says 'Format'.

For Body text, **Left indent** should be 0: after all, this is the text that runs in your regular columns. The same goes for **Right indent**.

First Line, though, could be 0, or it could be (if you click the double arrow) half an em (50%), an em (100%) or two ems (200%). An em is a notional width traditionally (but not always) the width of a lower case 'm', being the widest letter, as opposed to an en, which is the width of an 'n', being a typical letter.

There are essentially two standards for paragraphing. Use one, but not both. Books, newspapers and magazines tend to use an indent at the beginning of every paragraph. For this you would usually set First Line as one em, but you might set half an em or two ems if it works better.

The other standard is to have space between each paragraph. This is commonly used in technical manuals, is familiar from the web, and is also the natural way that word processor users and typists will work.

In a word-processor, you are usually limited to having either no space or a full line between two separate paragraphs. QuarkXPress allows you to set the space before and the space after. True believers in grids would say that this space should be an exact multiple of the Leading (we'll

My first document

come back to the Leading), but, to my mind, a couple of millimetres usually works better both visually and in terms of economy. For Body Text, I would usually specify this as **Space After**, to avoid trouble with titles.

Now, what about '**Leading**'? Leading comes from the metal 'lead', so it's pronounced 'ledding', not 'leeding'. It no longer means what it used to mean.

In today's usage, 'leading' is the distance from baseline to baseline. If the font is 10 point, and the leading is 10 point, it is 'set tight'. With metal letters, that would be the minimum leading, and used to be referred to as 'no leading'. With computer fonts, the leading can actually be less than the font size. This can work for titles, but be careful.

Generally, the leading should be 120% of the font size for most typefaces in most text, though 130% is common in novels and other books.

The letter grid, if you are using that, is set in lines of the height of the leading. If you stick to that type of grid, inter-paragraph spacing must be a multiple of the leading.

All sound a bit complicated? If you leave it on 'auto', QuarkXPress will ensure that the leading is good.

Alignment can be left, right, centre, justified, or forced justified. Left aligned text is generally seen as the most legible. Printed books are still often set justified. Right and centred text are only for by-lines and titles respectively, and forced justified is a special effect. Try them all, and then stick to left aligned.

H&Js refer to the Hyphenation and Justification controls. This should usually be set to Standard, until someone complains, at which point, turn it off. Almost all professionally printed material uses hyphenation, but clients complain about it frequently.

Character alignment should be baseline unless you know a good reason why not, such as for the spine of a book.

On the right, **Drop Cap** creates a dropped capital of a certain number of characters covering (usually) two or three

With moveable type, the point size would be the total height of the lead body on which the letter form stood. This body had to be high enough to accommodate the lowest descender and the highest ascender, which would typically be a capital letter, or, if the printer supported it, a capital letter with an accent. To improve legibility, additional lead was placed between the lines. Today, however, 'leading' is used for the baseline-to-baseline distance.

Inter-line ='old-fashioned' usage of 'leading'

Notional font size, descender to ascender. Note that the caps height is lower than the ascender

Leading, as used here, = baseline to baseline

A dropped cap is a well known device for signifying the beginning of a section of text. They went out of fashion during the late 20th century, but have come back in with the evolution of DTP.

Rules can be applied to a paragraph, above, below, or both. You can set the length to the margins, the indents or the text, and further refine this with From Left and From Right. Offset refers to the percentage of the leading that the rule is offset from the text. Rules can be any style of solid or dashed, any width, any colour, any shade, and any opacity.

lines. If you want it to be in a different font as well, you'll need a Conditional Style. Don't put a dropped cap in your Normal style.

You can opt to **Keep Lines Together**. Leave it off for Normal. For Body text, we will want to set this to on, but not 'all lines', which will cause all the text to vanish. Instead, set to Start 2 and End 2. This will stop unsightly widows (single lines at the end of a page) or orphans (single lines at the beginning of a page) from appearing.

Do not set **Keep with Next** to on. All your text will instantly disappear if there's more than one page of it. Only use this for titles or for groups of text such as bullets. If you do group your bullets this way, make sure that the list is always shorter than a page.

You can set **Lock to Grid** if you want. My recommendation would be only to do this if you are sitting a typography exam.

Hanging Character Set allows some special refinements. For a full explanation, and some useful tricks, see Part 5.

•/123 allows you to specify bullets or numbering. You wouldn't want this in Normal, but it can be useful elsewhere.

3   Create structured titles

So much for the Body Text. What about the titles?

You construct the titles the same way you would the Normal character and the Body text paragraph styles. Doing it in a structured way can save you a lot of grief later on.

My preferred approach is to create the biggest title I am going to use in the document, and call it Title 0. For Title 0 I also create a new character style which is Title 0 at the right size, and the right font, if it isn't the same as Normal. I may use the Rules tab to set a rule (not an underline) below or above the title. However, note that ruls above do not appear at the top of a page, and ruls below don't appear at the bottom of the page.

My first document

Once I have Title 0 sorted, I then base smaller titles on it, creating a Character Style for each size, based on the Title 0 style, and a paragraph style based on Title 0.

Pro tip—most palettes have a search function. If you type in Title, only the styles with 'Title' in them will appear, making it much easier to work with.

4   An easier way to do this

Does all this sound complicated or even tedious? I've gone the long way round because it's worth explaining it. But there is a much easier way.

If you format some text using the Measurements panel, you can Ctrl-click/right-click on the Style Sheets palette, either in the paragraph section or the character section, and a sub-menu comes up. If you click 'New', it will create a new style sheet for you based on the formatting you've just given it. If you click 'Update [name of the style you're on]', it will update that style sheet to what you've just formatted it as.

Pro tip—How to know if you've applied local formatting: when there is a '+' by the name of the style in the Style Sheets palette, it means you've changed something.

Remember, when doing this, that the style sheet you are creating will be based on 'no style'. This means that it will not change with the Normal or Title styles when you change them.

New...

Edit Body text...
Duplicate Body text...
Update Body text
Delete Body text

Apply Style Sheet & Retain Local Type Styles
Apply Style Sheet & Retain Local Type & OpenType Styles
Apply Style Sheet & Remove Local Formatting
Apply Style Sheet & Remove Local Paragraph Formatting
Apply Style Sheet & Maintain Appearance

Apply Using Next Style
Apply Using Next Style & Retain Local Type Styles
Apply Using Next Style & Retain Local Type & OpenType Styles
Apply Using Next Style & Remove Local Formatting
Hide Search

Above: Ctrl-click/right-click on the paragraph or character styles and a sub-menu comes up allowing you to update the style sheet.

Keyboard shortcuts speed up the workflow dramatically. You can set your own in File—Preferences. Some keyboard shortcuts that are best kept as they are and used a lot include:

Cmd/ctrl-B	*Bold*
Cmd/ctrl-I	*Italic*
Cmd/ctrl->	*Larger text*
Cmd/ctrl-<	*Smaller text*
Cmd-opt-shft-[	*Less tracking*
Ctrl-alt-shft-[	
Cmd-opt-shft-]	*More tracking*
Ctrl-alt-shft-]	

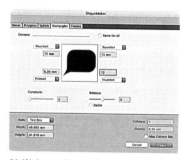

Frame set at one angle, text in frame at a different angle. Clearly you would want a good reason to actually do this.

Utilities—ShapeMaker allows you to create all kinds of unusually shaped text boxes, including speech bubbles.

7 Ad hoc formatting

Ok, so, now you know that you should, as a general rule, work with style-sheets, not have random bits of formatting all over the place. But, of course, in the real world, there are plenty of times when you do need to do ad hoc formatting. To do this, use keyboard shortcuts, or the Measurements panel. You can also use the Style menu.

1   Measurements panel

The Measurements panel at the bottom of the screen has a number of tabs, which change contextually depending on what you're doing. The Home tab, on the left, contains the most generally useful things.

On the left, you have X: and Y: and W: and H: for the position and width/height of the frame you're working in.

Next to them, you have the angle of the frame ∡ and its skew ◰. Interestingly, you can set the frame at one angle and the text within the frame at a different angle—that option is in the Text Box tab as ∿.

In the fourth column you have a control for the radius of the corner ⌐, for rounded boxes, and, below it, a button to suppress output ⊘, which means the frame won't print or export.

The radius affects all four corners, and you can change it at any time. If you want to have differently rounded corners, you can go to Utilities—ShapeMaker and create your own from there. Alternately, you can use the drawing tools ✑✎✐✏✒✕⇲ to make or modify a shape.

My first document

Next in line you have the box colour ◣. Crossed-out ☒ means no colour, which is the default. Click on the crossed-out box, and up comes a list of all the colours you've defined—more on that in a moment. Next to it is the shade of the colour.

Underneath this you have opacity ▣ (or transparency, if you prefer). At 100%, the colour is solid and everything underneath is obscured. At 0%, the colour—but not the contents—is completely transparent and the box is essentially uncoloured. Between the two you have varying degrees of transparency. This is very useful when you have text over part of a photograph, but the photograph is itself too busy and distracting and interferes with the letters. Creating a white coloured box with transparency at 50% gets round the ugliness of a white box obscuring the middle of a picture, but also makes the text legible.

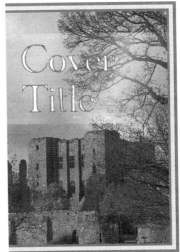

Above: a transparent color blend is used in this guidebook cover to deal with the problem of a distracting photographic background.

If you're working in a text box, you'll have the column ▦ gutter ▦ and font controls next. When you're not in a text box, these won't be there.

The columns control ▦ is set to 1 in this example. Below it you set the gutters ▦ between columns. By default, these match the settings you put in when you created the layout.

Next you have the name of the font, with Bold, Italic, Underline, *f* for a sub-menu with more effects, Open Type features and a nifty little paint-brush ✔ which allows you to copy formatting from one place to another (though you *know* that it's better to create a character style…).

With the font, if you've got thousands of fonts installed, it's quicker to click on it and start typing the name. Once you've got to more or less the right place, you can then select the exact variant.

Pro Tip—the Font Styles—Bold, Italic, etc—can be a trap for the unwary. If you bold a font which does not have a bold weight installed, QuarkXPress will create a 'faux' bold.

Underline style settings, applied.

Below, the f sub-menu. This gives a set of useful, albeit brutal, type effects.

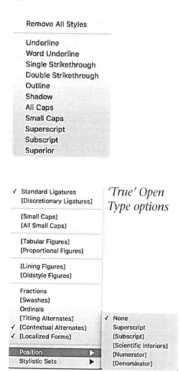

'True' Open Type options

A little warning will appear beside it. This may or may not output properly, but, either way, it will look poor compared to a proper bold version of a font. The same goes for italic: QuarkXPress will make the Roman version oblique, but it won't create a true italic font.

You really shouldn't use Underline, but, if you must, you can control how it looks by creating an Underline Style in the Edit menu. I have to say I can never remember how this works, and always end up hunting around for it. Once you've created an Underline style, you apply it from the Style menu with Style—Type Styles—Underline Styles—*name of your style*. Unfortunately, the U underline in the measurements panl only does common-or-garden black underlining.

If you press the *f* icon, you get a sub-menu of type-effects. Probably the most useful option is 'Remove All Styles'. What it's important to know is that all of these are 'fakes', being constructed by QuarkXPress to simulate true typographic outlines, shadows, small caps, and so on. In the old days, you would rarely find any font which contained true typographic versions of these, but new, OpenType fonts, often have some or even all of them.

For the 'true' versions, click the green-coloured *O*.

Here you will see an array of options. Some are in square brackets [...], which means they aren't supported by the particular font you are working in. Those that aren't in square brackets are available, which means that they have been designed into the font. Typographically, this is golden.

The version of ITC Stone Serif this book is set in, purchased from Monotype in about 2007, includes Fractions ¼, ¾, Superscript [1], and Standard Ligatures, such as fl. For some reason QuarkXPress thinks it offers ordinals, though it actually doesn't. You can access all the lettertypes, or just browse them, in the Window—Glyphs palette, which is also useful if you want to insert a Dingbat or Symbol character from another font.

My first document

Finally on the Home tab of the measurements panel, if you're working in a text box, you get font size Tᴛ, leading ⇕, alignment options ≡ ≡ ≡ ≡ ≡, tracking ↔, baseline shift ⌐A, font colour ■, and font opacity ▣.

If you click on the double arrow on the left of the font size box Tᴛ, you get a list of QuarkXPress's recommended font sizes. It's usually best to go with those, except that 11 point is generally the most legible size, and Quark never offers it. For the rest, work within the harmonic series. Designers are always taught not to use half point sizes. QuarkXPress will allow you to, but you shouldn't.

The leading control ⇕ is underneath the font size control. This does exactly what we discussed earlier under Styles, except that you can watch what happens as it goes up and down. If you type in '0', it doesn't give you zero leading (which would be silly, as the lines would be on top of each other), but the automatic leading. This is normally 20% on top of the font size, so it would be 12 points from baseline to baseline if the text is 10 point. If you want to change this, for example because you are setting a novel, you can do it in Preferences—Print Layout—Paragraph—Auto Leading. You can also change the defaults for superscript etc while you're there, but don't.

For continuous text, don't play with the leading unless you are actually going to increase it. Increased leading assists legibility and can give a luxurious feel.

You can decrease the leading in titles to increase the apparent weight of the text. Do this in combination with tight tracking, otherwise rivers of text will open up between the letters. We'll come to tracking in a moment.

Next you have the various kinds of justification. We covered that under styles.

The ↔ control is for tracking, though QuarkXPress insists on calling it 'kerning'.

When choosing font sizes, work to a harmonious sequence, eg,

9 point

10 point

12 point

18 point

24 point

36 pt

Increased leading assists legibility and can give a luxurious feel to text, especially for text is set in narrow columns.

Tight leading works in titles, when letters are tightly tracked

Left aligned text has the highest legibility, and is fairly modern in feel.

Fully justified text is the norm in printed fiction and newspapers, but be careful of narrow columns: rivers may open up between words.

Right justified is only for by-lines—it is hard to read in long copy.

The same goes for centred.

Forced justification is a special effect. Use scarcely.

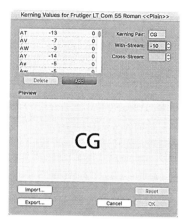

AT	-13		0
AV	-7		0
AW	-3		0
AY	-14		0
Av	-5		0
Aw	-5		0

Kerning Pair: CG
With-Stream: -10
Cross-Stream:

Delete   Add

Preview

CG

Import...   Reset
Export...   Cancel   OK

Above, editing the kerning pairs in Edit—Kerning Pairs—Kerning Pair Edit (click on a font to select).

Below, tracking text tightly makes more of an impression but is harder to read. At large sizes for signage, wide tracking is a distinct advantage, but looks affected in ordinary text.

Tracking -20
Tracking -10
Tracking -5
Tracking 0
Tracking +5
Tracking +10
Tracking +20
Tracking -20
Tracking -10
Tracking -5
Tracking 0
Tracking +5
Tracking +10
Tracking +20

Kerning, properly, is setting the gaps between difficult letter combinations such as AV, ij. This is normally done by the font designer, though on free fonts it may have been done badly or not at all. In QuarkXPress, you can edit the kerning pairs in Edit—Kerning Pairs. You would normally only do this if there was a particular collection of letters that was giving you trouble, such as the abbreviation CCG in Frutiger. 'CCG' is an important abbreviation in the UK's National Health Service (NHS), and Frutiger is the NHS font, but CCG always looks wrongly spaced. To fix it, you would need to edit the CG pair and the CC pair for each weight of Frutiger you were using.

If you're trying to use a font (perhaps one that you found and loved on a free font site) and there's more than a couple of bad pairings, abandon it and find something else. Kerning an entire font costs thousands of £, $ or € and takes masses of time and skill.

If you're using a commercially available font and the kerning is bad, ask for your money back.

The control in the measurements panel, despite being called 'kerning', is actually tracking. Tracking is varying the space between letters uniformly across a selection of text.

If you select some text, by dragging the mouse across it, you can then play with the tracking.

As you'll see, reducing the tracking by up to -5 still looks reasonable and legible. In fact, if you turn Full Justification on in the alignment (above), this is one of the tricks that QuarkXPress uses to fit the words on a line. You can adjust exactly how it does that in Edit—H&Js.

If you reduce it to -10, the text will looked cramped in body text. In titles, though, especially (see above) with reduced leading, this can create more weight and impact. Even in titles, -20 is going to be difficult to read.

Increasing the tracking beyond +5 starts looking like a special effect. It was very popular to have wide tracking on letterhead paper in the 1990s. Now it just looks a bit dated.

My first document

If you are (against all aesthetic sense) trying to fit more words onto a line using tracking (we've all done it—just never admit you've done it), then the shortcut keys Cmd-opt-shift-[and] (Mac), or Ctrl-alt-shift-[and] (Windows) allow you to change it 1% at a time. That might sound like a lot of keys to press down all at once, but once you've learned the combination, you'll find yourself using it all the time. Just remember not to admit it.

Do not, under any circumstances, make the font narrower to fit on the line. You *could* do this in the Character tab of the Measurements panel with A̅ or A̲ but it spells design disaster, except as a special effect. The reason is that the letter-type as given is optically as perfect as the designer could make it. Distorting it makes it less good (ie, bad). If you need an extended weight of a font, then these do exist for the larger type families such as Helvetica and Frutiger. Changing the width of the letters just makes it look cheap and nasty.

Underneath the tracking (or 'kerning') control is a control for shifting the baseline up and down ᴬ. There are all kinds of valid reasons why you might want to do this. Experiment to see what it does.

Finally, on the right of the Home tab in the Measurements panel, you have the character colour ◼ and opacity ▣ . This works just like the box colour and opacity.

Other things to play with in the Measurements panel are Character controls—most of which are in the Home tab—Paragraph, which essentially mirror what we discussed in style sheets, Rules, also discussed in Style Sheets, and Tabs. Tabs work like they do in word processors.

Once you've formatted some text the way you like it, you can Opt/Alt-click on the styles palette to save it as a Style (character or paragraph), or update the style you're working on. Remember—consistency is key to good publications.

Special effects:

Outline
CHANGING THE WIDTH
Shadow

They all look rubbish if overused.

Below: Helvetica Neue family. The weights are numbered based on their appearance on the page, which is why extended weights have lower numbers.

27 Ultra Light Condensed
25 Ultra Light
23 Ultra Light Extended
47 Light Condensed
45 Light
43 Light Extended
37 Thin Condensed
35 Thin
33 Thin Extended
57 Condensed
55 Roman
67 Medium Condensed
65 Medium
63 Medium Extended
77 Bold Condensed
75 Bold
73 Bold Extended
87 Heavy Condensed
85 Heavy
83 Heavy Extended
97 Black Condensed
95 Black
93 Black Extended
107 Extra Black Condensed

2   Text Box

While we're still on the Measurements panel, there's a couple more things to look at. More or less in the middle, if you're working on a text box, you'll see the tab '⊞ Text Box'. Click it, and a row of stuff comes up. The first half of it you've already seen on the home panel. It's the second half we're interested in here.

A vertically justified text box fills out all of the space, increasing the leading and the inter-paragraph to achieve this.

Generally, you want to have some extra inter-paragraph space, because this will help legibility.

From about the middle of the tab, you'll see icons for vertical placement of text. Normally this would be set to 'top', which is the first icon ⊟, but you can also set it to bottom ⊟, to centre ⊟, and to vertical justification ⊟, which spreads the lines across, adjusting the leading and inter-paragraph to suit. If you do select this, the greyed-out icon below becomes active ⊟, which lets you specify the inter-paragraph maximum. Generally, a larger value will give a better result, though the default, somewhat unhelpfully, is zero.

You wouldn't normally set narrative text using anything but 'top', which is why it's the default, but if you are doing text boxes for captions, diagrams and other things then these are highly useful.

When using a frame with a text box, it is best to have some insetting. You can set this in the Text Box tab of the Measurements panel. You can choose uniform insetting, or you can set them separately.

Next along you'll see two check boxes, one above the other. The first one ▣, when checked, opens up separate inset values. We'll come to that next. The box below turns off 'run text around all sides' ⊞. It does what it says—it can be useful if you've got a box over your text, and it's giving you trouble.

Insetting ▣ is a bit more useful. If you've got a frame (see next section), then you don't want the text butting up to it. The same goes for text on a coloured background. You can either set the insetting to be uniform, or, with the check box we just covered, change each side.

My first document

This is so useful that you'll probably want to use exactly the same insetting on all of your text boxes in frames or on coloured backgrounds. You'd think there would be a style system for this, and, you know what? There is.

Go to Window—Item Styles and click on the big green ✚. All of the settings of your box are now copied over. It works more or less like the Paragraph and Character styles. If you click through the tabs in it, you can turn off the things you don't want copied over to new items, or turn them on.

Every box you now create just requires you to click on the style to format it like your first box. If you later change the style, all the boxes update.

After the insets, you see character angle ⬩ and character skew ⬩. We looked at character angle before. Character skew is a great wickedness, even worse than changing the width of characters. Try it and you'll see why. Then deny that you ever tried it. However, you could use it with box skew ⬜, where the box skew skews the box, and this rights the text.

Next to it are a couple of little arrows ▣▣. These flip the text vertically or horizontally. Very useful if you are doing window stickers, and worth including in an item style, so that you can flip everything once you're happy. If you are flipping things to talk to old image-setting devices, use the Print options instead.

Finally on the right, you have Ascent ⬩-and baseline shift ⬩. The Ascent can be changed to Cap Height or Cap+Accent. It essentially controls how the baselines are set. Leave it on Ascent, unless there's a good reason not to.

Underneath it you have baseline shift ⬩. This is not the same as the baseline shift in the character tab. It moves the baseline for the entire text box. It's useful when you need it.

Item styles are massively useful. Most things that can't be held in Paragraph or Character styles can be set and reused here.

Box skew -20% with character skew 20%—could be useful for doing labels (as on page 34) where you don't want to spend all your time lining up text.

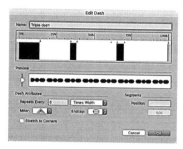

Edit—Dashes and Stripes

Editing a new dash, and the result, below.

Below, layering a triple dash in white on top of dots. Someone, somewhere will have a use for this...

3 Frame

We just mentioned frames, and you may be wondering where they are. They're in the Frame tab. If you're coming over from InDesign (well done, welcome), then you might be expecting this to be called 'Stroke'. It's all quite self-explanatory. Have a bit of a play.

Where it says ⊡ '0 pt', you set the width, where it says '—— Solid' you set the kind of stroke. Frame colour ◼ and opacity ▣ are as elsewhere. If using a dashed stroke, you can set the colour of the Gap ⊠ and its opacity ▣ separately.

What you might be thinking is: these strokes aren't very exciting—why can't I have my own types? Well, you can. Go to Edit—Dashes & Stripes, and select New, for a new dash or stripe. You can now play around until you like what you have. Use Endcap if you want rounded dashes (ie, dots).

You can't have dashes which are also stripes, though you could achieve this by overlaying two lines on top of each other, one with dashes and the other with stripes. Why you would want this is up to you.

4 Clipping and Runaround

Two other tabs to look at, especially for graphics, are Clipping and Runaround. They function in quite similar ways, and can read each other's settings.

We'll start with Clipping. Click on the box marked 'Item'. You are offered Item, Embedded Path, Alpha Channel, Non-White Areas and Picture Bounds. Try Non-White Areas.

This changes the tab to look like this:

My first document

Above, a scanned illustration from a Victorian book in the British Library, with, below, Non-White Areas clipping applied. Use the threshold and noise controls to get the exact result required.

You can now use the threshold, noise and smoothness controls to complete the cut-out. If you have a scanned line illustration, turning 'Outside Edges Only' off allows you to remove that background from the scan.

This won't achieve what you want with everything, but it means that many images which would otherwise require substantial editing in Photoshop, and the addition of Alpha channels or embedded paths, can be managed.

The Runaround menu operates in much the same way, except that if you have set up clipping, and you click on Item, it will offer you 'same as clipping'. The 0pt boxes allow you to increase the gap around an item when the text runs round it, or, just as interestingly, decrease it, for if you want part of a picture to interact with the text.

Generally speaking, you won't want text butting right up to an image, so a bit of runaround padding is good. Save as an item style so that you can use it consistently throughout the layout.

5 Picture Box

While we were doing that, you probably noticed another tab which wasn't there previously: Picture Box.

Everything on the left will be familiar from the Home tab—it's essentially the same stuff as for a text box. On the right, though, are some interesting things.

Ad hoc formatting

X% and Y% allow you to set the proportions exactly. You can drag them using the image tool, as we saw earlier, but if it's a bitmapped image such as a JPEG, TIFF or PSD, you could be headed for trouble later on. Generally speaking, bitmapped images need to be scaled to 100%, 50%, 25%, and so on, but not 19.72% or other funny numbers. When reproduced on a laser printer or commercial offset printing, moiré occurs, which is when the dots of the image don't align well with the dots of the reproduction. It produces funny patterns that distract.

You can also click on the little chain item 8 and uncouple 8 X% and Y%, allowing you to distort the image. By default, the two are linked (unlike Word, which by default allows you to distort a picture, resulting in all the funny shaped logos you see in word processing layouts). You shouldn't do it, unless there's a reason to.

The X+ and Y+ allow you to precisely move the image inside the box. You normally do this with the image tool, but sometimes you need to do it accurately.

The next pair of controls are for rotating 4 the image—especially useful if someone sends you a picture of the sea with a rotated horizon, which always looks silly—and skewing it 口, which is generally even more dangerous than distorting. The next pair of arrows flip the image horizontally or vertically. Horizontal flip is very useful, unless there's visible text on an image, in which case it looks silly.

In the middle of the tab you see 'Composite'. With PSD images you can use saved layers.

Underneath, and the most important of all, you see 144 dpi. For most purposes, you need at least 300 dots per inch for a bitmapped image to reproduce well. If you want to get technical about it, you need to oversample against your output device's line-screen by 2x, although, at a pinch, we used to work with 1.25x when no straight lines were present in the image. Most print these days has a line-screen of 150 lpi, which gives you 300 dpi. If you've got a more fine-art look, at 175 lpi, 300 dpi will still usually work.

Above, although distorting a picture as a lazy attempt to spice up an otherwise dull layout is always wrong, the skew control can be highly useful if used correctly. Here, an isometric book cover preview requires only one image, pasted into two separate boxes. It can be automated using item styles. This will naturally not produce the same results as a 3d design package, but for quickly showing mockups of many publications, it can be invaluable.

My first document

What doesn't work is a line-screen of 150 lpi (lines per inch) and an image which is 150 dpi. Sharp lines will be pixelated and horrid.

What absolutely doesn't work is 72 dpi, which is the size most images come off the web. This is 72 dpi at final output size. A lot of times, an image will be pulled off the web and then stretched to fit a space, giving more like 37.2 dpi. The result will be blotchy and rubbish.

Returning to our 144 dpi image, this is clearly not enough to reproduce well. The image either needs to be scaled down, or replaced with one at higher resolution.

Finally, on the right hand side, you can set the colour of the image ◼, its opacity ▣, the colour of the image background ◼ (not the same as the box colour) and its opacity ▣. The image opacity is very useful and works for all images. The other three only work for bitmaps created in a particular way. This used to be very popular up to about 2005, when full colour reproduction got so cheap that two colour reproduction went out of fashion.

If you've got a 1-bit TIFF monochrome image, you can set the image colour to one thing, and the background colour to something else. The only reason you would do that these days is either for a design project, or for a real 1950s retro look. Otherwise, best left alone.

At the far end, you've got the button to suppress output, ◉. This suppresses the output of the image, but not of the box. This could be useful if you are working with comp images and want the frame to appear, but not the comp.

Above, this is a crop from a much larger image, shown at 300 ppi (top), 150 ppi (middle) and 72 ppi (bottom). The original was not quite sharp, so the downsampled 150 ppi image is no worse— for blurred images and shadows, oversampling is not needed, though many RIPs will flag it up as an error. A sharp image , would have unpleasant stepping artefacts which you won't see on your computer screen. Always check the true resolution, rather than just going by appearances.

The bottom example would be typical for the resolution of an image copied from a website. You may not spot the degradation on a laser printer. 80% of readers will not spot it in print, but it will subtly devalue your publication.

Drop Shadow

Blurred

Glowing

Now, I don't know how you feel about Drop Shadow. It's a special effect, but it's one which is now so widely used that it looks 'real', rather than affected.

Click on Apply drop shadow, and you get a nice drop shadow.

Pro Tip—be careful when you come to export, because QuarkXPress will try to send this at 150dpi. This is actually fine for a standard shadow, because it has no sharp lines. However, many imagesetters or print houses will complain, so you may need to change it in the PDF Export options.

If you play with the controls, you change the angle of the shadow ☉, its distance ⬕, scale ▤, skew ⬐ and spread ⬕.

If you're coming from InDesign, you may be wondering where glowing edges, blurs and other things are. You can achieve these using the drop shadow controls.

If you want to blur some text, turn 'Inherit Opacity' off, and set the opacity of the text itself—in the Character tab or the Colours palette—to zero.

For Glowing text, turn 'Multiply Drop Shadow' off, set the colour to white (or your preferred glow colour) and move the measurements until it lines up nicely.

You can also create glowing or blurred lines or boxes by the same means. You can only have one kind of drop shadow per box, and if the box has a background colour—including white—the shadow will be from the box, not the text.

If you intend to use drop shadows, it is worth saving them as Item Styles, with all other parameters turned off.

7   Colours and blends

We're going to move off the Measurements panel now, and look at the Colours palette.

If you're coming from InDesign (and other applications), you may be a bit cross with the colour palette. Before you can use a colour in QuarkXPress, you must define it. Why not just pick colours you like, when you like?

Well… how long have you got?

Essentially, even with the best calibrated screens like the one I'm using right now, there is no real guarantee that the colour you are seeing will reproduce well on the printed page. The technologies of screens and pages are totally different. At best, you are getting an approximation.

What is more, your eyes will see colour differently at different times of the day, and with different ambient light. You may think that two reds are identical, and on your screen they may be absolutely identical, but when printed out, one might be a muddy russet, and the other a winter red.

For entirely historical (but still useful) reasons, designers tend to specify colours from the Pantone books. Pantone would love to sell you all of their swatch books, but the main two are the Coated and Uncoated PMS books.

Pantone colours are actually about how printers' inks are mixed, but they are now so standard that all kinds of processes offer 'official' Pantone simulations. Four colour (ie, full-colour CMYK) print will never be *quite* the same as a Pantone colour that it's trying to represent, and RGB and web-hex colours appearing on a screen will never be exactly the same either, but the Pantone standard is nonetheless what most people use.

If for some reason you don't like Pantone, you can define colours in lots of other specifications. Most brands, though, are specified with Pantone colours, and, if you are working professionally, you will want to look at the client's Visual Identity specification before you start.

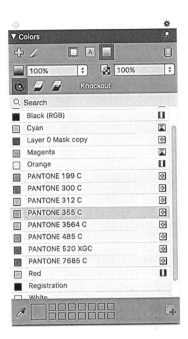

The Colors palette, in Window— Colors, is something you will have open a lot. Here colours can be defined, applied to frames, text, pictures and boxes, deleted and otherwise used and abused.

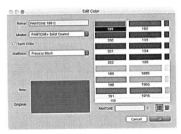

Defining the Pantone 199 C colour.

Pantone Coated colours represent what happens when particular ink mixes are put on coated paper. Uncoated are the same mixes but on uncoated papers. The results are sometimes quite different. If you are just using Pantone to specify colours that will eventually be output some other way, this shouldn't worry you. If you are actually printing in Pantone, you can't mix the two: no paper can be both coated and uncoated on the same side.

Below, a swatch as it would appear in the Pantone book (except in colour). The values on the right are for mixing Process Blue and Reflex Blue. 'C' means the swatch is on coated paper.

| **PANTONE** | PANTONE Pro. Blue | 81.30 |
| **300 C** | PANTONE Ref. Blue | 18.70 |

When colour is critical, or you have doubts about the colour accuracy of a process, for example when specifying signage from a company you haven't worked with before, it is standard to supply a colour chip for matching purposes. Pantone sell books of these and also single-colour replenishments.

Go to the Colours palette, and Cmd/ctrl-click. A new dialogue opens allowing you to edit the colours. If you delete one, you can have all occurences replaced with a different colour—for example, if you have two similar shades of green but just want one. For now, press 'New'. You can short-circuit all that by pressing the ✤ in the palette.

Up comes a dialogue which allows you to specify the colour you want.

For now, let's put in Pantone 485—one of my favourite reds: not as cheesy as Pantone Warm Red, but not as in-your-face as Rubine or other pink-influenced reds.

To do this, click on 'Model', which is the second line down. Up comes a long, long list of colour models. You'd think that was surely every colour specification in existence, but it isn't. There's no RAL there, and some other industry-specific models are missing. That's not a problem, you'll just have to consult conversion tables if you want to buy matching paint for decor and signage.

Click on Pantone Coated V3. This is the latest version and contains the most Pantone colours.

In the bottom right hand of the window, type '485'. You can browse through the colours with the slider on the right as well, but, seriously, the chances that your monitor is exactly right are exceedingly slim. Use Pantone books to get the colours you need.

You've now got Pantone 485 C. Save this, and it will appear in the Colours palette.

Pro tip—often when you're working on a document and importing a lot of graphics, especially from Excel or Word, your colour list will get full of odd things that you don't want. At the end you'll probably want to delete all of them and have them transfer to your official colours. In the meantime, if you type 'Pantone' in the Search, just above the top colour, only the Pantone colours will show up.

What if you don't like Pantone, don't own Pantone books, don't have anyone to borrow them from, and just want to make a lovely document, perhaps with pictures of horses?

My first document

New in QuarkXPress 2016 is the eye-dropper tool ✎. It's at the bottom of the Colours palette.

The easiest way to work with the Eye Dropper is to import a photograph and use it as a basis for your colour palette by clicking on the dropper and then on various places in the picture. The new colours appear in the eye-dropper's own mini palette. When you're happy, you can transfer them to the main palette with the ⊞ on the right hand side.

This is a good way of building up a palette of colours for a one-off document where the brand colours haven't been specified. For example, if you were doing a brochure about turf-houses in Iceland, you could use the green of the turf-roof, the brown of the interior wood, and the blue of the sky to give you the colours you will use for the rest of the document.

The eye-dropper ✎ is at the bottom of the Colours palette. Click the dropper, then anywhere on your Quark screen and a colour is added—for example from a photograph like the one below. When ready, click on a colour and press the ⊞ on the right. Your colour is added to the main palette.

8 Back to 'My First Document'

So, we've had a bit of a look round various things.

If you've been playing as you go (though, if you're reading this on a train or in a library you are still warmly welcome) then you should now have a page which has got margins, maybe a grid, a couple of pictures, some text, some paragraph and character styles defined, and maybe an item style and some colours.

That covers about 80% of what you'll be doing most of the time in QuarkXPress, though you've only covered 20% of the features. That's the old 80-20 rule at work again.

The next thing to do is to print it, and export it.

9 Print it!

Press Cmd/ctrl-P. You can do this from File—Print if you want, but nobody ever does.

The Print dialogue seems rather daunting. It is, and there's a good reason for it.

While your computer normally makes lots of nice assumptions about how you want to print—and some very irritating ones, such as always trying to shrink PDF files to fit the page even when there's no need—QuarkXPress absolutely does not want to assume anything. If you are printing direct to an Imagesetter, then you won't see any result until the film has been output and developed. Even then, with CMYK separations, you'll have four separate films that are hard to evaluate. The first time you'll see that what the computer guessed you wanted wasn't actually what you wanted is when things come rolling off the printing press.

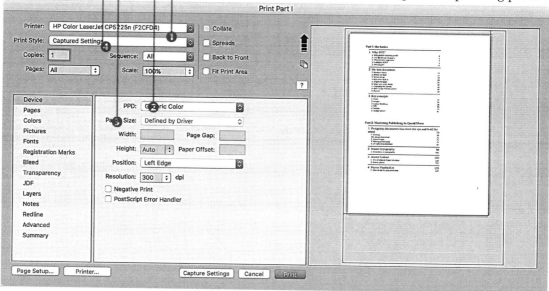

Your Printer
Choose PPD here
Choose paper size
Save as a new Print Style

Above, although apparently complex, setting up your printer just requires three steps: choose the PPD, choose paper size, and save as a new print style. After that, you can keep returning to the print style in any document.

So, Quark leaves nothing to chance, and neither should you.

To be fair, most people are now exporting to PDF, and just using a laserprinter to proof, so things aren't as scary as they might be.

The first thing to do is to select your printer's PPD file. (See illustration)

54   *My first document*

In the middle box, you'll see PPD, which stands for Post-script Printer Definition. Click on where it (probably) says 'Generic Colour'. Up comes a long, long list of printers. Scroll down it (you'll only do this once) until you find your exact printer. If it really isn't there, choose Generic Colour.

Then choose the paper size that is generally in your printer. You can change it later, but it's going to be most convenient this way.

Now, go to Print Style, which is underneath Printer at the top, and choose 'New Print Output Style'. Give it the name of your printer. You can come back to this every time you want to print, and you don't have to go through the PPDs again, which is just tedious.

Now that you've done that, go on to Pages, on the left. Here you choose Portrait or Landscape.

Back to the top, you can have Spreads turned on or off, for example to print a full page spread (you knew that), or Collate, but not both at once. You can print back to front, meaning last page first, which is good if you have an older printer that prints face-up, thereby always having the pages come out in reverse order. You can also Fit Print Area, if you are proofing a larger document on smaller paper.

Everything else, for now, you can leave as it is. If you want to print a selection of pages, you can choose odds or evens in Sequence, or, in Pages, you can type 1,3-8,9-14, and it will do that. If you've got sections with different kinds of page numbers, it understands that as well.

10 Exporting

Exporting as a PDF is a lot easier. Just choose File—Export—Layout as PDF, and pick one of the PDF Styles from the menu. For more details on this, go to Part 5: Menus, File, Export. For now, any of the presets will suffice. If you don't pick a preset or set the Options, the file will be 'as is', and potentially very large.

Congratulations, you have completed 'My first document'.

What is a PPD? Essentially it's a printer definition file. It should normally be installed when you install your printer, though if you installed your printer some time ago, you may not have the latest version. Google to find the current one. A bad PPD file can potentially crash QuarkXPress, so if you are finding that printing causes problems, it's probably time to check for the latest PPD.

Below, the File—Export—PDF dialogue, showing the PDF Styles menu, bottom.

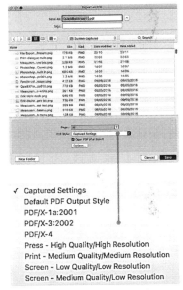

✓ Captured Settings
  Default PDF Output Style
  PDF/X-1a:2001
  PDF/X-3:2002
  PDF/X-4
  Press - High Quality/High Resolution
  Print - Medium Quality/Medium Resolution
  Screen - Low Quality/Low Resolution
  Screen - Medium Quality/Low Resolution

PDF export styles. Press is for going to press, print is for office printers. PDF/X-4 is a verified, pre-checked style.

The key concepts we will look at in this section are:
- *Fonts*
- *Images*
- *Colour workflow*
- *PDF files*
- *Vector Graphics*
- *Output devices*

A lot of this comes into the category of 'lore'—things that are passed on by word of mouth and often left unexplained. Many readers will already know everything in this section, and can pass it by. Others, though, will have found some things confusing but perhaps never dared to ask.

3 Key concepts

So, in this introductory section we've looked at where DTP is coming from, and taken a gander round the most common things you do with a document.

In the other Parts we'll dive deep into some of the most powerful aspects of QuarkXPress.

First, though, an awful lot of the problems you'll face in publishing with QuarkXPress (or, let us be honest, any decent DTP application) can be overcome by getting to grips with some key concepts.

Like lots of things in the world of computers, these were introduced gradually over many years. If you happened to be there at the time, they were exciting new things. If you're new to professional publishing, there's a lot of stuff which everyone expects you to know but no-one ever takes the trouble to tell you.

1 Fonts

The first, most troublesome thing is fonts. Fonts have gone through a quiet revolution over the last thirty years, from the bitmapped fonts supplied by Bitstream for use in the original HP laser printers to today's Open Type fonts which can potentially contain thousands of glyphs.

2 Open Type—OTF

The current gold standard in fonts is Open Type Format. These may be named OTF, but they can also be named TTF—even though the old style TrueType files have the same extension.

Pretty much every font you buy these days should be an OTF font, but OTFs vary in their capabilities and contents. Fonts such as Gabriola, Scriptina Pro and Vollkorn, available for free, contain numerous alternate glyphs which can be accessed through the Open Type features either in the

Style menu, or the Measurements palette, of from the Character styles palette.

FF Chartwell is an OpenType font which goes beyond that. It turns what you type into charts and graphs.

QuarkXPress 2016 supports all the current Open Type features, including Stylistic Sets and Multicolour transformations, though you have to turn this on in Preferences—Project—General. Previously, multi-coloured transformations, used by FF Chartwell, didn't work, and stylistic sets were not supported.

Stylistic sets are likely to become more common in future, with the prospect of true historic fonts where different sizes and weights have slightly different designs.

3   TrueType—TTF

Before OpenType there was TrueType. This was actually invented by Apple, but mainly adopted by Windows. Older .ttf fonts have a limited number of glyphs, which means you will often find that non-European characters are missing. Many of the 'free' fonts on the internet are actually old ttf fonts no longer distributed by their creators. This does not necessarily mean they are genuinely free, and you may run into copyright problems using them.

4   Postscript Type 1

Adobe Type 1 fonts are the basis on which Open Type was built, but Open Type has evolved a long way. Many of the older Type 1 fonts are no longer compatible with Windows 10 and Mac OS X. If you are having trouble with an older file, check first what fonts are there. You may be able to do an upgrade deal with the font provider.

5   Bitmap

QuarkXPress does not support bitmapped fonts, neither the old Bitstream ones, nor the current crop of photo fonts in colour.

Using FF Chartwell rings, 44+85+63 becomes a ring diagram like this:

Chartwell is a good example of clever programming in Open Type that uses substitutions to create a highly useful system.

All fonts are computer programmes, but Open Type takes this to its logical conclusion with a complete programming language which is bespoke to its system, though it brings in the elements from earlier specifications, including TrueType. Open Type fonts can swap letters around, replace strings of characters with symbols, replace entire words with other words, automatically create fractions and ordinals, create handwriting which still joins up when you change the size of some letters, and do many other things.

While Open Type offers the holy grail as far as typographers are concerned, which (for them) is fonts which change their letter characteristics based on size, thus reproducing the uniquenesses of different sizes of hand-tooled metal type, it must be remembered that few designers are programmers, and few programmers designers. An advanced font may still be typographically dreadful.

2 Images

1 JPEG vs TIFF

The most popular image formats are JPEG and TIFF. JPEG stands for Joint Photographic Experts Forum, and TIFF stands for Tagged Image Format File. There are basically two differences. JPEGs are 'lossy' compressed files. Based on the opinion of the experts, JPEGs lose detail in order to save space, but the detail they lose is generally detail the eye doesn't discern. JPEGs also have additional compression built in. The result is that a JPEG file can compress what would be 8MB into about 429KB. An 8MB file is too big to email—once it's been converted for the net, it's over 10MB and most corporate servers will kick it back. At 429KB, you could send fifteen or twenty JPEGs. For that reason, JPEGs are hugely popular, both on the web and for supplying graphics to designers.

TIFF files also allow compression, but only lossless compression. This is, inevitably, much less effective, so a TIFF file is automatically much, much larger. What's more, TIFFs can also contain layers, alpha-channels, and greater bit depth. A multi-layered TIFF file, captured in 36 megapixel on a Nikon D800 can easily end up being 1.5 GB—too large to even fit on a CD-R.

Quark generally does not export things as TIFF unless you insist that it does. It downsamples everything to 300 dpi, even at press resolution, and compresses as JPEG. This is fine, because this is the final conversion before print.

However, if you need to work on the file, keeping it as TIFF for as long as possible is better. PSD (below) is better still.

2 Raw

The highest possible resolution coming out of the camera is Raw format. This is, literally, the raw data from the camera. All raw files are proprietary formats. Nikon raw files are NEFs, for example. QuarkXPress doesn't interpret raw files directly. You can process them in Capture One, Lightroom,

Key concepts

DxO, Photoshop, or straight through Mac OS. If you have access to the raw files, you don't necessarily need to keep TIFFs, because you can always redevelop them later. On the other hand, if you are doing extensive photo-editing or manipulation, you'll want to keep your intermediate TIFFS or PSDs.

3 PSD

Photoshop's proprietary format is PSD, but it's so ubiquitous it's now a standard, QuarkXPress can import PSDs directly, and, depending on how they were saved and what is in them, do some final tweaking.

PSDs are essentially uncompressed TIFFs with enhancements. They store more information, including Photoshop's own layer effects information. They are the best intermediate format if you are editing a file. Like TIFFs, they can be huge.

4 GIFs

GIF—Graphic Interchange Format—is an old web-standard which has had a new lease of life with animated GIFs. No GIF should ever appear in a print document. Not only is the resolution usually terribly low, but GIFs discard most of the colour information, producing a grainy, bitty image.

5 300 ppi rule and Output Sharpening

As noted earlier, you should aim to have all images appear at 300 pixels per inch (ppi, sometimes dpi, though this is not technically correct) or greater in your QuarkXPress document. Quark will downsample to 300 ppi, but, for optimum quality, you are best having the pictures sized to be exactly 300 ppi at output size, as used in Quark. This also allows you to do Output Sharpening, which can lift your nice-enough pictures to something which absolutely glistens with sharpness when printed.

Also in the news…
PNG is a lossless bitmap format which web-browsers can read and which, unlike JPEGs, allows for transparency. PNGs are generally much larger than JPEGs, but substantially smaller than TIFFs. QuarkXPress outputs a good many PNGs when exporting for HTML5 publications, as they are the preferred graphics format for devices.

GIFs and the now defunct PCX format used Indexed Colour, which meant that, to fit within an 8bit graphics format, only 256 colours were used. Originally these were the original 'web-safe' colours, which meant that almost all images were horribly discoloured. To overcome this, an index of colours was placed at the start of the file, which meant that an 8-bit file could store any 256 out of 16 million colours. This could look quite good on a website during the 1990s, but could never produce the colour resolution necessary for CMYK print. You can set up JDF rules—see Part 4—to automatically detect and reject indexed colour if, by some error, an indexed file has been introduced into your workflow.

Colour formats

CMYK *is Cyan, Magenta, Yellow and blacK. Most commercial print and most colour laser printers and copiers use the four CMYK colours for their ink plates or toner.* **RGB** *is Red, Green, Blue, and relates to the colours of pixels on monitors and in cameras.*

sRGB *is a web-standard for displaying consistent RGB. Most digital cameras will produce sRGB unless you tell them otherwise. sRGB is fine for bringing images into QuarkXPress.* **Adobe RGB** *is an alternate RGB format more suitable for intensive image processing. This is also fine for QuarkXPress. However, make sure that the profiles are properly embedded—you can check in Photoshop if not sure. If the colours in QuarkXPress look different from those in Photoshop—and you have correctly calibrated your monitor (see opposite column), then the most likely culprit is the profiles not being embedded, or the wrong profile being used.*

L*a*b *stands for Lightness, a and b. L*a*b is a very high quality method of specifying device-independent colour. It doesn't have any exact analogy with processes we're used to, though, so is harder to understand.*

Greyscale *refers to files that only contain luminance information, usually 8 bit but possibly 16 bit if coming from a high-end camera.*

Duotones *are an attempt to reproduce a greater colour range by printing in different coloured inks, usually browns and blacks.*

Output sharpening is the ultimate trick in the quality toolbox. These days, you should only output sharpen for offset printing. If printing digitally, many digital printers incorporate their own output sharpening. If in doubt, experiment.

The formula for output sharpening is this:

Radius for Unsharp Masking = Viewing Distance inches x Resolution ppi x .0004.

If that makes no sense to you, then you can take advantage of other people having done the hard work either with Photokit Sharpener for Adobe Photoshop, or the NIK plugins which, at the time of writing, are being made available for free by Google. This is explored further in Part 2.

3 Colour Workflow

Now, about CMYK. In the old days, before computer image-setting, images (or, preferably, transparencies) were photographed with four separate colour filters to produce the separations needed for each printing plate. No further conversion was possible.

When imagesetters came in, drum scanners were used to record tremendously high resolution images in CMYK for inclusion in imagesetting files.

Meanwhile, actually establishing flat colour in CMYK was relatively difficult. Reds, greens and blues were fine, but, pre-imagesetters, orange had a nasty habit of turning out brown.

From the 1990s, computer imagesetters, together with advances in press technology such as straight-through CMYK presses—effectively four printing presses in one—meant that virtually any colour which could be reproduced by the process could be reproduced relatively consistently.

16 million colours were promised, as a result of the technology being 32 bit[2]. The eye can distinguish a lot of colours,

---

2 Technically, this should have produced 4 billion colours, but people always talked about 16 million. In reality, the number of useful colour differences which can be reproduced is dramatically less than that. CMYK can only show 55% of the Pantone range, which is why

Key concepts

but the overlap between gradations that CMYK can (supposedly) produce and what the eye can see is not especially brilliant, which is why additional solutions such as six colour presses, called Hexachrome, were introduced.

In the meantime, sRGB became the standard on the web, while Adobe RGB became a standard for image processing.

So, what is true colour?

The answer is that no device can truly represent what the eye sees. 'Plain' RGB has lots of values for colours our eyes can't discern, but gaps, especially in the greens, where the eye sees a difference. sRGB and Adobe RGB map the colours differently to make the most of the colour space.

CMYK, on the other hand, is a simple statement of what ink is going to go onto the press, or toner from the Laser printer drum. Different presses and different printers will produce different colours.

This brings us to the importance of colour workflow. Every device you use should be calibrated with an ICC profile. You can assume that the printing press is, you know that Pantone numbers are, and photographs are either calibrated or the exact colour is unimportant. The weak links in the chain are your own proofing device, usually a laser printer, and your monitor.

Uncalibrated, your monitor and printer will mislead you .

The only way to properly calibrate a monitor and printer is with a calibration device, such as those made by Spyder or X-Rite. If you don't have one, you may be able to borrow one. Either way, you are just guessing with colour if you don't.

Bit depth

Related to colour is bit depth. Early colour computers used 8-bit colour, which meant that only 256 colours could be stored in a file. GIF files still use this, with what is known as Indexed Colour.

Pantone has developed its XGC Extended Gamut colours, using a seven colour press.

How to bring your calibrations into QuarkXPress.

First, calibrate your printer and monitor using a device such as an X-Rite Color Checker.

Once this is done, go to Utilities—Profile Manager. Your new profiles should appear on the list. If not, you can specify the folder in which they are.
Now go to Edit—Colour Setups—Output. Choose 'New'.

In Edit Output Setup, name your device, specify the mode, which will usually be composite, the model—As is is okay for most printers—and, under Output intent, select the Profile which you have created for your printer. You may need to create a different profile for every combination of printer and paper.

Finally, go to Edit—Output Styles. Choose the printer output you created earlier. In Colours, select the output setup you just created.

'True' colour is 8-bits per colour per pixel, which in RGB is 24 bits, and in CMYK 32 bits. However, advances in camera technology mean that RAW files are now usually output in 16-bits per colour per pixel, confusingly known as 16 bit, although, counted the same way as before, it is 48-bit. Only 12 or 14 bits of this are actually recorded by the camera, but that gives a potential 281 trillion colours. This genuinely is more than the eye can perceive in one go (though, with its self-adjusting iris, the eye is capable of determining extremes of light that no camera can capture), and is also vastly more than the alleged 16 million that CMYK can reproduce. The job of RAW development software is to choose which of these values is actually going to be displayed, and which will simply be compressed or discarded.

4 PDF

Originally designed as a portable way of viewing files, Portable Document Format, PDF, is now the sole standard for transmitting complete layouts across pretty much everything. Unlike sending a Word file, which will reformat itself based on what fonts are on your system, a Microsoft Publisher document which almost no-one can open, a PowerPoint document which suffers the same problems as Word, or an InDesign or QuarkXPress document which depend on sending all the supporting files, a PDF is completely self-contained, including all the pictures, colour profiles and fonts.

Almost all fonts these days allow embedding in PDF. If you have fonts that don't, just get rid of them, as they are more or less useless.

QuarkXPress 2016 imports and exports PDFs, and it can also (for the first time) break down PDF files into native objects. For this Ctrl-click/right-click on a PDF you have imported to bring up the contextual menu, and choose Convert to Native objects. Leave all the settings in the dialogue box that comes up as they are. Your file is now converted to a group of Quark native objects. You can ungroup these, recolour them, edit the text, and so on. A fair few

What can go wrong in PDFs?

Different devices treat PDFs in different ways. Some are ultra-sensitive to errors in fonts, bad transparencies, and so on. Unfortunately the most sensitive devices are the most critical in publishing: image-setters and plate-makers. This means that a file that displays perfectly well on your screen, and may print perfectly well on a laser printer, may crash an imagesetter, holding up every other job in the queue. Even a file that does, eventually, execute may take many times as long.

QuarkXPress is well-behaved as regards PDFs, but it is at the mercy of the fonts and graphics you import into it. The most common culprit is transparencies, which some applications create in a haphazard fashion. If struggling, try turning transparencies off when outputting for press. This makes the file less editable, but editability is not important at that stage of the workflow.

Key concepts

kinds of software will import PDFs, but there is very little out there which will convert them with the power and smoothness of QuarkXPress 2016—though even Quark doesn't get it right all of the time. Some applications just create very strange PDF files.

As importantly, QuarkXPress exports PDF files, which is the main way now that stuff is sent to printers. Selecting the Press output style when you go to File—Export—Layout as PDF is generally the best option, but if things are going wrong, you can export as PDF-X, which is a verified, standards compliant file for the pre-press industry. However, anything odd about your file, such as dodgy fonts, dodgy graphics and so on will cause the validation to fail (after all, that's what the validation is for). If in difficulties, use the JDF Job Jackets to pre-flight your file, and fix whatever is broken. See Part 4 for an explanation.

PDF files combine images, vectors, fonts and text. They can also (though not in QuarkXPress, yet) be turned into fillable forms which can be used to gather information. If you create a form in QuarkXPress with fill-in boxes, it can be easily converted into a fillable form in Acrobat Professional.

5 Vectors

For illustrations, vector files are the best, because they can be continously resized without blurring or creating unwanted jagged edges. There are three formats, all of which work fine.

1 EPS

The oldest vector format still widely used is Encapsulated Postscript, or EPS. Postscript is the invisible language computers use to instruct high-end printers, and an EPS file was originally simply a printer Postscript file encapsulated so that it could be inserted into a document. Essentially, when a Postscript printer encountered an EPS, it stopped what it

PDFs can contain programming language snippets, videos, interaction, sound and other elements not suitable for printing. Some applications use PDFs as a container for PNG or JPEG files rather than sending across their information as editable vectors.

Computer graphics were originally all bitmaps. The format is easy for computers to manage and process and requires no complex mathematics. However, bitmapped images, where every pixel is described by a set of binary digits, have a fixed size. Printing them above that size results in stepped images, for 1-bit black and white bitmaps, or pixelated images. Mathematical vectors, using Bézier or spline curves, can be infinitely scaled, and require a relatively small file size. However, the processing requirements are much greater, so office applications such as Word will only display the bitmapped previews of vector files such as EPS, though most applications now display files in the PDF format, a descendent of EPS.
Below, the same curve, much magnified, as vector and bit-map.

was doing, processed the EPS file like a separate job, and then went back to what it was doing.

EPS files cannot be directly viewed by programs like Word. Usually they have low resolution previews, which Word can see, and they print out at low resolution on anything but a Postscript printer.

EPS files contain the fonts embedded in them. However, if you edit an EPS, those fonts disappear unless they are separately installed on your computer. For this reason, logos and other static text are usually converted to text outlines before distribution.

QuarkXPress 2016 interprets EPS files so you see the real content, not the low resolution preview. EPS files do not support transparency, so it will often be better to use Style—Convert to Native Objects if transparency is required.

2   AI

Originally the native format of Adobe Illustrator (although that is really now PDF), AI is a flavour of EPS which was implicitly more editable, though Adobe EPS files generally are editable in Illustrator and other illustration applications. Anything that Illustrator can do, AI can store. QuarkXPress can convert AI files but, just as with EPS files, the fonts will disappear if not otherwise on your system.

3   PDF

As well as its other uses, PDF is now becoming the standard for vector graphics. A PDF can contain images, like its predecessors AI and EPS, but if it only contains vectors and fonts, the total file size might well be just a few kilobytes. The exception is PDF files that have come from mapping applications, which contain millions of vectors. Quark can happily import these PDFs, and will convert relatively simple maps. Once maps start reaching into the 1GB or above, Quark tends to grind to a halt. Best to do all the manipulation in the mapping software and leave them in PDF format.

Key concepts

6 Output device

Unlike Word files, which may never actually be printed off but just looked at on a screen, QuarkXPress files are meant to be viewed by people who haven't got a copy of QuarkXPress. Traditionally this has been print media, though Quark is also at home now producing eBooks, Kindles, HTML5 publications, native apps and web pages.

1 Laser Printer

Office laser printers and printer-copiers are quick, relatively high resolution, and found everywhere there are computers. While home users may prefer inkjets—cheap to buy, expensive and slow to use—businesses prefer lasers.

A black and white laser printer with a nominal resolution of 600 dpi will print black and white images that look somewhat like the images you had in mind. In principle you can control this and lower the line screen so that the resolution is rougher, but the images are better—see Part 2 for more on this—but most modern laser printers have got so many built-in tricks to marginally improve the result that this doesn't work. You can try it, using the File—Print—Colors dialogue and changing 'frequency' to 60, but, nine times out of ten, the printer will override this and do what it was going to do anyway.

When designing for office lasers—for example a staff magazine which you will send to each site and have printed off—just be aware that while black and white lasers *could* produce great photos, they probably won't.

Colour laser printers and colour printer-copiers are something else. You can calibrate either of them using a calibration device and they will generally produce some pretty good pictures. If uncalibrated, the pictures might well be heavily coloured towards red or blue. High end printer-copiers, such as Xerox Digital Presses, will come with calibration, and all you need to do is load the profile onto your system.

2 Digital Press

A digital press is a fancy word for a very big, very good colour laser printer, usually with options for SRA3 paper, which means that you can trim it afterwards for full-bleed. They are usually auto-duplexing, and most of them will impose documents for you if they are simple booklets. Anything more and you will either have to buy your own imposition software, or do it 'by hand' in QuarkXPress, for which Composition Zones will be your best friend.

Digital Presses are usually Pantone colour matched.

You may actually have a digital press at the office, and just be thinking it's 'the photocopier'. Rather than spending £75 and waiting a week for 1,000 DL leaflets, you could be be sorting it all in-house.

There are basically three differences between 'the photocopier', if it is the same machine, and the results that a print house will give you on digital print.

First, paper. If you're printing on A4 copier paper, then the result will look like A4 copies. Investing in some reams of 130gsm and 150gsm silk, gloss and art matt SRA3 paper will suddenly lift your output to a much more professional level. Keep the paper in SRA3 plastic boxes, or keep it wrapped, unopened in its original packing.

Second, maintenance. The office copier is probably only maintained when it goes wrong. People who make their livings with digital presses are much more careful with them—and pay for proper servicing, as well as following all the cleaning and clearing instructions.

Third, finishing. A printer's manual guillotine can be had second hand for not a great deal. This will allow you to trim a ream of paper to perfection. A school type hand guillotine may well produce a decent result with up to ten sheets when it is new, but the edge quickly blunts, the components get out of line, and the result soon disappoints.

The same goes for stitching (a printer's word for stapling). A decent stitching machine is not hugely expensive, and will sort out hundreds of documents in an hour.

Folding machines take you to a different level. Essentially, there are two types of folding machines: air-machines, and machines that don't really work. The kind of office folding kit that you see in stationery catalogues will ruin one sheet in ten, and none of the folds will be particularly good. Hand folding is almost always better.

3   Offset

The classic way of printing is Standard Web Offset Press, SWOP, usually referred to just as 'offset'. This is real printing, quite possibly with machines that are seventy years old but still kept going with care and attention.

In the old days, you would have to go to a pre-press bureau to produce film from an image-setter, and then take this round by hand (or courier it) to the printers, who would make the plates from the films and do the job.

By the mid-nineties, most print houses had their own imagesetters. These days, many printers work straight from PDF file to plate without going through film at all.

SWOP printing has a fixed plate size. Generally, this will be quite big, as the printer would have to turn down bigger jobs if stuck with a small machine. Presses which are SRA3 in size are small, SRA2 is common, SRA1 is quite usual. You can find presses that do SRA0. If a printer is keeping an old press going—often for black and white jobs—it may work to sizes with names such as Emperor, Grand Eagle, or Double Elephant (which is 678 x 1016mm).

What all this means is that your 85mm x 55mm business card job is not going to be the only thing on the press. Usually, a printer will try to Impose your job so that the entire press is used. Imposition is done these days semi-automatically in software, another reason for wanting PDF files. Provided that you have specified everything correctly, the printer will then print the minimum number of pages, with a few extra for spoils, and then fold, trim and stitch to your finished size.

To SWOP or not to SWOP? SWOP is, technically, web-offset, which means printing from rolls of paper rather than sheets. However, SWOP has become a standard term for describing how you should colour calibrate a job, even when the printer will actually be using a sheet-fed press.

Setting your colour calibration in View—Proof Output is more a guide for you than anything which will affect the printer. PDF composite workflow, now preferred, means that you will be sending all the colour profiles for everything in the document as part of the PDF file (you don't have to do anything for this— Quark does it). When the printer receives your file, the colour profiles will be interpreted by the Raster Image Processor (RIP), and the correct colour calibration applied.

SRA0	900	×	1280	mm
SRA1	640	×	900	mm
SRA2	450	×	640	mm
SRA3	320	×	450	mm
A1	594	×	841	mm
A2	420	×	594	mm
A3	297	×	420	mm
A4	210	×	297	mm
A5	148.5	×	210	mm
A6	105	×	148.5	mm

| DL | 99 | × | 210 | mm |

DL is A4 cut or folded in three.

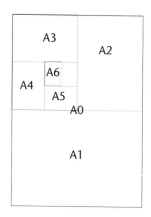

Above, the A system is based around a sheet of paper, A0, which is exactly one 1m² in area, and where the width is 1/√2 of the height. These proportions, 1:1.414, though artistically inferior to the golden section, which is 1: 1.618, mean that if a sheet of paper is folded or cut once in half, it stays the same shape. A1 is therefore half A0, A2 is half A1, and so on. SRA sizes are have additional width and height to allow registration and trimming.

A pretty typical minimum economic quantity is about 750. This means that if you are doing a DL leaflet, which is A4 folded into 3, and the printing press is SRA2, printing 750 sheets will produce 3,000 DL leaflets. The printer will normally impose it so that only one plate is made, and the stock (paper) is turned or tumbled so that it prints correctly on the other side. If this is not possible, for example because you perversely decided to save costs by having one side in CMYK and the other in black and white with a spot colour, it may actually cost more.

Always ask your printer for advice. When asking for quotes, ask for several quantities. The total price always goes up the more you want printed, but the price per sheet drops, up to about a million sheets, after which it no longer drops. Typically. Again, each printing house is set up differently, and some will be competitive on some kinds of jobs and not on others.

4 Risograph

Beloved by political parties and small charities, the Risograph is the lowest possible quality printing device still in use. Essentially an electronic stencil duplicator, it produces rough prints onto standard copier paper at very low cost in small quantities. Check with a local printer about costs of offset for different quantities: you may be surprised at how few you have to have printed for offset to be cheaper than Riso.

If you're not already wedded to Risograph, my advice is to steer well clear of it. The price in terms of volunteer man-hours is steep, even when the cost of operation is limited.

If you do need to produce for Risograph, see if you can get hold of a Riso profile from the manufacturers, or else get an exact specification of how you should send the job. Many Riso operators do a lot of experimentation for the right settings. You may need to do the same, even with an ICC profile, because the process tends to wander quite a lot.

Key concepts

5   Flexo

Once little better than Riso, flexoprint, which uses rubber plates and is popular in packaging, has come on dramatically in the last years, to the point that today's flexo can rival the offset of fifteen years ago. For producing millions of copies of something, flexo is by far the cheapest solution, which is why packagers love it. It is also generally more tolerant of substrates like cardboard that offset printing can't or won't touch.

Flexo customers tend to be incredibly brand-aware, so flexo print houses are generally very clued up on colour management, and will either send you the profiles on request, or specify how they want the PDF to arrive so they can apply their own profiles. Always take your print house's advice seriously. Just because the best flexo printer on the market can rival offset for quality doesn't mean that any print house you deal with actually has one of those machines. If the flexo house sales rep says it won't work, then it won't— and if you're printing a million of anything, you'd better believe it.

This doesn't just apply to colour reproduction. If you are printing for packaging, take advice on whether particular fonts or artwork will display well. White bold text reversed on green on the side of a package at six point on the cheapest flexo printer you could find anywhere in the world could well be utterly illegible—which could leave you legally liable if it's the bit that says 'don't take this if you are pregnant'.

6   Thermal

There is actually one process which is, potentially, even worse than Riso, and that is thermal printing. You will remember this from fax machines, but thermal paper is still in use for labelling, and it's doing very well. Essentially, you cannot have any fine lines, and you can't have any shades of grey. If you do, it will just look like nothing. Try it before committing the design.

Print terms that may confuse
Printers have their own terminology. The problem is not when you don't know what they mean, but when you think you do, but they are using a word differently.
Bleed—*3mm or 9pt extra around the artwork to allow for trimming.*
Board—*200 gsm or up.*
Camera Ready—*finished artwork, usually now a PDF.*
Colour separations—*CMYK (not usually used for spot colour).*
Composite—*colours supplied in one file for later separation.*
Coverage—*how much ink on the paper. 300% is usually too much.*
Creep—*movement due to binding.*
Die—*a cutting or scoring tool.*
Dot Gain—*darkening of the artwork due to dots 'blooming'.*
Drill—*punch holes.*
Equivalent paper—*non-branded version of what you specified.*
Imposition—*mounting your artwork into plate-sized sets.*
Moiré—*unpleasant interaction of two half-tones. Always wrong.*
Panel—*one side single folded face.*
Prepress—*everything between your PDF and the printing press.*
RIP—*Raster Image Processor, the main prepress software.*
Score—*press a line for folding.*
Self cover—*cover is same stock as the rest of the document.*
Spot—*colours such as Pantone that are additional plates.*
Stitch—*staple.*
Stock—*paper (or board).*
Trim Size—*the final size of the paper, prior to folding.*
UV coating—*a gloss varnish applied as a spot colour and hardened with ultra-violet light.*

Thermal is also the technology used for printing ribbons (often using machines originally designed for bar codes) and for print ID badges. You don't often see a nice looking ID badge, but it is possible to design them if you are careful to observe the strictures of the medium. For ID card machines, you can print in colour, but not fine lines, and everything will be degraded and a bit blurry.

7   Roll printers

At the other end of the universe from Thermal are roll printers. These 56" wide machines, often with six or eight ink cartridges, tirelessly churn out roll-up banners, printed cloth, vinyl, sticky labels and almost any other substrate that bends. There are also even bigger machines which can print onto non-bending surfaces.

Roll printers are capable of astonishing colour rendition, potentially much better than offset. However, it depends a lot on the substrate. The best vinyl and silk substrates are gorgeous. Incidentally, the rep will use that when he demonstrates the machine. Cotton canvas, on the other hand, though a fantastic feel, doesn't take colour well.

Use the ICC profiles that come with the machine and/or the substrate, and make sure you have View—Proof Output turned on in QuarkXPress, and select the appropriate profile to view with. You may need to pump up the colours in Photoshop if you want your images to glow on canvas.

Roll printers almost always come with their own RIP software (for Raster Image Processor) and also do their own imposition—important if you are printing 1,200 15×15mm stickers.

8   Outdoor advertising

For outdoor advertising, you will never actually get to talk to the print house—it's all done via the media sales agency. You can be generally fairly confident that if you provide the PDF file the way they specify it, the colours will come out right. Do ask questions though about what the best type

Key concepts

size is. Media companies have astonishingly detailed research on what works and what doesn't. According to David Ogilvy, founder of Ogilvy & Mather, 99% of advertisements don't work. The reason: simply failing to stick to the basic formula of doing the job right.

Usually, outdoor adverts are designed at a fractional size, either 1/4 or 1/10, which makes proofing rather easier.

9 Digital devices

Kindles, eBooks, HTML5 publications, native apps and HTML5 web pages are now all within the range of QuarkXPress 2016. We'll explore that in Part 3. However, just as it's worth understanding the processes for print to avoid expensive misconceptions, understanding the strictures of digital is essential.

These days, tens of thousands of companies produce bespoke apps to promote their products. However, the vast majority of apps on the Apple and Google stores are never downloaded by anyone. Making them free doesn't actually help.

When you produce a piece of print, or an advertisement, sticking it in front of someone's face is relatively simple. When you produce an app, there is no intrinsic reason why anyone will ever find it. If they do find it, you are asking them essentially to allow it to take up residence in their personal space. To do so, you need to make a very good case to them about its usefulness.

QuarkXPress-generated digital content will tend to be informational. You really wouldn't want to try programming a racing game with it. The question, then, is what there is about your information which makes them want the app rather than the PDF, and the PDF rather than the piece of paper, and the piece of paper rather than just the intention that they might one day visit your website.

Off-topic:
how advertisements work
The basic formula for advertisements is AIDA. This is:

Attention
Information
Decision (or desire)
Action.

Essentially, the first thing someone sees or hears needs to be the attention grabber. The next thing is the information which tells them what it is you are offering. The fourth section is text, images, sounds or any combination which makes them decide to buy (or whatever else it is you want them to do). Some people prefer to say 'desire', as this is also the section which makes them think 'yes, I want that'.
The final section is action, usually in the form of a direct response they can make there and then. It could be 'click the link', or 'ring 0800 etc now', or something as nebulous as 'make a mental note'.

Next time you watch a TV ad, or see a print ad, follow through the logical sequence and see if you can identify the steps. Advertisers are extraordinarily creative in how they do these things, but you will (I think) be surprised at how slavishly the formula is still followed.

Part 2: Mastering Publishing in QuarkXPress

The first part introduced QuarkXPress, the basics of creating a document, and some of the key concepts that you need to know. Part 3 will look at digital publishing, and Part 4 some deep features of QuarkXPress. In Part 5 we will go through every tool, palette and menu.

This part—possibly the most important section in the book—will look at mastering print publishing. Much of it will apply to any DTP application. It will refresh and explore some of the concepts touched on in the first part.

As with the previous part, much of this will be familiar, if you have been working in design or desk top publishing for a while. Once again, I include it because my experience is that many people who are otherwise highly competent designers, typographers, photographers or pre-press specialists sometimes lack a crucial piece of information.

1 Documents that draw the eye and hold the mind

A book everyone interested in design should read is Universal Principles of Design by William Lidwell, Kritina Holden and Jill Butler. This section picks up a number of his ideas.

The same format of paper and print process can present an eye-catching, compelling, argument that changes the world, or a lifeless reproduction of some tired old slogans with off-putting photography. Great design is, quite literally, by design.

1 Strategy

No document should ever be published without a purpose. Sadly, many are. All too often, publishing a document was a step in some departmental project plan. By the time the project got that far, no-one could remember why, just that their job evaluation depended on doing it. The results usually speak for themselves, or, rather, they don't.

Publishing is about communicating. Any kind of communication relies on knowing four things: Outcome, Audience, Messages, Delivery.

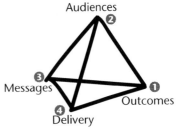

1 Outcome

If your document achieves its purpose, how will the world be different? Your outcome may be something as humble as people filling in the correct form when they ask for a library ticket, or as grand as presidents signing a major peace treaty. Let the purpose which the document is to accomplish drive everything else.

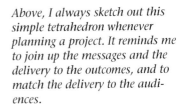

Above, I always sketch out this simple tetrahedron whenever planning a project. It reminds me to join up the messages and the delivery to the outcomes, and to match the delivery to the audiences.

2 Audiences

For that to happen, who is it that you need to persuade? Almost certainly not everyone. Who are the people whose decision will directly achieve your purpose? They are your

decision makers. Be aware also of who else is going to read it. Who might be influential in recommending it? They are your **influencers**—sometimes journalists, sometimes politicians, sometimes sales staff, sometimes just the woman who knows everyone else in the village. Who might not like what you're doing and try to put a stop to it? They are your **gatekeepers**. A document which is a bit brash or otherwise insensitive may stir up resistance, whereas one which is a bit sweeter or simply less offensive may be more effective.

What do you know—or could you know with a bit of research—about your decision makers, influencers and gatekeepers? Imagine you are trying to do a leaflet for teenagers. Your first thought might well (and should well) be, 'exactly which teenagers are we talking about?' If you are a 36 year old parent of nine-year-olds, teenagers may look like a homogenous and rather scary group. Teenagers to themselves are in many kinds of groups and streams, and some are iin the group which is proud to be part of no group.

The more research you can do about your audiences, the better you can reach them. True insights into how they think will give you true insights into how to reach them.

If stuck, remember this: ultimately, you are going to have to divide up your audiences by how you reach them. If your document is going into schools, it's going to be policed first by teachers who are the gatekeepers. It's going to reach teenagers while they are at school, and, if it comes through the school, potentially be seen as 'official', and therefore dull and irrelevant. Clever design, though, can turn that on its head.

3   Messages

The great thing about Desk Top Publishing is that you can be working on the text while working on the design. If you are both writer and designer, then figure out—before you start designing or writing anything—what your key messages are. What will persuade those audiences, which you now understand so well, to do what it is you want them to

Documents that draw the eye and hold the mind

do? Boil them down to just three or four crisp phrases. Make them memorable. It is much easier to design well from memorable messages than to try to spice up messages which are vague, dull or commonplace.

If someone else has written the text, don't be afraid to ask them what the key messages are. They will become the structure of your document. Whether it's a three hundred page report on the price of fish in the North Atlantic, or a one sided invitation to a May ball, there should be around three key messages. If the writer doesn't know, it's worth sitting and brainstorming with them until you both know. If you don't, whatever you design will be wrong anyway.

4 Delivery

How are your messages going to get into the hands, and therefore into the minds, of your audience? I'm always amazed at how many people want a document designed in a particular way, but have never bothered to work out how they will distribute it. A sales leaflet relies on people actually handing it out. That 500 page report needs to be sent to the people who need to read it—but do they even accept unsolicited reports? If not, it may be necessary to organise a special event to invite them to, in which case you're not just designing a report, you're designing an event.

The method by which your document reaches you audience is going to be fundamental to its format. Form must follow function. The way you want them to respond is also crucial. If your document does not include a method of response, you can assume that there will be no response.

Only when you have pinned down Outcomes, Audiences, Messages and Delivery are you ready to start designing.

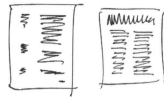

2 The design thumbnail

If you want to create great documents in QuarkXPress, don't start with QuarkXPress.

You may wonder what application you should start with, but it isn't any application at all, it's a sheet of paper. Rough out ten or fifteen thumbnail sketches of a document—advertisement, report, brochure, form, whatever—that will satisfy the requirements of your Outcomes-Audiences-Messages-Delivery brief. Refine these down to just a couple which will do all the work you need to be done. Draw them out again, but larger, and mark in where the bits of information like headers, page numbers, contact details, coupons or whatever you need go. These outcome-essential bits and pieces can wreck otherwise pristine designs if they aren't considered carefully together.

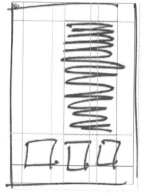

3 Master Pages

Once you have your worked up thumbnails, create a new document in QuarkXPress. Use the layout dialogue to set out the size, margins, columns, and whether it is single page or facing page, and whether there will be automatically flowing text, or a fixed number of pages.

Once you've done that, go to Master Pages at the top of the Page Layout Palette (Window—Page Layout). Double-click to open one, and start transferring your thumbnails onto it. QuarkXPress is pretty good at not getting in the way, but, if it does, remind yourself: **Never Let Software Dictate Design** (NLSDD).

Using the first Master Page as a basis, create other master pages until you've laid out all the thumbnails you need.

Pro-tip—take a picture of your thumbnails on your smartphone, import them and use them as a guide. It's much quicker, and it will help you to stay true to your design.

Thumbnails, above, inspire an unconventional grid with three narrowing columns.

Documents that draw the eye and hold the mind

1　Grid systems

At this point you will have to decide whether you are going to stick to a grid system, work organically, work harmonically, or a combination of all three.

Grids we looked at in Part 1. Pre-DTP, they were more or less a necessity for creating any kind of consistent artwork. These days you can compromise more, depending on what you're trying to achieve. A grid will give you the most strongly designed look. However, it doesn't have to be the kind of grid you find in Swiss books from the 1950s. Any kind of wacky thumbnail you've created can be the grid, as long as it's executed consistently.

Use your Master Pages and guidelines, either made from the Guides palette, or dragged from the rulers, to create exactly the grid you want. Grid purists lock down not only every column guide and box, but also where the lines of text are allowed to go. Turn on View—Page Grids to see these. You can edit these either in the Window—Grid Styles palette, or, only while editing a Master Page, in Page—Master Guides & Grid.

2　Organic

On the other hand, you might want to go for something much more organic. This is a much more Anglo-Saxon approach, where the content of the photographs and the shape of the titles determines the flow of the page. You will still need underlying consistency, but for this you can lean either on the grid or on the harmonic system.

For organic working, the eye-dropper tool will help you conform colours to photography, and dynamic guides will help you keep things from jarring with each other by being just different.

3　Harmonic

The harmonic system is about creating a set of harmonious typefaces and sizes and letting them set their own rhythm

Above, grid purists lock down where the lines of text are allowed to fall. To see this, turn on View—Page Grids. To force your text to behave this way, go change the Paragraph Style to 'lock to grids'.

Below, faced with a single, overpowering image, it may make more sense to position the text organically. The grid, if used at all, is subverted to the needs of the page.

as they flow through the document. A grid exists only to the extent that the margins and possibly main columns are consistent. Everything else is up for grabs.

Grid advocates may say that this is merely using a poor-man's grid, and the whole thing would be improved by having a proper grid. However, when you are setting a style across a group of documents—which is what brand Visual Identities do—a consistent set of typefaces, sizes and colours will strongly create a sense of shared identity, even though the grids are, of necessity, very different.

If working harmonically, the specification of styles should be carried over from document to document. A JDF is a good way to do this—see Part 4.

Harmonic systems are particularly useful when working with long documents that keep changing. No matter how much you want to stick to a grid, when a particular chart has to go between two lumps of text, someone has just turned up with a new wodge of text to go ahead of it, and you're under pressure to keep the overall page count down, the constraints of the design grid may put you on a collision course with the needs of the client.

When working harmonically, you can set a keyboard shortcut for each style, and blast through hundreds of pages clicking the titles into place.

Most designers mix aspects of grid, organic and harmonic designs.

4 Making photos pop

The ubiquity of digital cameras means that more and more design is photographically led. However, though almost everyone these days owns a camera, designers are not necessarily photographers. Making a promising image work with the layout can be an issue, which is why, increasingly, designers reach for stock photography available online.

With few exceptions: NUSP—Never Use Stock Photography.

Why not? Stock photography is the clip-art of a new generation. Millions of images are available. They cover every subject and therefore no subject, and they have only one style: ubiquity.

As any photographer who has tried to sell stock images will tell you, even the broadest-minded stock warehouses are pretty sniffy about what they accept. They want images which are generally applicable, without things that bind them to one particular circumstance. In other words, they want images that they can sell again and again. Stock houses don't want images which are relevant, they want images which are never irrelevant.

In stock images, everyone is usually perfectly dressed, has perfect teeth, perfect skin and perfect smiles. The exception is news archives, where you can pick up retro images of days gone by.

It is always better to have an image shot specifically for what you are doing. Clothing styles, skin tone, weather conditions and light will be subtly right for your audience, whereas in stock they will be tailored to match the average.

However, the quality of pictures available via stock is usually much greater than those shot for a purpose. How do you overcome that?

Above, relatively anonymous image of two men and a bow.

Below, the same image cropped to just include the man's face. In this case, layout permitting, a longer crop would have emphasised the directionality of the arrow.

1   Cropping

One of the basic rules we teach beginners is 'if your pictures aren't good enough, probably you aren't near enough'. Beginners tend to try to capture the whole scene, rather than capturing the main interest.

Shooting for layout, you want the photographer to go the other way, leaving generous borders on all sides so that you can crop the image to be right for the layout. However, this is really just leaving the editorial decision until later. The best way to turn a so-so image into a powerful image is to crop, ruthlessly.

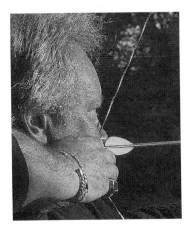

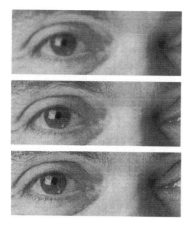

Above, the same image with the eyes slightly blurred (top), as the image came out of the camera (middle), and with a slight decon-volution filter applied to refocus.

Below, the best image with output sharpening applied, via NIK Sharpener Pro 3.

2 Pre-sharpening and output sharpening

Even the best photographers with the best cameras tend to produce pictures which, at the pixel level, are slightly soft. This is because digital cameras generally have anti-aliasing filters. Pre-sharpening the image with an Unsharp Masking radius of 0.5 pixels tends to overcome this, and should be the first step before processing an image.

For those looking to maximise focus quality, a true decon-volution filter such as FocusMagic actually refocuses a very slightly blurry image. The result is quite extraordinary. Photoshop's own Smart Sharpening can produce a similar result, though the effect is not as pronounced.

For most photographs which are imperfect, the problem is not usually that the image is out of focus, but that the focus is on the wrong thing. Images where the background is sharp but the foreground is blurry—all too easy when photographing people, because autofocus prefers to latch on to strong geometric shapes rather than people's faces—should be discarded. However, for many otherwise well executed images of people, the tip of the nose is sharp but the eyes are slightly soft. This gives a tired, disinterested look. Focus Magic and Photoshop Unsharp Masking (USM) can help here. It can also help if you slightly blur the rest of the image, which makes the eyes comparatively sharper. If the eyes still look blurry, discard the image.

Much more important than the absolute sharpness of the image is its apparent sharpness when reproduced. For optimal sharpness, resize the image in Photoshop to the final output size at 300 ppi resolution. Then convert to the output colour space—CMYK for colour print, greyscale for black and white. Now apply Output Sharpening, which means setting the radius for Unsharp Masking at 1.5 pixels. This will produce an image which looks oversharpened on screen, but prints much better.

If you actually know the line-screen of the final output device, you can do better. Resize your image to 2x the line-screen, so if it is is a rough 70 lpi, for Risograph or old fashioned newsprint, your image should be 140 ppi. If your

Documents that draw the eye and hold the mind

line-screen is a fine art 200 lpi, your image should be 400 ppi. Do this even if it means upsampling in Photoshop. Then apply your Unsharp Masking at:

Viewing Distance inches x Resolution ppi x .0004.

The normal viewing distance is the diagonal of the sheet of paper (or billboard, or anything), so if your paper is an A3 magazine spread, the diagonal in millimetres is:

$\sqrt{(420^2 + 297^2)} = 514$mm or 20.24 inches

because diagonal^2=side A^2 + side B^2

For a fine-art line-screen of 200 lpi, your image resolution is 400 ppi, and the formula is thus 20.24 x 400 x 0.0004, giving you an Unsharp Masking radius of 3.2.

If this is too much maths, either download (currently for free) the NIK filters from Google, which include Sharpener Pro 3, which does everything automatically, or buy Photokit Sharpener.

For ultimate sharpness, print on coated paper and have a UV varnish applied.

To summarise on sharpness:

1. Start with a sharp image, particularly sharp on the centre of attention, which, with people, is *always* the eyes.
2. Improve the sharpness with capture sharpening, FocusMagic or Photoshop's Smart Sharpen.
3. Output sharpen. This is by far the most important step.
4. Consider coated paper (often cheaper than uncoated because of shorter drying time, though cold presses can't print on coated).
5. Consider UV varnish—more expensive, but gives the maximum sharpness if all the other steps are followed.

There is no point trying to use an image which still looks soft once output sharpening is applied. Discard the image and find something else.

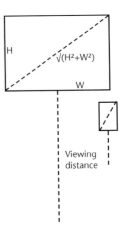

Above, normal viewing distance whether for a 48-sheet billboard or a piece of paper in front of you is the same as the diagonal of what you are viewing. Use Pythagoras theorem to work this out. If that seems all too difficult, you can scale it down and use Quark's Measurements panel to tell you the length.

Below, halftone is produced by changing the size of the dots.

Screen resolution =
printer resolution/√grey levels

For 256 levels of grey,
maximum lpi is
Laser printer   300 dpi   =   18.75
Laser printer   600 dpi   =   37.5
Risograph   600 dpi   =   37.5
Imagesetter 1200 dpi   =   75
Imagesetter 2400 dpi   =   150
Imagesetter 4800 dpi   =   300
For Platesetters (computer to
plate) the calculations are the
same.

Typical screen values:
Screen Printing   45–65 lpi
Laser Printer (300dpi)   65 lpi
Laser Printer (600dpi) 85–105 lpi
Risograph   106 lpi
Offset Press
(newsprint paper)   85 lpi
Offset Press
(coated paper)   85–185 lpi

Mono lasers and Risos only achieve those values by offering limited levels of grey, which is why photographs look grainy.

3 Resolution

In the above, we touched on resolution. An image should generally be 2x the resolution of the line-scren for halftone output such as offset and laser printers.

To explain a little: to have an effective line-screen of 150 lines per inch (lpi), which is magazine quality, the imagesetter needs to be imaging at 2400 dots per inch (dpi), because it is printing smaller or larger dots to give the impression of shades.

An old fashioned mono laser printer at 300 dpi can only produce 256 levels of grey—which makes the levels continuos to the eye—at 18.75 lines per inch. At that, the dots are very clearly visible, but the image, unless the viewing distance is enormous, is generally not. Billboards are done at about that level of lines per inch, but you tend to look at them from 20 feet away. If you stand close to one, you can see the dots, but you can't make out the picture.

Current laser printers play all kinds of tricks to overcome this, with fancy names like RET. Even so, the best monochrome laser printers still produce fairly rubbish looking photographs.

The 1980s Linotronic imagesetters could produce 1200 dpi, giving a line-screen of 75 lines per inch, which was more or less the best that newsprint paper could do. Newsprint has improved now, and you can easily achieve 85 lpi, and do it in colour, which, though it doesn't actually quadruple the resolution (for all kinds of reasons), does make the pictures better. Indeed, colour laser printers do quite well with monochrome photographs because, although their native line-screen may only be 40 or so lines per inch, by printing monochrome photos using four colour toner, and various other tricks, the effective resolution reaches up to the 120 lpi level.

The 1990s imagesetters were typically 2400 dpi, and could therefore easily produce 150 lpi. This is the standard at which most printing is done, because above 150 lpi it becomes progressively more difficult, even on art or coated paper, to keep the print clean.

Documents that draw the eye and hold the mind

Imagesetters have now been largely replaced by Platesetters, which go straight from computer to plate without intermediate film. These will often be 4800 dpi—for a maximum line-screen of 300 lpi, which, if you can find a paper good enough to print on, will seem like a photograph. In practice, 150 lpi is still the standard for coated papers, which is why images are generally expected at 300 ppi, as halftoning halves the resolution.

We did some experiments during the 1990s, encouraged by Kodak who were pressing the advantages of PhotoCD, and found that if you don't have sharp, straight lines in your image—for example because you are photographing people rather than product boxes—you can get away with 1.25x oversampling. However, you will still have to explain that to your print house: the proprietor is likely to tell you that your images are 'too low resolution'.

To summarise all this:

1   If you supply photos in their final size at less than 300 ppi, your print house is likely to complain.

2   If you supply photos in their final size at less than 2x the line-screen, and your images contain sharp, straight lines, they will look 'stepped' and otherwise poor.

3   If you supply photos in their final size at under 1.25x the line-screen, they will look poor whatever you do.

'Logical' screen resolution on a Mac is 72 ppi, and on a PC 96 ppi. Retina displays work to a much higher actual resolution. Even so, images which look brilliant on the screen at 100% will in almost all cases be far too small for print.

4   Lab adjust

Do your images look a little dull? If they look dull on the screen, they will look even worse once printed in CMYK. If you are depicting industrial machinery in professional grey, then this may not trouble you. If you are doing a brochure for holidays in sunny Spain, it may work against you.

The eye typically takes in six megapixels (MP) from an image at normal viewing distance. This means that a full page or billboard image needs to be 12 megapixels, because halftone requires 2x oversampling. Today's cameras typically shoot at 16 MP–24 MP, which allows for some cropping. The Nikon D800 series shoots at 36 MP. Medium format cameras such as Hasselblads are often 56 MP plus.

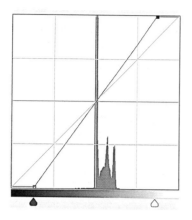

Above: tucking in the 'a' in LAB colour, using the curves function in Photoshop. Do the same for 'b', and then convert back to RGB.

Below,
left, dull image;
centre, tone-mapping applied;
right, too much tone-mapping.

In Photoshop, you can up the saturation, and, in Photoshop's Raw mode, you can even increase the 'vibrance'. However, the result is often that you produce lobster-faced people with unreal looking skies.

Professional photographers often employ this trick: In Photoshop, or any other application that supports it, convert your image from RGB to 'Lab', or 'L*a*b' colour. Then go into the Curves adjustment, and go to 'a'. The curve, to begin with, will be a straight line. Move the bottom rightwards about 1/8 of the way, and move the top leftwards the exact same amount. You can see this because the centre grid-lines still cross the middle of the curve. If that line isn't on the middle, it creates a colour shift. Then do the same thing for the 'b' curve.

Once done, convert the image back to RGB and continue working.

To see the results, make sure you have View—Proof Output set to your final output process in QuarkXPress. This will inevitably be duller than what Photoshop is showing you. If it is significantly duller, turn View—Proof Output off: the image should now be the same as in Photoshop. If it isn't, then either the monitor calibration is switched off in Photoshop or QuarkXPress, or the colour profile has not been correctly assigned in Photoshop.

Assuming all is fine, turn View—Proof Output back on in QuarkXPress. Does the image look overcooked? It is better to have a slightly duller image than one which is oversaturated. However, using Lab colour to do the adjustments will keep you away from most problems of oversaturation.

5   Tone-mapping

An image which is still dull may be rescuable through a process called tone-mapping. Photoshop can do this natively, and so can a number of plugins and stand-alone applications, most notably Photomatix Tonemapping. The process is otherwise known as 'Pseudo HDR'.

Documents that draw the eye and hold the mind

Tone-mapping is intrinsically dangerous. It is good for rescuing an image where the lighting is either too dull, or too harsh, and restoring details. However, it is easy to go overboard, giving effects that would belong better on a fantasy film-poster.

Reshoot the photo…

The best advice I have ever been given when wrestling with an image that just didn't work was 'reshoot the photo'. Whether you are creating an obesity campaign and your fat bloke isn't fat enough, or a brochure with cute furry animals that look more savage than cute, or a poster for a romantic weekend and your couple look like they've just had a row, there is no Photoshop filter that can possibly fix your problem.

There are times when you've gone to the trouble of setting up a studio shot with paid models. You've done everything right. When you get back to the layout, it just doesn't work.

There are three possibilities here.

First, there may have been technical errors in the execution of the photograph. You should be able to spot what they were immediately. It may be possible to fix them in post-processing, but if there are a lot of images, it is often quicker and cheaper to reshoot.

Technical issue	Fixable	What to do
Blurred image	Maybe	FocusMagic, Unsharp Masking
Colour cast	Yes	White balance setting in Curves
Two colour casts (from mixed lighting)	Maybe	DxO, Mask and edit Curves, or use as monochrome
Distracting background	Yes	Mask out background
Cluttered image	Maybe	Crop out clutter
Wrong facial expression	No	Reshoot
Too tightly cropped	Yes	Set the image in a border
Blown out highlights	Maybe	Go back to Raw image, redevelop
Wrong camera angle	No	Reshoot
Unexpected reflections	Maybe	If minor, clone out. Else, reshoot.
Dust and spots	Yes	Use the spot fixer

Photoshop filters you wish they made:
"The look of love"—makes couples seem more devoted to each other.
"Cuteness"—adds a touch of Landseer to any animal.
"Fat/thin"—perfectly reproportions any human to some unrealistic standard.
"Sincerity"—turns that manipulative grin into something grandmothers swoon over.

Secondly, the image may just not work, creatively. It's supposed to be obvious that it's something, but it isn't. Or, it's supposed to be something the viewer only sees on the second go, but it's too obvious. There are lots of other things that can be creatively wrong with the image. Often this is because the visual idea just wasn't strong enough. In that case, brainstorm again, and come up with a better idea.

The third possibility is that the brief is simply wrong. This is especially likely to be the case when you're fairly sure you've done what they asked you to do, and they come back asking for ever more creative changes. In my experience, this is often a sign that the person you have been dealing with is not the real decision maker.

At this point, it is worth reviewing:

Is the **Outcome** realistic? I've often been asked to provide a logo which 'makes customers buy the products'. No such logo can exist.

Is it the right **Audience**? Do the people evaluating it understand who it's for? Very often, marketing materials are designed to appeal to the people who pay for them, not the people they are actually aimed at. You may need to 'educate the customer', including showing evidence for your design choices.

Are the **Messages** right? If the image you are working with effectively puts over the agreed messages (or one of them), but the layout as a whole doesn't work, there's a good chance that the messages themselves just weren't very effective.

Is the **Delivery** right? Is the image right for the delivery? People have often come to me with images they desperately want included, but the final document is being reproduced in black and white. The image is clear enough in colour, but in monochrome, it's just a load of grey. You, as the layout designer, appreciate that what you see on your screen is never quite what appears in print—and, in any case, you've turned View—Proof Output on in QuarkXPress to match the final output.

5 25 rules of composition

The rules set out here are 25 rules which I have picked up from books, seminars, web-discussions and in teaching over the last thirty years. They are more comprehensive than you generally find, but there are doubtless others I have missed. They are rules in the sense that they show what happens when something is done. There is no moral imperative to follow them, and they can be deliberately combined in competition with each other to produce interesting effects, or to initially mislead the viewer. The rules are primarily created for photography, but can apply equally to general layout.

1 The eye moves naturally from dark areas to bright areas.

2 The eye moves naturally from indistinct to distinct forms.

3 The eye comes to rest at the point two lines cross.

4 The eye is drawn to the point at which two lines *would* cross, if only they were long enough.

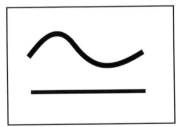

5 The eye is more attracted to curving shapes than straight shapes.

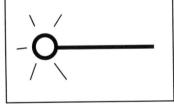

6 The eye will begin at a centre of attention, and then follow lines leading away from it.

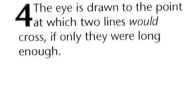

7 Rotary motion tends to bring the eye into the centre of an image, and then back out again.

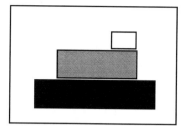

8 Where darker and larger shapes are underneath lighter and smaller shapes, the result is harmonious.

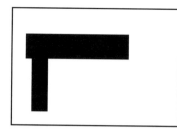

9 Where shapes would appear to 'topple', the result is one of tension.

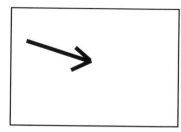

10 The eye follows implicit direction and motion, such as an arrow or a gaze. Where space is left for it, the result is harmonious.

11 When a pattern is disrupted, the eye is drawn to the disruption.

12 In a rectangle, the eye will naturally come to rest at the Golden Section points, about 61% from the far side.

13 When a shape within a frame mirrors the shape of the frame, the result is harmonious.

14 A single item of primary interest draws the eye.

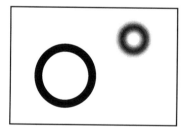

15 Where a secondary item, less dominant by means of colour, focus or position resembles the first, the result is harmonious.

16 Multiple items which draw the attention equally are competing interest, which confuses the viewer.

Documents that draw the eye and hold the mind

17 Lines leading out of the frame will tend to take the viewer with them.

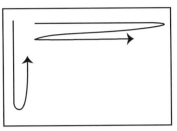

18 For viewers used to reading left to right and up to down, the eye naturally follows a reading path across the image.

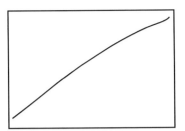

19 A line sloping upwards across the frame is perceived as optimistic, a line sloping downwards as pessimistic.

20 The eye is drawn to human faces, or things it can interpret as human faces, more than other interest.

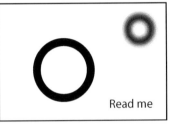

Read me

21 For literate readers, the eye is drawn to text at the expense of the image.

Speling

22 Once a 'mistake' in an image has been identified, the viewer is unable to appreciate the rest of the image.

23 Negative space can play as powerful an effect as positive space.

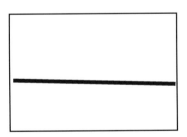

24 Where lines are not quite vertical or horizontal, tension is created. Skew lines such as water horizons are perceived as errors.

25 When two shapes overlap, they tend to create a new shape in the eye of the viewer, even when this is unwanted or inappropriate.

2 Master typography

The first printers were typographers, and typography remains one of the most important skills of the desk top publisher. Good typography makes reading a pleasure. Poor typography makes reading difficult or impossible, losing the interest of the reader.

At the most basic level, a publication is successful when people who start reading it continue to read it until the end. A publication which people give up part way through is, in that sense, a failure. Although no typography can rescue bad content, bad typography will limit the impact of even the very best content.

The three most important books for typographers:
The Elements of Typographic Style, Robert Bringhurst
Why Fonts Matter, Sarah Hyndman
Reading Letters, Sofie Beier.

Why Fonts Matter examines the emotional impact of letter types. Reading Letters summarises all of the research on legibility.

1 Legibility

The first duty of the typographer is legibility.

This comes down to eight things:

- Typeface
- Type size
- Leading
- Kerning and letter spacing (tracking)
- Line length
- Justification
- Colour
- Print Process

Cap height, t-height, x-height, baseline and descender. The most important physical aspect of letter legibility is having a high x-height compared with the t-height or Cap height.

1   Typeface

Sofie Beier summarises more than a century of research in her book Reading Letters.

There are four key findings to do with the letters themselves:

- Familiarity is key. Familiar letter-types are more legible. Even German Black-Letter is highly legible for those used to it. This is why some studies indicate that serif fonts are easier to read, and other studies indicate that sans-serif fonts are easier to read. Italics are unfamiliar.

- A high x-height in proportion to t-height (or Caps height) improves legibility for the same point size.
- Slightly wider letters are more legible than slightly narrower letters. Condensed fonts are therefore less legible.
- Strokes which are uniform and slightly heavier are easier to read than strongly differentiated strokes.

Additionally, some fonts have easy-to-confuse letters, such as lower case l with upper case I and the number 1.

High legibility	Lower legibility
Helvetica Neue	Bodoni
Frutiger	Adobe Garamond Pro
ITC Bookman	Helvetica Condensed
Candida	Futura Book
ITC Franklin Gothic	Gill Sans
Plantin Standard	TRAJAN

In the examples above, Helvetica Neue, Frutiger, ITC Bookman, Candida and ITC Franklin Gothic all have relatively high x-heights. Plantin, Candida, Frutiger, Helvetica and Franklin Gothic all have even strokes. Bookman Medium, although the strokes are more differentiated, is a slightly heavier weight and is wider than most fonts—almost like an extended font.

Bodoni, Adobe Garamond Pro, Futura and Gill Sans all have low x-heights. They would need to be 1-2 points larger to have the same legibility as the more legible fonts. Bodoni has very strongly differentiated strokes, which make reading difficult. Helvetica Condensed is too condensed to make comfortable reading. Trajan is available only as a Caps/Small caps font. It is widely believed that capitals are intrinsically harder to read and take up more space than mixed case, but the research says the opposite— what makes capitals harder to read is merely that we are less familiar with them.

Beyond a certain expected legibility, it is possible to make text over-legible, which reduces its credibility, and can even

Easily confused letters:
In many fonts, one or more of the following are easily confused with other letters from the same line.

e	c	a	s	n	u	o
i	j	l	t	f		
O	Q	D	C	G		
V	Y	W	M	K	X	
T	I	J	L			
F	B	P	E	T	H	
H	N	M	(Futura)			

Helvetica, Futura and Bodoni, showing the differing proportions and stroke variations.

Above, printer's letters at the Plantin Museum, Antwerp.

In moveable type, the point size is the height of the body, which is a fixed size for all letters for easy racking, and so must accommodate the highest capitals—possibly with accents—and the lowest descenders.

In computer fonts, the 'point size' does not depend on a physical body. Generally it conforms to the physical measurements, but sometimes poorly.

Setting for people with visual impairments.
Depending on a person's vision, they may be unable to read text smaller than 14 point, 18 point, or even 24 point. However, 14 point text is too large to be easily legible by normally sighted people. The best thing is to produce a separate version or versions in large-print. Ideally, users should be asked for their preferred type size. A generic large print version should be 18 point.

come across as patronising. Designers need to combine the different elements of legibility judiciously—Futura, Bodoni and Adobe Garamond may sometimes be better choices than their more legible peers.

2 Type size

David Ogilvy's research[1] indicates that the most legible type size is 11 point. However, that depends a bit on the optical size of the letters.

aaaaaaaaaaa   eeeeeeeeee
bbbbbbbbbbb   fffffffffff
ccccccccccc   gggggggggggg
ddddddddddd   hhhhhhhhhhh

In the examples above, all the letters are set at 12 point, in fonts Adobe Garamond, Bodoni, Bookman, Candida, Frutiger, Futura, Gill, Helvetica, Helvetica Condensed, ITC Franklin Gothic and Plantin. The optical size of the letters varies dramatically. This is clearest in the x-height—as noted above, low x-height means less legibility—and in the ascenders.

Frutiger set at 10 point appears as large as Futura at 11 point, except in the capitals.
Adobe Garamond needs to be 12 point to appear the same.

or, put another way,

Frutiger set at 10 point appears larger than Futura at the same size, except in the capitals.
Adobe Garamond appears even smaller.

As a general rule, fonts with high x-height and otherwise good legibility can be set at 9-11 point. At 12 points they seem overlarge, and legibility suffers. Fonts with lower x-heights can be set from 10-12 point for body text. Fancy fonts may need to be as large as 14 point to be legible at all, and should never be used for body text.

1 In Ogilvy on Advertising, Orbis, 1983. A book everyone in the business of communicating ought to read.

Master typography

3   Leading

As discussed earlier, leading refers to the gap between the tops of the bottoms of the descenders and the tops of the ascenders on the next line. In past times this was measured by the amount of extra lead which needed to go between the bodies of the letters, but since the advent of computers leading is usually taken to mean the distance from one baseline to the next—partly because of the difficulties of agreeing what the actual height of the font is. The old meaning of leading is now covered by 'line spacing'.

In QuarkXPress:
Leading   =   distance between baselines
          =   font size + line spacing

QuarkXPress 2016 defaults to automatic leading of 20% in addition to the font's own height. You can change this in Preferences—Print Layout—Paragraph. If setting narrative fiction, you might want to make the automatic leading 30%. Incidentally, and somewhat confusingly, this 30% is actually using the *old* meaning of leading, as the extra space, rather than the total space.

If you are using a grid, and locking your text down to it, the baseline position may be important. By default, the baseline is set to 25% above the bottom line, but you can also define it, either using Window—Grid Styles, or, when in Master Pages, Page—Master Guides and Grid, to be based on the top line or centre lines. You can also have it read from the font itself, to correctly position your baseline. I have to say that I have never, ever made use of this facility, but, then, I'm not a grid purist.

More usually, you would set the leading in Paragraph Styls—Format, or using the Measurements panel.

Text which is 'set tight'—with no additional leading—is only marginally legible, though it can work in titles where reduced leading gives more weight to the text. During the 1970s, 80s and 1990s, U&lc magazine popularised improving legibility by reducing the font size and dramatically increasing the leading. It looks a bit dated now—especially with narrow fonts—but could well be due for a comeback.

The grid style panel

The leading used to be the additional gap between Bottom line and Topline of the next row of text. These days, it usually means the total space from Baseline to the next Baseline—but not always.

During the 1970s, 89s and 90s, U&lc Magazine popularised the idea of setting text in smaller sizes but with exaggerated leading to improve legibility while getting more words into the same space. This was often in conjunction with electronically narrowing the font. Although 90% width is properly a font faux pas, the enhanced leading is well worth considering.

A' ac Ac AC ad Ad ae Ae af ag Ag
AG Ao AO ap ap Ap Aq AQ at At AT
au Au AU av Av AV aw Aw AW ay Ay
AY b, B, b. B. BA Bb BE Bi Bk bl
Bl BL BP br Br BR bu Bu BU BV BW
by By BY C, C. ca Ca CA ch ck CO
Cr CR d, D, d. D. da Da DA dc DD
de DE dg Dl DL DMDN do DO DP DR
dt du DU dv DV dwDW dy DY e, e.
ea EC ei el em en EO ep er et eu
Eu ev Ev ew ey f, F, F, F; F: f.
F. F. fa Fa FA FC fe Fe ff FG fi
Fi fl fo Fo FO Fr Ft Fu Fy g, g.
ga ge GE gg gh gl go GO GR Gu GU
hc hd he He hg ho Ho HO hp ht hu
Hu hv hw hy Hy ic Ic IC id Id ie
ig IG io Io IO ip Iq it It iu iv
j, J, j. J. ja Ja JA je Je jo Jo
JO ju Ju ka kc kd ke Ke kg ko Ko
KO Ku L' la lc LC ld le lf lg LG
lo LO lp lq LT lu Lu LU lv LV lw
LW ly Ly LY M ma Ma mc Mc mdMd
me Me mgMGmn mo MoMO mp mt mu
mv my N, N. Na nc NC nd ne Ne ng
NG Ni no NoNO np nt nu Nu Nu nv
nw ny o, O, o. O. Oa OA ob Ob OB
OD OE of OF oh Oh OH Ol oj ok Ok
OK ol Ol OL omOM on ON op OP or
OR OT ou OU ov OV ow OW ox OX oy
OY p, P, P; P: p. P. pa Pa PA Pe
PE ph pi pl PL Po PO pp PP pu PU
PY qu QU r, r. ra RC rd Rd re Re
rg RG rk rl rm rn ro Ro rq rr rt
Rt RT Ru RU rv RV RW ry RY RY s,
S, s. S. sh Si Sl SM Sp st ST su
Su SU t, T, T; T: t. t. T. ta Ta
TA Tc TC td te Te Ti to To TO Tr
Ts Tu Tw Ty U, U. ua Ua UA uc UC
ud ue ug Ug UG Um Un uo UO up Up
uq Us US ut uv uw uy v, V, V; V:
v. V. va Va VA vb vc VC vd ve Ve
vg VG Vi vo Vo VO Vr VS Vu vv vy
w, W, W; W: w. W. wa WA WC wdWd
we wg WGwh Wi Wmwo WO Wr Wt Wu
wx Wy xa Xa xe Xe xo Xo Xu Xy y,
Y, Y; Y: y. Y. ya YA yc YC yd Yd
ye Ye Yi yo YO Yp YS Yu Yv ZO

If you want to do this, consider using Vertical Justification, in the Measurements—Text Box tab, which will increase the leading to fit the text box.

4   Kerning and Letter Spacing

For good legibility, fonts need to appear evenly on the page, and they need to have adequate spaces between the letters and the words. Too much space, though, combined with too little leading, will open up rivers of text and the eye will get lost.

Kerning is how the spacing between individual pairs of letters is adjusted. This is done by the font designer, and often takes more time and skill than creating the fonts in the first place. Commercial kerning houses charge large sums to kern fonts accurately.

The reason for kerning is because the shapes of the letters themselves either open up gaps or appear to crowd each other when the font side-bearings are consistent. In the days of moveable type, printers would often have special glyphs which combined two hard-to-kern letters. Sometimes these would be joined, to create ligatures, such as fl or fi. These are often present in modern fonts, and can be turned on in QuarkXPress Character Styles—Standard Ligatures or Character Styles—Discretionary Ligatures, or through the Open Type settings in the Measurements panel. In Preferences—Print Layout—Character you can specify how many characters will be ligatured together, though few fonts offer too much in this regard, and whether 'ffi' and 'ffl' should be ligatured.

You can also specify at what size kerning begins. The default is 4 point, which is also too small to be legible—in other words, QuarkXPress always kerns text. You should not normally need to adjust this.

In QuarkXPress, you can fix one or two bad kerning pairs in Edit—Kerning Pairs. If there are any more than one or two, it becomes virtually impossible to do it consistently in QuarkXPress—you are as likely to create problems as to

Master typography

solve them. You can export and import your kerning edits from the Edit Kerning Pairs window.

A specialist font design utility such as FontLab Studio is better placed for this, but only if you are the copyright holder of the font—in which case you most likely created it in FontLab or a similar application. Even then, great amounts of time and skill are needed.

Pro tip—No matter how much you love a font, if the kerning is bad, discard it.

Tracking is the general space between characters—confusingly called 'kerning' in the Measurements panel. Fonts have been constructed normally to have the optimal tracking when set at ordinary body text sizes, 9–12 point. When using Justified text, QuarkXPress will ordinarily adjust the tracking by 2% in either direction to fit the text onto the line. This is set in Edit—H&Js. With Standard H&Js, Quark will expand or reduce the space between words to a greater extent, as this is generally easier on the eye.

However, at larger sizes, for example for titles, most fonts benefit from having the tracking reduced a little. You can do this on an ad hoc basis by using the A͞V control in the Measurements panel, on a stylesheet basis by adjusting the Track Amount in the Character Styles panel, or, in an altogether more refined way, by adjusting it per typeface across all sizes in Edit—Font Tracking Tables. This does not affect the font itself, only the QuarkXPress document. If you want to do this across all your documents, make the edits to the Tracking Tables with QuarkXPress open but all documents closed.

When designing text to be read at a distance, legibility increases if the tracking is wider, up to 50%, after which there is no improvement.

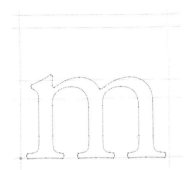

Adobe Garamond Pro 'm', showing sidebearings.

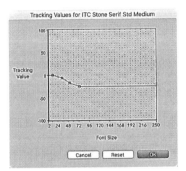

In Tracking Values, you can specify tracking consistently across the range of type sizes.

Below, Stone Serif Medium 8 point with 0% increased tracking, 10%, 30% and 50%. Legibility is increased for distance reading at 50% extra tracking. Notice also that the letters actually appear larger.

Legibility at a distance
Legibility at a distance
Legibility at a distance
Legibility at a distance

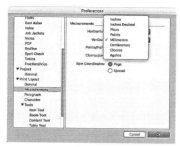

*Preferences—Print Layout—
Measurements.*

*Most people will naturally choose
millimetres or, if in the USA,
inches, as their measurement.
However, Picas, Points, Ciceros or
Agates may also interest you
when working out line lengths.*

Point:	*0.35 mm, 1/72 inches*
Pica:	*12 points*
Cicero:	*4.5 mm, or 12 old French points, 12.9 computer points*
Agate:	*5.143 points, considered to be the smallest size legible in newsprint. Called a 'Ruby' in the UK.*

*In QuarkXPress, you can enter
any measurement no matter what
your default units are, as follows:*

Point:	*pt*
Millimetre:	*mm or m*
Centimetre:	*cm*
Pica:	*p*
Cicero:	*c*
Agate:	*a*
Inch:	*" or i*

5   Line length

The length of the line has a significant impact on legibility. If the line is too long, the eye loses its place. If it is too short, the eye has to keep jumping to the next line, and it becomes harder to follow, especially where there are frequent hyphenations.

Importantly, the length of the line and the length of the words and sentences go together. No word should ever be hyphenated twice onto three lines, and no sentence should ever be on more than three lines, except in the most literary texts, such as the first page of Umberto Eco's *Baudolino*. This is one reason why newspaper journalists write such short sentences, because their columns are so narrow.

For English:

- The usual length for a single column page is 45–75 characters.

- The ideal length is considered to be 66 characters.

- When set in columns, 40–50 characters is generally acceptable.

- For margin notes, the minimum line length is 12–15 characters.

This book has 58 characters per main column line, and 37 per line for the marginal comments. You would not generally want to set extended narrative text in a column that narrow.

With generous leading and discontinuous text, such as in footnotes, 85–90 characters might well be legible. Even with good leading, more than 75 characters will be hard going in narrative text.

When setting in narrow columns, hyphenation becomes almost compulsory, and it is generally best to set flush left, ragged right.

Master typography

6 Justification

Text which is set flush left, ragged right, also known as **left justified**, is the most legible.

Text which is set flush right, ragged left, known as **right justified,** and text which is **centred**, is illegible, except in very short sections.

Text which is fully justified, or, simply, **justified**, is flush left and flush right, with the spaces between the letters and words automatically adjusted by QuarkXPress based on the H&J settings selected, either in Styles—Paragraph—Format, or in the Measurements Panel, Paragraph tab.

You can edit the H&J settings, as well as looking at the standards supplied, in Edit—H&Js. There is not a great deal of benefit in playing with the settings, unless you are under extreme space constraints. Standard will do for most purposes. In narrow columns you may need to use Narrow Measure or Very Narrow Measure.

By default, QuarkXPress has Standard H&Js on, even in left justified text. Many people don't like this, as they find even occasional hyphens distracting in text they are paying for. See below, *Hyphenation.*

When to justify
Printed fiction and narrative non-fiction is still generally set flush left and right, or 'fully justified'.

Dictionaries, technical manuals and academic writing have traditionally always been printed fully justified, but there is movement towards Flush left, ragged right (left justification).

Newspapers are generally printed fully justified, and often in narrow columns with small fonts.

Magazines were traditionally set fully justified, but are now frequently set flush left, ragged right.

Advertising, marketing and promotional material is still occasionally set fully justified, but more usually flush left, ragged, right.

Flush left, ragged right:
Yesterday afternoon set in misty and cold. I had half a mind to spend it by my study fire, instead of wading through heath and mud to Wuthering Heights. On coming up from dinner, however, (N.B.—I dine

Justified:
Yesterday afternoon set in misty and cold. I had half a mind to spend it by my study fire, instead of wading through heath and mud to Wuthering Heights. On coming up from dinner, however, (N.B.—I dine

Flush right, ragged left:
Yesterday afternoon set in misty and cold. I had half a mind to spend it by my study fire, instead of wading through heath and mud to Wuthering Heights. On coming up from dinner, however, (N.B.—I dine

Centred:
Yesterday afternoon set in misty and cold. I had half a mind to spend it by my study fire, instead of wading through heath and mud to Wuthering Heights. On coming up from dinner, however, (N.B.—I dine

Forced Justification:
Yesterday afternoon set in misty and cold. I had half a mind to spend it by my study fire, instead of wading through heath and mud to Wuthering Heights. On coming up from dinner, however, (N.B.—I dine

(Emily Brontë, Wuthering Heights)

Edit dialogue for the H&Js, standing for Hyphenation and Justification. Standard is right for most jobs. Narrow or Very Narrow Measure fits more in, but looks scrappy.

When flowing text round a picture, always have the text on the left and the picture on the right, as in this example.

When text is on the right and the picture is on the left, it becomes hard to read, and also looks excessively dated.

Slanted justification by skewing a text box may well be marginally more legible than right justified or centred, but why would you ever want to inflict anything so ugly and wasteful on your long-suffering readers? Remember—just because you can do it, doesn't mean that you should.

Hyphenation Exceptions for Part 2
aren't
didn't
doesn't
weren't
won't
wouldn't

Language: English (International)

Add   Delete   Cancel   Save

Edit hyphenation exceptions to prevent bugbears like "didn't" from breaking across lines.

Essentially, the more formal and traditional the document, the more likely it will be set fully justified. The more contemporary and 'designed', the more likely it will be set left justified.

Invitations are often set centred, with parts left and right justified, so that everything falls nicely on the page. Centring really only works for single lines of text, as you would find in an invitation or on a poster. The eye finds it hard to locate the next line, slowing reading speed and making it more likely that reading ceases.

Right justified should only be used when it is formally required, such as in addresses on correspondence, for lining up figures or words in tables, or for single lines such as captions and by-lines. It is very hard to read several lines when right justified.

During the 1980s, it was fairly common to see text flowing round a picture, sometimes on both sides. This was because it was a new feature available in Aldus PageMaker (Mac) and Xerox Ventura Publisher (PC), and from version 5, in Word and WordPerfect.

When the picture is on the right and the text is on the left, the result is generally good, as long as attention is paid to problem areas.

When the picture is on the left and the text is on the right, it becomes very hard to follow the text. The result is generally scrappy.

Hyphenation

In narrow columns, or when fully justifying text, hyphenation is generally necessary to avoid huge gaps opening up.

QuarkXPress hyphenates well in a number of supplied languages, and Xtensions are available for others. However, it isn't always perfect. You may have noticed in the Harry Potter books that "didn't" is frequently hyphenated as "didn't", which just looks ridiculous. To prevent this happening, go to Utilities—Hyphenations Exceptions—Edit. You can add as many in as you like. If you prefer to do all your hyphenation manually, but are unsure of the rules,

Master typography

you can turn off H&Js in the Paragraph Style—Formats panel, and use Utilities—Suggested Hyphenation to tell you what the hyphenation should be. Cmd/ctrl-hyphen in front of a word prevents it from hyphenating. Cmd/ctrl-hyphen inside a word hyphenates at that place, if hyphenation is turned off, or at that place or another suggested place if hyphenation is turned on.

You can also use Utilities—Insert Character—Special and Special (non-breaking) to insert breaking and non-breaking characters.

Some punctuation is troublesome with breaking. Em dashes— and slashes / may not behave as you want them to. The quick fix is to use Find/Change to insert zero-width spaces, as \z—\z or \z/\z, \z being the code for a zero-width breaking space. A more cunning method—see overleaf, *Hyphenation niceties*, is to specify breaking sets.

Hanging Character Margin alignment

If you want to make your text truly beautiful, you might consider using Margin Alignment. Edit this in Paragraph Style—Format—Hanging Character Set, and apply it in the Measurements panel, paragraph tab ¶, shown as ▦ (underneath H&Js), or in a paragraph style.

See the section under Menus in Part 5 on Edit—Hanging Characters, which explains how to create hanging character classes, and combine them into Sets.

What's this for, what does it do, and how do you do it?

Essentially, when you justify text, the computer lines up where everything goes based on the instructions provided by the font file. However, while electronically correct, the result is not optically correct, especially at large sizes.

QuarkXPress lets you create a Hanging Character Class, which is either trailing or leading, which allows a character to hang over the margins. The most obvious use for this is to allow punctuation, such as a full stop, to be right on the right hand margin, rather than forcing the entire word onto the next line. In a long document, that could save you a couple of pages.

Above, suggested hyphenation reminds you of the rules for the language you are working in. If you are a cautious hyphenator, then turning auto-hyphenation off and working through Utilities—Suggested Hyphenation may save more time than it costs.

Below, editing Hanging Character Class to produce optical margin alignment.

Margin alignment in action:

Where are you going, my pretty maid?
I'm going a milking, sir, she said.
May I go with you, my pretty maid?
You're kindly welcome, sir, she said.
What is your fortune, my pretty maid?
My face is my fortune, sir, she said.

And not in action:

Where are you going, my pretty maid?
I'm going a milking, sir, she said.
May I go with you, my pretty maid?
You're kindly welcome, sir, she said.
What is your fortune, my pretty maid?

English nursery rhyme

If you want absolute control over which characters are allowed to break a line, turn on East Asian Functionality in QuarkXPress—Preferences—East Asian. You will need to quit and relaunch for this to take effect. This will bring up additional options, including in H&Js, where you will see "Non-breaking Char Set". There are a number of options, but if you want to edit one, go to Edit—Non-Breaking Character Set, where you will see that Simplified Chinese Standard has rules for which western punctuation cannot begin or end a line, or is non-separable. If you duplicate this, and call it 'Standard', you can make your own adjustments.

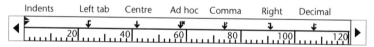

If you then go back to H&Js and select the Non-breaking Character Set you just created, you can apply it to various H&J settings.

Here's the clever bit. Having done that, if you now go back and turn East Asian functionality off in the preferences, and relaunch QuarkXPress, all the additional (and confusing) extra menu items have disappeared, but the changes you made are still active.

In each class, you specify which characters are affected, whether it is hanging, trailing or dropped cap margin alignment, and what percentage adjustment to make.

Once you have created your classes, you combine them into a set. You cannot include the same character in two different classes within the same set (which would, after all, be giving contradictory instructions).

For basic use, turn on the Punctuation Margin Alignment and see what it does.

If, when you look at your text closely, you are not happy with the alignmet of particular letters, you can create a new class (or more than one) and, effectively, nudge those letters a little—perhaps 7% for leading character alignment for W and Y. This is more important for larger text, where the differences are more obvious.

You can set up as many different Classes and Sets as you like, with different combinations of Classes in different Sets. However, you can only have one Set applied per paragraph style.

Using tabs for in line justification

You can use tabs to separately justify text within a line. This is often preferable to constructing a table, because the text remains running text, and the information often arrives in tabbed format.

If you select the text, and then go to Measurements—Tabs, a ruler will pop up. You can then use left, centre, right, justify on decimal, justify on comma, and align on other character. You can also add fill characters. When done, Cmd/ctrl-click on Paragraph Styles to save as a new style.

Project	Begins	Ends	Work	Predecessors	Cost
Prisoner of Zenda reprint	12 May 2016	14 June 2016	72h	5,4,67	£8,200.00

In this example, dates are centre tabs, Work and Predecessors are right tabbed, and Cost is tabbed to line up on the decimal point.

Master typography

7 Typographic Colour

Even in monochrome, fonts have their own colour. This can complement or interfere with other colour ideas that you have in your layout.

The most basic colour of type is the shades of grey it creates on the page. Bold text, and black text especially, has a much darker colour, but even in body text, differing fonts bring a different colour to the page. Too heavy, especially in a solid page of single column text, such as a novel, with relatively parsimonious margins (every additional page is a reduction in the publisher's profits), and it can seem over-bearing and off-putting. Too light, especially on gloss or silk paper, and the lack of contrast makes reading a strain.

All this is exacerbated by printing words in colours, or on colours, or, worst of all, in colours on colours. When reliable, cheap CMYK printing first became widely available in the 1990s, all kinds of colour combinations became popular. Now that we have rather got over ourselves, black text on white, with perhaps titles in some strongly contrasting colour, has become common again. It used to be a common stereotype—the client who, since he was paying for full colour, wanted all the colours of the rainbow in his brochure.

We'll take a look at the emotional impact of colour later: it is important. Here, we will just consider legibility.

Essentially, black text on yellow is the most legible—in small quantities. After a while it seems over-imposing.

Black on white has the best overall, long-term legibility. For very short text, acuity of white on black is slightly better, though this drops off quickly with prolonged reading.

The most important factor is **luminance contrast**: black on dark colours such as strong red, or white on light colours, such as pastels, substantially slows reading.

Within that, the colours at the ends of the spectrum—blue and red—slow reading more than the colours in the middle of the spectrum.

Bauer Bodoni left, Bookman right

Above, Adobe Garamond, Candida
Below, Helvetica Neue, Futura

Text—The Prisoner of Zenda,
Anthony Hope

From most legible to least:
Black text on white
Black on yellow
White on blue
Blue on white
Yellow on red*
Black on red
Black on red has 50% legibility compared with black on white.

(from Journal of Design Communications, Virginia Tech, 2003, issue 4: Bix, Lockhart, Cardoso and Selke)
*The oldest age group found yellow on red less legible than black on red.

—

—

Colour contrast, such as red on green, does not improve readability.

When a coloured background is used, the lower the saturation, the more comfortable it is for extended reading.

8 Print Process

On the internet, all colours are more or less equal in terms of how well they will be reproduced. In print, legibility of particular colours is strongly influenced by the print process.

In Spot Colour printing, every main colour is printed with the appropriate ink, so all colours are effectively equal in terms of reproduction—their legibility is solely a result of the factors we discussed in the colour section.

In CMYK print, every colour except for Cyan, Magenta, Yellow and Black is produced by combining coloured dots, which are typically offset from each other at angles of 105°, 75°, 90° and 45°. The colours indigo-blue, bright red and strong green are produced by combining, respectively, Cyan and Magenta, Magenta and Yellow, and Cyan and Magenta at 100%.

In high quality print processes, the four process colours plus indigo, red and strong green can be considered to be safe for text: as long as the registration is accurate, they should be legible. Where there are questions about registration, for example in office colour laser printers, or attempting process colours on a Risograph, only the process colours themselves are safe, and, of these, only black is genuinely legible. The exception is when printing over a solid colour background. If flat yellow has been laid down, then red (100% magenta + 100% yellow) is safe, as is green.

For high quality print with good registration, the legibility of other colours depends on the line-screen of the printing process. At 150 lines per inch, the standard for most print these days, titles and bold text will generally be safe in most colours, and black text on a light toned background will also be safe, but smaller text will tend to dissolve into a sea of dots. If in doubt, ask the print house for samples of work they have done before in colour. Just because the equipment is technically capable of producing the result you want, doesn't mean that the print operators are going to take sufficient care of your job to make it work.

Stock

The stock on which you print has a significant impact on legibility. Unfortunately, it runs in two opposite directions.

All ink print is beset by issues of dot gain. Dot gain is the way that an ink dot blossoms out when applied to paper. Laser printer users do not wrestle with this, but anyone who has owned an ink-jet knows what happens when you try to print fine lines and gorgeous colours onto ordinary copy paper: the lines blur, the ink sinks into the paper, and everything turns into a world of soft pastels. Dot gain is now dealt with in the pre-press software (the RIP), but there are still limitations on the maximum vibrance achievable.

There are essentially nine main types of paper in common use for offset print:

Coating	Type	Photos	Dot gain	Legibility
Coated	Gloss	Excellent	Lowest	Poor
	Silk/Satin	Good	Low	Medium
	Matte	Acceptable	Low	Good
	Dull	Acceptable	Medium	Good
	Newsprint	Acceptable	Medium	Good
Uncoated	Wove/smooth	Weak	Higher	Excellent
	Laid	Poor	Higher	Excellent
	Linen	Poor	Higher	Excellent
	Newsprint	Marginal	Highest	Excellent

Coated papers are treated so that the ink is not absorbed and dries on the paper. Gloss dries fastest and gives the most vibrant colours, because it has the lowest dot gain. However, the shininess of gloss makes it hard to read.

Don't worry about dot gain... usually

In the past, it was necessary to adjust photographs and halftones to take account of dot gain. These days, CMYK pre-press software usually makes the adjustments at the final stage.

*For printing in black and white it can be a bit more trial and error. Ask for an example of other monochrome work your printer has done. **In mono, all text will look ten times as good as on your screen, and images will look half as good.***

You can overcome this to an extent. For photographs, in the Levels dialogue in Photoshop, 'tuck-in' the top and bottom levels and move the middle level down by about ⅛. Nb, this is only for controlling dot-gain when the pre-press software will not do it. Generally, leave things as they are.

Below, bringing the levels 'inwards' in Photoshop. Any photo editor should be able to do this.

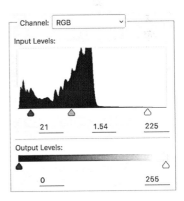

Hot press versus cold press

Modern printing presses are typically heatset, with an 'oven' or dryer built into the press, so that the ink evaporates. Coldset offset, or 'cold press' relies on the ink soaking into the paper. Coldset, in principle, can only be used for uncoated papers, though UV inks or an additional drying tower can be added.

Web versus sheet-fed

Web-fed presses, such as all the classic newspaper presses seen in films, use rolls of paper. They can print at 80,000 cut-offs an hour, with each cut-off being the circumference of the roll. However, this means that the cut-off must always be the same size. An economic quantity is in the region of 30,000 A3 trim-sized.

Sheet-fed presses can cope with a wider variety of paper sizes, though the absolute size of the plate determines the maximum. Sheet-fed can generally produce higher quality images than web-fed. An economic print run might be 5,000 A3 trim-sized, but printers often 'gang-up' more than one job. Especially in the summer and over the Christmas period, printers may accept shorter runs or charge uneconomic prices in order to keep the presses running and to cover overheads.

Silk or satin (depending on who you ask) is a compromise between gloss and matte. It gives generally good photographs, low dot gain, and is more legible.

Matte art paper is generally more expensive (gloss is actually the cheapest coated paper). Dot gain is still low, and legibility is good. Matte art is usually the best choice for crisp, promotional literature where text predominates, although the photographs will not be as good as gloss. They can be greatly improved, though, with a spot UV varnish, which effectively makes the pictures glossy and the rest of the document matte.

Dull papers are a step beyond matte. Colour pictures are never particularly good, dot gain is poorer, but the paper's intrinsic legibility is good.

Coated newsprint has come to the fore since around 2000. It has enabled most national daily newspapers to regularly print decent quality colour photographs, without having to run a special magazine section. It is much shinier than traditional newsprint, but generally retains good legibility. Dot gain is much higher than other coated papers, which is why the pictures in newsprint can never compare with magazine pictures. Because of the dot gain, font choice is important: fonts which are insufficiently robust will lose their way.

Wove paper does not come across as woven at all—that paper is linen. Wove is smooth, uncoated stock, like copier paper. Colours are generally dull because the ink soaks in, and fonts have to be carefully chosen because of dot gain. However, provided that the text is well transferred and the dot gain controlled, it can be highly legible. It is generally a poor choice for CMYK.

Laid paper has a prestigious feel, and is often used for business stationery. It is not recommended for CMYK printing, and business stationery is usually done with spot colours.

Linen is another prestigious paper, which shares the advantages and drawbacks of Laid.

Master typography

Uncoated newsprint paper has the worst dot gain, but is highly legible if the dot gain is correctly controlled. It is for black and white reproduction only.

Digital printing

Digital printing is essentially done with the same technology as laser printers, but the machines are generally better kept, able to deal with a wider range of stock, and are Pantone matched and colour calibrated. Digital can produce the same quality as standard 150 lpi offset.

The enormous advantage of digital is that there is no dot gain and no drying time. Genuinely gripping images can be presented on stock which is little better than cheap copy paper. Even so, using matte art paper or silk will enhance the result considerably. There are very few advantages to using gloss paper. Because toner is laid down onto the paper, photographs tend to have a glossy finish anyway, and there are no drying time benefits. Gloss is intrinsically the least legible paper, so should only be used when absolutely required. Many digital printers will actually print less reliably onto gloss than onto silk.

Risograph

The bargain basement of the printing world, Risograph has enormous amounts of dot gain, to the extent that printing at a lower size than 11 point is generally a risk: on at least some of the copies, the result will be too blurred to read. There is a certain excitement and sense of authenticity about Riso printed materials, a little like Lomography and home made wine.

Excursus:
Credibility and Relevance
If we only cared about legibility, we could do worse than set everything in Univers 11 point. However, even a font as beautifully functional as Univers would make our lives dull if used too much.

Choosing typefaces which are appropriate to the subject matter enhances relevance. We are drawn to things that look like other things we are interested in.

Interestingly, credibility is actually higher if the typeface is slightly harder to read—providing that it is still legible. Whether this is intrinsic or something we have just got used to has not been established. However, we all know that the headline of a newspaper article, in big, bold text, is never as complete or accurate as the smaller print of the article itself. We expect the 'small print' of an agreement to be what is legally binding, whereas anything which is large and obviously intended for us to read first we tend to dismiss as marketing fluff.

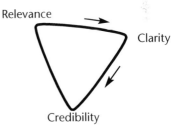

Relevance — Clarity — Credibility

The order of perception is usually 'does that look interesting' (relevance), 'what does it say?' (clarity), 'do I believe it?' (credibility).

2 Desirability in typography

The typographer's first duty is legibility, but, because type plays the principal role in most publishing, it also has an enormous impact on desirability. Designers want to—and should—create beautiful documents which are functional in terms of legibility, but also a pleasure to own, read and treasure.

Truly beautiful typography is an artform.

Some of the needs of beautiful design are in tension with the needs of legible design. But, as we saw earlier, too much legibility is a bad thing. Beyond a certain level of 'readable in the length and complexity of the content', additional legibility is a bit like shouting louder or speaking r-e-a-l-l-y s-l-o-w-l-y a-n-d c-a-r-e-f-u-l-l-y: it slows down the conversation and annoys the listener.

Put another way, for most tasks, there is a range of freedoms between the limits of ugliness at the one end and illegibility at the other. Clearly, if you are designing safety signs for a building site, being legible and eye-catching is the most important thing, and a result which is ugly but effective is better than one which is beautiful but not absolutely clear. On the other hand, if you are designing a wedding invitation, you can expect that the recipients will be willing to invest a little time puzzling out (or guessing) what it actually says.

Beauty in typography comes from three things:

1 The shapes of the letters
2 The rhythm of the page
3 The aesthetic of the design.

The shapes of the letters—as we will see in the next section—impact us through a combination of the intrinsic, the implicit, and the associative.

The rhythm of the page is much more about the abstract shapes which type creates, not only the flowing body text, but also the ornaments and apparatus such as headers, footers and page numbers.

Below, basic anatomy of a letter. There are numerous classification systems in use, some of which use similar terms to describe different things, and vice versa. It's important to recognise that the overall impression of a letter in text is quite different from one gathered by analysing its constituent parts.

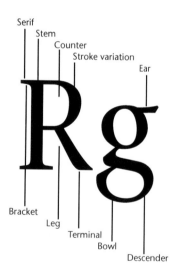

Serif
Stem
Counter
Stroke variation
Ear
Bracket
Leg
Terminal
Bowl
Descender

Master typography

Design aesthetic very much goes with a theoretical understanding of typography. In that sense, while most readers may have a vague appreciation of it looking and feeling 'just like it should', only other designers, perhaps only other designers with an understanding of the history of publishing, will truly appreciate what you have done.

2 The shapes of the letters

All fonts have an impact on us. That impact is greater if we do not realise that it is happening.

Fundamentally, it comes down to three things.

- **Intrinsic**: the actual shape of the letters (in titles) or the shapes they create collectively have a compositional effect, like those described in the Rules of Composition.
- **Implicit**: the features of the letters, such as evenness of stroke, serifs and stroke direction implies how the letter was created, which says something about it.
- **Associative**: the fot reminds the reader of something else, usually the contexts in which they would normally expect to see that font.

Intrinsics

At very large sizes, the graphical shape of the individual letters play a major role in composition. At body sizes, it is their effect as a group which is more pronounced. The overall slant of the characters, for example, could be leaning backwards (Renaissance fonts such as Plantin), vertical (Bodoni and other Romantic fonts), or leaning forwards, as in almost all italic and oblique fonts.

One reason why Comic Sans is both the world's most derided font and also one of the most popular is that people actually like the optimistic forward slant. However, like almost every font which draws attention to itself, this initial attraction quickly turns to distaste.

We looked at the colour of the text on the page under legibility. Each font also has an intrinsic regularity (or irregularity), which translates into a particular kind of flow on the page.

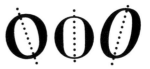

Above, Plantin, Bodoni and Stone Serif Italic. Plantin, named in honour of the Flemish typographer Plantijn, is Renaissance in spirit. Bodoni is a Romantic font. Stone Serif Italic is an Italic. Each has a particular direction of axis, one of its intrinsic characteristics.

abc | abc

Futura (left) and Franklin Gothic. Futura is a geometric font, built around fundamental shapes constructed with ruler and compass. Franklin Gothic is much more human in its proportions. This, too, is intrinsic to the letter shapes.

Gab | Gab

Gill Sans (left) is intrinsically irregular, unlike the archetypal Swiss font Helvetica (right). The irregularity of Gill Sans is one of the things which has made it attractive to a wide variety of official purposes, including, perhaps unwittingly, the British railway service.

Implicitly:
STONECARVED: TRAJAN
Artist crafted: Bodoni
Old printshop: Bookman
Crafted: Garamond
Drafted with ink: Gill
Pen Written: Hypatia Sans
Constructed: Futura

TR

The forms of Trajan, above, were taken from Trajan's column, Rome. Below, in the non-Latin Armenian alphabet, the same techniques are clearly seen in this engraving in Stepanavan.

Implicits

Fonts all share some characteristics. They all have strokes, they all have terminations of those strokes, they all create negative space within and around the font, and they all have places where lines join.

How these things come together implies something about their origins. Of course, these implications are pure fantasy: all fonts are collections of numbers which are delivered by computer to a printing machine. Nonetheless, in exactly the same way that a particular combination of digital wave-forms tells you a clarinet is playing, or a double bass, or a child warbling, the forms of letters give you an irresistible impression of where they 'really' came from.

The origins of the letterform Trajan are clear: the font was defined from the carvings on Trajan's column.

Bodoni looks like it was drawn by a rather romantic artist.

Bookman looks like it might have come from an old fashioned printer's workshop.

Garamond, on the other hand, suggests that the letters were individually crafted in metal. Their forebears probably were.

Gill looks like the work of a draftsman (it was).

Hypatia Sans looks like it might have been carefully written with a pen, by someone with absolutely immaculate penmanship.

Futura looks like it was constructed on graph paper.

Implicitly, fonts tend to reside somewhere on each of these three continua:

Human	. . . .	Machine
Transitory	. . . .	Permanent
Ornamental	. . . .	Functional

The more a font suggests that it has been written, drawn or crafted, the more it appears human. The more it suggests that it is part of an industrial process, has been computer

Master typography

generated or has been constructed geometrically, the more it appears machine made.

The more a font resembles handwriting, the more it appears transitory. The more it seems to have been carved in stone or made by another costly process, the more it seems permanent.

The more flourishes and features a font has, the more it seems ornamental. The plainer it is, the more it seems functional.

- heavy serifs suggest super-definiteness and authority, being reminiscent of stone carving
- serifs suggest permanence, authority, prestige
- sans-serifs suggest personal, human
- strong variation in stroke-width implies calligraphy—prestigious, expensive, old but also human
- weak variation in stroke-width implies handwriting with a ballpoint or marker—personal
- no variation in stroke-width implies computer or machine production.

An interesting thing about implication: it only has to be slight to have a powerful effect. If you set a page of text in Trajan, it would authentically resemble Latin carved inscriptions, but it would also be rather ridiculous. Set a page in Palatino, which is designed to reflect Renaissance forms, themselves heavily inspired by Classical Latin carving, and the result will be authoritative and classical, but without the ridiculousness. The UK Parliament would concur: it has had a corporate font commissioned based on Palatino.

This is the main reason why of the hundreds of new, commercial, fonts published every year, most resemble each other or existing fonts very closely. Free, enthusiast-published fonts tend to be much more demonstrative. When setting an entire book, the tremendously subtle difference of fonts which are almost like each other but not quite is enough to make a substantial impression. Demonstrative fonts are just too much, even when used only in titles.

THE CHIEF BEAUTY OF THIS BOOK LIES NOT SO MUCH IN ITS LITERARY STYLE, OR IN THE EXTENT AND USEFULNESS OF THE INFORMATION IT CONVEYS, AS IN ITS SIMPLE TRUTHFULNESS. ITS PAGES FORM THE RECORD OF EVENTS THAT REALLY HAPPENED. ALL THAT HAS BEEN DONE IS TO COLOUR THEM; AND, FOR THIS, NO EXTRA CHARGE HAS BEEN MADE. GEORGE AND HARRIS AND MONTMORENCY ARE NOT POETIC IDEALS, BUT THINGS OF FLESH AND BLOOD—ESPECIALLY GEORGE, WHO WEIGHS ABOUT TWELVE STONE. OTHER WORKS MAY EXCEL THIS IN DEPTH OF THOUGHT AND KNOWLEDGE OF HUMAN NATURE: OTHER BOOKS MAY RIVAL IT IN ORIGINALITY AND SIZE; BUT, FOR HOPELESS AND INCURABLE

Above, setting extended text in Trajan: actually quite ridiculous.

The chief beauty of this book lies not so much in its literary style, or in the extent and usefulness of the information it conveys, as in its simple truthfulness. Its pages form the record of events that really happened. All that has been done is to colour them; and, for this, no extra charge has been made. George and Harris and Montmorency are not poetic ideals, but things of flesh and blood—especially George, who weighs about twelve stone. Other works may excel this in depth of thought and knowledge of human nature: other books may rival it in originality and size; but, for hopeless and incurable

Above, setting in Palatino implies authority without bombast.

| Happy families are all alike; every unhappy family is unhappy in its own way. Everything was in confusion in the Oblonskys' | Happy families are all alike; every unhappy family is unhappy in its own way. Everything was in confusion in the Oblonskys' house. The | Happy families are all alike; every unhappy family is unhappy in its own way. Everything was in confusion in the Oblonskys' house. The |

Above: almost identical, but different enough to have a major impact on extended text. Helvetica, left, Univers, centre, Frutiger, right.

(Texts: Three men in a boat, Anna Karenina)

Above, Broadway (upper), the 'obvious' 1920s font, works far too hard, especially in conjunction with a 1920s-style illustration (Karen Arnold, Public Domain) and a thick-thin border. A better choice would be Goudy Old Style (lower), a font more commonly used in the 1920s than any of the stereotypically 1920s fonts.

For setting the title of a 7th century book, the correct answer is Pfeffer Mediaeval. Use Open Type stylistic set 2 for authentic English as opposed to continental letters. You may wish to compromise a little: readers will appreciate the curved back 'd', but not the 's' and 'r', which bear no relation to modern letters.

Continental d
Inſulaɾ ð

Associations

Associations are in the eye of the beholder, but a designer can usually take a fairly good guess at the kind of associations that readers will make.

The easiest associations to discuss are those linked with a particular time period, so we'll begin there. However, associations are much more powerful when evoking feelings—of safety, warmth, adventure, and so on—where you are engaging with the reader's visual sense, without triggering them to intellectually identifying what you are doing.

Generally speaking, the more obvious the association, the less impact it has. Want to be reminiscent of the 1920s? Setting in an Art Deco font such as Broadway is a bit like carefully explaining a joke and then saying "D'ya geddit? D'ya geddit?" Much better choices would be Goudy, Gill Sans or Cheltenham. They will feel subtly appropriate, without shouting at the reader.

Over-obvious font associations are often a result of perfunctory research. If you are designing the cover for a book set in the 7th century in England, then you might be drawn to a font such as Trump Mediäval, largely on account of the name, or possibly Goudy Medieval. Neither have anything in common with the lettering of the 7th century. Anybody actually interested in the subject matter would be likely to spot this immediately.

The correct answer is Pfeffer Mediaeval, a free-to-download font[2] with a vast 800 authentic characters, accessed via Open Type stylistic sets 1-6, which offer continental, insular, Gothic and runic scripts. Interestingly, Pfeffer Mediaeval looks much less obviously 'medieval' than many faux-black letter fonts.

In the past, a vast knowledge of fonts and their associations—built up by constant observation, careful note-taking, and months spent browsing through font books—was necessary in order to take a good guess at what fonts would have the right associations, without stepping into obvious traps such as Broadway or Trump Mediäval.

2 From robert-pfeffer.net.

These days, it is much easier. Use Google images to find pictures of design associated with the impression you are trying to create. Then use MyFonts—WhattheFont or another internet utility to tell you what font is in use. There's also a WhattheFont app, which is convenient if you are visiting a museum as part of your font research.

As well as telling you what the font is, these utilities will also offer you a number of alternatives, which is particularly helpful if you are trying to make useful combinations with fonts in your budget.

As a rule of thumb, the impact of a font on the reader (or viewer) is 1×Intrinsics + 2×Implicits + 10×Associations. What the font reminds us of is hugely powerful.

2   The rhythm of the page

When it comes to page rhythm, good typography and good design can go hand in hand—but they don't necessarily.

Designers tend to think of abstract shapes on a page. What works as abstract shapes does not necessarily work as good typography, either in terms of legibility or desirability. Type creates its own rhythm, and the two may conflict.

For example, a seven column, fully justified, page is enormously attractive from the designer's point of view. Odd numbers of things generally give better design than even numbers. For something imposing, almost imperial, it has much to recommend it: no matter how heavy the title, it will sit stably on these seven pillars. Unfortunately, the days of broadsheet newspapers at 749 by 597 mm are in decline, and on tabloid or A3, the largest format now in common use for print, seven columns even at nine point text get just 21 characters to a line—far too short to fully justify, and fairly ridiculous when justified flush left, ragged right.

A seven column underlying grid can be better used with three double width columns, set ragged right, and a narrow column in a larger font. Setting ragged right creates its own rhythm, and allows the page to breathe, allowing narrower margins. The result is more pleasing, and more efficient.

Above, a seven column page has a magnificent stability, supporting a sumptuous headline, enhanced by setting fully justified. However, even on A3 paper and 9 point text, this gives column widths of just 21 characters, which, fully justified, create a spiky right margin full of hyphens, and lines where the letters are spaced impossibly widely, opening up rivers of white on the page.

Below, a more sensible use of a seven column grid, ragged right.

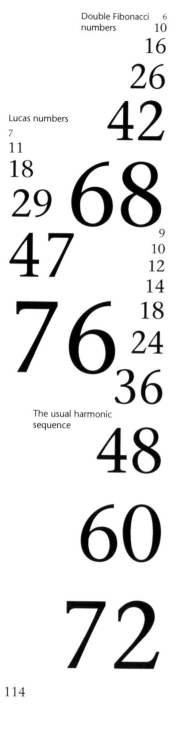

Double Fibonacci numbers 6 10 16 26 42 68

Lucas numbers 7 11 18 29 47 76

9 10 12 14 18 24 36

The usual harmonic sequence 48 60 72

3 Aesthetics

There are three fundamental aesthetic considerations to do with typography. First, the balance of sizes and weights of letters. Second, the combinations of different typefaces. Third, the use of typographical conventions that match the chosen letter types and purpose.

Sizes

If you are setting with just one typeface—something which requires a lot of confidence, but usually pays huge dividends, then a harmonic series of sizes, such as 9,10,12,14,18,14, 36 will serve you well. If you click on the double arrows next o font size in the Measurements panel, QuarkXPress will offer you just such a series, which is also what it does if you use Cmd/ctrl-< for smaller or Cmd/ctrl-> for larger.

9,10,12 etc is not the only aesthetically pleasing sequence. You may prefer to use the Fibonacci series, with its links to the Golden Section, which goes 1, 2, 3, 5, 8, 13, 21, 34. To make these practical for fonts, double each number and start from 3x2=6, thus deriving 6, 10, 16, 26, 42, 68.

Lucas numbers will give you a different set again: 7, 11, 18, 29, 47, 76, 123.

As no non-mathematician can possibly be expected to re-member these, or other sequences, you can define them as sets of character styles, and, if you are going to make this part of your regular practice, include them in Job Jacket JDFs. See Part 4.

Weights

It is tempting to have the body text set in a book font, the subtitles larger and heavier, the titles larger and heavier than that, and the chapter titles largest and heaviest of all. Typefaces with a lot of weights tend to encourage you in that direction.

However, the titles will often balance much better if the larger the font, the lower the weight. For most typefaces, this is a problem, as there is generally only one weight or no weight at all lighter than the standard version. When

Master typography

two typefaces are used together, it can make sense to have the smallest titles set in black, the next titles in bold, the titles above that in roman, and the largest titles in light.

Combining different fonts

The base rule as always taught is: never more than four fonts on a page. By font is meant: never more than four literal fonts, which is to say size/weight/typeface combinations that you would lift out of a font (or fount) when preparing moveable type. Excitable new users of word-processors have been known to have that many in a single sentence.

Subverting the rule, designers for U&lc Magazine were often challenged to include a dozen or so fonts on the same page and yet still make it look good, coherent and cohesive.

Generally speaking, it is now common to set text in a pair of contrasting or harmonious fonts. Unschooled newbies combine fonts with abandon, up until the moment that someone points out that their combinations simply don't work. At that point, they go scurrying to find books of acceptable typeface combinations. The problem is, even books that offer them do so for precious few pairs of faces, many of them not available on the aspirant publisher's computer.

Everybody who designs would love to do so in a world of infinite budgets, but in the world we live in, choice of typeface is usually constrained by i) what's on my computer right now, ii) what can I find for free on the internet and iii) would could we possibly afford to pay for?

This has been improved a little by the arrival of font-rental services like Typekit, but they make the corresponding problem worse: too much choice, not enough knowledge.

The simplest thing to do is to set a document in fonts designed to go with each other. This book is set in Sumner Stone's Stone Serif, with Stone Sans as the variant font. There is also a Stone Informal. Each of the fonts is designed to go together, and they are provided in a decent set of weights.

36 Point
24 Point
18 Point

12 Point

Titles in progressively lighter versions of Helvetica Neue, from 55 Roman at 12 point through 45 Light at 18, 35 Thin at 24 and 25 Ultra Light at 36 point.

Above, below: what a 'font' literally looks like. A 'font' or 'fount' was the place where all the letters of a single size-weight-face combination were kept, occupying the space of a big desk. (Plantin Museum, Antwerp)

Lucida bright
Lucida grande
Lucida casual
Lucida sans
Lucida sans typewriter
Lucida console
Lucida handwritten italic

Lubalin Graph
Avant Garde Gothic

Should you do this...?
Apparatus bellis verecunde imputat
ossifragi. Matrimonii insectat ossifragi,
quamquam suis corrumperet syrtes.
Catelli vocificat adfabilis zothecas.

Univers title, Palatino text

Going with a single super-family was important, because, by its nature, this book was going to include examples of lots of other fonts, and it was important to minimise clashes.

Another choice would have been the Lucida family—available in Bright (meaning Roman, book font), Sans, Casual, Sans Typewriter, Console, Handwritten, and even Grande. I seem to remember learning at some point why the Grande is called Grande, but it's slipped my mind.

Lubalin Graph is the serif version of Avant Garde Gothic, though it's been quippingly pointed out that the only text which looks good in Avant Garde Gothic are the words 'Avant Garde Gothic'.

If you are short on budget, several highly useful free weights of the Museo super-family have been released by the creators, Ex ljbris. I liked them so much that I bought the entire set. Unfortunately, Museo has been such a hit (because of Ex ljbris's generosity, perhaps) that you now see it everywhere, including many places where its slightly playful Dutch origins (the letter 'U' looks like plumbing) are utterly inappropriate.

What to do, though, if you want to combine, say, Univers with Palatino? They are both well-worn fonts, and a couple of minutes searching on the internet will show you that the world is not full of warnings against. But how would you know?

- **Contrast**—when combining fonts, they should look substantially different from each other. Univers is a sans, Palatino is a serif, so we win there. Univers with Arial or Univers with Helvetica would jar disastrously. If in doubt, set the two fonts at significantly different sizes and weights.
- **Shared characteristics**—two faces which are otherwise very different but have something distinctive in common will often work. Bodoni can work well with Futura, because, despite being very different in spirit, they both have extended ascenders and low x-height by comparison with most other contemporary fonts.

Master typography

- **Same period**—Gill Sans and Goudy, being of the same period, naturally share some characteristics which, a hundred years later, make them look like a good pairing. You should not rely on this too much. Bauhaus with Gill Sans just looks silly.
- **Similar spirit**—Univers has humanistic forms, and so does Palatino. But Palatino is also referencing the Renaissance, whereas Univers is a modernistic face.
- **Same designer**—Fonts by Hermann Zapf often go with other fonts by Hermann Zapf, fonts by Adrian Frutiger often work together.

If you're willing to pay for it, there is a very nifty utility called TypeDNA, which scans all of the fonts on your system and works out which ones go with each other. Unfortunately it doesn't tell you why they work together, though its recommendations are generally fairly solid.

To return to the question, Univers and Palatino? Probably not. Univers Bold 65 or Univers 75 Black with Palatino would offer better contrast. In this particular case, Helvetica would be a better pairing than Univers.

Knowing your typography

By default, the output from QuarkXPress is history-aware. It turns on ligatures unless you tell it not to, kerns text properly, assigns a decent amount of leading which is right for print rather than just typewriting, and insists that you make design decisions such as paper size, margins, columns and pagination when you first create a document.

There are basically three levels of typographic skill and knowledge which are obvious in any document. Quark gives you the first one for free, while word processing applications tend not to.

The second level is about using correct typographic characters. Computers now generally correct inch marks to 'smart' quotes, but still get other typographic symbols wrong.

Above—when in doubt, consult the Window—Glyphs palette, which will also identify alternates for a particular selection.

	Name	Usage	Mac	Windows
—	em dash	punctuation	opt-shift-hyphen	alt-0151
–	en dash	range, 5–7 etc	opt-hyphen	alt-0150
-	hyphen	joins/splits words	hyphen key	hyphen key
−	minus	mathematics	use glyphs palette	
×	times	mathematics	use glyphs palette	alt-0215
÷	divide	mathematics	opt-/	alt-0247
±	plus minus	approximation	opt-shift-=	alt-0177
·	mid point	punctuation	opt-shift-9	alt-0183
•	bullet	punctuation	opt-shift-8	alt-0149
°	degree	angles, °F	alt-shift-8	alt-0176
æ	(various)	vowel sound	opt-'	alt-0230
º	Ordinal	Nº	opt-0	alt-8470
'	Quote	Open single	opt-]	alt-0145
'	Quote	Close single	opt-shift-]	alt-0146
"	Quote	Open double	opt-[	alt-0147
"	Quote	Close double	opt-shift-[	alt-0148
…	Ellipsis	punctuation	opt-:	alt-0133

On Windows, use the alt key and the numeric keypad

Open Type fonts are able to conduct automatic transformations. The Chartwell fonts do this to produce charts on the fly from number.
Handsome Pro does this to more accurately reproduce the variation in handwriting:

Handwritten irregularity is essential in a credible handwriting font.

Not all fonts support the full range of typographic symbols, and only the most common ones are given here.

Where possible, true small caps, ordinals, super- and subscripts should be used. These are available in Measurements—*O* (open type features). While QuarkXPress does its best to create small caps, etc, on the fly, the proportions are always inferior to designed versions.

Increasingly, Open Type fonts also provide Stylistic Sets, now fully supported in QuarkXPress 2016. With stylistic

Master typography

sets, swashes and other alternates can be selected, or, in some cases, entire alternate versions of a font.

With careful planning, it is possible to create sets of linked stylesheets and conditional styles which take the options offered by Open Type stylistic sets further—for example, by specifying that the first capital in a paragraph takes a swash, but not others.

Typographical niceties

The third level of typographic skill is having a genuine appreciation for the typographic conventions which go with the kind of document that you are producing and the kind of fonts that you are using.

- **Separating paragraphs**—modern convention is either to indent the first line or to put space between them, but not both. Renaissance examples exist with either, with both, and with neither.

- **Justification**—not all Renaissance books are justified, but when they are not, the ragged right is like a smoothly torn piece of paper, not the radical difference of length which a computer will tend to produce (even QuarkXPress): the true typographer goes back and re-works abrupt line differences.

- **Slugs and dropped caps**—books as far back as medieval illuminated manuscripts used slugs, which are the first few words of a paragraph in bold, a different colour, capitals, italics or a larger size, or dropped caps, or both. Slugs can easily be produced in QuarkXPress using conditional styles. There is an automatic setting for Dropped Caps in Style Sheets—Paragraph—Formats. However, this will not produce a Renaissance dropped cap, which should be in a different font and even a different colour. Use Conditional styles to specify what the first letter should be.

- **Bullets, outlines and section heads**—paragraph and section headings have a long history. Bullet points are more recent. Numbered sections in books are really a product of the last hundred years. Because all of these

Gabriola offers several stylistic sets, in addition to small caps.

AaBbCcDdEeFfGgHhIiJjKkLlMmNnOoPpQqRr

AaBbCcDdEeFfGgHhIiJjKkLlMmNnOoPpQqRr

AaBbCcDdEeFfGgHhIiJjKkLlMmNnOoPpQqRr

AaBbCcDdEeFfGgHhIiJjKkLlMmNnOoPpQqRr

AaBbCcDdEeFfGgHhIiJjKkLlMmNnOoPpQqRr

AaBbCcDdEeFfGgHhIiJjKkLlMmNnOoPpQqRr

AaBbCcDdEeFfGgHhIiJjKkLlMmNnOoPpQqRr

Creating a separate character style for Gabriola with Open Type Stylistic set 7 allows us to set the first character of a paragraph to a swash, as below.

Gabriola example. Gabriola's ordinary 'G' is simpler.

*Quintilian of Albertus Manutius, 1514, with indents **and** spaces.*

There are several conventions for abbreviations. Consistency within a document is key—often a problem when the document is the product of many authors. The recommendations at the top of this list are the most universal, those at the bottom least universal.

1 Never use apostophes for plurals. Eg, MPs, not MP's.
2 Never use two full stops at the end of a sentence, eg, 'Brian has his Ph.D.', never '...Ph.D..'
3 Use a comma after an abbreviation only where the sense demands it.
4 Words that have entered the language like laser and radar are no longer abbreviations, and do not take full stops.
5 Brand names are given as their owners use them, eg, BBC, IBM, not B.B.C or I.B.M.
6 Acronyms do not usually take full stops, eg, ICBM, not I.C.B.M.
7 Where the first and last letter are given (contractions), don't use a full stop, eg, Dr, Mr, but Prof., Rev. (UK usage—US usage says do include a full stop).
8 Where permitted, do away with full stops in abbreviations, therefore eg, ie, etc, rather than e.g., i.e., etc.
9 Don't put a full stop by a middle initial unless the person insists on it. Eg, Martin M Turner, not Martin M. Turner.

are relatively new, their usage is often defined by a corporate style guide, rather than a general rule. If in doubt, use the Oxford Style Guide, which is available as a free download. Generally, only the final bullet takes a full stop, unless one or more of the bullet points contains two sentences (and therefore includes a full stop), in which case, every point in that particular list takes a full stop. This does not transfer to other lists in the same document.

- **Punctuation**—punctuation has changed considerably over the last hundred years. The em dash, —, and the ellipsis, …, are now firmly established as modern punctuation, not only in dialogue where they originated, but in writing of all kinds. At the same time, the semi-colon and the colon are disappearing. Most often when a semi-colon appears, it is used inappropriately. It's worth comparing the crisp, lucid prose of Francis Bacon (1561–1626) with the way semi-colons are used today.

- **Abbreviations**—these have gone through all kinds of typographical fads and phases in the last two thousand years (the Romans *loved* abbreviations, especially in stone engravings), and the rules in the UK and the USA are different. It's fair to say that if you were to set text according to Renaissance rules, even when using Renaissance type and page design, you would confuse half the readers and get complaints from the other half. Nonetheless, having a firm understanding of how abbreviations are used today, and in what contexts, will substantially improve your typographic aesthetic.

- **Titles and headings**—titles are often set in Title Case, which means that every important word is capitalised, but not usually two-letter words or prepositions mid-sentence. Thus, The Lord of the Rings, not The Lord Of The Rings. Automatically engaging 'title case' in Style—Change Case—Title Case will get this wrong. Titles do not usually take a full stop.

- **Capitals**—except in titles and when setting in all capitals, decapitalise as much as possible when setting in

English. Modern business writing has become full of caps used to emphasise, dignify jargon, or raise a function to the level of a proper noun. While the Board may be a proper noun, the board meeting on Wednesday is not, and should not be given capitals. The Chair and the Trust may both be proper nouns, but when the Chair is chairing a meeting, 'chairing' should not be capitalised.

- **Dates**—these should follow the house style of whoever commissions the document. However, where there is no house style, use 3 April 2016, rather than 3rd April, April the 3rd, etc.

- **Units**—get units right! These are especially confusing with computers, where Kb is kilobits, but KB is kilobytes (8× as great). °F and 360° in a circle, but C and K, except when dealing with historical °Centigrade (it is now Celsius, without the degree marker). Units such as mm, cm do not take full stops.

- **Ligatures**—where ligatures are available in the font, use them. Where they aren't, don't worry about them.

- **Figures**—where available, use Old Style figures, which drop below the line, in running text, as they create less interruption. In tables, use Tabular Figures if available.

- **Numbers**—numbers from one to ten should be written out, and 11 upwards given as numerals. The exceptions are that ranges are always given as numerals, eg 3–7, and dates are given as numerals except in narrative fiction, where it is also common practice to write out numbers up to one hundred. Additionally, where a number is not being used to denote a quantity, but for some other purpose, it should be written out. For example, "People often say 'twenty' when they mean, simply, 'a lot'", or "in Old Testament Hebrew, 'one thousand' may be used to denote a military unit, much as a Roman Century, without implying 1,000 individuals present".

Em Space	⌥⌘6
En Space	⌥⌘5
3-per-Em-Space	
4-per-Em-Space	
6-per-Em-Space	
Thin Space	⌥⌘7
Hair Space	
Word Joiner	
Flexible Space	⌥⇧⌘Space
Figure Space	
Punctuation Space	⇧⌘Space
Standard Space	⌘5
Ideographic Space	
En Dash	
Em Dash	⌥⌘=
Hyphen	⌘=

Above, non-breaking spaces in Utilities—Insert Character—Special (non-breaking).

QuarkXPress has a full range of spaces to control how text breaks and how it does not.

But I cannot tell; this same truth, is a naked, and open day-light, that doth not show the masks, and mummeries, and triumphs, of the world, half so stately and daintily as candle-lights. Truth may perhaps come to the price of a pearl, that showeth best by day; but it will not rise to the price of a diamond, or carbuncle, that showeth best in varied lights. **—Essays, On Truth, Francis Bacon**, *one of only a few writers to use semi-colons effectively.*

- **Spaces**—use the full gamut of spaces available, breaking and non-breaking, to control the text. Mathematical expressions need non-breaking spaces if they are not to become nonsense. Em dashes, which are often used without spaces around them, may need zero width spaces on either side, otherwise they will prevent a word cluster from breaking across two lines.

- **Typewriter features**—as noted earlier, underlines do not belong in typeset text, the only exception being when you use a pseudo-typewriter font, such as American Typewriter. Tabs are typewriter features as well, but they have evolved to serve a different purpose in QuarkXPress. Strikeouts should not be used, nor should faux-effects such as Quark's outline and font shadow (though Drop Shadow is fine). These are really legacies from the early days of desk top publishing.

3 Master Colour

When we see something for the first time—a document, an object hurtling through space, a jar on a shelf—the first thing we see is movement. The second thing is colour. After that form, and, finally, content. Our ancestors clearly benefited from this. The things to look out for are things which are moving. Once we have seen something is moving, colour helps us determine whether it is a roaming sheep, which we might kill and eat, a wild boar, which will put up a fight, a sabre-tooth tiger, which might well eat us, or a falling rock or tree. In the case of a sabre-tooth tiger, confidence and experience might help us decide whether to fight or flee. In the case of a falling boulder, we should always flee: no matter what fight we put up, the rock will always win.

The psychological impact of colour is more immediate and greater than anything else in the designer's armoury (since we cannot create movement, though we can imply it). Before we come on to examining the technicalities of colour in QuarkXPress 2016, it's worth understanding the way colour works on us.

1 Emotional impact of colour

Like fonts, the impact of colour is partly intrinsic, partly implicit, and partly associative, but the weighting is quite different.

1 Intrinsics of colour

Colours at the low end of the spectrum hit our eyes with more energy. They have the largest and most direct effect on us. These are reds, oranges and yellows. Colours at the high end hit us with less energy. These are blues, indigos and violets.

Our eyes identify colour in a particular way. By 'eye', I am talking about the complex optical-cortical system, not just the physical retina. Our eyes are equipped with rods and cones. We have about 120 million rods in the retina, which are highly sensitive to luminance, but not to colour at all. 6–7 million cones give us our colour sense, and these are concentrated in the centre of the eye, where there are no rods.

This is why everything appears to go grey in low light, because we rely on our grey-only rods, why (though we don't usually realise it because the brain compensates) things on the edge of vision don't have much colour, and why everything gets blurrier in low light—we rely more on the rods which are not in the high-resolution, central fovea. For the same reason, we associate strong colours and sharp focus with wakefulness, and weak colours with blurred focus with drowsiness.

Rods also don't see red very well, so red objects appear to lose luminosity much more in low light. On the other hand, the rods are much better at spotting motion.

The rods take a lot longer to respond than the cones do, which is why it takes a while for our night vision to engage.

The cones are in three groups: blue, red, and green. The brain then interprets this information giving us perception of the entire spectrum, though, because of the overlap, we have much more ability to perceive greens and yellows than cyan-blues and violets. What we perceive as colour is what the brain deduces from comparing the response of each of these pigments.

2 Implicit effect of colours

The universal human experience means that particular colours imply particular things to everyone. Red always carries the implication of blood, and with it danger. Sky blue implies fine weather, whereas stormy blue (as you would expect) implies bad weather. Bright green implies verdance—well watered grass in good condition. Dark green we associate with tree leaves. Yellowy-green suggests dying vegetation. Ochre and browns imply autumn, or earth. Particular browns have particular resonances of muck.

However, it is not 'blue' that reminds of sky, but only very exact and particular blues. You will only ever see a navy blue sky if you are watching the zenith round the time of sunset. You will never see a turquoise sky, though, if you have been to the Caribbean, you will have seen impossibly turquoise sea. Blood has a very distinct colour, somewhere between Pantone Warm Red and Pantone 485. Other reds are more likely to remind us of fire, or perhaps fire-engines.

When the colours are exactly right, implicit impact of colour is high, but when they are a little off, the impact vanishes. Nobody would ever mistake lemon-yellow for sunset yellow, even if they don't have separate words for the two colours.

3 Colour associations

From the moment we start to learn to distinguish things in the world around us, we begin to build up colour memory. This is not just for things that are thrown at us day after day—the implicit meanings of colours—but for the exact shades of favourite toys, the covers of books, the table cloth at home. A colour which is no longer in use can trigger a tidal wave of nostalgia when it is reintroduced.

In addition to our own personal responses to colour, there is a fairly established body of knowledge about which colours tend to be interpreted in which ways. This is to some extent cultural, and particular cultures. Orange means the Dutch nation if you are Dutch, but Halloween if you are from the USA. The table presented on the next spread provides (for the first time, I believe), an easy look-up for helping to choose single colours to imply attributes.

4 Creating colour palettes

Transmuting the research-based impact of single colours presented here into full palettes is outside the scope of this book. However, there are hundreds of smart-device apps, web-apps and Mac or Windows applications which will do it for you, including Adobe Illustrator and Pantone's own MyPantone app.

As a reference to the list on the next page, Pantone numbers to illustrate the colours. These are not definitive, or even the best colour to represent the word, but should help to deal with any confusions.

Terracotta	7580
Brick Red	484
Burgundy	7420
Bright Red	Bright Red
Orange	165
Gold	7555
Golden Yellow	130
Bright Yellow	Yellow
Light Yellow	100
Cream	7499
Beige	468
Taupe	7529
Earth Brown	464
Coffee or Chocolate	462
Black	Black
Charcoal Gray	446
Neutral Gray	423
Silver	428
Pure White	White
Red Purple	248
Deep Plum	7648
Bright Pink	Pink
Fuchsia	807
Orchid	245
Light Pink	Magenta 0521
Peach	162
Dusty Pink	Red 0331
Mauve	Violet 0631
Grape	2583
Lavender	522
Blue Purple	267
Navy	2748
Cobalt Blue	7691
Bright Blue	2728
Electric Blue	285
Sky Blue	297
Light Blue	277
Aqua	284
Light Green	351
Turquoise	3115
Teal Blue	321
Dark Green	341
Olive Green	7761
Bright Green	354
Bright Yellow-Green	7488
Lime	375
Greenish Yellow	389

Acidic	Greenish Yellow · Lime	Fruity	Peach · Greenish Yellow · Lime	Safety	Bright Yellow
Aggressive	Bright Red	Fun	Bright Pink · Fuchsia · Orange	Sandy	Beige
Airy	Pure White	Futuristic	Blue Purple · Silver	Secure	Earth Brown
Artsy	Bright Yellow-Green	Fuzzy	Peach	Sensual	Fuchsia · Red Purple
Attention-Getting	Bright Pink	Gaudy	Bright Yellow-Green	Sentimental	Mauve
Authoritative	Navy	Ghostly	Neutral Gray	Serene	Navy
Autumn	Golden Yellow	Glistening	Pure White	Serious	Black
Babies	Light Pink	Glowing	Orange	Service	Navy
Basic	Navy · Black · Taupe	Grass	Bright Green	Sexy	Bright Red
Bland	Beige	Gregarious	Orange	Sharp	Bright Yellow-Green
Bold	Bright Yellow-Green · Black	Happy	Bright Pink · Orange · Light Yellow · Golden Yellow · Sky Blue · Bright Blue	Sheltering	Earth Brown
Bright	Fuchsia · Pure White			Sickening	Bright Yellow-Green
Buttery	Golden Yellow			Silent	Pure White
Calm	Light Blue · Light Green	Harvest	Orange · Golden Yellow	Slimy	Bright Yellow-Green
Calming	Sky Blue	Heavenly	Sky Blue	Smooth	Cream
Camouflage	Olive Green	Heavy	Black	Sober	Black · Neutral Gray
Casual	Beige · Earth Brown · Light Blue · Neutral Gray	Heritage	Earth Brown	Soft	Light Pink · Dusty Pink · Mauve · Peach · Light Yellow · Cream · Beige
		High Energy	Fuchsia		
Cheerful	Light Yellow · Bright Yellow	Homemade	Terracotta · Coffee or Chocolate		
Childlike	Orange	Hope	Bright Yellow · Golden Yellow		
Classic	Cream · Beige · Deep Plum · Navy · Olive Green · Black · Charcoal Gray · Neutral Gray · Taupe · Silver	Hot	Bright Red · Bright Pink · Fuchsia · Orange · Bright Yellow	Solid	Charcoal Gray
				Soothing	Aqua · Light Green
		Industrial	Bright Yellow · Neutral Gray	Sophisticated	Grape · Charcoal Gray
		Innocent	Pure White	Spirited	Bright Pink
Classy	Teal Blue	Innovation	Teal Blue · Electric Blue	Spiritual	Blue Purple
Clean	Light Blue · Pure White	Intense	Electric Blue	Spring	Bright Green
Comforting	Golden Yellow	Inviting	Peach	Stately	Dark Green
Confident	Navy	Invulnerable	Black	Sterile	Pure White
Conservative	Navy	Irish	Bright Green	Stimulating	Bright Red
Constant	Sky Blue	Jewellery	Turquoise	Stirring	Bright Blue
Cool	Light Blue · Sky Blue · Aqua · Dark Green · Neutral Gray · Silver	Juicy	Orange	Strong	Brick Red · Navy · Black
		Lemony	Greenish Yellow	Subdued	Mauve
Corporate	Neutral Gray	Lightweight	Pure White	Subtle	Dusty Pink · Grape
Country	Brick Red · Terracotta	Liquid	Aqua	Sun	Golden Yellow
Cosy	Dusty Pink	Lively	Bright Green · Lime	Sunbaked	Golden Yellow
Creative	Red Purple	Loud	Orange	Sunny	Light Yellow
Credible	Navy	Luminous	Bright Yellow	Sunset	Orange
Cute	Light Pink	Luxury	Golden Yellow · Red Purple · Blue Purple · Pure White · Black	Sunshine	Bright Yellow
Delicate	Light Pink · Lavender			Sweet	Light Pink · Peach · Light Yellow
Delicious	Peach · Cream · Coffee or Chocolate	Magical	Black	Sweet Scented	Lavender
		Masculine	Earth Brown	Sweet Taste	Lavender · Grape
Dependable	Sky Blue · Navy	Mature	Burgundy · Charcoal Gray	Tacky	Bright Yellow-Green
Dirt	Earth Brown	Meditative	Blue Purple	Tangy	Orange
Discreet	Coffee or Chocolate · Deep Plum · Charcoal Gray · Neutral Gray · Silver	Military	Olive Green	Tart	Greenish Yellow · Lime
		Modern	Silver	Tasty	Burgundy
		Money	Dark Green · Silver	Technology	Electric Blue
Dominant	Cobalt Blue	Mysterious	Black	Tender	Light Pink
Drab	Olive Green	Mystical	Blue Purple	Timeless	Neutral Gray · Taupe
Dramatic	Bright Red · Bright Blue	Nature	Dark Green	Traditional	Navy · Dark Green
Durable	Earth Brown	Nautical	Navy	Tranquil	Sky Blue
Dusky	Dusty Pink	Neutral	Cream · Beige · Aqua · Light Green · Taupe	Trendy	Bright Pink · Bright Yellow-Green
Dynamic	Bright Red			Tropical	Orchid · Turquoise
Earth	Earth Brown	Nighttime	Black	Trustworthy	Dark Green
Earthy	Brick Red · Terracotta · Beige	Nostalgic	Lavender	Uniforms	Navy
Electric	Bright Blue	Nurturing	Peach	Unique	Red Purple · Teal Blue
Elegant	Burgundy · Deep Plum · Black · Charcoal Gray	Ocean	Turquoise · Aqua	Valuable	Silver · Gold
Enduring	Charcoal Gray	Opulent	Gold	Vibrant	Bright Blue · Electric Blue
Energetic	Bright Pink · Bright Blue	Outdoorsy	Bright Green	Vital	Orange
Energising	Bright Red · Orange	Peaceful	Light Blue	Warm	Brick Red · Terracotta · Light Yellow · Golden Yellow · Cream · Beige · Earth Brown · Gold
Energy	Bright Yellow	Pleasing	Teal Blue		
Enlightening	Bright Yellow	Powerful	Bright Red · Deep Plum · Black		
Essential	Beige · Neutral Gray	Practical	Neutral Gray · Taupe		
Exciting	Bright Red · Bright Pink · Fuchsia · Red Purple	Prestige	Black		
		Prestigious	Black · Gold	Water	Light Blue
Exotic	Orchid	Professional	Navy · Charcoal Gray	Welcoming	Terracotta
Expensive	Burgundy · Deep Plum · Teal Blue · Black · Charcoal Gray · Silver · Gold	Provocative	Bright Red	Wheat	Golden Yellow
		Pure	Pure White	Whimsical	Orange
		Quality	Neutral Gray · Taupe	Wholesome	Terracotta · Earth Brown
Faithful	Sky Blue	Quiet	Mauve · Light Blue · Navy · Light Green · Dark Green · Neutral Gray	Wild	Bright Pink
Fantasy	Blue Purple			Woodsy	Earth Brown · Dark Green
Feminine	Light Pink	Radiant	Gold	Youthful	Bright Pink · Electric Blue
Flags	Bright Blue	Refined	Burgundy		
Flamboyant	Red Purple	Refreshing	Dark Green · Lime		
Floral	Lavender	Regal	Deep Plum		
Flowers	Golden Yellow · Orchid	Restful	Sky Blue · Dark Green		
Foliage	Bright Green	Rich	Burgundy · Golden Yellow · Cream · Coffee or Chocolate · Teal Blue		
Forest	Dark Green				
Formal	Pure White · Black	Romantic	Light Pink		
Fragrant	Orchid	Rooted	Earth Brown		
Fresh	Aqua · Bright Green	Rustic	Earth Brown		
Friendly	Orange · Bright Yellow	Safari	Olive Green		

Essentially, you need to make a list of the attributes you want to represent. Work through the colours from the one attribute with the longest list—this will be your reference list—going through every single colour harmony model on offer, until you find a colour that includes a shade which approximates to at least one colour from each of the others.

This can take you a couple of hours, but it's rewarding work. If you end up with no harmony model offering something for all of your attributes, you will have to distil them a bit further and have fewer of them.

You can try with different hues of the colours in your reference list. Doing it with a Pantone swatchbook is highly recommended: your computer monitor will easily mislead you, even if well calibrated.

Once you've decided what you like, you should have a palette of four to seven colours to work from.

A shortcut—maybe

Does this seem tedious to you? Or do you have an attribute which is not on the list, and which is key? An alternative is to find an image which represents to you all of the emotional impact you want to create. You can use Google images, Flickr, browse your back catalogue, or even wander round the streets with a camera.

When you have the image, load it into QuarkXPress and use the Eye Dropper tool ✐ in Window—Colours to extract a range from different parts of the image. It will still be worth sanity checking it against some colour harmony models: it is possible that it works in that image, but nowhere else.

Facing Page
Based on Leatrice Eiseman's Pantone Colour guides, and my own research, the table offers the colours which naturally represent the attributes given. While there are many tables available showing what the impact of a colour is, to the best of my knowledge this is the first table where you can begin with the impact you wish to create and find the colour that creates it.

Colour harmony models supported by Adobe Illustrator:
Analogous
Analogous 2
Complementary
Complementary 2
Split Complementary
Compound 1
Compound 2
High Contrast 1
High Contrast 2
High Contrast 3
High Contrast 4
Left Complement
Monochromatic
Monochromatic 2
Pentagram
Right Complement
Shades
Tetrad
Tetrad 2
Tetrad 3
Triad
Triad 2
Triad 3

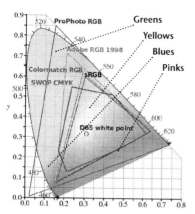

Above, CIE 1931 colour space diagram (image—Wikipedia), showing how various colour spaces map onto the visible spectrum, which is the largest area.

Below, Utilities—Usage—Profiles. You can select which profile to view, and you can also reassign profiles, though this is a sign of a problem elsewhere.

2 Colour spaces

We touched on colour spaces earlier. Colour can only enter a computer in one of two ways: either through a sensor device, such as a digital camera, or by someone entering the colour on computer using numbers—albeit entered via a graphical interface—and then comparing it to a target colour. The first depends on the calibration of the camera and lighting environment, the second depends on the calibration of the monitor, the viewing environment, and the colour skills of the operator. Either way, it's a mixed business.

The computer's output, on the other hand, is a very simple matter. It instructs the output device either to fire its red, green or blue illuminators, or to lay down coloured inks or toner on paper or some other substrate. At some point some calibration should have taken place so that the computer takes account of the inconsistencies of the process, but it is all very much by the numbers.

Now here is the problem. A monitor will illuminate up to 256 levels of Red, Green or Blue, and, assuming a near perfect print process, the printing press, inkjet or toner-based printer will lay down up to 256 levels each of cyan, magenta, yellow, black, and/or other inks, for a supposed four billion colours.

The problem is that the eye does not perceive colour—as we saw earlier—by anything remotely like this process. The result is that there are shades of red which a computer can print that the eye really can't distinguish, but also shades of green which the eye sees as very obviously different, but which fall between the shades a computer is able to offer.

The shades which a monitor can display, a printer can print or the eye can see are the gamut. No output device can match the gamut of the human eye, and, even more importantly, no input device can either. Additionally, because the technology of a monitor is so different from a printer, no printer can print all the shades a monitor can display, but neither can a monitor display all of the Pantone colours which can be created by mixing different inks—especially not neon and metallic colours.

If that seems a long explanation, it should at least give some idea of why there are so many colour specification systems, and why colour is such a tricky business.

There is, unfortunately, more, and it is quite critical. When a camera, such as a Nikon D800, captures an image, it does so on Raw data, which is essentially meaningless without a computer model of the camera to interpret it, because a digital camera has different numbers of sensors to capture reds, greens and blues. This raw data needs to be transmitted in a form that other devices can understand, which means mapping what the camera has recorded into a colour space which other devices can interpret. The 'best' format for photographs is ProPhoto RGB 16 bit. However, this carries much more data than can ever be used. If the image is never going to be viewed off a computer monitor, and specialist software is invoked to display differing aspects of the image—for example in astrophysics—then ProPhoto is a good bet. Otherwise, when going from Raw to Tiff, PSD or JPEG, the extraneous data is discarded and either sRGB is chosen as the Colour Space, or, if the image is likely to go through significant processing, Adobe RGB, which retains more data. The advantage of sRGB is that it is the native colour space for most monitors, and so is the most widely available and what is 'expected' by devices such as web browsers that do not manage colour properly.

Normally, the colour space is attached to the file. When it reaches QuarkXPress, Quark makes the relevant adjustments, and everything works smoothly. Any image that comes with an ICC profile will be outputted correctly.

—Except when things go wrong. Sometimes profiles get detached, are incorrectly assigned, or are mistakenly converted to something else during processing. Each device and application is then left to guess what the intention was. The good news is, once set up correctly, a colour workflow should keep working without difficulty.

CMYK print can only reproduce 55% of the colours in the Pantone PMS matching system. However, the Pantone Extended Gamut colours, which are supported by QuarkXPress as Pantone Gamut, allow up to 95% reproduction[1]. Extended Gamut adds three additional colours to CMYK, being orange, green and violet, which is one more than the 1990s Hexachrome standard. When printing for XGC, include the spot colours unconverted the composite workflow for the XGC RIP to sort out. Naturally, check with your print house about their requirements. XGC is a specialist process and relatively few print houses currently support it, though Pantone predicts that up to 50% of print houses in the USA will support XGC by 2020.

---

1 According to Pantone's web seminar. Esko gives a figure of 80%.

Below, ensure the calibration for your proofing device is checked in Utilities—Profile Manager.

Below, in Edit—Color Setups—Output, name your device and assign your calibrated profile.

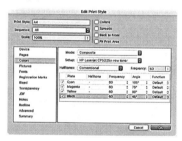

Below, in Edit—Output Styles—assign for your device the Color Setup you created in Colors.

Below, you can now select your device in View—Proof Output.

1 How to calibrate your system

1 Calibrate your monitor and proofer, eg, laser printer, using an X-Rite device, a Datacolor Spyder, or alternative. If you don't have one, use the profiling software that came with your computer and the supplied printer profile.

2 Ensure that the source camera has been set up to embed a profile. Normally this should be sRGB or Adobe RGB. If the source camera does not allow profiling, it is most likely fixed on sRGB.

3 Ensure that the software which develops the image initially assigns an appropriate profile. This software would normally either be Lightroom, Photoshop, Capture One, DxO or another raw developer, or else software built into the system.

4 Import the image into QuarkXPress 2016. Go to Utilities—Usage—Profiles. At the top, where it says 'Profiles', select the profile that you believe your image should have. If it's not there, go through all the options until you find it. If the profile is correctly attached to the image, your colour workflow is working.

5 Go to Utilities—Profile Manager, and ensure that the profile of your output device (eg, SWOP, for Standard Web Offset Printing) and for your proofing device are ticked.

6 Go to Edit—Color Setups—Outputs, and create a new style for your proofing device. Leave the defaults as they are, but choose your calibrated device's profile in 'Output Options—Profile'.

7 In Edit—Output Styles, create an output style for your proofing device (or edit the one you have). In the Colors pane, in Setup, choose your calibrated profile.

8 In View—Proof Output, select your proofing device.

9 Print something—camera colours, your screen, and the output from your proofing device should all match up.

2 Specification systems

QuarkXPress supports a number of colour specification systems. RGB stands for Red–Green–Blue and specifies colours in the same way a camera would capture them or a monitor would display them. HSB is Hue–Saturation–Brightness, a more intuitive way of working with colours. LAB, or L*a*b stands for Lightness, A and B. Lightness is obvious but the other two, while powerful and device-independent, do not correspond with our intuitive idea of colour. Adobe Illustrator uses LAB as its internal colour system.

CMYK and Multi-Ink are specifications of what ink goes onto the page. Multi-Ink includes Hexachrome support.

Pantone is the most established specification system. Only the Solid Coated and Uncoated swatch books are widely used in print, as most systems including QuarkXPress will automatically convert to CMYK on demand. Pantone also provides swatch sets for fabric and for hard substrates such as plastic. From QuarkXPress 2016, Extended Gamut Colours can now be specified, though, again, the real benefit of Extended Gamut is being able to print up to 95% of Pantone PMS colours on a six-plate press (technically, Extended Gamut is CMYK + Green + Orange + Violet, but no more than six plates are ever used to reproduce any particular colour).

DIC, Focoltone, Toyo and Trumatch are alternate swatch-based specification systems, like Pantone in some respects. They have more localised popularity and support in various parts of the world.

Web Named Colors represent the colours that Cascading Style Sheets understand. Web Safe Colors are an old standard for what all monitors could be expected to reproduce, though this is really no longer necessary.

3 Swatch books

If you are working with colour, purchase the swatch books. Though expensive, they are the only real shared colour currency in the print world.

Below, QuarkXPress 2016 supports thirteen different systems, including the complete and up to date Pantone systems.

RGB
HSB
LAB
✓ CMYK
Multi-Ink
DIC
FOCOLTONE
PANTONE + Solid Coated-V3 M0
PANTONE + Solid Coated-V3 M1
PANTONE + Solid Coated-V3 M2
PANTONE + Solid Coated-V3 M3
PANTONE + Solid Uncoated-V3 M0
PANTONE + Solid Uncoated-V3 M1
PANTONE + Solid Uncoated-V3 M2
PANTONE + Solid Uncoated-V3 M3
PANTONE Gamut Coated
PANTONE Gamut Coated D50
PANTONE Gamut Coated Polarized
PANTONE Gamut Coated UVC
PANTONE+ CMYK Coated
PANTONE+ CMYK Uncoated
PANTONE+ Color Bridge Coated
PANTONE+ Color Bridge Uncoated
PANTONE+ Pastels and Neons Coated
PANTONE+ Pastels and Neons Uncoated
PANTONE+ Premium Metallics Coated
PANTONE+ Solid Coated
PANTONE+ Solid Coated-336 New
PANTONE+ Solid Uncoated
PANTONE+ Solid Uncoated-336 New
PANTONE® GoeBridge™ coated
PANTONE® Goe™ coated
PANTONE® Goe™ uncoated
PANTONE® color bridge CMYK EC
PANTONE® color bridge CMYK PC
PANTONE® color bridge CMYK UP
PANTONE® metallic coated
PANTONE® pastel coated
PANTONE® pastel uncoated
PANTONE® process coated
PANTONE® process coated EURO
PANTONE® process uncoated
PANTONE® solid coated
PANTONE® solid in hexachrome® coated
PANTONE® solid matte
PANTONE® solid uncoated
TOYO
TOYO COLOR FINDER
TRUMATCH
Web Named Colors
Web Safe Colors

Colour spaces

4 Master Production

So, your job is done when the PDF file is emailed to the printer? Of course not (you knew that).

1 How to talk to your print shop

SWOP stands for 'standard web offset printing'. The funny thing is, I've never yet found a 'standard' print shop or print house. Some of the best printers I know own no equipment: they farm everything out. I've known printers who ran 19th century presses in their garages and could do any amount of pristine work as long as it was no bigger than tabloid and no more than two colours. There are print companies with brochures telling you how their new investment makes them the most competitive, despite never being able to match anybody else's price, and printers who suck on their teeth and say 'that's going to be expensive', before giving you the sharpest price for hundreds of miles around.

Most printers these days use software to help them work out the price for your specification. Even so, they quickly learn whether you are someone who provides entirely finished artwork, makes quick decisions, and doesn't change their mind half way through the job, or someone who dithers, demands endless changes, and then pays late. Print houses often operate special prices for both of these categories of customers.

Being able to specify a job correctly enables you to get things right from the outset. Printers like that.

Process
Professional printers will generally use one of four processes: Offset, Digital, Flexo, or high-speed inkjet.

Offset is the descendent of Johannes Gutenberg's original printing press. At each pass, a plate is inked and pressed onto the stock, which is then taken away and a new sheet or pass of the roll put in its place. At one end of the scale,

Letterpress is done almost entirely by hand, and the 'plate' is, in fact, a collection of metal or wood letters. At the other end of the scale, four printing presses in a row make up a CMYK press, which is quite possibly as big as a truck.

Digital means a high-speed, calibrated colour, printer-copier capable of handling a wide range of stock. They will often do their own duplexing, and even stitching, drilling and folding (as long as it's simple). With the correct preparation, digital jobs can be individually tailored, for example with names and addresses.

Flexo is an extremely high-speed process that evolved for printing packaging using rubber plates, but can now deliver passable quality which can rival the offset of twenty years before.

High-speed inkjet is usually used for customising print produced by offset, for example by adding names and addresses onto leaflets for the post. Mailing houses make frequent use of these.

Additionally, sign-makers and specialist repro-houses offer roll-printers, also called Plotters, which are Raster Image Processor (RIP)-driven ink-jet or solvent printers, typically 56" or more, able to print on a wide range of materials including vinyl and cloth. They can be combined with cutters.

Colour Production

CMK (as you well know) stands for Cyan—Magenta—Yellow—blacK. It's the standard for 'full colour' print.

CMY is a cheaper way of producing colour if black text is not required, and if darker colours are not hue-critical. It is seldom used in offset these days, but Flexo printers often print in CMY, and package designers may specify colours that take advantage of it.

Spot colour is a press run of a particular colour. Spot colour is normally run as a colour plus black, and the colours are almost always specified as Pantoe PMS, or just PMS. As mentioned elsewhere, but worth repeating, PMS, Pantone Matching System, is by far the most widely used colour

Other processes
*In addition to offset, digital, flexo and high-speed inkjet, there is also **rotogravure**, for 300,000 or more impressions, **screen-printing**, for less than 250, **letterpress**, for a truly artisan quality, **stencil duplicator** (though the same effect can be achieved with Risograph), **rubber-stamping**, **thermal printing**, impact **dot-matrix**, and **potato-printing**. Commercial photography, such as for wedding albums, is often printed with **dye-sublimation**, which provides a true continuous tone image, though for fine art a **Giclée** is preferred—originally a separate process, but now usually done by inkjet printing. Each has its own merits. You can also make stencils and hand-spray with an **airbrush** or a spray can. This leads us on to sign-making. For this, as well as commissioning commercial 3d signmaking—either with a 3d printer or by traditional processes—you can cut out letters and art in expanded **polystyrene** using a hot wire, or **roll-print** onto a wide variety of substrates. Often a designer is called on to create artwork for promotional items, which are typically applied by **dye-sublimation** onto plastic, though they might be machine (or even hand) **stitched** onto cloth, or **laser engraved**. In the UK, Structiv can have your artwork made into **woven steel** fence panels. We once had a light-engineering company produce **bronze** keyrings in the shape of a town's silhouette—unique, and cheaper for 100 than any promotional catalogue item.*

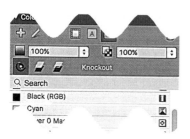

Above, Multi-ink allows you to specify mixtures of Pantone PMS with CMYK or Hexachrome or each other. Pantone 485 at 30% and 7685 at 50% produces an ugly shade of puce.

In Window—Colours, the Knock-out line is greyed out except for Spot colours—background colour. The default is usually correct, but over-print and knockout can be selected if necessary.

QuarkXPress no longer offers choke controls, choke being the area of overlap specified for knock-out colours. This is normally done in-RIP. If you really need to increase the choke—for example because you are printing to Risograph and the registration is very loose—create a frame of the same colour as the box of the lighter colour. If you need to refine this further, create a multi-ink colour using the two colours for the choke frame.

matching system in the world, but it isn't intrinsically a colour specification at all. Pantone specifies what inks should be mixed to produce the relevant Pantone colour. The result will vary marginally on every different kind of paper. Two swatchbooks are provided: Pantone U, for uncoated paper, and Pantone C, for coated paper. Pantone CV stands for coated and varnished.

A quick look at the swatch books will show that the uncoated colours are not just duller for the same number, but might also have an apparently different hue.

UV varnish is generally specified in the same way as a spot colour, and is often referred to as 'spot UV'. To specify the UV varnish, create an additional spot colour, for example as RGB bright green, and name it 'UV Varnish'. Put all your varnishes on a separate layer, which you can keep turned off when your not directly editing it. Liaise with your printer about exactly how this should be communicated.

It's possible to overprint Pantone colours (or any ink), to produce other colours. I have to say I have not actually been involved in a multi-ink project using this technique since 1989. CMYK print is now so cheap that if you want more colours, it's generally cheaper to do a CMYK job than to play with multi-ink. The exception would be when you have to use two Pantone colours as a result of your brand specification (it may be time for a new specification).

Be that all as it may, you can play with multi-ink, and specify it you want, in the Colours—Edit Colour—Model: Multi-ink dialogue.

Even if you don't actually want to do this, you can use the combinations to work out what will happen if you over-print or choke two colours, for example 30% Black with Orange.

Hexachrome is a six-ink high-colour process, that was 'the next big thing' in the 1990s, but is now mainly seen on high-end ink-jet printers, including roll printers. Hexachrome adds orange and green. You can specify hexachrome colours directly in the Multi-ink dialogue, but ask your printer if you intend to use it: you may be better off

Master Production

leaving them specified as Pantone, RGB or CMYK and letting the RIP do the conversions. This is the workflow you are advised to follow, in any case, when exporting for a Pantone Extended Gamut output.

Conventional versus Stochastic rendering

Conventional printing is done with a half-tone screen. It is possible to print much higher resolution images if instead of a grid of dots of different sizes, the dots are all the same size and are placed by the computer in exactly the right pattern. Ink-jet printers generally use this technique, which is called stochastic rendering. 'Stochastic' means random.

Stochastic rendering was going to be the next-big-thing after hexachrome in the 1990s. However, the process for printing it is much more difficult, and flat colours come out poorly unless they are first roughened. We commissioned one job in 1999 with stochastic rendering, decided it was no improvement, and never did it again. Best avoided.

Other halftone screens

Something with more pedigree is non-conventional halftone screens, which can be literal lines, ellipses, squares or tri-dots. You set these in the Colours pane of the File—Print dialogue. Unfortunately, the chances of actually being able to make use of this are fairly slim. While the LaserJet III we had in the 1990s was well-up for having its line-screen changed, the HP CP 5225n in my office right now has all kinds of special tricks to create its pseudo-magazine quality prints, and ignores all attempts to change the line-screen or the dot function. This is, in any case, a Postscript function only: ink-jets and non-Postscript lasers will not do it. Alternate screens are specified in-RIP, so if you want to use this feature, you will need to tell your print house to set it up for you. They will probably ask, 'Why?' The line-screen on imagesetters is too fine for it to be visible, and a screening setting must apply to the entire job, not just one image. You would also be taking a huge risk if it was a CMYK job. If you want to achieve the look of 1960s art-print, you might be better advised to apply it in Photoshop to each individual image, using Convert to Greyscale fol-

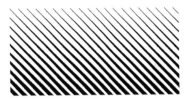

In the Colours pane of the File—Print dialogue, you can set the type of line-screen using Function. However, when exporting for PDF, this has to be set in-RIP.

Above, diagonal lines instead of conventional dots (at 15 lpi). This can give a 60s pop-art or art-book look, but is better created per image in Photoshop, by converting first to Greyscale and then to Bitmap, and selecting the required halftone screen.

Paper feels different depending on how many times it has been through the press.

70 gsm	Flimsy, feels cheap
80 gsm	Copy paper
120 gsm	Luxurious in mono-laser, flimsy in CMYK offset
130 gsm	Flimsy in CMYK offset
150 gsm	Substantial in CMYK offset, feels stiff in laser
160+ gsm	'board'
250 gsm	2 colour business cards
350 gsm	CMYK business cards

CMYK two sides has had eight times the pressure applied to it as a single side of black and white. If (as is most likely) this is on coated paper, there will be an additional loss of volume because the heat drying process will also expel some of the moisture in the paper. By contrast, the heavier the colour in colour laser printing or in digital printing, the thicker the paper becomes. As a result, you must be careful of cracking along any folded edges.

lowed by Convert to Bitmap, which will then offer you a choice of halftone screens.

Stock

Moving on from esoteric considerations of halftone screen, which your print house will not normally expect you to specify, you must always specify the print stock. This is best done by first asking the printer what they recommend for the job you have in mind.

The table on p105 sets out the various kinds of stock in general use. Except for producing business stationery, offset benefits from coated stock, whereas digital creates its own gloss-like coating, though a coated stock will still produce a better result as uncoated is prone to mottling.

Weight

If you generally print with an office laser one-sided onto 80gsm copy paper, you might expect to get the same result when printing to offset. Things (as always) are a little bit more complicated. Laser printers roll the paper, compressing it slightly, and lay down an extra thickness of toner. Offset compresses the paper much more, and every pass means more compression (it is, after all, a printing *press*). This means that 150gsm which is ridiculously thick on office-laser, and thicker when printed two sides in heavy colour, feels only ordinary when printed CMYK both sides via offset. This is because it has been through the press eight times. Take your printer's advice on this: the stock they use and the way their press is set up may require a heavier or lighter paper, and the effect of gloss, silk or matt will also have an impact.

Generally speaking, for mono offset jobs, 120 gsm matte will give a nice finish, but for CMYK 130 gsm is really the minimum, with 150 gsm giving a more substantial feel. If you are mailing, work out the weight of the paper *before* you finalise the specification. An A0 sheet is exactly 1 square metre. The A series is designed so that each size is exactly half the preceding size, by cutting or folding once, so A1 is ½ a square metre, A2 is ¼, A3 half of that, and A4 one sixteenth. Therefore, to find out what your A4 sheet will weigh, divide the weight in gsm (g/m²) by 16. In the

UK, where the cut-off for the cheapest rate of post is 100 grams, you can put 8 sheets of 150gm A4 into an envelope, unless the envelope is particularly heavy.

Up to a point, heavier stock will give more sense of authority and importance to your document than anything you can accomplish with the layout. However, after that point, it becomes ridiculous. Major multinational companies tend to have business cards on comparatively flimsy 275 gsm stock. One-man startups can easily be lured into 350 gsm or even 450 gsm. Having a really thick card appears to give weight, but, in fact, it simply signifies 'one-man business'. Likewise, unless you are royalty, business letters on anything more elaborate than vellum 120gsm will look silly. 100gsm white copy paper is as prestigious as most business letters need to be, and choosing a stock that produces that same feel for your CMYK or spot-colour jobs offers the 'sweet spot' of substantial without appearing vain.

The best thing is to ask the printer for a sample of a similar document. An 80 page catalogue can be printed on 90 gsm silk and still feel substantial, whereas a single-page flyer on that stock would feel cheap.

Deadlines and drying times

Printers will usually give you a one or two week turnaround, depending (often) on their previous experience of how reasonable a customer you are. If the job is digital, 3,000 copies can be printed and finished in a morning, when haste is needed. Offset print may require drying time. Different stocks and different processes have different needs. Yellow ink dries faster than most other colours.

In desperate circumstances, most printers will provide you with a part-order early—though they may want you to collect it or pay for additional delivery. You can also get a few hundred copies done digitally, though, of course, you are now paying the higher per-unit digital cost in addition to your offset cost.

Finishing

Finishing refers to folding, cutting, trimming and stitching, or any other binding you want.

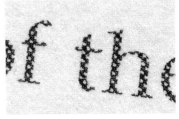

Always give them what they ask for

Printers may specify something which 'ought' to give the wrong result, but, in their process, gives the right result. The proof-PDF for this book was sent to CreateSpace, the on-demand printer and distributer, with profile Grey 100K.

When the proof arrived, it seemed fine, until we noticed a very slight greyness to the text. Imaged at 600%, we realised that the CreateSpace RIP had interpreted 100K Grey (ie, black not made up of CM overprinting K, which is 'rich' black) as a request for 90% black, and had therefore output it it as above.

Rechecking the specifications, we found that the instruction was to send 'as is', with no colour conversion. Hopefully, the version you have received is now imaged correctly...

The moral of the story: whatever the printer asks for, give it to them. They know their process, and the adjustments that need to be made. If you correctly satisfy their specification and the job is wrong, it's their fault, and they will rectify it. If you 'correct' their specification to what it 'should' be, and the job goes wrong, it's your fault.

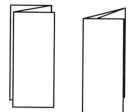

DL Z-fold (left) and roll-fold/envelope fold/fold inside.
Note that the panels should be slightly different sizes to fold correctly. See Part 4.
Below, opposite: other standard folds.

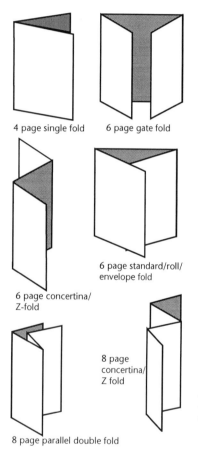

4 page single fold

6 page gate fold

6 page concertina/
Z-fold

6 page standard/roll/
envelope fold

8 page
concertina/
Z fold

8 page parallel double fold

Essentially, you have two choices here. You can either use the standard folds, cuts, trims and stitching that your print house does (or find another printer that does what you want), or you can specify something unusual.

Standard folds vary from printer to printer. Virtually anyone can do you a DL Z-fold or roll/envelope fold (fold inside). Some printers will be unhappy if you want A3 folded to A4 and then DL folded. Those offering specialist folding, however, can do all kinds of weird and wonderful things, which may include accordions, twists, tulips and pop-outs.

If you are printing digitally, remember that heavy colour on a fold line will cause cracking.

The same is true for **trimming** and **cutting**. All print involving bleed is trimmed, usually being printed on SR sizes of paper, such as SRA3, which are oversized to accommodate crop and registration marks. Most printers will be happy to produce a final document at any size smaller than their press.

Additionally, most printers will have some standard die-cuts, such as for presentation folders. They will happily supply you with PDF templates for these.

For about £60, €80 or $60, you can get a die made. This generally takes a couple of weeks. You specify the die using a separate spot colour layer. Ask your printer for exactly how they want this specified. Expect to go through several stages of proofs before the printer is satisfied that you are satisfied. If you incorrectly specify the die cut, or fail to include enough bleed (reckon 6mm rather than 3mm on each side, and at least 3mm safety inside), the result will be unusable. This will be your responsibility, but printers are well used to difficult customers, and won't want to take the risk.

Once a die has been made, it can be used again and again, so the price drops considerably.

As part of a marketing campaign, a well-conceived die-cut piece of print can have dramatically more impact than a brochure, and will typically be hand-sized, for easy distribution. This means that you can print perhaps four or five for the same amount of paper as a DL leaflet. If your quantities are large enough, this can be substantially cheaper.

Fancy folds are usually done by hand, but the folds are pressed (the printer calls it 'scoring') using essentially the same process as die cutting. All the same considerations apply. Typically they will be delivered flat for you to fold yourself. You can ask the printer to fold them for you (at a price), but you will then find that they occupy 5–30 times as much space to store.

Stapling in print is called **stitching**. It is the cheapest and most obvious way of holding the pages together. Above about 32 pages of A4 ('pages' always refers to a single printed side at the final folded size, as your page numbering would give), **saddle-stitched** documents start looking a bit cheap. **Side stitched** documents always look cheap. You can't saddle-stitch more than half an inch total thickness, and you would be mad to try.

For a more refined look, for example for an Annual Report, **Perfect binding** looks like a 'proper book'. More than six mm spine means you can include a spine title. Perfect bound books will fall to bits eventually if much used.

Tape binding and plastic **comb binding** are fine for information you want to refer to often, but are far too ugly to ever hand to anyone else. **Spiral** (wire) binding, by contrast, gives a very prestigious feel, especially in music books. Commercial spiral binding can be had for up to 300 sheets, but office spiral binders only do about 125.

Case binding, usual for hardback books, is the highest standard that you would normally aspire to, with the folios sewn together in blocks of signatures, glued to linen tape and wrapped in a hard-cover. Beyond that, you are into cloth-boards and leather binding.

There is one other binding choice which you might try once, but not twice: screw and post. This creates an industrial, elegant, high art feel.

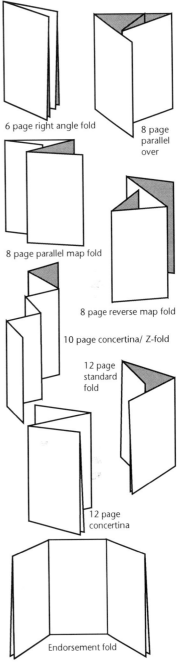

6 page right angle fold

8 page parallel over

8 page parallel map fold

8 page reverse map fold

10 page concertina/ Z-fold

12 page standard fold

12 page concertina

Endorsement fold

 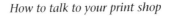

We tried this one year for an annual report. The result was highly prestigious, but it also destroyed the covers of other books that stood next to it on the same shelf.

For shorter documents, you might consider **swatch books**, like the Pantone books. After numerous errors of proof-reading, including frequently failing to spot incorrect telephone numbers, we gave one client swatch books with all of the things they needed to check. You would normally hand-assemble these, but you can specify to the printer where the hole should be **drilled**.

Finally, you might consider supplying some documents on four hole drilled paper. Again, ask the printer to drill for you. This is very useful if you want to create the impression that the information you are sending is valuable, but that it will also be periodically updated. Actual experience suggests that only a small proportion of recipients will, in fact, replace the pages in the original manual you sent out, but the impression you create is a powerful one.

Delivery and Storage

Always specify the delivery and storage for your print. Many printers will offer a call-off service, where they store your print and deliver it as needed. There will be a cost attached to this, though it may not be much. Standard delivery—but always specify this—is to one address in [name of area]. You can't usually save much by going to collect the print yourself, but you can strengthen your relationship with the printer, which is often worth the cost of the petrol.

Attn: W. Caxton
From: G. Chaucer

Dear William, further to our conversation, please would you quote for the following:

1,000 ex
5,000 ex
15,000 ex
CMYK + UV 4pp A4 brochure, full bleed, from our SRA3 finished PDF artwork, on 150 gsm silk or similar (please advise), printed R/V, trimmed to size and folded to A4 with spot UV varnish specified in our file as a separate plate.

Proofs: PDF
Delivery: 1 address, Warwickshire.

Please could you advise on timescales?

Attn: G. Chaucer
From: W. Caxton

Dear Geoffrey, further to your instruction, I am pleased to provide the following quotation, valid for 30 days and subject to sight of the artwork:

From your camera ready SRA3 artwork supplied as compatible PDF for separation in-RIP including additional plate
4pp A4 two sides, 150gsm silk, CMYK with spot UV coating
Finishing: folded and trimmed to A4
Delivery: 1 address Warwickshire

1,000 ex   £115 excl VAT
5,000 ex   £140 excl VAT
15,000 ex   £170 excl VAT
Turnaround 10 days from approval of proofs (PDF).

Alternatively, we can provide 1,000 ex printed digitally at £85. This will not be UV varnished, but digital technology will give a glossy look to images. Turnaround 5 days.

Rules for asking for quotes:

1 Spell everything out.

2 Always include: colours, additional plates, stock weight, final folded size, how many pages, how you will supply the artwork, whether one-sided or two-sided (recto/verso).

3 Always specify how you are going to proof it. PDF is common these days. You can also specify laser-proof or Color-Match, among others. Color-Match is the most expensive, but worth it if the job is critical.

4 Specify where you want it delivered.

5 Ask for turnaround times, rather than dictating them.

6 Include any special instructions.

Printers love comprehensive specifications, and will generally give better prices if everything is spelled out correctly.

You will usually get a quotation back which is worded slightly differently from what you asked for—this shows (among other things) that the printer has correctly interpreted your specification. The quote will normally be standard from whatever estimating software the printer uses, and will probably be in the order of the processes involved.

*Saddle Stitch, Perfect Bound and **Spiral** or **Wire-O** are suitable for 'finished' organisational publications. Watch out for page creep when saddle-stitching. Anything over fifty pages might be better perfect bound.*

*__Perfect Bound__ (paperback) and **Case Bound** (hardback) are standard for published books. They are the only types with printable spines.*

*Although ugly, **tape-binding** may be the best choice for in-house manuals.*

*__Loop stitch__ is mainly for multi-installment documents. Sewn or **pamphlet** stitch is prestigious, but labour intensive. __Screw and Post__ is either overly fussy (if metal) and damages other books, or looks unappealingly cheap, if plastic. However, a single plastic screw and post looks spectacular if you present something in swatch-book format.*

*__Plastic grips, stab/side__ stitch and **comb bound** are only for **transitory documents**. Media sales companies, for some reason, seem to believe that comb-binding, if supplemented by a transparent plastic cover, somehow improves the value of a document. It doesn't.*

If the answer is 'comb bound', you asked the wrong question.

If you are tempted to upgrade the value of your document with case binding, don't: it will look like vanity publishing. As a simple rule of thumb, if you are giving it away for free, never bind with anything more prestigious than perfect binding.

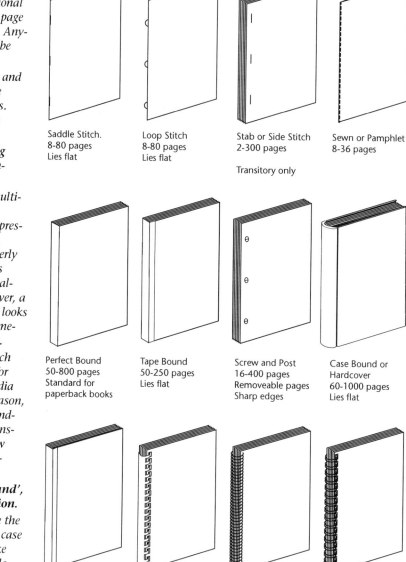

Saddle Stitch.
8-80 pages
Lies flat

Loop Stitch
8-80 pages
Lies flat

Stab or Side Stitch
2-300 pages

Transitory only

Sewn or Pamphlet
8-36 pages

Perfect Bound
50-800 pages
Standard for
paperback books

Tape Bound
50-250 pages
Lies flat

Screw and Post
16-400 pages
Removeable pages
Sharp edges

Case Bound or
Hardcover
60-1000 pages
Lies flat

Plastic Grip
2-250 pages
Removeable pages
Transitory only

Comb Bound
2-250 pages
Lies flat
Always wrong.

Spiral Bound
16-275 pages
Lies flat

Wire-O Bound
16-275 pages
Lies flat

Master Production

Part 3:
Live Digital

Digital Publishing has quite some history: it goes back even before the times of the world wide web. However the invention of web, which most people call 'the internet', meaning the display of graphical pages and typography, is probably where we see the start of the modern electronic publishing. It has evolved a lot since the '90s: using HTML5 it's possible to create a rich layout that almost resembles the richness of layouts in print. Typography can be applied, which is also very similar to what you know from printed matter. Now that we have a medium that is capable of rich design, we can use it to design pages. However, the audience of the internet is different from print; information is often consumed in snack-sized packages, such as a short tweet, a Facebook post, a snippet of news on a website. Still, the need, desire and effect of a well-designed page and well-written long article is still there, even in electronic times.

So where's the challenge? Can't you just use the browser or device as a RIP, as you can in print?

The difficulty of Digital Publishing is in two parts: display and distribution.

With Display (or device) I mean the 'Player', in other words, the technology displaying your layout. That can be the browser, but it is often also a different technology, such as an eBook Reader or a Kindle device, an app, or a PDF Reader like Adobe Reader. All of these have different limitations that either come from hardware (like the black & white Kindles not having a fast processor or a capable graphics engine to display effects), or from software, like a good ePub v3 Reader on Windows or Android. What your reader will see depends a lot on the platform they use for reading. Can you make assumptions about your reader's reading device? It's almost back to the early days of the web, where you needed to determine which Internet browser was used, Internet Explorer or Netscape. Otherwise, you have to fall back to the lowest common denominator, which means reducing design and typography, even color.

The second challenge is distribution. Not everybody wants to give their content for free. So if you charge for your digital publishing, there's a few distribution channels that are either impossible to use or have a steep implementation hurdle that you need to jump yourself. Maybe you want to distribute a recurrent publication, such as a monthly newsletter or magazine. That's impossible to do in some distribution channels, so you are forced to a specific one, which—to make things worse—dictates or excludes certain file formats.

So the decision process in Digital Publishing often comes down to: what distribution model do I want to use and what are my readers using? That dictates file format. Which dictates design and interactive possibilities. Kind of back to the 90's.

Matthias Guenther, Head of Desktop Publishing at Quark Software Inc.

Print is not dead. PriceWaterhouseCoopers predicts that, by 2019, 72% of book revenues will still be from printed books[1]. Digital, though, is definitely on the rise, and will account for 28% of all book sales, exceeding 40% in the US, UK, Singapore and South Korea. It is now the norm rather than the exception to publish books and shorter documents in both digital and printed formats.

The obvious attraction of QuarkXPress for digital publishing is the ability to reuse content and layout. At a deeper level, the real benefits come from being able to use QuarkXPress workflows. While there are many development tools out there, and many people willing to turn a PDF file into an app for a modest fee, the background both of the tools and of the people is in programming and web-development. As technology has advanced, it has become progressively easier to achieve any result that can be imagined, but the process of producing typographically good layout and assuring the workflow from design through proofing to publication requires the same set of skills and tools as for traditional print publishing.

QuarkXPress 2016 allows you to create native apps for smart devices, to create HTML5 publications for smart devices and personal computers, to output HTML5 pages which can be used standalone or as the basis for a template to build a WordPress, Concrete5 or Drupal theme, to output fixed format ePubs, to output reflow format ePubs and Kindle books, to output hyperlinked PDFs, and to output HTML text.

This section will explain the benefits and drawbacks of each, how to create them, and how to refine them.

---

1 Global entertainment and media outlook 2015–2019, PwC, Ovum.

Digital
In print, 'digital' means a Xerox DocuPress or other short-run laser-based printer-copier calibrated to press standards. In the world of 'digital', 'digital' means everything which is not physical print.

The dropped cap
QuarkXPress 2016 now supports dropped caps in Kindle and ePUB output, as well as when saving text as HTML.

1 Planning for digital

If you have legacy content in QuarkXPress, you can publish it for digital quite quickly. What you do will to a large extent be dictated by the layout and content you already have. When starting from scratch, it is important to plan in the same way as you would plan a print document, establishing Outcomes, Audiences, Messages and Delivery as we saw in the previous section.

In my experience, it is at this planning stage that things most often go wrong. Many otherwise hard-headed businesses, charities and public-sector organisations become overly excited at the prospect of producing an app or other electronic publication. Sensible planning goes out of the window. Part of this is the lure of 'free'. Digital content can be issued without cost (or so it would seem). Another part is the lure of 'new': our business/charity/body must be at the forefront. A third part is the lure of 'cool': an interactive app would be so much more in touch with our customers, supporters or users. Finally, there is the lure of 'urgent': if we don't do this, then our competitors will. The result is that the world is awash with poorly conceived apps and e-publications, most of which are never downloaded or read. Because they are enthusiasm-driven, they tend to use the very latest technology, which becomes dated a few months later and no longer supported two years after that.

Question 1: What is our outcome?
What is it exactly that we are intending to achieve, not in terms of producing a publication, but in how we will influence the world around us?

Question 2: Who are our audiences?
Who do we need to reach in order for that outcome to be achieved? With reference to digital, what is the uptake of what kind of technology in this group? Figures are widely available for many demographics in most countries—who has internet access, who has smart devices, their browsing and reading preferences, and so on. Although most smartphone users have Android or iOS devices, there are still many businesses which only issue Blackberry phones

Planning for digital

and refuse to let users bring their own device. If you are targetting that particular sector, a PDF document or web page may be the best option.

Question 3: What is our message?
In three lines, what are we trying to communicate?

Question 4: How will it reach our audiences?
Delivery is the most common problem in digital publishing. Although transmission may be as simple as clicking on a link to download, this is not the same as reaching the recipient. What equipment is supported? What proportion of our audience has that equipment? Is it necessary to reach the rest of the audience by another means? If you are doing a sales promotion to a million people, you might be quite pleased if 1% of them downloaded your app and looked at it. If you were trying to inform 200,000 people of an imminent flu pandemic, you would need to find a reliable way to reach all of them.

Assuming that they do access your content, how much of it will they read? If you send it as a Reflow ePub or Kindle, they are likely to start at the beginning and carry on until they get bored. How far are they likely to read? If you send as a PDF, they are most likely to search for the terms they are interested in, unless the document is very short. If it is short, will it contain all the information they require? If you are creating an app, what will the User Experience (UX) path be? Will this take them by the right route?

1 Comparing digital options

1 App Studio and HTML5 publications

App Studio is a Quark-provided platform to produce digital issues of publications as downloadable apps on the Apple and Google App stores. It is a paid service, and there are also costs to making apps available.

HTML5 publications, new in QuarkXPress 2016, are accessed via websites and respond on smart devices and com-

Is this the right project?
It's always worth making your content available electronically, even if it's only as a PDF. Searchability extends your reach. Anything more complex needs careful thought. Many organisations have invested large sums in apps that are never downloaded by anyone but the organisation's own senior management team.

Free or paid?
Is making a profit or covering costs one of your intended outcomes? It is much easier to monetise an App Studio app or a Kindle publication than an HTML5 app or a PDF.

Regular or one-off?
If you've successfully reached your audience once, will that make it easier to reach them again? For regular publications, App Studio may be better.

Is a publication the right kind of delivery?
QuarkXPress creates publications, be they print, ePub, app, PDF or web page. However, publications are only one kind of digital experience. Would a YouTube video, a Twitter campaign, a Facebook page or a utility app be better? Would syndicating content through RSS reach more people?

puters like native apps do—provided that the server can keep up with user demand.

App Studio apps and HTML5 publications are identical in terms of supported content. They offer the maximum amount of interactivity, including 360° images, animation, audio, buttons, picture zoom, scroll zones, slideshows and displaying separate web content.

To produce an App Studio or HTML5 publication, you need to work in a digital layout, from Layout—New... choose type: Digital. You can preview them as you work using the globe icon at the bottom right of the screen. Deployment is through the App Studio palette (Window—App Studio Publishing) or File—Export—Layout as HTML5 Publication.

2 HTML5

If you export a layout as HTML5 Publication, as above, and then open the folder which has been produced, you can locate fully-formatted and feature complete HTML5 pages in the html5output folder. You could, in principle, upload that folder to a web server and it would immediately be one or more linked and functioning web pages. It would lack refinements, such as responsiveness (ie, that it would resize itself to the device), but, if you needed a website quickly and wanted to use QuarkXPress typography, it might serve you well.

More usefully, this makes an ideal set of templates to convert in Concrete5 or using an application such as PineGrow to turn it into a template for WordPress. You can achieve the layout, look and feel that you need rapidly and easily in QuarkXPress, and then introduce the Content Management System features you are interested in subsequently. This is dramatically faster than the 'old fashioned' way—creating layouts in Photoshop, exporting them as slices, and then extensively reworking them.

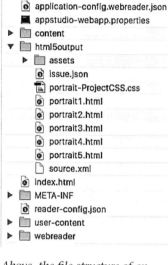

Above, the file structure of an HTML5 publication. If you want to open the html files, you must go to html5ouput and choose one of the files such as portrait1.html. Just going to index.html in the root folder will not work.

Planning for digital

3   ePub and Kindle

ePub and Kindle are formats for publishing to reader apps (ePub) or Amazon devices (Kindle). Both ePub and Kindle have two formats: fixed layout and reflow.

Fixed layout

Contrary to what you would expect from the name, fixed layout is the most advanced format. With fixed layout, you can use any design or typography you like, and it will come across pretty much exactly as you designed it. As far as is possible in the format, text will come across as searchable, and clicking on it in Kindle will produce online dictionary help, as well as providing the ability to add annotations. To create Fixed layout, you must be working in a digital layout (File—New... choose Digital).

The ePub format supports a very wide range of interactivity. You can have buttons, audio, video, and so on. Audio and video can be via links or embedded, though, naturally, this substantially increases file size. You can expect ePub to support most things that an HTML5 app would. However, the reader experience depends on the device: any feature which is missing on the chosen device (or version of the reader) will have an ugly "Audio Content not supported!", or similar tag over it. Even supported features may behave differently—for example, animations may go slower. Note that OpenType features are not supported by HTML5.

The Kindle Fire—essentially an Android device—supports ePub and its interactive features, but the other Kindles do not. QuarkXPress output to Kindle produces a Kindle Mobi format which is compatible with all Kindle devices. Mobi supports fixed layouts, but not interactive features. If you want interactivity and want to reach Kindle Fire users, create as ePub, which the Kindle Fire can read.

Reflow layout

The original ePub and Kindle readers were purely text reading devices, and reflowed the text to suit the device and the reader's preferences. You can turn any text into Reflow layout by clicking Layout—Add Pages to Reflow. You do not need to be in a Digital layout to do this. Reflows do as you would expect—they reflow. You can create a chain of articles and components so that pictures and call-outs appear in the right places. Anchored pictures in the text will usually display at the right place (though only if they have files behind them—pasted pictures will not), though they may come across at the wrong size.

QuarkXPress 2016 supports fonts, colours and some typography in reflow layout. For example, dropped caps come across nicely. However, anything involving complex use of fonts, such as charts made with FF Chartwell, will fail, because reflow layout does not support Open Type options.

On the other hand, both Kindle and ePub offer maximum compatibility in reflow layout. Kindles (apart from the Kindle Fire) do not support ePub, so if you want to make a reflow layout available on both platforms, you need to provide both types of file.

Reflow is extremely good for long narrative text, such as you would find in a book, and handles footnotes well. A book which relies on graphics may fare poorly—even when correctly embedded, graphics will be displayed in the early Kindles in 1 bit format, which makes most images barely distinguishable.

4   PDF

PDFs are intrinsically interactive, because they are searchable. Subject to export options, QuarkXPress will bring across all hyperlinks and anchors, and will automatically connect lists and indexes. You can create page features, such as empty boxes, which can be converted later into fillable forms which then send their data back for collection (use Adobe Acrobat Professional or an equivalent utility).

The biggest advantage of PDF is that it is a format everyone is comfortable with. A proportion of any audience will refuse to use your HTML5 app and look askance at offers of an ePub or Kindle file. However, most will be happy to view a PDF. PDF retains your document layout and typography exactly. Additionally, you don't need a special licence to be allowed to use your fonts in it.

5 HTML text

Easy to overlook because it isn't in the File—Export section, you can save HTML text from File—Save Text, choosing HTML as your output format. HTML text is ready format-ted. It will not (usually) include graphics, though in certain circumstances it will include anchored graphics, but it will correctly format your titles and dropped caps. Fonts are not transmitted via HTML text, so do not rely on particular font features.

HTML text has the lowest gloss but the highest reach. You can put it into an RSS feed, paste it into a WordPress post, or allow it to format via FlipBoard on someone's tablet, and you have instantly reached people in the way they prefer to be reached. It takes seconds to accomplish. Whatever out-put options you choose, it is always worth doing HTML ad-ditionally and getting it onto a website.

Method	Best for	Conversion time	Interactivity	Typography
HTML text	RSS, CMS	Seconds	Links	Dropped caps, fonts, colours
PDF	Email, download	Minutes	Links, auto-indexing	All
ePub reflow	Smart devices reading	1 hour	Footnotes, links	Dropped caps, fonts, colours
Kindle	Older Kindles	1 hour	Footnotes, links	Dropped, caps, fonts, colours
ePub fixed	Smart devices, Kindle Fire	1/2 day	Extensive but device de-pendent	All
Kindle fixed	Newer Kindles	1/2 day	Limited	All
HTML5 Page	CMS template	1 day	Full	All
HTML5 App	Any device app	1/2 day	Full	All
App Studio	App store app	2 days	Full	All

Left, our sample guidebook, which we want to make into an ePub.

Above, Reflow Tagging palette 'as it comes out', for a sample guidebook layout.

Component 1	CoverTitle
Component 2	Gulosus suis...
Component 3	The Red Cas...
Component 4	MMT_7198...
Component 5	MMT_6528...
Component 6	Fiducias co...
Component 7	Fiducias co...
Component 8	Chirographi...
Component 9	110557053...
Component 10	Umbraculi ci...
Component 11	111986808...
Component 12	111426107...
Component 13	Lascivius ma...
Component 14	Cathedras a...
Component 15	Chirographi i...
Component 16	_MMT6194...
Component 17	112024864...
Component 18	MMT_7201.jpg
Component 19	112886968...
Component 20	Octavius inc...
Component 21	Aegre perspi...
Component 22	Rures imput...
Component 23	110440071...
Component 24	Apparatus b...

2 Easy Digital Workflow

The choices on Digital may be relatively difficult, but the workflow is straightforward.

There are essentially two workflows you can pursue, Reflow and Fixed/Interactive. The Reflow is conceptually complicated (but we'll explain it), and may seem, when all is done, a bit intricate for what it produces. The advantage is it plays on any device. The Fixed/Interactive is simpler and offers control of the layout, though it too relies on the Reflow concept, so we will begin with that.

1 Reflow workflow

To create a reflow document, do this:

1   Open any document with autolinked[1] text and some pictures.

2   Go to menu Layout—Add Pages to Reflow, choose add all to one article.

3   Go to menu Layout—ePub Metadata and add some basic information.

4   Go to File—Export—Layout as ePub. Export using the defaults.

5   Open the file and take a look. Job done... or not.

If you flick through the ePub produced, you'll see that the main narrative seems all in order, but all of the images are at the back of the document with no particular context for the text.

Go to Window—Reflow Tagging. You should see a long list of components.

Look for the one which begins with the first words of your main text. It should normally have a link icon, showing you that it is the document's auto-linked text.

---

1 It doesn't need to be autolinked to work, but we'll be looking at the particular issues of an autolinked document in this section.

Easy Digital Workflow

If you go back to your ePub, you will see that all of this text, after the cover title, is one long flow, and every other item has been put after it.

Now go to View—Story Editor. This gives you a text-based view of the document, which is useful for editing long text without having to worry about its format, or for sorting out issues in text which has been formatted in a way which is hard to edit.

You'll see that it has precisely the same order as the ePub you've generated. This is helpful, because it means you can work here without having to export to see what happens.

For our Guidebook, we are going to need to chop the text up into pages, if the graphics and their captions are going to be in more or less the right place. However, this is going to be annoying if we want to edit the book again later, so let us first clone the document to a new layout, using Utilities—Cloner and choosing the 'new layout' option.

We now need to chop it up—we wouldn't do this if we were setting a novel, but, for a guide book, it is going to be essential. To do this, go to Utilities—Linkster, select All Pages, and choose the first icon to unlink them. This means we now have one story per page. If you check the Reflow Tagging palette, you will see that it is clear: the reflow articles have not transferred with the cloning.

Go back to Layout—Add Pages to Reflow, and choose 'one article per story' which will keep things organised.

Go.

You will see in the Reflow Tagging palette that a lot of articles have come in again. However, at least on my example, the pages which are no longer in the flow did not come in. Also, not everything is in the order I want. Not a problem. Click on each page and then add as Item (not article) in the Reflow Tagging palette. Then, using the green arrow keys at the top, sort everything including these articles into the right order. You can try dragging, but that doesn't always produce reliable results, which is why the arrow keys are there. The View—Story Editor may not immediately refresh,

Cloner, above, Linkster, below.

Below, the Reflow palette with everything reorganised

Above, the ePub now reads like a book.

ePubs and Kindles must have covers. Therefore, QuarkXPress always sends the first page of the document as an image, which is interpreted as the cover. If your document does not have a cover, then the first page of text will actually go as an image—almost certainly not what you intended.

QuarkXPress depends on the current KindleGen for its Kindle export. Always get the latest version. If it does not produce a result as good as the ePub export, consider creating first as ePub and then converting to Kindle Mobi with an application like Caliber. Although the most recent KindleGen does appear to work better than the last one, Caliber will give you more options.

so close it and open it again when you're ready. You can now export for ePub again.

This time the result should be much more what you are looking for.

There are a couple of refinements that still need to be made.

If you didn't add the ePub metadata in Layout—ePub Metadata, the file will have come across as an anemic 'ePub made in QuarkXPress'. This needs to be finished.

Text which is very small will have been sent across as an image. This is probably not what you want, so you may need to change the font size.

The ePub Table of Contents will have names like 'Article 1, Article 2', etc. You can edit these by going to each article in the Reflow and changing its name, but these articles are really just a convenience so that you can manually put the graphics on the correct pages.

A better way is to use a list from the Window-Lists palette to create a Table of Contents. See Palettes—Lists in Part 5. When you export, choose Options—Table of Contents… Use List as ToC palette. This will then extract your list, which should relate to the chapter headings.

So, to summarise:

Basic workflow—Add pages to reflow, change metadata, see if it's worked. As long as you add a table of contents built from a list, this workflow will be more or less right for long narrative text, such as a novel.

Advanced workflow—Clone the document, unlink the pages using Linkster, add pages to reflow, one Article per Story, add in any missing pages. Reorder to suit. Create a list for Table of Contents. Export, fix any errors, job done. This is suitable for more complex books with advanced layout.

However, neither of these are interactive, beyond the basic interactivity that comes with an ePub reader or a Kindle.

2 Fixed Layout Workflow

The advanced workflow we just tried is a bit of a halfway house between 'proper' reflow and fixed layout. You need to be working in a digital layout for this section.

To turn your print layout into a digital layout, you need to use Layout—Duplicate Layout and choose 'Digital' in the dialogue. You can't do this through Utilities—Cloner.

Let's go back to the guidebook for a moment, and return to the questions of outcomes, audiences, messages and delivery.

Outcomes: what are we trying to achieve? If we are (for example) a major national publicly- and member-funded organisation that runs castles, we probably want to get more people visiting castles, and we want them to get more out of each visit and tell their friends. Our audience, therefore, is people who visited the castle and are prepared to pay a bit more to know a lot more. Our key messages—not necessarily spelled out, but communicated through the medium, are going to be: 'there's even more than you thought there is' and 'take part in history'.

How are we then going to plan this? We may have a set of gorgeous photographs shot in superb evening light at 36 megapixels or more. We almost certainly have an archive of old documents that relate to the castle, some of which are on display, but can't be touched. We have maps. We may also have recordings and videos. Set against that, we have to actually get our document into people's hands. That could be via Amazon Kindle—but then we are restricted to things which Kindle supports—via our own website, or, perhaps, via a wifi server where they can download while they are in the gift shop. For any of these, we need to control the document's size, which means a restriction on video, audio and massive images.

Let's focus for a moment on the messages: 'there's always more', and 'take part in history'.

While we may have some good audio and video, the thing that people are most likely to want to look at is interactive maps that they can pinch and zoom. Maps in books are al-

That font you like…

QuarkXPress 2016 asks you first about exporting fonts. Many now have separate licensing agreements (and prices) for inclusion with eBooks or on the web. Given how easy it is for someone to Google for breaches of the font licence, it's better not to take chances.

Also, be aware that eBooks and HTML5 do not support OpenType special features.

Below, using fixed layout you can exactly reproduce the look of your booklet. There are also some obvious interactive improvements— provided that the ePub reader supports them.

Small text can become a button to show a pop-up at a more legible size.

Making a map pinchable and zoomable (use an image) is an obvious improvement for little effort.

Small images benefit from being zoomable and scrollable.

Vista images can gently change using a slideshow, for example showing seasons.

A digital layout is much easier than working with a reflow layout. You do not need to divide things up into articles, as this is done for you by virtue of creating boxes on the page. Everything exported as a fixed layout will appear where you placed it. As long as you stay within the limitations of your target devices, your added images, animations, buttons, picture zooms, slideshows, scroll zones, videos and web view should function correctly.

Above, our map did not work as an EPS. Converting to native objects allows more interactivity.

ways too small, and being able to get our fingers onto one is going to make things much more interesting. The obvious way to do this is to add a Picture Zoom action from the HTML5 palette in Windows—HTML5. We need to be careful here. Trying out our EPS map via export on an iPad Pro, we discover that, although it zooms, pans and pinches very nicely, the background has turned black. We'll try a bit of fixing, but we may need to opt for an image, albeit a high resolution one.

We can also zoom and pan the images. To do this we need to have everything in the zoom and pan window in the visible picture box.

Something that the very best archaeology museums now do is have exhibits for all to see in glass cases, and pull-out drawers underneath, where there might be twenty of the same thing for experts to examine. Scroll Zones, also in the HTML5 palette, allow the reader to access what is, in fact, another layout, scrolling through it while remaining on the original page.

If we want people to come back, then we might want to have a web view which links them to a place on our website which constantly updates with the latest special events, or, at least, opening times. On the other hand, we need to plan this properly so that if the user has no connection, they are not suddenly facing an obviously missing area on the screen.

It might be worth running an audio loop of birds singing, perhaps punctuated by the sounds of swords swinging. A good loop can create a strong impression without necessarily costing us much in the way of storage space or download time. This can be added using the Audio function, with autoplay turned on, loop, and hide controller.

Our experience has quickly become immersive. The question is then: do we need our original eight pages, or are we going to concentrate everything into just a couple of highly interactive pages? Almost certainly the answer is a mixture of both. If you set up one page of, say, a map of the castle where each building is a button that shows a pop-up with more information (which, to us, is a new layout), you can have children playing with it for hours. However, older readers may be more interested in reading extended narrative, which they are expecting because there is no limit on the length of text. The castle in our example is Kenilworth Castle. You could potentially include the entire text of Sir Walter Scott's novel Kenilworth, which is now long out of copyright.

If pressed for time, we could take our Guidebook layout, copy and paste every part of it onto the pages of a digital layout, quickly add a couple of audio files, make all the pictures zoomable, put in a pane for our website, and the job is done. This could potentially be accomplished in less than an hour.

We would then need to test it—and it is the time required to test our ePub on iPads, iPhones, Kindle Fires, Android tablets, Macs and PCs, and then to sort out any little niggling problems that would make it worth our while to construct the entire ePub from the ground up, perhaps by building it around the physical castle so that people can wander round and move the map to where they are, and see everything as it is there.

The workflow, either way, is very simple:

1 Create a digital layout or duplicate a print layout and select 'digital' in the dialogue box

2 Put everything where you want it

3 Add interactivity using the HTML5 palette

4 Export as ePUB, layout: fixed (using a list for Table of Contents, perhaps)

5 Test, test and retest—on as many different devices and readers as you can find.

Knowing your limits: is QuarkXPress the right tool?

To a hammer, it is said, everything looks like a nail. Fixed layout interactive ePUBS and HTML5 or native apps are so powerful that you might be tempted to try to do everything with them.

Currently, QuarkXPress apps can't gather user data (though they can show a web view that does, or create a new email). Although they are interactive, they are not interactive in the way a racing game is. They can't access a device's camera, and they can't make sense of tilting or the GPS, though they can collect data via Google Analytics.

QuarkXPress interactivity is superb for creating books and publications that go beyond the printed page into a new space. For other things, other development suites are better. When planning an interactive ePUB or an app, be aware of the limitations.

3 HTML5 publications and App Studio workflow

HTML5 publications are browser-based apps which are fully HTML5 compliant, and will work in any current browser. If the browser doesn't support a particular standard feature, then it will have its own mechanism for gracefully declining to show it to you. App Studio apps are the same, but they go one step further: they are tuned by the pay-to-publish App Studio site (Window—App Studio Publishing) into native apps for iOS and Android smart devices. There are additionally steps you have to take to get your apps onto the iTunes App store and Google's App stores.

The advantage of App Studio apps is that you can have complete confidence that what you intended is what the user experiences, with no problems about internet connection speed since everything is on the device. You can also access certain device functionality, and it is much easier to monetise your content. The disadvantage is that you have a whole marketing job to promote your app before anyone actually downloads it. Consider: how often have you seen 'Get the App' and not bothered to download it? The psychological barrier to putting another app on your device is much greater than simply visiting a website.

Aside from that, the content of HTML5 publications and App Studio Apps are functionally identical.

If we go back to our guidebook example, then we see at the bottom left of our screen an icon ⊕ at the end of the row which was not on our print layout screens:

Clicking on that takes us to a preview of the HTML5 publication, which will appear in our regular web browser. Immediately we should feel this running a little bit faster than an ePUB. Controls which may not have worked—depending on our device—now respond instantly. You may feel you have suddenly arrived in the promised land. Don't get too carried away. You are viewing a preview of the app

Above, the HTML5 palette offers an array of interactive elements.

Easy Digital Workflow

when viewed via Quark's micro-web server running locally on your computer. When you upload the full app to the web, a fast connection with a relatively concise site will still make it pretty brisk. A slow connection, or a slow server where you underestimated your app's popularity, especially if you have lots of audio and video files, will make everything slow right down.

Still, if it all feels like magic, it very nearly is.

Essentially, an HTML5 publication or App Studio app is your digital layout ePub, but it behaves on any device the way you expect it to behave, without having to test it on everything. It is as interactive as you want it to be.

Exporting it is the only difficult bit.

If you go the paid route via App Studio, follow their process via the website, through the App Studio Publishing palette.

If you are going down the HTML5 publication route, go to File—Export—Layout as HTML5 Publication. Make sure that you choose a new folder, otherwise it will spray files into whatever folder you put it all into. It will take a bit of time to process all the files. When done, you will need to up load them to a web server via FTP. If you don't know how to do this, find someone who does. Note that you can't simply click on the files and expect them to do something, as your local machine won't be configured to serve files in the way a web server does. Again, uploading will take a few minutes. Then navigate to the URL it is uploaded to with your web browser, and enjoy.

Quite possibly if you want to sell a downloadable app, an HTML5 publication version is the best selling tool. Give people full access for free on the web, and offer them the opportunity to buy it as an app to sit on their device. Somebody who likes your web app will work out fairly quickly that it is going to be more convenient to walk round a castle with the app on their phone, rather than hoping that there will be enough signal to use the web app when they most want it.

Working with interactive elements

If you click on the interactive elements in the HTML5 palette one by one, they are quite self-explanatory in what they do. However, this doesn't mean that it is necessarily obvious how they work.

To explain: each object only does exactly what it specifies, and nothing more. If you set a Button to show a pop-up, it will do exactly that. When you test it, you will find that the pop-up pops up—actually displaying the contents of a new layout, though the users don't know that—and the pop-up hangs around. You need to configure the pop-up itself to be a button to hide it again.

If you create only a portrait layout, when you turn a smart device, it will display that portrait layout, but in a landscape box. If you want turnable interactivity, you have to create a second, landscape layout as well.

Whatever file format your graphics are in, QuarkXPress will convert them to PNG, if transparency is required, or to JPEG. OTF and TTF fonts are embedded. Check your licence agreement for the fonts you intend to use. HTML5 does not support Open Type features stuch as stylistic sets.

4 Using HTML5 as is

Once you have exported as HTML5, you can go into the html5output folder and look for documents that end with .html. Each one of those is a web page, and you can click on them to bring them up in your browser. In principle, you could upload any one of them and they would operate as one page websites, though links and some functionality would not necessarily come across. This may be just what you want. If you are creating an online version of a publication, and you want to retain the impression of reading a book, then the app versions will work better. If you want a highly immersive single page, where all of the additional information is done via pop-ups, which place another layout onto the page, then the interactive features of the book-reader will just be getting in the way.

As mentioned previously, you can also use this as a template for conversion into a WordPress, Drupal or Concrete5 theme.

3 Three Digital Publishing Projects

In this chapter we will look at three digital publishing projects, all using HTML5 publications.

As well as showing how the layouts work, I've tried to give some consideration to how the projects come about. All three are based on 'real life', though only the final one is a live project.

1 The Staff Magazine

Here is the scenario. You have been producing the staff magazine for as long as you have been with the company. Articles come in. The internal communications officer reads them, edits them and forwards them to you. You also receive a collection of photographs of suspect quality, and occasionally go out with a camera to collect some rather more inspiring images. Everyone is happy.

Then, senior management decrees that it is far too wasteful to be printing thousands of copies of the magazine every month. The whole thing must be sent round electronically. You see the writing on the wall—there's a young lad in IT who has been saying that he could do a much better job using Dreamweaver, and he's desperate to try it out. Your boss suggests that maybe just doing what you do as a PDF might work—except that a bit of research done last year shows that no more than one person in twenty in your organisation actually reads emailed PDFs.

The answer we're going to pursue is replacing the 16 page magazine (which, seriously, was a chore to fill half the time) with a four page HTML5 publication, which is going to be delivered via the corporate intranet, and also be available online for anyone who has the URL. Your target reader is using a web browser on a desktop or laptop, but you also want to make sure that senior management, who all have iPads, see what a first rate job you're doing. You're rather cheekily going to tag your publication "the most news and information packed four pages you will ever find, anywhere. Fact." With that as your strapline and underlying message, you are going to rechristen the magazine, previously entitled some dull corporate name such as 'Inner View' or 'Corporate Focus', simply as, 'Fact.'

The layout, right, is an iPad double spread, centre, or single pages for back (below) and cover (bottom). The hook is in the outrageous claim that the publication is information packed, when the cover is mostly blank. Inside and back page, the visible stories are just teasers, leading to pop ups or scroll windows. All images are interactive in some way. By repurposing a previously made but unpublished magazine, development time was 2 hours.

Right, as it appears on a web browser, spreads intact. An iPad will show the spread in landscape or individual pages in portrait.

Cover—the cover makes the outrageous claim that it is the most information packed four pages anywhere, which challenges the reader to prove it wrong—even more so because the cover is mostly blank. The secret is inside: all of the stories are scrollable or pop-upable, and some rotate.

All stories are scrollable or pop-ups—**Scroll zone** or **button**

Flixel video clip—moving image—**Video**

Easter egg—clicking gives discount to coffee shop—**Button**

Web viewer pane to intranet/website—**Webview**

Comedy animation here—**Animation**

Opinion piece swaps around every few minutes—**Slideshow**

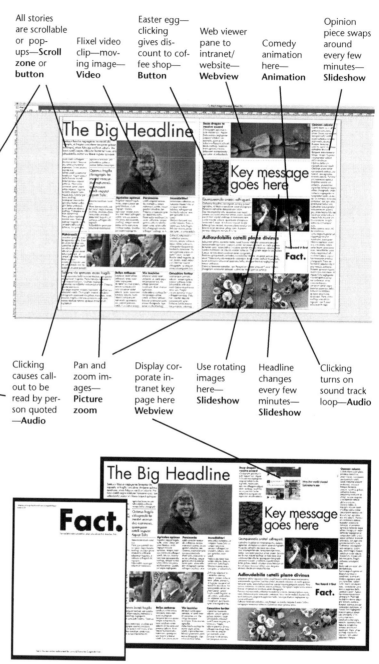

Clicking causes callout to be read by person quoted—**Audio**

Pan and zoom images—**Picture zoom**

Display corporate intranet key page here—**Webview**

Use rotating images here—**Slideshow**

Headline changes every few minutes—**Slideshow**

Clicking turns on sound track loop—**Audio**

Three Digital Publishing Projects

2 Castle Walkaround

After seeing the way you turned the guidebook into an ePub, the manager of the castle visitor's centre wants a one page walkaround. She's seen the same thing at a cathedral while on holiday in Spain, and thinks it will bring in more visitors. The idea is to have the HTML5 publication for free on the web, but sell the smartphone app. You only get to hear about this, though, when someone rings you up to ask you if you could send over all the assets so they can tender it out. A quick conversation later, they agree to let you 'have a go'—if they like what you've done, you can do the job. Otherwise, it's going to an app design company.

You decide to take up the challenge. Right now we are only pitching for the work, so we're just going to do the iPad version. However, if successful, we'll need to complete the HTML5 version in portrait and landscape, and, for App Studio, produce a separate version for each of the standard screen shapes: 16:9, 4:3, 15:10. Assuming we get that far, we'll be using Shared Content (Window—Shared Content) to keep everything synchronised in the same layout.

People's expectations of interactive are now much more than just 'press a button and an animation happens'. By contrast with the staff magazine, which is deliberately and ridiculously shouting at the reader 'look, we're interactive!' (staff magazines need to retain a strong sense of poking fun at themselves—if they don't, their readers will simply mock them), the castle walkaround needs to be seamless, and feel like we are running our fingers over a map.

When pitching for a job, it's essential to keep everything 'magic'—if the client gets the idea that they can see how you did it all, they might decide that they can do this themselves, or they might go online to try to find the cheapest person who will do more or less what you are doing. If you can get the interactions just right—usually by tweaking the exact way in which animations take place—the whole thing will seem impossibly good. Once the client has signed a contract, it's fine to go with drafts and beta versions, but, when pitching, never take anything which does not work absolutely flawlessly.

Above, the digital layout can create automatic Portrait and Landscape versions, linked. App Studio allows several different sizes to be bound together in one document. For HTML5, it's best to create a separate version for each type of device and assign them different web-links: iPad versions do not scale down to iPhone size, which means that some of the information will be off the page. If that's too ungainly, a bit of clever editing at the code level can make it all auto-select the correct device— that's out of scope of this book, though.

After the madcap but relatively simple staff magazine, this layout is much richer in terms of interactions, so it is important to keep the User Experience (UX) as simple and clean as possible. Many actions must be accomplished by using a button with a popup to open an entirely different layout—which looks identical to the user, but which allows an audio file to play while a slideshow takes place, and so on.

Designing this can easily get out of hand. The map itself is quite complex, and, once converted to native objects, draws more system resources. Use layers to help sort things out, and lock the layers when you aren't working on them. You can colour code the layers to match the colour coding of your interactive areas. Also, keep all the text on one layer—this will help when you do other language versions.

Controls such as zoom, full screen (for a desktop browser) and app help are created by QuarkXPress automatically, so you don't need to worry about them.

You can put all the interactive elements onto the map in about an hour, but you will then need to tweak them all to make sure they 'feel' right. This is about speed of interactions and transitions. For example, when changing to different historical periods, use a fade, but don't use it elsewhere.

Use layers to keep track of different interactions

Webview appears if relevant, eg, events today

UX—Use multiple layouts for interactions

UX—different colours =different interactions

UX—leave some spaces uninteractive

UX—use compass as a help menu

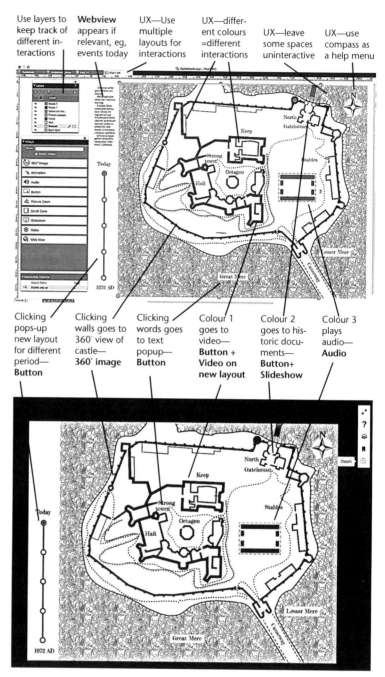

Clicking pops-up new layout for different period—
Button

Clicking walls goes to 360° view of castle—
360° image

Clicking words goes to text popup—
Button

Colour 1 goes to video—
Button + Video on new layout

Colour 2 goes to historic documents—
Button+ Slideshow

Colour 3 plays audio—
Audio

Three Digital Publishing Projects

3 Promotional EP web-app

A singer-songwriter has put together an EP, which she'll be selling at gigs. The app is a strictly zero-budget project. You've offered to help with the cover design, but now there's the question of promoting it on social media. As your friends in the music business have told you, the sole purpose of the CD cover and anything else is to interest people in playing the songs—we'll want to keep it simple, then.

Setting the back picture as button—popup creates a new layout.

Below, using black borders and only one page simplifies the experience, putting the focus on the artwork.

In this case, there's no point giving people the idea that they are reading a book, so we opt for identical vertical and horizontal layouts which are simply the cover and back cover of the CD. The back cover is set to be a button which opens a pop-up—in fact, an entirely new layout as far as QuarkXPress is concerned. It's important to use a pop-up rather than a 'go to page' button, because going to a page has a page shift effect, which will ruin the interactivity. When the popup appears, it covers the CD cover. Clicking on each song then plays a short clip from the song, using the Audio command. Clicking on the back cover again closes the pop-up, taking us back to the original screen. The only other refinement here is that the master pages are set to have a black background, kept locked with a layer, so that there is no apparent page when viewed on a tablet. A separate set of layouts is needed for other device profiles, and a bit of html code needs to be inserted to switch between them. Alternatively, you could just link to the HTML5 output.

Above, the screen as it first appears, below, with the popup.

When you open an HTML5 publication, the QuarkXPress logo comes up. You can have your own logo, or anything else. Dig into the folder you put your app in, and you'll find a folder called 'web-reader', and in it, 'images'. The 'loading-logo.png' is the one you want to change, though you may feel like changing all the others as well. You can change this for the entire application in Quark's XTension folder, webapp.

Have a care for the URLs
No matter how seamless your app is, if it is reached by going to http://yourcorp.co.uk/interactive/ webapps/serial207898, or something similar, then many users will be put off. You can buy a domain quite cheaply, and you can also use a subdomain of your main domain—search engines don't like these, but you may not want your publication exposed to the search engines anyway.

Warn me first!
If you are directing someone to a web app, warn them first that is what you are doing. If someone believes they are just going to a web page, and then sees the loading icon (and they may well not recognise it), they may think their computer is being hacked. If in doubt, have a web landing page which links to the app, with a short explanation about what to expect.

4 Digital wrap up: is it really that easy?

The first few times I tried the HTML5 app publishing functions, I thought I must be doing something wrong. Could it really be *that* easy? The answer: it really is. Just remember not to make life too complicated for yourself. A couple of interactive features will make most documents exciting. Twenty interactive features—except on something like the castle map single page—may make your users feel overwhelmed. Back when I used to program video games—does anyone remember The Frozen Heart for EV Override?—I learned that the magic of making things seem real was to test, tweak, test, tweak, and keep on tweaking until it felt just like using a real object.

The other side of this is that you need to do a set of layouts for every type of device you are going to support. At the moment, going the App Studio route enables the device to select its correct layout, but the HTML5 route doesn't. It should take a web-techie about ten minutes to write some code to slip in which will swap these for you, but the exact code will depend on which devices. Any layout will work on any device—it just won't be as nice, and it's perfection which will make it stand out.

The other, other side is that what is now very easy to do in QuarkXPress is actually very hard to do by other means.

Part 4:
Deep Publishing

1 Workflows that speed results and reduce errors

This section is about workflows. It's possible to produce page layouts in Microsoft Word or PowerPoint. People used to wander into our office all the time with publications they had done that way, in the hope that we could 'just tweak them a little bit'. The problem with Word and Power-Point (for this purpose—they are fine for what they are designed for) is that while it may be possible to achieve something, it's slow, cumbersome, gets more and more unstable the more that is in it, and almost impossible to fix quickly and reliably when something is wrong.

Desk top publishing—and QuarkXPress, I would argue pre-eminently—is the right tool for the job.

However, just because you are using QuarkXPress doesn't mean you are using it optimally. Most workflows can be improved.

1 Design—Layout—Editing—Publication

Publishing a document, be it a one page invitation or a 350 page technical manual, basically falls into four or possibly five processes. It is possible to go back and change things later, but it is more effective to get things right in order.

(Brand) ➔ Design ➔ Layout ➔ Editing ➔ Publication

2 Design (and Brand)

Usually the Brand is already in existence before design begins. Brand is much more than a visual identity or a logo: a brand is a promise of an experience, and what is referred to as 'branding' is making that promise palpable. Unless working on a truly ad hoc document, always ask for the visual identity specification before starting off. If they don't have one, ask for some of the materials they use a lot: nine times out of ten, the brand will reveal itself through them.

Design is about solving a problem of matching style to purpose in a compelling, attractive, and, above all, useable way. The adage of the Bauhaus—form follows function—is one every designer should work to.

For most publications, you have three inputs: purpose, content and production.

Purpose covers the things we discussed earlier under strategy: intended outcome, target audience, key messages, methods of delivery. This is the function part—it invariably includes 'and stick to the brand' even when this is not spelled out.

Content is usually words and pictures, though, as specified by the visual identity document, it may also include characteristic graphics.

Production is the method of publication, be it print, digital, or both. Production is linked heavily to budget, though practicality may play a larger role.

The designer's job is to find a way of making those fit together. In the early days of print, production dominated: there were only a limited number of ways of getting the text onto the page. Hot metal typesetting created much greater freedom, and later phototypesetting set designers free to do pretty much what they wanted. This freedom was tamed in the 1950s by the Swiss system of using a design grid—effectively expanding upon the traditions of print, but bringing order to what otherwise might have been chaos.

Desk top publishing, with its ability to set consistent type without requiring a grid, frees up designers again, though, as they get older, many designers do return to grids, seeking a cleaner, purer and more consistent design.

Visual Identity Document
A visual identity document will usually contain a minimum of logo, specifications for its use, typeface(s), colour palette, and characteristic graphics. It may also contain examples and specifications for photography, standard layouts, tone of voice and guidance on overall editorial style, which may also be a separate 'house style' document. Always stick to the brand, even if you detest it.

Working in QuarkXPress, the designer's role (though it may easily be the same person who also does the layout and the editing) is to set the Master Pages and the core style sheets, including body text, titles, variants, such as our margin annotations, and item styles for characteristic rules and boxes.

1 Master Pages

Master Pages give the consistency of a grid, even if the designer is religiously opposed to using grids. We could conceive of a Master Page with guidelines constructed entirely using the Golden Section—for example, by beginning with the Golden Spiral available in Utilities—ShapeMaker—Spirals.

Hard core grid makers will want to lock text to grid in the paragraph style sheets, and set an absolutely consistent grid from page to page. Although admirable, this ship may well be wrecked on the rock of production: most processes will give a millimetre or so of shift in any direction when the paper is trimmed, enough to rob the page of total grid formality.

If you are prepared to compromise, the Window—Guides palette (see Palettes—Guides in Part 5) allows you to construct Guides to a grid system, while you remain freed to have text flow where it will, choosing inter-paragraph and inter-title spacing by what looks right to you, rather than by grid calculations. If you are happy to have text take up whatever space it likes, you can still set titles so that they only fall at particular places by locking them to a grid. See Window—Grid Styles for information.

One of the particular problems of modern design is that we expect much more in the way of illustration, and we expect a closer relationship between illustration and text than we did thirty years ago. Few readers will now put up with 'See Fig. 1', and have to look backwards or forwards a few pages to find Fig. 1. This was common practice still in the 1980s, but we now expect graphs, charts and tables to come at the right place in the text. Given that these kinds of illustrations bring their own rhythm to the page, which may dis-

Workflows that speed results and reduce errors

rupt its natural proportions, the designer needs to come up with a solution.

For this book, we have chosen to fit pictures of dialogue boxes either across the main column, which is two grid columns and a gutter wide, or in the margin column, which is one grid column wide. As the dialogue boxes and palettes come in many different proportions, this means scaling them differently. This, of course, is inconsistent, but we chose to have inconsistent scaling rather than randomly shaped boxes interrupting the page. This is itself based on the design aesthetic that the eye first sees overall shapes, and only afterwards the specifics.

To get the job done, the designer needs to have a good grasp of what kinds of content are going to be provided, and needs to understand what the production constraints are going to be. This includes recognising the inherent properties of different kinds of print, the amount of ink that different weights of paper can take up, the level of detail that can be achieved once dot gain has been accounted for, and so on.

When the designer will also be doing the layout, there can be an ongoing process of refinement until a publication is finished—at least, the first time. For most tasks, it will be more economical to give the job of updating, recreating or imitating a design to a more junior team member.

Designers, as a rule, dislike the task of documenting what they have done. However, for a speedy and consistent workflow in QuarkXPress, specifying the design requirements in a Job Jacket JDF (see later in this chapter), and setting evaluation rules, will help layout artists enormously in sticking to the task and getting it right every time.

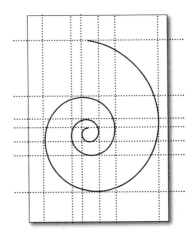

Above, off-grid with a Golden Spiral. Although this bears little relation to the Swiss grids of the 1950s, it can be used to produce organically consistent documents—provided there are enough pages for the consistency to shine through. The shorter the document, the less the need for an exciting grid, and the more the risk that it all just looks messy.

2 Style Sheets

With the Master Page(s) sorted, setting style sheets is a matter of choosing fonts and making some formatting decisions, such as whether paragraphs should be separated by a space, as is common on the web and in most technical documents, or identified by an indent, which is almost universally used in narrative fiction. Setting with a space means that you almost certainly cannot use a fixed text grid, as a whole line space looks too glaring on the page for most purposes.

See the Window—Style Sheets section in Part 5 for more on this.

For a strongly designed look, it is worth refining optical margin alignment. See Part 5, Edit—Hanging Characters for instructions on setting up margin alignments, as well as an alternative form of ragged right justification.

It's best to set overall hyphenation at this stage as well, but this will need looking at on a line by line basis during editing.

3 Colours

Colours should be defined early using swatch books, not simply taking a guess at what looks nice on the screen. See Palettes—Colors in Part 5. It's for the designer to check that the desired colour is reproducible on the planned process. CMYK produces only about 55% of the Pantone colours. Specifying a colour that cannot be reproduced in CMYK may require an extra spot plate or using seven-colour Pantone Extended Gamut (XGC). Equally, Pantone colours are specifications for mixing ink, not guarantees of what the result will be on your particular stock.

4 Rules, Bullets and others

You can set up dashes and stripes with Edit—Dashes and Stripes. More interestingly for consistent design, you can delete the presets (for a document or Job Jacket) so that the layout artist doesn't use the wrong rule by accident. The same goes for Bullets, Inline Table Styles, Footnotes and Callouts. For a single ad hoc document, this is probably more work than is needed. For a document which will become the exemplar for a consistent suite of publications, it is essential.

Workflows that speed results and reduce errors

5 Specifying layout evaluation

Although you cannot pre-flight everything, JDFs allow you to specify many more for checking that the publication conforms to the design. This can identify lines that are too narrow or shades which are too light to print, accidentally skewed boxes, text which is smaller than the minimum specified, fonts which are not in the allowed set (by specifying what is allowed, rather than listing every font which isn't), fonts which are not at specified font sizes, and so on. These rules can be applied whenever it is convenient, rather than interrupting the workflow while someone tries out an alternate font size. See the JDF section below for details.

6 Name things structurally

You can help the layout artist (or yourself, if you are the same person) a great deal by giving things consistent names which are easily searchable and don't rely on having to look things up. You may know that the corporate colour is Pantone 300, but the layout artist, who may be a temporary worker because the regular artist is off sick, probably doesn't. You can rename it to 'Corporate Pantone 300'. Naming style sheets consistently will also help. 'Title 1, Title 2, Title 3' will be a lot easier to find than 'Title, subtitle, paragraph header'. Even better would be 'Title 1 - Part, Title 2 - Chapter, Title 3 - Heading' etc. This means that the layout artist does not have to remember which titles go with which kinds of text.

3 Layout

Layout is the task of putting all of the content into the design. If you are the designer *and* the layout artist, you can carry on fiddling with the design as you do it—but quite possibly not when you are on the second publication of a series.

If you are doing just layout, the task can be interesting enough for a one-off short document, but what about 3,000 pages of text? What about laying out 170 DL sized leaflets all of which are eerily similar?

1 Auto insert pages

For laying out a lot of text, turn auto-insert pages on in Preferences—Print—General. If this is off, when pages overflow, they will not create new pages. You might want to turn this off again later, when a rogue overflow might cause every page to hop to the right or left, involving an annoying amount of resetting.

2 Document automation

Document automation is the friend of the layout artist. For QuarkXPress, making full use of Conditional Styles, Item Styles, automatic paragraph numbering, Content Variables and Shared Content can turn a tedious task into a relatively rapid one. As importantly, it becomes much easier to consistently make changes if, for example, half-way through your epic DL leaflet project, a new corporate identity is unveiled.

Each of the following is explained in Part 5:

- Bullet, Numbering & Outline Styles
- Conditional Styles
- Content (shared)
- Content Variables
- Cross References
- Item Styles.

3 Shortcut keys

You can set shortcut keys for Paragraph Styles, Character Styles, Item Styles, and, on a Mac, any menu command.

Workflows that speed results and reduce errors

In terms of workflow speed, with a well-defined set of styles, setting shortcut keys is by far the biggest time save. Compared to clicking on style sheets in the palettes, it can take less than one tenth of the time to format a long document.

For Macs, as well as having some standard shortcut keys, you can use an easy-on-the-fingers shortcut key as a liquid key—just keep changing it in Preferences—Key Shortcuts to whatever you need most at the time. I use Cmd-~.

4   Palette searches

Several palettes have a Search line at the top, which finds all of the items in that palette that contain the characters you specify. If the designer has named things structurally, you can enter 'Title' and all of the title styles will come up on the list. This applies to style sheets, items styles, colours, hyperlinks and anchors and content variables. You can also search for individual glyphs in the Glyphs palette, though you can't rename them.

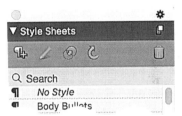

Above, the Search line in the Style Sheets box filters out everything but its own characters. If you have structured your style sheet names, you can easily find related sets.

5   Lists for navigation

Lists (Window—Lists) are ordered lists of items based on paragraph or character styles. You would normally use a list to create a Table of Contents, but lists are also clickable ways of navigating round a document.

6   Name objects with HTML5

Even if you have no intention of digital publishing, you can name items using the HTML5 palette without having to assign an action to them. Like lists, these then become findable by clicking—great if you've lost track of where something is.

7   Multiple layouts

QuarkXPress 2016 allows you to have many layouts in the same project. Provided that you aren't at risk of putting too many eggs in one basket (certainly turn on auto-backup in the preferences!), multiple layouts offer huge savings of time. If you are creating new paragraph or character styles (using 'based on'), they will automatically stay synchronised. You can easily share content from one to another.

8   Flag incomplete items with a style sheet

It's not uncommon to be given a document to be laid out which isn't finished (that doesn't mean it's a good way of working). As you work through the text, you encounter marks such as "£xxx", or "new text from George goes here" or "make sure this text is replaced". I usually define a special character sheet called 'Highlight for Replacement' which sets these sort of sections in bold, red, italics. The reason for using a style sheet rather than just formatting it is that you can then use Lists (See Part 5—Palettes—Lists) to produce a page-numbered list of all the issues. I usually put this at the back, but you can put it over the cover if you want to. As the issues are dealt with, you reformat them back to regular text, and they disappear from the list. Eventually, the list is empty.

4 Editing

When the layout is done, it is time to edit. This can be the work of one person, or a whole department.

Editorial tasks include:

- Supplying missing information and sections
- Proof reading (or commissioning it)
- Table of Contents and Indexing
- Copy-editing
- Improving typography and page layout
- Dealing with loose lines
- Condensing the document to suit the agreed format.

In newspaper terminology, people operating QuarkXPress would often be termed 'sub-editors'. The sub-editor takes journalistic copy, fits it into the space available and constructs a clever headline. Sub-editors also get to choose what pictures go with the text, before submitting it all to the editor.

In many desk top publishing environments, the editor is you. Your job is to make the document consistent and correct. Here are the steps.

1 Typographic editing

Injudicious editing can do more damage to a document than leaving it alone. You can greatly improve speed and reliability by going about things the right way.

Above, the Redline palette. While generally abused and misused for document collaboration in Microsoft Word, redlining can be extremely helpful when entering proof corrections—not so much for the ones you intend to enter, but for checking that you haven't also made unintentional changes to the text.

First, get the author or editor to read through the document. There will be times when you set documents you don't understand at all: for example, the Finnish translation of a document you've been working on in English. This read-through is not the same as proof-reading (next step), but obviously you should deal with any spelling or other mechanical errors that are brought to your attention.

I personally don't like redlining, but using it to track your changes at this stage could be crucial for the aforementioned Finnish job. See **Part 5—Palettes—Redline**.

Find/Change is invaluable, but also very dangerous. This is improved somewhat by being able to do **Edit—Undo** immediately after a Find/Change that has, for example, replaced the letter 'a' with 'the' throughout, thus giving you words like 'Thendrew', 'thend', 'theuthor', and so on. Undo will restore all of them, and the second time round you can make sure that you have 'whole words only' checked—and go through them one by one.

Don't forget **Edit—Item Find/Change**. It's generally safest to use it to find rather than change, but if you discover that you've got the wrong frame colour on more than two boxes, Item Find can help you locate all the problem issues.

It's probably too late at this stage to use the spell-checker. The best time to use it is when you first import the text. If in doubt, skip: although Quark's is better than most, there are far too many examples of words like 'Alister' being replaced with 'alligator', and worse.

Use the **Utilities—Line Check** to automatically pick up on problems of bad justification, possibly problematic or fossil hyphenation, widows, orphans and overflowing text boxes.

Line Check can only take you so far. At a particular moment, once you are sure that there will be no significant changes except for proof corrections, print everything off and go through line by line, checking that it looks right. No matter what the computer says, if it doesn't look right, it isn't.

Hyphenation is a particular problem. You shouldn't really have more than three hyphenated words in a paragraph. You can set QuarkXPress to limit the number of consecutive hyphenations, but the only way of managing the entire paragraph is to check visually and adjust.

Use JDF rules, under **File—Job Jackets—Evaluate Layout** to discover layout problems which are hard to spot. See the next chapter for more details. You can pick up incorrect fonts, badly resized graphics (all your images should be at 100%, and should be saved at 300dpi), slight rotations, off-sized text, rules too thin or shades too light to print, and many other issues.

2   Proof reading

You cannot proof read a document you have been working on. You always need to get someone else to do it. You need to have the proof reading done before the other editorial tasks—or, at least, before you finalise them—because poor spelling can ruin your indexes, tables of contents, typography or even line length. Proof readers will sometimes find whole sections of text which have been repeated from elsewhere, or identify gaps where text has clearly gone missing. Proof reading is a profession in itself. However, a lot of desk

Say 'no' to spell checkers
Somewhere in the early evolution of this book, 'publishing' was somehow changed to 'publishig'. Had this been added by accident to the auxiliary dictionary? When we checked, it wasn't there. Nonetheless, we found fifteen incidences: a rather embarrassing error if it had made it to publication. Using a spell checker may help in the early stages of authoring, but any errors you 'keep' will become structurally embedded.

If you have a House Style Guide, or you have decided to use someone else's, such as Oxford University Press's, then make sure that you give this to the proof reader with the document, otherwise they are liable to mark endless queries on your use of, for example, 'eg' instead of 'e.g.,'.

Workflows that speed results and reduce errors

top publishers, especially if working in a team, are often asked to do ad hoc proof reading.

Here is what to look for:

1. Missing, repeated or incomprehensible text, including markers such as "[insert job title here]" or "$xxx".

2. Spelling and grammar

3. Punctuation and spaces

4. Consistency of usage—eg, title case, space around em-dashes, words with more than one correct spelling, bullet points and numbering, attributions, footnotes, captions

5. Declaration of abbreviations and consistency of use

6. Inconsistent typography—eg, font changes, use of inchmarks instead of typographical quotation marks, inconsistent inter-paragraph spacing

7. Adherence to corporate style.

Professional proof readers use specific marks to indicate problems in the text. The most common ones, published in the Chicago Manual of Style among other places, are listed on the right. They should give an indication of the kind of issues proof readers are supposed to spot.

Do not run a spell-checker to make automatic corrections after the proof reader has proofed it—you will potentially undo a lot of valuable (and expensive) work.

Something your proof reader will not do, but you (or someone) needs to is actually ring any phone numbers listed, visit every website, and email every email address. Even if the telephone number is correct, there is no guarantee that the person who will answer it will be aware that they are speaking to a member of the public.

Proof Marks
(Chicago Manual of Style, et al)

℮	*Delete*
x	*Remove blemish*
stet	*Leave as is*
∧	*Insert here, or superscript*
∨	*Insert here, or subscript*
⊂	*Close up, delete space*
℮	*Delete and close up*
tr	*Transpose*
=	*Straighten type*
‖	*Align vertically*
(⁄)	*Insert parentheses*
;⁄	*Insert semicolon*
⊙	*Insert full stop*
:⁄	*Insert colon*
∧	*Insert comma*
∨	*Insert apostrophe*
∨	*Insert apostrophe*
∨	*Insert double quotes*
∨	*Insert double quotes*
=	*Insert hyphen*
?⁄	*Insert question mark*
N	*Insert en dash*
⌒	*Insert em dash*
eq#	*Equal spacing*
hr#	*Insert hair space*
ls	*Letter space*
□	*Indent one em*
[	*Move left*
]	*Move right*
⌐	*Move up*
⌴	*Move down*
⁆⁅	*Centre*
fl	*Flush left*
fr	*Flush right*
ital	*Set as italics*
rom	*Set as Roman*
bf	*Bold face*
lc	*Set in lower case*
sc	*Set in small caps*
caps	*Set in capitals*
wf	*Wrong font*
sp	*Spell out*
¶	*New paragraph*

Building an index is a workflow in itself—especially if working in a QuarkXPress Book. A Book will coordinate an index across all the chapters, but you have to create an index in each chapter.

Step 1: *Determine scope*
Determine the level of detail and comprehensiveness the index will operate at.

Step 2: *Tag your keywords*
Either working through your document, or using an imported list in a separate frame, tag the keywords using the Index palette and the Add ⬚ button. Only use the Add All ⬚ button if you are building an exhaustive reference (ie, a concordance).

Step 3: *Build the index and print off a copy—check it for consistency and comprehensiveness, based on your planned scope.*

Step 4: *Add in additional keywords, subsetting them in the index palette as appropriate so that they sort with the main keywords.*

Step 5: *Use the Find Next Entry ⬚ button in the Index palette to work through every entry. Check for consistency and comprehensiveness.*

Step 6: *Build the index again and print off. Mark up the instances which need to be formatted in a different way, using the Reference—Style or Scope options in the Index.*

Step 7: *Make the changes from step 6, rebuild the Index, print and review it. Refine manually.*

3 Table of Contents and Indexing

Longer documents may require a Table of Contents (ToC) and possibly an index. You will probably regenerate the table of contents several times. Create the ToC using Lists, for which see Part 5—Palettes—Lists. The index is a rather trickier matter. The mechanics of it are explained in Part 5—Palettes—Index. How you generate an index, though, has a lot more to do with the document's function and target audience. A true academic index, of the type you would find in F.M. Stenton's Anglo-Saxon England, has varying degrees of focus and explanation based on the relative frequency and importance of the subject matter.

Before computers, indexes were drawn up by hand, and were often as valuable as the text itself.

If you take the proof-read version of the document, save with a different filename, create an auxiliary dictionary and then run the spell-checker **only adding spellings, not, under any circumstances, accepting them** you will then be able to open your auxiliary dictionary in a text editor, such as Text Wrangler. A little trimming of the XML headers (use a copy of the file to do this) will give you a list of all the words the spell checker did not know, which is a good start in identifying all unusual proper nouns. These would be worth indexing.

There are also numerous utilities, including WordCloud, available online which identify all the unique words in a document and calculate their frequency. You, or the author, can go through the list and identify what the important ones are. Only index important words.

Something simpler than an index, and much easier to manage, is a gazetteer. If you have a well-structured document, you can use the Lists function to generate an alphabetical list of all your section titles. You might need to play with this a little. You can also use it as the basis for indexing.

5 Production

You need two things to proceed from the finished layout to production. The first is the go-ahead—in writing, with a signature if at all possible—of the document owner. This may be the original author, the commissioning editor, the budget holder, or just whoever it is on the client side that is dealing with you. The other is the formal approval of the publisher. Many clients—internal and external—may think you are being far too punctilious in asking for both. That is, up to the moment when things go wrong. People can be very blasé and say, on the phone, 'oh, it's all fine, I'm sure you've done a good job'. When the job comes back from the printer with the Chief Executive's name misspelled, or to the old brand specification one day before the new specification is announced, you may find all fingers pointing at you. This is easier if you are working as an external designer, because you would normally (should, must) have written agreement to go ahead. In-house, I have had some very sticky moments when it turned out the person I thought was authorising something did not (after all) have the authority to do so.

1 Negotiating with printers

Every print house is set up slightly differently. Back in one organisation, we had a list of 116 different printers who had contacted us pitching for work on at least one occasion. We always used to get three quotes, and we would always get a fourth quote from any new printer who contacted us. If they weren't close to the best price on three occasions, we put them to the bottom of the pile. However, we were careful to ask if there was anything they were particularly competitive on. One printer we found couldn't touch anybody else's price on anything, except for NCR pads (people really still use them). On NCR pads (that is, whatever replaced carbon paper), they were half the price of anybody else, and were happy to accept short print runs.

Ensure that you are comparing like with like when you get the quotes back. Check carefully any quote which is dra-

Document governance

In any kind of corporate environment, governance is crucial. Who has the authority to do things? What happens if they get it wrong?

For publishing, the best method is the author-editor-publisher approach. This is built into many Content Management Systems online.

Essentially, someone creating content is the author. Someone doing layout, copy-editing, proof-corrections or just running a spell checker is an editor. You can have all kinds of editors, and newspapers often have several layers of them.

The publisher is the person who is authorised to have the document issued. They take on a legal responsibility: if the document defames someone or otherwise breaks the law, it is the publisher, not the author or the editor, who is responsible.

In the author-editor-publisher setup, the publisher must not make changes to the document. They can ask the editor to make them, but the moment they start working on it themselves, they have become an editor, and are no longer objective enough to be the publisher. The simple rule is: no-one can sign-off something they have had a hand in. That means, at a minimum, two people must be involved: the author, and the publisher.

matically cheaper than the others: it could be that, like our NCR specialist, the job they are quoting is exactly what they are best suited for. It could also be that they can't fulfil your specification and have quoted for something which looks a bit like it. We found that High Street printers, especially when part of larger selling groups, often quoted for CMYK when we were asking for spot colour. Also watch out for printers who want to charge you for pre-flighting or other normally free extras. Once, when we wanted to get scratch cards printed, the price was ludicrously low, but the printers wanted to charge extra for the pre-flighting. We told them that if they gave us the specification, we would ensure our PDF was compliant. Unsurprisingly, they found lots of 'errors' in it, largely based on things which weren't included in their published specification. By the time we had gone to and fro with them a few times, it was too late to go to any other printer. We paid the pre-flighting charge, and the job suddenly became achievable. The total was slightly over the second-best quote, but we felt like we had been tricked (and probably were).

2 Printer's Proofs

Printers these days offer PDF proofs as a first choice, and only ColorMatch or similar if you insist. PDF is usually perfectly good: it will be the printer's fault if what they deliver does not match the PDF. If you are concerned about colour, check with them that they can achieve your Pantone specification, or something near it, if simulating in CMYK. They may tell you that they can't, in which case you need to decide how critical it is, and whether to run an extra plate. We found (and still use) a sign printer who was ridiculously cheap, and relatively local. After receiving delivery of a 3m x2m sign board that turned out to be a sort of reddish-orange rather than the Pantone 165 we had specified, we discovered that he didn't have a set of Pantone swatches at all, and really preferred to work to RAL colours. He was very good, and delivered us a new sign at no extra charge. We, in turn, purchased a RAL swatchbook and afterwards specified everything that way. We still use him—but we are always extra careful to check the colours.

As well as proofs, you may want to ask for examples. If you are having, for example, a CD reproduced, you will want to know that the repro house understands that you are looking for production quality, rather than duplication quality—if they mainly produce CDs for the IT industry rather than commercial music, you could be in for a shock if you have not previously seen a sample of their output.

Workflows that speed results and reduce errors

Using a PDF workflow, there really should not be any issues with the proofs, but check them properly anyway. Look out especially for:

- unauthorised font substitutions
- text reflowing and hyphenating poorly
- text reflowing and becoming lost
- graphics appearing pixelated, or missing
- colours that are different on screen from what you are expecting.

With colour issues, even if your monitor is poorly calibrated, the colours going in should match the colours coming out. When they don't, you have a breakdown in the colour workflow somewhere. Check the PDFs you are sending first: has the colour shift already occurred? You may need to go back to your original photographs if you have them. Use Utilities—Usage—Profiles to check what profiles have come across with the files. A general dulling of colour, or, conversely, a violent vibrancy, is usually a mark that the colour profile has got lost somewhere.

Assuming that the printer's proofs are satisfactory, get your internal or external client to sign-off that you can go to print.

3   But what if…?

Anyone who has been doing print for a while will have experienced at least one disaster scenario which requires reprinting. In one dreadful week, I once had to have a document reprinted twice, as progressive layers of senior management each decided that there were critical changes that had to be made. Mercifully, I had everything in writing. I still felt like an idiot going to the printer to ask for a reprint. (He, of course, was very happy, since we paid for all three versions.)

My rules for this are as follows:

Media companies, sign-makers, middle-men, eBook distributors, packagers and others

The text here is mainly about sending publications to printers. Most of the same things apply when going to production through a third party, or for a non-print output. If working with a middle-man, such as a media sales company, some of the burden is lifted from you, but still don't assume anything.

Two mantras worth repeating:

"Two pairs of eyes on every document"

and

"Nothing leaves this building without my signature on it."

No matter what the urgency, no document should ever go to print without a second person checking it, and no document should ever go to print unless authorised by someone who has the authority to do so.

Minor typographical errors are to some extent inevitable in long documents. A document should be reprinted if:

- *there are critical factual errors*

- *there are errors in titles or headers*

- *there are brand errors, such as stretched logos*

- *there are contact detail errors*

- *there are more than three spelling errors on a page*

- *there are consistently misspelled words.*

When I am working in an organisation where I have final authority in terms of publishing (except, of course, for documents which I have had a hand in) I actually get these rules approved by the board, along with a set of other communications policies.

You will often find that the emotional impact of a bad print job vastly outweighs the financial cost. I have seen people in tears, shouting, and generally behaving as though calamity had befallen. Many printers will help you rush through a job when something has gone wrong, and I've known a fair few who don't charge for the reprint at all. Take it all in your stride, be professional, stay calm, and get on with fixing the problem, rather than apportioning (or avoiding) the blame.

As a word of friendly advice, even if you can absolutely prove that it was not your fault, do not attempt to do so. You won't win any friends, and no good will come of it.

4 Archiving

Make sure that you get a copy of whatever is printed, and keep an archive of it. Use File—Collect for Output to store a complete set of files somewhere you can reliably get them back—preferably somewhere that is itself regularly backed up. On no account should you try to back them up yourself and delete the originals. I once had a graphic designer working for me who did that—and then discovered all his DVD backups were corrupt, and the files were gone.

Retrieving old documents
Even when you can get old documents, it doesn't always help. You can use Quark's Document converter (a free download) to convert version 3–version 6 files, and QuarkXPress 2016 will natively open anything more recent. But what about old PageMaker files? Ventura Publisher? Microsoft Publisher? With QuarkXPress 2016, it is usually easiest to convert a PDF file to native objects. No PDF? Scan it, and remake.

Workflows that speed results and reduce errors

2 Job Jackets and JDF

JDF is an industry-standard method of specifying a set of print jobs and publications from start to finish.

If you don't already use JDFs, there are three very specific workflows I want to cover where they can help you a lot: brands, document automation, and pre-flighting.

1   How Job Jackets work in QuarkXPress

Before we go any further, we just need to look for a moment at how it all fits together.

If you open up Utilities—Job Jackets Manager, and have a poke around, you'll see that there are two layers: Job Jackets, at the top, with the QuarkXPress logo, and Job Tickets, underneath them. You have probably already noticed that File menu offers File—New Project from Ticket.

Essentially, it works this way.

Ticket: everything
If you create a new project from a ticket, **everything** in that ticket goes into your new project. That could be something as innocuous as a rule that says 'never print anything below 6 point', and warns you if you try to, or it could be six layouts of sixteen pages each, all ready created with Master Pages, style sheets, hyphenation exceptions and auxiliary dictionaries. If those six layouts are in the ticket definition, all of them will be created in your new project.

Jacket: anything
Anything in the job jacket can be loaded into a ticket, but nothing is unless instructed to.

2   What this is like

The Job Jacket is like a brand, whereas the Job Ticket is like the brief for a particular job. When you're handed the brief, you should always ask for the brand's Visual Identity. However, you might forget to, or just ignore it: I've known designers who did that.

What it is:
Job Definition Format is an XML document structured in a particular way. XML itself is just a way for computers to talk to each other and make sense of content without actually having to understand it (which, despite advances in Artificial Intelligence, is still a very long way off). QuarkXPress uses XML in several different ways.

Below, the Job Jackets Manager dialogue. We will go through it step by step.

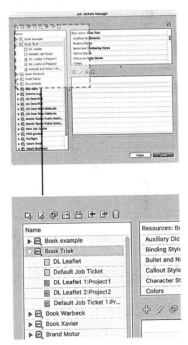

A brand, according to the UK's Intellectual Property Office, is a promise of an experience.

*More exactly, a brand is made up of three components: what is **promised**, what is **delivered**, and how it is **presented**. Consistently fulfilling the promise strengthens the brand. Failing to fulfil the promise weakens it—perhaps catastrophically. Strong brands are absolutely seamless: everything about the presentation underlines the promise, and the customer gets exactly what they were expecting.*

For a new brand, that's all there is. However, as a brand becomes established, its reputation begins to outweigh everything else—up to the point when enough people have experienced it and made up their own minds. Even then, reputation can make them imagine they are having a great (or terrible) brand experience.

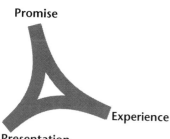

Promise

Experience

Presentation
- Name
- Logo
- Visual Identity
- Written style
- Deployment (eg, packaging, signage, publications, design of product).

Nothing in the brand *makes* you do what it says. It's just that it will be wrong if you don't.

The Job Ticket is like a template for the job you're going to do, or perhaps even a previous document that someone has cleared of all content and sent to you. All the styles, dictionaries and everything else are already there for you.

It may be that you still need to go back to the brand specification—for example because you know there's a specification for a DL leaflet, but you've only been sent the A4 staff magazine. For that, you would go back to the Job Jacket, and pull in more of the things you want.

1 Using a job jacket to work with a brand

Imagine you have three clients (or three brands, if you are in-house). We'll call them Jean-Claude Xavier, Trisk Agility, and Perkin Warbeck Pears.

Jean-Claude Xavier is an elderly gentleman of very distinctive habits. You think he may have taken part in the 1960s Paris riots. He comes round to your studio and tells you things like 'no text which is not set in either Futura or Bodoni is worth the paper it is printed on', and 'it is the mark of a fool that he uses a grid—an artist uses his eye alone'. You think Jean-Claude Xavier might be slightly mad, but someone pointed him out to you at a conference last year and said he was one of the world's most respected typographers.

Trisk Agility has a twenty-four page Visual Identity document, and they made you sign a contract promising that you would never disclose its contents to anyone. You are not entirely sure what Trisk Agility does (or makes), though you think they may supply automation software for one of Ikea's competitors, and possibly administer the Norwegian pension scheme.

Perkin Warbeck Pears is an old family business. Every season they demand that you produce something 'radical and new', but, every time you do, they reject it, and you end up going back to a very slightly altered version of what they had before. On the other hand, the work is steady, they are not a particularly difficult client, and they pay your invoices promptly, without question.

All three of these are brands, even though only Trisk has a Visual Identity document. Monsieur Xavier's brand is a very defined concept which is in his mind. He knows when you achieve it, and he will tell you when you don't—even though he is not always willing to tell you how to achieve it or what you are doing wrong when you don't.

Trisk Agility has rigid, perhaps over-rigid specifications. The brand manager may not be aware that their Pantone colours will come out differently under different processes.

To understand Perkin Warbeck Pears' brand, you need to look at the last fifty years of their leaflets and advertising. Setting the text one point larger or one point smaller is the limit of the innovation they are looking for.

For Xavier, you are starting every document with a clean sheet in terms of the page design, but the typography is going to be absolutely constant: Futura and Bodoni, both of which require extra leading. All the jobs will be in monochrome: the underground presses were not printing CMYK in May 1968, and Xavier is not going to allow it now.

For Trisk Agility, you need to specify in your JDF every one of their twenty-four pages of rules. There may be some that even JDFs won't cover, so you will probably want to have them stapled to the front of your Trisk folder.

Warbeck's brand is the sum total of all the print they ever produced. They always have an extra plate for 'Warbeck's Green'—a spot colour that predates Pantone, which only a dozen local printers knows how to mix.

JDFs will help you with Xavier, Trisk and Warbeck's—but the workflow to get there is different in each case.

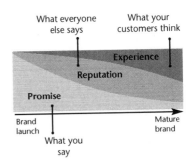

Below, how brands develop over time.

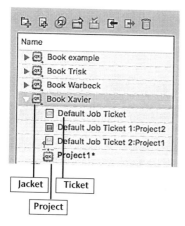

Jean Claude Xavier's brand is an example of starting with an exemplar document and turning it into a Job Jacket, and a single ticket which you will use for almost everything. The ticket is fairly loose—just a few bits of typography, but it will help you to keep track of M. Xavier's preferences, many of which are hard to remember—though he can spot when they have not been followed merely by glancing at a page.

Opposite:
Moving things 'upwards' from a project to a ticket automatically puts them into the jacket as well. When creating a new ticket for a new kind of job, you have to move things 'downwards' from the jacket into that ticket: only the things you explicitly put into the ticket will be used to create a new job. You can keep using the same ticket to create more jobs, and they will synchronise (paper tickets, of course, wouldn't).

1   Jean-Claude Xavier's Typographic Brand

To put Xavier's brand into a JDF, take any layout that he has pronounced 'acceptable'. You probably have a long history of him being not entirely satisfied, so pick the one that he seemed the most pleased with. If this is an old document, made in QuarkXPress 2.0, or, heaven help you, Page-Maker, then you may need to open a PDF and convert it to native objects, or even scan a document and match up the font sizes and leading. Hopefully there will be some paragraph styles that you can create. Any other things that he likes, such as characteristic dashes and stripes are worth keeping as well.

Load up the document in QuarkXPress 2016.

Now go to Utilities—Job Jackets Manager.

Have a look down the list of Job Jackets (left). If you haven't used this before, there shouldn't be very many. You may need to peek into a couple of them by pressing the arrow, until you find your project, which is 'inside' a job jacket. It also has a ticket assigned to it.

If you don't do anything, this will only stay in the Job Jacket Manager for as long as the project is open.

What we want to do is turn Jean-Claude Xavier's typographical rules into something which we can use as the canvas for any new project we do for him.

You'll see there is a 'ticket' already attached to the project. If you click on the project, you'll see that there are various things in the big pane on the right which have numbers with them. These are the style sheets, colours, H&Js and so on which are saved with your project.

If you now click on the job ticket attached to the project, you'll see there are no numbers: the ticket is empty, and does nothing.

What you need to do is move the resources you want from the project into the ticket, which will move them into the jacket. They will still be available to the project, but they will also be in the ticket.

Job Jackets and JDF

How do you do this?

With the project selected, click on any resource which has a number by it. We're interested in paragraph and character stylesheets, but all of the resources work in the same way.

On the left will be what the resource is, a particular colour, a paragraph style, and so on. On the right it will say 'In Project'. Click on that, and change it to 'In Ticket'. You'll notice that the description on the left now goes bold. If you click on the Job Jacket, which is the top icon of that particular group, you'll see that the styles you just moved are now in the Job Jacket as well.

Work through the list, moving everything across which is relevant. You will certainly want to include your character and paragraph styles, and you should take the H&Js with them. Only move colours that you want—in M. Xavier's case, that will be no colours, as the jobs will only ever be in monochrome.

When you've done all this, duplicate the entire Job Jacket with the ⊛ icon at the top, and give it a name like Xavier Brand. Save and close. Now close your document. If you go back to Job Jackets Manager, Xavier Brand is still there, but the job jacket for the project you were working on has vanished.

So, if you now create a new project from ticket, and use Default Job Ticket, all the styles in the Job Jacket will appear in your new document, right?

No. Remember, *everything* in the Ticket goes into the Project, and *anything* in the Jacket can go into the Ticket. At the moment, all of our styles are in the Jacket, but we haven't put any of them into the ticket. To do that, we need to go back to Job Jacket Manager and click on our resources in the Default Job Ticket. At the moment, all of them will say 'In Job Jacket'. We need to move the ones we want to 'In ticket'.

Sound a bit confusing?

Everything that is in the ticket goes into a new project. The ticket is the complete set of instructions for that new job.

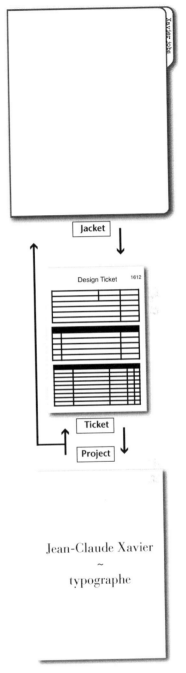

Using a job jacket to work with a brand   189

*Will M. Xavier be happy?
Not entirely. Artist and expert typographer that he is, he has stood
over you and supervised your
manual kerning of every letter
pair in Bodoni and Futura that he
is unhappy about, using Edit—
Kerning Pairs. Unfortunately, although you can export and import
these, they are not a feature of
JDFs and Job Jackets.*

*On the other hand, M. Xavier is
never content with the Bodoni you
are using. Every few weeks he
finds yet another version of the
font that he now believes is superior, and insists that you print off
a dozen examples for him to have
a look at. By changing the In
Ticket paragraph styles, all of the
documents will be synchronised,
making the job relatively painless.
Sometimes he changes his mind
and wants it all back again.*

Everything which is in the ticket is also in the jacket, because the jacket encompasses all the tickets. Nothing is in
the ticket unless you put it there, either 'upwards' from a
project, or 'downwards', from the job jacket.

Let's say we do that. Every time we now create a new project from ticket, and use that default job ticket, all of those
styles will be in our new document.

For M. Xavier's brand, that is more or less it. You can go
back to any other project which has, for example, different
features, and use File—Job Jackets—Link Project to attach it
to M. Xavier's job jacket. From there, you can move in
things such as conditional styles. They don't even have to
be from M. Xavier's brand. If you have a really clever conditional style that you have developed for Trisk, you can
move that into the Xavier jacket. It will automatically bring
style sheets with it, so you may need to go into a project,
and correct them to the right fonts. If there is a conflict,
QuarkXPress will ask you whether you want to keep the existing style, use the new one, or rename the new one and
use it.

Just one more word before we leave M. Xavier's brand. If
you change a style which is in a ticket, then that ticket is
changed, which will change styles in other documents as
you open them. If you don't want to do that, after you
have created New Project from Ticket, go into the Job Jackets manager and, for that project, move those styles to 'In
Project', instead of 'In Ticket'.

There's one more refinement to this brand, but we'll look at
that when we come to look at pre-flighting and rules.

2 Trisk Agility: the Style Guide Rules

Trisk Agility is almost the opposite of M. Xavier. They have
an exceptionally detailed style book, even specifying what
sizes of paper are to be used (A3, A4, A4 cut lengthwise in
two, and A4 folded into four. A5, A6, and DL are all forbid-
den). Their colour book is exacting, and there are even
specifications about what kind of bindings are allowed. On
the other hand, you often wonder if the marketing team ac-

tually understand the rules, or can tell when they are not being followed. Your contract specifies that you won't be paid if the rules are breached. However, on the couple of occasions that you made a mistake, no one seemed to notice.

For this, we are going to start at the Job Jacket level and create specifications. We will later create rule sets, with which we can measure our adherence to the brand specification, and so be confident that our invoices will be honoured.

Go to the Job Jackets Manager and create a new Job Jacket. We are now going to work down the list, setting everything we can. Many of the options will remain obstinately blank—we can only create them by using a project, but we will do what we can for now.

1   First, create an auxiliary dictionary in Utilities—Check Spelling. We are going to build up a vocabulary of odd Trisk words that are otherwise strange to the dictionary, as well as the proper nouns of their many products, which are called things like Og, Ur, Ull, and so on.

2   In Contacts, set the job contacts. These will include the manager you deal with at Trisk, yourself, and the print commissioning manager, based in Stockholm. You are never actually allowed to talk to the printers yourself.

3   Set the External Resources. These should include all versions of the logo, standard pictures, standard text such as business details, and anything else which you will want to have ready in the Content palette (see Part 5—Palettes—Content).

4   Trisk's style manual includes a list of words you are never allowed to hyphenate. You've previously put them into a hyphenations exception file. Load this in the Hyphenation Exceptions box.

5   If there's a formal Job Descriptions system, you can apply it here.

6   Layout specifications is where you are going to copy in all of the exacting descriptions of what

Trisk Agility is an example of starting with a Visual Identity document or Brand Specification. You need to work from both ends—work from an exemplar document upwards to set the colours, styles and so on, and work from the Job Jackets downwards to set characteristic layouts and rules on bindings and production.

Any External Resources you specify and subsequently include in a Job Ticket will appear in the Content Palette for the new project whenever one is created from File—New Project From Ticket. This can include graphics, text and Composition Zones.

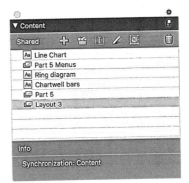

Above, the Content palette. See Part 5—Palettes—Content

paper sizes are allowed, instructions on when it is appropriate to comb-bind (the correct answer is 'never', but Trisk permits it for internal documents where the audience is fewer than 17), and special layouts for staff magazines, the Jöl promotional advertisements, and so on. If it's in the manual, put it in the JDF. You'll notice that you can specify CMYK and spot colours, but there aren't yet any on the list to choose from. We'll need to put those in via a project in the next stage.

7   The Publication Layout Target is a text field which may or may not be important, based on their manual. Leave blank unless there's a reason not to.

8   Leave Publication Specifications blank, unless they have actually sent you this information (they might well do). This is really production-level stuff, some of which QuarkXPress can read, but not write.

9   Rules and Rule sets are going to be very important, but we'll come back to them later.

10 Leave the rest blank.

Once you've done that, it's now time to create a project and put in some resources, in the same way we did for M. Xavier. This time, once we've created it, we will link it to the Job Jacket using File—Job Jackets—Link Project.

The resources we are most likely upload are a specification for Normal (paragraph and character), possibly a specification for their alternate font (though, for Trisk, everything is actually set in Siseriff, a Swedish font designed by Bo Berndal in 2002), and, most importantly, the colour palette. Trisk Agile has a palette of nine colours, each with specifications in Pantone, CMYK, and Pantone XGC extended gamut colours. There are also colour sub-sets for printing to Flexo, sign printing, banners and vehicle liveries. You will never want all of these variations in a single layout, but they all need to be in the specification. Give them names which will help you identify them, such as 'Flexo Trisk Green', 'Flexo Trisk Indigo', 'Offset Trisk Green', and so on. Transfer everything from 'In Project' to 'In Ticket'.

Trisk's colours include Pantone 7501 and 2718. If you import their PDF, these should come in automatically.

You may also be able to use an imported PDF with Style—Convert to Native objects to bring in a range of their type styles and other elements. Be careful, though: there are numerous examples of visual identity documents which are subtly different from the guidelines they declare.

If you have the Visual Identity PDF file, you can quite possibly short-circuit a lot of this by importing the PDF and converting to native objects, which may well (depending on how they set it up) automatically bring in the correct colours.

We are now ready for the final step (apart from Rules—see later). You won't want to create a job ticket for every conceivable layout in the book, but you will want to for the ones you do regularly—staff magazine, advertisements, promotional leaflets, packaging.

For each kind of job, create a new job ticket. You can define these more or less flexibly depending on what they are. Every job will need the Normal paragraph and character styles loading, as well as any alternates. Load in the colours for the type of job it is: there is no point cluttering the staff magazine with Flexo colours. Include relevant external resources: the type of logo for the layout, standard pictures and text. This will appear in the Content Palette. This can also include composition zones: very useful if you have an elaborate masthead. The magazine will have an exact number of pages, specified margins and Master Pages, possibly even a text grid. You can't create any of these things in the ticket—all you can do is choose to make things 'in ticket' which already exist in the Job Jacket.

The ones you are most likely going to concentrate on are Layouts, Paragraph and Character Styles, Dashes and Stripes, Hyphenation Exceptions and Auxiliary Dictionary.

3   Perkin Warbeck Pears: brand is production

Perkin Warbeck Pears don't know how to define their visual identity—they would probably ask you to do it for them if they had to—but everyone knows what the Perkin Warbeck brand is. A distinctive colour that you see nowhere else, a hand drawn logo from the 1890s which has undergone slight simplifications over the decades, each one the cause of a protracted boardroom battle, and a font which was absolutely cutting edge when they introduced it in 1914, and

Perkin WARBECK Pears

The Perkin Warbeck brand. The illustration uses four colour plates—but none of them are CMYK. These days you can get away with three Pantone colours for the ochre, terracotta and blue, but Perkin Green has to be specially mixed. You are eagerly hoping that Pantone Extended Gamut colour printing will be arriving soon, and you will be able to consistently reproduce the colours. You may not actually tell Warbeck you are doing this.

went through a brief period of renewed popularity in the 1970s, but which you rarely see these days. Most people confuse the bold weight, which Warbeck love, with Cooper Black, but it is actually ITC Souvenir, Ed Benguiat's digital take on Morris Fuller Benton's classic. They don't have a marketing department ('waste of money—never needed one before'), and you get invited to all their Christmas parties.

There is an artisanal quality to the Warbeck brand, which leads us nicely on to production.

The basics you can get right by following the steps for Trisk Agility and M. Xavier. You'll probably want to start with some exemplar files, transfer them into the Job Jacket, and construct some of the layouts that you most often use—purely as a convenience for yourself: they know their brand is safe with you.

Production is a bit more tricky. Their main colour, Warbeck Green, predates Pantone. It has to be mixed specially, and only the six printers in Herefordshire, England, that they use are able to mix it—one mixes it for packaging, another for stationery, another for signage, and so on. They each call it something different, which led to numerous misunderstandings when you inherited the job from old Mr Dodds, who was still doing cast-offs and sending copy to the printers typed when he finally gave up Warbeck in 2002 ('can't be doing with those computerers').

It's here that you start using the fields we didn't touch—Job Descriptions, where you are going to log the exact instructions for the printers that Mr Dodds gave you (and, by the handwriting, he probably had them from his predecessor and they belong in a museum), Publication Specifications, and much more. I should say at this point that this is not at all what JDFs are designed for: the format is designed to automate and assure production among very large print players. However, anyone who has been doing desk top publishing for any length of time knows that an awful lot of the skill comes down to negotiating with small players who will do a job that the big players can't or won't touch.

Logging all your knowledge about the process will also help to future-proof your work. One day, one of those printers in Herefordshire is going to buy up the others. They will install new presses, the old-timer who knows how to mix the ink will be gone, and with him a vast wealth of knowledge about how the brand is controlled. The more you can specify this in a JDF, using standard printer's terms, rather than terms that are known nowhere outside of Ledbury, the easier you are going to make the transition to big print processes, perhaps, with XGC colours, able to produce a passable imitation of Warbeck Green.

4 Wrapping up on JDFs for brands

Branding is, of course, something I'm personally very engaged with. Every designer and publisher is involved with brands in some way, perhaps more so than they are involved with print output processes. The JDF format was designed for controlling print jobs. I've chosen to illustrate it with these brand examples because I think that makes more sense for most publishers and designer than trying to explain meta-processes and printer-provided JDF templates. The processes, though are essentially the same.

I've also chosen the persona of a rural designer working with a few rather disparate clients. Again, I felt this made the explanation work better. However, the larger the team, and the more people with specialised functions or who take on parts of a project temporarily, the greater the benefits of JDFs. The senior designer may not have time to explain to the temp all the intricacies of Warbecks or the strictures of Trisk Agile, but a JDF can do the hard work for them.

Watch out!
If a style sheet is in the Job Jacket, and you create a new document from ticket, and change the style sheet, it changes for the entire Job Jacket. This helps with consistency, but means you should make new style sheets using 'based on' if you want a different body font size, and so on.

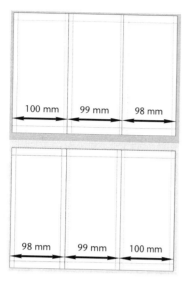

Above, setting a DL roll-fold
Contrary to popular belief, the panels of a DL roll-fold should not be 99mm equally, but 100+99+98 (outside), 98+99+100 (inside), to take account of the folds. This is tedious to set up.

Use a Job Jacket with a DL layout specification for six panels. In QuarkXPress, all the pages in a layout must be the same size, so create six master pages at 99mm x210mm with LR margins 7-6,8-5,9-7 (mm outside), 7-9,5-8,6-7 (mm inside).

You will still need to drag the master pages into position as 3-panel spreads, but it is a lot easier, quicker and more reliable than moving guides manually. This is for 7mm lateral margins. Alternatively, set margins of 0-0,1-0,2-0 (mm outside), mirrored for inside. This will give a 1mm fold zone.

2 Document Automation

As you have probably gathered, JDFs can be as simple as setting up a document with the correct colours, and fonts, or they can be used to automate an entire print job which takes place over multiple layouts including digital.

There is always a trade-off with automation: if you are going to produce a suite of 300 new DL brochures, then you can save vast amounts of time by setting up Master Pages with the correct margins and gutters (though you will still have to drag these onto the pages). If you are doing a 16 page staff magazine four times a year, it may be (and is) very exciting to see every page propagate itself with all of the relevant Master Page spreads, but it may be more convenient to simply reuse the last edition.

In my view, the most important things for consistently creating large numbers of documents are:

The layouts—especially with fiddly things like DL roll-folds (see margin). If you are doing a promotional package of leaflet, billboard, bus-rear, bus-inside, Adshel and flyer, then having all these created together makes for a fast, consistent workflow. Also, all your special paper sizes for various types of outdoor media don't have to be in the QuarkXPress list of paper-sizes, which will all be reset to the defaults if you have to delete preferences.

Colours, dashes, structural paragraph and character styles—remember that if the style is in the ticket rather than in the project, changing it will change it for all the jobs with that ticket. It's best therefore to have a few brand-specified styles, including Normal, in the ticket, and make project-level styles for particular purposes. You can always move them to the ticket later if they prove useful.

Content—if you have a lot of different versions of a logo and have to check every time which of the colour variants you are supposed to use, it is much easier to have the correct one for the document.

Conditional Styles—clever conditional styling can format an entire document at the click of a mouse button.

Job Jackets and JDF

3 Rules, evaluation and pre-flighting

Have you ever sent a PDF to the print house which was a page longer than it should have been because of an unexpected overflow? Most offset printers will ring you up and ask for a new PDF. If it's a digital-press job, though, they might well have printed a hundred copies of your supposedly 16 page staff magazine before spotting that it's now twenty pages and the last three are blank.

QuarkXPress can be set up to automatically evaluate the job before output, to check that it conforms with the ticket specification—such as being exactly the right number of pages—and also a number of other rules that you can create.

With a ticket-based job open, go to File—Job Jackets—Evaluate Layout. If you run the evaluation, it will tell you if your document fails any of the criteria you have set. For example by being a page too long. You can set QuarkXPress—Preferences—Job Jackets to run automatically on open, close, save or output (which would be my choice), so you will always be warned if you are about to PDF a job of the wrong length.

There may also be things that you want to check which are not in the specification. For example, the Job Ticket can automatically insert your character and paragraph styles, but it doesn't stop you using other fonts. There is no Find/Change to find fonts *other than* the correct ones, although you can use Usage, fonts, if you remember to.

Go to the Job Jackets Manager and into the main job jacket. There you can specify rules, and rule sets. Once you've made a rule, it needs to be in a rule set for you to be able to load it into a Layout in the Job Ticket, which you'll use to create new compliant documents.

In the job jacket, create a new rule. Call it 'Must be [name of font]'. In the drop down menu, pick 'character', and choose 'next'.

Above File—Job Jackets—Evaluate Layout, showing the Staff Magazine passing its page count evaluation of 16.

Text Characters: Search for all Text Characters where:

▼ Font Name	is not ◇	Siseriff LT Std Light	⬍		⊕
		Siseriff LT Std LightItalic	⬍	⊖	⊕
		Siseriff LT Std Regular	⬍	⊖	⊕
		Siseriff LT Std Italic	⬍	⊖	⊕

| Cancel | | < Back | Next > | | Finish |

For the Trisk Agility brand, body text must be in the Siseriff font. The rule, above, fails when the font *is not* one of the fonts specified. A rogue bit of Helvetica, for example copied from another document, will be flagged up when the evaluation is run, as will any other off-book fonts.

You can combine several of these into a single rule. For example, if your body text font is Siseriff 11 point regular, and you always want this to be set in black 100%, you can construct two rules, one to flag up if that font size and weight is not black, and another to flag up if that font size and weight is not 100%. You will put both of these into the same rule set, which you might name 'Body Text', and load them into the Layouts of the job ticket.

You might also want to create rules that evaluate box rotations, images which are too small, images which are GIFs or Indexed colour, lines which are too thin to print, and so on. These can be a mixture of things which a specialist preflight utility would find—which you might combine into a single rule set and use in all your job jackets—and things which are specific to the brand, or even to a particular layout. When setting for billboards, for example, no text below a certain size is legible, and you would want to make sure that was rigidly observed.

Enforcing evaluation
You can set the Preferences to automatically evaluate your layout on Open, on Save, on Close or on Output. On Output is the safest option, though you may want to temporarily leave it on something else if you are trying out lots of different outputs while initially constructing a document.

3 Database publishing with XPress Tags

XPress Tags is a gobbledegook format which QuarkXPress and a few other applications understand. With the right converter, though, you can turn reams of uninteresting Excel spreadsheets or database files into pristine, perfectly formatted layout, without ever needing to touch the style sheet palettes or conditional styles.

In essence, XPress Tags (not to be confused with XTags, which is a third party Xtension) is a plain text format with markers for changes in paragraph and character stylesheets, as well as local formatting. It can specify the formatting for stylesheets, colours, and a wide collection—though not complete—of other QuarkXPress text features.

You can see how much XPress Tags code is needed to specify the word 'Text'.

Clearly, nobody would want to spend their time writing the tedious code to produce that.

However, as far as a computer is concerned, automatically writing all that code is no more nor less difficult than any other task.

From a workflow point of view, there isn't a great deal of point in using XPress Tags to define stylesheets. The real power is in using it to tag text with the right style.

As a general rule, I use FileMaker Pro to generate tagged text. However, you can do it just as effectively (though nowhere near as easily) in Excel or any spreadsheet, if you don't happen to own a copy of Filemaker.

1 Publishing a Who's Who from a database

Consider the problem of a database of people. The information has been collected from a website without any formatting (though with appropriate consent). The intention is to

Text

Above, the word 'Text', in this book's Normal style sheet. Below, the Xpress Tags code that specifies that.

```
<v12.00><e8>
@Normal=<Ps100p100t0Y1h100
z10k0b0cKf"StoneSerifStd-
Medium"n2o("Calt","liga","locl")L
0G0>
@Normal=[Sp"","Normal","Nor-
mal"]<*L*AL*h"Standard"*s"Non
e"*m"None"*bn(7.2)*kn0*kt0*ra
0*rb0*d0*p(0,0,0,0,0,0,g(P,S))>
@$:Text
```

A note on this example
What follows here exposes the workings of XPress Tags as much as possible, using software—Excel—that almost everyone has. In practice, you wouldn't choose Excel to do it (get a copy of Filemaker Pro), and, once you'd done it, you would forget all about it and the the XPress Tags do all the work for you. I rely on XPress Tags workflow every day, but it's so seldom I actually edit the code that I always have to look it up.

XPress Tags can be used to publish catalogues, do mail merges, automate the layout of a magazine or even a novel. Currently, XPress Tags does not support footnotes. The easiest thing to do is to mark them up as [Note] and then use Find/Change to go through. Microsoft Word import does support footnotes, and if a document is footnote-rich, it may be easier to work with Word rather than XPress Tags.

create a Who's Who. Not only is the business of formatting an entire Who's Who tedious, it's also fraught with error.

Title	Given Name	Surname	d.o.b.	Education	Career	Honours
Prof.		Moriarty	04/12/1872		Consulting Criminal	Soc Thieves
Mr	George	Smiley	12/12/1923	Eton, Oxford	Secret Intelligence Service	KG (not used)
Mr	Robinson	Crusoe	15/7/1632	Various	Wastrel, slaver, castaway	Royal Geographical Society

You want it to look like this:

Prof. MORIARTY **born 04/12/1872** Educ., *Career Consulting Criminal* HONOURS SOC THIEVES

Mr George SMILEY **born 12/12/1923** Educ., Eton, Oxford *Career Secret Intelligence Service* HONOURS KG (NOT USED)

Mr Robinson CRUSOE **born 15/7/1632** Educ., Various *Career Wastrel, slaver, castaway* HONOURS ROYAL GEOGRAPHICAL SOCIETY

If there are a lot of entries, the business of going through each one intricately styling each part (even with character styles) is going to take you days, during which time you will progressively lose the will to live—I know this from experience. You will almost certainly make a lot of errors.

I will give the steps to do this in Excel. This complicates things a little, but it will mean that you should be able to follow even if you don't have a database application. Any other spreadsheet will do if you are not an Excel user.

Here's how.

First, open your Excel Spreadsheet.

Across the top you will have the list of headers. Copy those and paste them in the same row after the headers have finished. Then, in what you've just pasted, put <@ in front, and >§ behind for each of the cells. In front of the first one also put "@Entry:

The result will look like this:

Database publishing with XPress Tags

@xEn-try:<@xTi-tle>§	<@xGiven Name>§	<@xSur-name>§	<@xd.o.b.>§	<@xEduca-tion>§	<@xCa-reer>§	<@xHo-nours>§

High level process for XPress Tags
1) *Acquire your data*
2) *Set up a way of tagging the data with XPress Tags, using* **@name:** *for paragraphs and* **<@name>** *for character styles*
3) *Apply this to the whole dataset*
4) *Import into a plain text document with the XPress Tags header* <v12.00><e9>
5) *Import into QuarkXPress*
6) *Format your styles*
7) *Tidy up.*

In my example I've added an 'x' in front of each because I want to keep all the styles together, and don't want them mixed up with the rest of the book styles. If you're working in a new document, you don't need to do this.

What you have done is created XPress Tags character tags with the name of the header as the style sheet. In addition, in front of the first one you've created an XPress Tags paragraph tag.

Although the example of the word 'Text' at the start of this section does not give this impression, the format for XPress Tags is actually very simple.

It's *@paragraph-style-name:* for a paragraph style, and *<@character-style-name>* for a character style.

The reason we had to put in " for the first one is because Excel will interpret '@' as an instruction, and try to interpret it. The inch mark " tells it to take the text.

We've put in § because we will want to add in some text. Until we've seen the file all laid out, we're not entirely sure what that text is going to be: do we want to put 'Title' in front of someone's title, or leave it blank? Do we need to write 'Honours', or is it self explanatory? We want to leave those decisions as late as possible.

So far we have created some tags, but we haven't connected them to the text.

Now here is what we do.

In Excel, in a new cell after the ones you created, on the same row, put in a formula which you are going to make by taking the cell-address of the tag, then "&", then the cell-address of what it refers to, then "&" again, until you have done all the cells.

While creating it, it's going to look like this:

=H1&A1&I1&B1&J1&C1&K1&D1&L1&E1&M1&F1&N1&G1

That may look annoying and complicated, but Excel will light up the cells you've clicked and give them different colours to make it easier. Do not use '+' instead of '&'. Excel will interpret '+' as an instruction to add the numbers together, which it can't, as the cells aren't numeric. It will give a #Value error, which tells you that you've done it wrong.

If you've done it right, when you come out of editing, you cell will now look like this:

```
@xEntry:<@xTitle>§Title<@xGiven Name>§Given
Name<@xSurname>§Surname<@xd.o.b.>§d.o.b.<@xEducation>§Education<@xCareer>§
Career<@xHonours>§Honours
```

Before going any further, let's test this.

In a plain text processor, something like Text Wrangler, copy the cell and paste it.

If you tried to import that now, QuarkXPress would not recognise it as XPress Tags. You need to add a very simple header first:

```
<v12.00><e9>
```

This is the header which informs QuarkXPress that the document is XPress Tags.

You now have a text document that looks like this:

```
<v12.00><e9>
@xEntry:<@xTitle>§Title<@xGiven Name>§Given
Name<@xSurname>§Surname<@xd.o.b.>§d.o.b.<@xEducation>§Education<@xCareer>§
Career<@xHonours>§Honours
```

Save it as 'anything.xtg'. If you are working in a text processor that can save in several formats, make sure you save as Plain Text.

Now, close down whatever files you are working in, because if the file is corrupt, it can cause QuarkXPress to quit unexpectedly.

Create a new file, go to File—Import—Text, and click on your file.

Do not press import yet! If all is well, you should see this:

Database publishing with XPress Tags

Type: XPress Tags

☑ Convert Quotes

☑ Interpret XPress Tags

Encoding: Unicode (UTF-8)

This tells you that QuarkXPress has correctly identified it as XPress Tags, and correctly seen that it is formatted as UTF-8, which is what the <e9> stood for in the header. If you are (for whatever reason) saving in some other Unicode format, then you need to adjust this. <e8> is UTF-16. A list of other codes is in the XPress Tags guide, which you can (and probably should) download from Quark.com.

If you try to import UTF-8 as UTF-16, or vice versa, then either the text will not import correctly, or else QuarkXPress will quit.

Assuming all is well, press Import.

What you'll see is this:

§Title§Given Name§Surname§d.o.b.§Education§Career§Honours

You may think that isn't very encouraging. However, if you click on it, each of those elements has its own character style, which is now visible in the Styles palette. One by one, go through the styles and change them, using one of them as the 'based on' style, so that if you decide to change the typeface or size later, everything will change together. That gives you this:

§Title§<u>Given Name</u>§Surname§*d.o.b.*§Education§*Career*§Honours

If you want, you can use Find/Replace to change the § to spaces for now.

Now here is the exciting bit.

Back in Excel, select all the tagging cells you've created (but not the original data cells). At the bottom right hand corner of your selection is a little marker. Drag this down and the cells will copy themselves. Keep dragging until you have copied your tagging cells and formula to the entire

The example given here is quite a difficult one, because it's a general case. However, there are many much quicker wins. The bibliography and citation manager software Bookends allows you to select a wide variety of bibliography outputs, and it also allows you to define your own. This means that you can easily insert XPress Tags among its own codes to reliably format any bibliography every time you want to update it. Many other software solutions provide their own customisable outputs: after all, a very high proportion of software these days uses either databases or structured formats such as XML to manage its own information internally.

This, in Bookends:

$@bibliography:$s
$@bibliography author:$a
$@bibliography extras:$ $ed++. $e, u2$ ed.$, $ Vol. v. $u13$ vols.$~ ~!:|~ ~u|~, ~d.$ $u12`.`
$@bibliography notes:$n

produces this in QuarkXPress:

On Brand
Olins, Wally
1st ed., Thames & Hudson, 2003.
Wolf Olins is to branding what David Ogilvy was to advertising. A lifetime of experience in this book.

Note that most software requires you to enclose your own text between special characters. For Bookends, this is $...$, so that it knows not to interpret it as its own specialist formulae.

list. If you check, you will see that the new cells have automatically changed so that they reference what is on their row.

Now go back to the column with your formula. You should be seeing an entire column of stuff where all the tags are the same, but the text in between them is different. Copy and paste the whole of that column into your plain text document, the one that begins with <v12.00><e9>.

If you now import that document again, you should see this (but many more entries):

§Title§Given Name§§Surname§*d.o.b.*§Education§*Career*§Honours

§Prof.§§Moriarty§*04/12/1872*§§*Consulting Criminal*§

§Mr§George§§Smiley§*12/12/1923*§Eton, Oxford§*Secret Intelligence Service*§

§Mr§Robinson§Crusoe§*15/7/1632*§Various§*Wastrel, slaver, castaway*§

Now it's time to replace those § with text you actually want.

In Find/Change, turn Ignore Attributes off, and enter the § sign along with the particular style sheet you are interested in. By the way, I'm using § because it is convenient on my Mac keyboard, top left, and it won't be used for any of the

Database publishing with XPress Tags

entries. You can use any symbol you like, as long as it doesn't appear in the data.

In Find/Change, make sure you have 'whole word' turned off. It's probably wisest to have Layout turned off as well.

As you recall, I slightly renamed my tags xTitle, xSurname, etc, so they wouldn't get confused with my book tags, and so they would all appear in the style sheet list together. This also makes them easy to find.

For each tag, simply use the Change field to turn § into something like, say, 'born', for d.o.b., 'educ.,' for education, and so on. New in QuarkXPress 2016, Find/Change remembers and makes a list of what you've done earlier.

Now we have this result:

Prof. MORIARTY *born 04/12/1872* *Career: Consulting Criminal HONOURS: ETC*

Mr George SMILEY *born 12/12/1923* Educ., Eton, Oxford *Career: Secret Intelligence Service HONOURS: ETC*

Mr Robinson CRUSOE *born 15/7/1632* Educ., Various *Career: Wastrel, slaver, castaway HONOURS: ETC*

That might all seem like a lot of work for three entries. If you have three thousand entries, you have just saved yourself about three days.

However—as you will well know if you've ever done a Who's Who—chances are significant that there will be some changes to the database itself before you are finished. Half-way through, you discover that all the Belgians have put in their surname where the given name would go, and vice versa. All the Americans have entered their date of birth in US format. All the Germans have capitalised words which, in English, you wouldn't capitalise.

When you point that out to the technical team who manage the database, they can usually sort it all out with a few clicks—but then you've got a new database file. Doing what we've just done, you can copy your tags and formula over to the new file, and leave the Find/Change only to the final version.

Alternative:
Conditional Styles

The workflow here is ideal if you are receiving the list as Excel or other database files. If you are receiving it as finished, edited text, with all of the 'born', 'career' and so on in, you would be better off managing it with conditional styles, where you set the styles to change when they encounter the trigger text—provided that this text is consistent.

As a halfway house, you can insert Conditional Style markers in a database file in the same way that you would insert XPress tags. This is intrinsically less reliable than using XPress tags, but, for a mid-sized list, it may be sufficiently less work to make it a better approach.

You can also combine the two. For example, if you were publishing a catalogue, there might be particular items you wanted to call out, and these might change regularly. Inserting a field in the database for the conditional style marker would allow that particular entry to be set in an above-and-below ruled box. Every time the catalogue was refreshed, the conditional styles would manage the new call-out items.

2   Is it time to get a proper database?

You can do all this in Excel, but would you want to? Microsoft Access, on Windows, Filemaker Pro, on Windows or Mac, or MySQL can manage the tagging for you much more easily, output a file with the header properly inserted, and even manage the bits of text between the entries, so you don't have to play around with § and Find/Change. There is a small investment of time to learn how to set up a database to do these things. If you are going to do one catalogue, Who's Who or other data-driven project once, or perhaps once a year, then the Excel route should work for you. If you are going to do it a lot, then a database will be better. The alternative is the XTags Xtension, which does everything we've discussed and a lot more.

More things with XPress Tags

The example above gives you the most basic use of XPress Tags. It's about as far you would want to go with Excel, but if you are running a database and can put your own formulae in, there are a lot more things you can do. This includes actually setting the style sheet formats, setting Open Type features on, working in multiple languages, and marking up text to be used in the index.

Going further, you will also need to take account of escaped characters, which are where you have a character in the text which QuarkXPress would interpret as an instruction.

The most current manual for XPress Tags is available for download from Quark.com, or do a web search for 'XPress Tags manual'.

The most obvious example is @, but the three that need attention are:
- @ use <\@>
- < use <\<>
- \ use <\\>

You can also specify a range of typographical characters which your database might not support directly. Check the XPress Tags manual for full information.

4 Shared layouts and composition zones

Deadlines are tight, but the team is willing. The only problem is, only one person can work on the same document at the same time, right? Well, of course not. QuarkXPress has enabled people to collaborate on a layout for quite a few years now. They don't even have to be working on the same computer network, now that we have DropBox and its peers.

Creating a composition zone is simple. Either draw a box with the Composition Zone tool, which is on the flyout menu for box drawing and looks like this, ⬚ or click on an existing item and then select Item—Composition Zones—Create.

Initially, your composition zone will create a new layout, which you can access if you choose Item—Composition Zones—Edit. Anything you put in it will update on the main layout.

That in itself can be highly useful—for example if you have a part of a document at 180° but you want to edit it right way up, for which simply create the composition zone, rotate it in the main layout, and then edit it in its own layout.

Another use is to crop things that otherwise can't be cropped. For example, if you have a map, drawing or diagram in native Quark objects, and you only want to show part of it, you can put it inside a composition zone, and anything off the layout will not show in the main document.

To share it, go to the Content palette (Window—Content, see Part 5—Palettes—Content) and, with the composition zone selected, click the ✛ to add. This will immediately bring up the Edit window, offering you the option of making it External, which creates it as a file which another user can open and edit. Once they have saved it, you can go to Utilities—Usage—Composition Zones to update it.

The Shared Item Properties edit box, where you can make a composition zone available to all open projects, or make it an external QuarkXPress file, available to any user to edit.

5 Image Grid

The Image Grid is an automatic layout tool which is much more useful than it might first appear. Ostensibly, it creates a grid of images rather like an old fashioned contact sheet, optionally with the file title and potentially image information for each file. It processes an entire directory, and then creates enough boxes and enough pages to do what has to be done.

Although it is called 'Image' Grid, it works just as well with PDF files and other graphics. The only requirement is that each graphic is a separate file. Provided that you can separate out a PDF into one file per page—which can be done with Adobe Acrobat Professional, or Apple's built-in Preview, you can populate the pages of an entire book with a previously created PDF. This is a quick fix if you need to change the headers, footers or page numbers on an existing PDF and you don't have the original QuarkXPress (or other) file, as you can set ImageGrid to scale and position the PDFs as you want them, and it is a fairly simple matter to remove the offending material and replace it with your own.

If you want to entirely recreate a document, you can combine this feature with Quark's new Style—Convert to Native Objects for included graphics (crop them before converting, which will make life easier). Copy and paste the text into an automatic text box, and you have every graphic in more or less the right place with the text flowing around it. For a long document, this could potentially save days of work, even taking into account the time you will lose cropping the pictures and adjusting them because of slightly different text flow.

ImageGrid is also a convenient way of importing a long list of graphics to add to your Library (from File—New Library).

6 Design Pad

If you have an iPad, you might want to download Design Pad, by Quark. The basic version is free, though you will need to pay a modest fee if you want it to create QuarkXPress documents.

Design Pad is a parameter- and grid-driven design tool. What is interesting about it is that it will continuously re-layout entire pages as you play with the parameters, something QuarkXPress would require lots of operations to achieve. This means that you can tweak (or entirely remake) a grid and see right away what that will do with titles, text, and so on.

In principle you could create an entire layout, complete with pictures and final text, on Design Pad and then send it to QuarkXPress. This might feel a bit like drinking from a long straw, but there are many initial tasks that are fairly easy to accomplish, especially if you need to create a suite of master pages all based around the same grid but each different from each other.

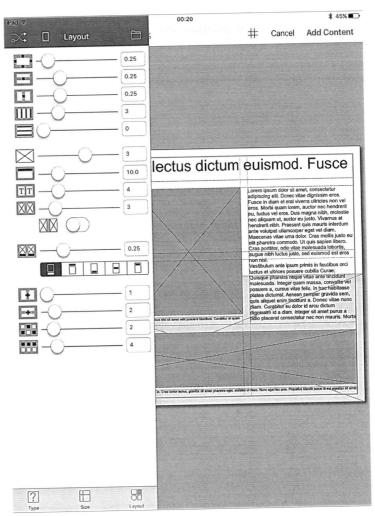

Above, Design Pad is a free-to-download parameter-driven layout application for iPad. By merely tweaking a set of controls, virtually any grid-based layout can be specified.

The app is capable of producing finished layouts with imported pictures and text. Its main use, though, is as a preparatory step to working with QuarkXPress.

Numerous templates are included.

209

Part 5: Power: Every function listed and explained

Tools, Measurements, Palettes and Menus

1 Tools

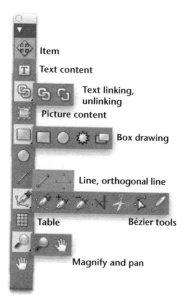

Item

Text content

Text linking, unlinking

Picture content

Box drawing

Line, orthogonal line

Table   Bézier tools

Magnify and pan

Above, all the tools with their flyout menus. By default in QuarkXPress 2016 several tools are already uncollapsed. Ctrl-click/right-click a tool to recollapse it if you prefer the layout of earlier versions of QuarkXPress. You can set default tool behaviour in Preferences.

The Text Content Tool also acts as a more general editing tool, giving you access to most of the elements of a table.

You can create text on a line by double clicking on the line. You can create text on a circle in the same way—double click on the frame. See Measurements—Text Box.

The **Item tool** ⊕ is generally used for moving boxes around the layout and for resizing or rotating them, by selecting the handles ⊸.

When moving, if you Opt/Alt-click after having started, a duplicate item will be created. Opt/Alt-clicking before you start temporarily invokes the pan tool.

If you Shift-click while moving, the object moves vertically or horizontally, but not both. You can combine Shift- and Opt/Alt-click.

When resizing, if you Cmd/ctrl-click, the contents are resized, but not proportionately. Combine with Shift-click to resize proportionately. Opt/alt-clicking while resizing resizes from the centre.

Resizing from the corners affects both dimensions. Resizing from the sides affects only that dimension.

If you hover over the corner handles, a reshape icon comes up which then changes to a rotation icon if you wait.

Shift-clicking while rotating constrains to 45° increments.

Pro-tip: the actual total rotation is given in the measurements panel.

If you double-click on a box, the selection tool turns into the relevant content tool for that box.

Shortcut—V

The **Text Content tool** ⊤ allows you to create a text box by dragging, and edit text by clicking inside a text box. Shift-clicking during creation creates a square box. Inside a box, if you put the cursor in one place and shift-click at another, the whole becomes a selection. You can do the same thing by clicking and dragging, but shift-click works over many—even hundreds—of pages.

While in the text tool, single letter shortcuts are disabled.

Shortcut—T

Tools

The **Text Linking tool** has a fly-out, accessed by holding down the black triangle⌐, which gives you a choice of link 🖺 or 🖺 unlink. You have to actually click the alternate tool to access it.

In use, the linking tool links two boxes together so that the text flows from one to the next. It can also link the 'chain' icon on a Master page to a box on that page, which will cause text to flow from page to page, with new pages created. This is the same as creating an automatic text box when beginning a new document.

To link multiple boxes, click the first, then the second, then the third. You don't need to hold down shift, or reselect (this is different in some earlier versions of QuarkXPress).

Unlink works in the same way—click on the second box to unlink it. This only unlinks that box, so a chain of boxes is not broken. You can't link to a box which already has text in it, but you can use Utilities—Linkster to link up boxes with text in them, retaining the text.

Shortcut—N (Mac), T (Windows)

The **Picture Content tool** 🖺 allows you to create a picture box by dragging (Shift-click constrains to a square), and once a picture has been imported, to use the round tabs using the round tabs, ⬤, to resize or rotate. Dragging with the tool on a picture shifts it in the frame. You can also use the arrow keys. Double-clicking on an empty picture box opens up an import dialogue. If you double click on an imported picture, it opens the update dialogue.

From QuarkXPress 2016, you can convert it to Native Objects with Style—Convert to Native Objects. This allows you to freely edit and recolour vector AI, PDF and EPS files.

By default, resizing a picture is constrained. You can turn the constraint off by clicking on the chain icon in Measurements W: and H: if you want to distort a picture.

Otherwise, the reposition content function works in the same way as with the Selection tool.

Shortcut—R

Linking the chain on the master page to create an automatic text box.

Above, the picture content tool produces rounded tabs, which can be used to resize or rotate the image. The frame tabs can also be edited in the picture content tool.

Above, double-clicking on an imported picture with the picture content tool opens a dialogue which allows you to update the original (if changed), edit it, or open the folder it is in.

213

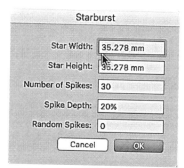

Clicking (rather than dragging) with the Starburst tool opens up a dialogue to specify the shape.

The Composition Zones tool ⊡ creates a new layout. Ctrl-click/right-click to edit.

The home tab of the Measurements panel offers X1, X2, Y1, Y2 for absolute coordinates of lines. If you change Endpoints to Midpoint, Left Point or Right Point, the panel changes to the coordinates of the point, the angle of the line, and its length.

The **Box Drawing tools** are set to the Rectangle Box drawing tool □ by default, but have a flyout for ovals ○, starburst ✳ and composition zones ⊡. If you hold down R while dragging to create, the content becomes Picture. If you hold down T, the content becomes Text.

The rectangle, oval and starburst use the same constraints as the Selection tool, and are simple drawing tools. For more complex shapes, use Utilities—Shapemaker.

The **Composition Zones tool** ⊡ uses the same constraints as the Selection tool ✛, but creates a holder for an entirely new layout. To edit this, Ctrl-click/right-click and the contextual menu offers you Composition Zones—Edit or Composition Zones—Convert to Picture. Edit opens up an entirely new layout box, which you then edit like your main layout.

This is highly useful if you want to separate out a part of the document to edit separately—for example because it is rotated in the finished document, but you want to edit it right way up. If you are coming from InDesign, and wanted to know how to rotate the document on the screen, this is how you accomplish that.

When finished, you can convert to a picture if you like.

You can make this shareable in the Content Palette. See Menus section, Item—Composition zones for more information.

Shortcut—B (On Windows, L selects Composition zones)

The **Line tools** and flyout offers a choice of orthogonal (right-angled) lines + or unconstrained lines ╱. You can use all of the same keyboard constraints as in the Selection tool. By default, lines come out at 1 point black. In the Measurements panel, you will see that the Home tab changes, allowing you to set coordinates, angle and length.

Shortcut—L (Mac) P (Windows)

Tools

The **Pen tools** flyout offers a selection of Bézier drawing tools. The default Bézier tool ✐ allows you to click from point to point, dragging as you do to establish the curve. If you complete the curve by clicking finally on the first point, it becomes a fillable shape, which can have picture or text as its content: Ctrl-click/right-click—Content to specify which. If you do not complete the shape, it remains as a line shape, which you can click with the Text tool to have text on a curve.

The second tool ✐ adds a point, the ✐ tool subtracts a point, the angle tool ✕ allows you to change the curve angle, the scissors tool ✂ allows you to cut the curve, the triangle tool ◮ allows you to move the points and reshape the curve, and the pencil tool ✐ allows for freehand drawing. Freehand is only useful if you are using a pen: on the mouse or track pad, it's quite fussy.

If you select a point or the whole curve with the triangle tool ✐ , you can then change the type of point with Item—Point/Segment type.

You can work on shapes created with the box drawing tools or with the text or picture box tools.

Shapes can be combined with Item—Merge or Split Paths.

Shortcut—P

The **Table tool** ▦ creates a table. To do so, select the tool, and then drag-click somewhere on the page. A new dialogue opens up, allowing you to specify Rows, Columns, whether the cells are text or picture, whether you want to auto-fit or not, what the tab order is, whether or not to link cells so that text flows through them as with the link tool, whether to maintain geometry, which means that the shape of the table stays put if you amend it, and whether to link to External Data. All of these except the external data can be changed retrospectively.

Linking to external data opens up a new dialogue, enabling you to browse to an Excel spreadsheet and then import a range from a sheet, specified with the name of the sheet—a

Using the freehand drawing tool, if you draw slowly, few points are produced, if you draw fast, many points are produced. Use this to your advantage if you want a very smooth curve which is easy to edit (go slow), or if you want a lot of points because you are then going to use them as a basis for something else (go fast).

The Table Properties dialogue. Clicking on Link to External Data opens the Table Link dialogue.

Above, the Table Link dialogue specifies how an Excel table is imported—either as a regular table, but linked to the underlying data, or as an Inline table, where all of the content editing is done in Excel, but all of the formatting is done by QuarkXPress Table Styles. You can also invoke this by using Item—Insert Inline Table.

list of options will be given—and a range in the format A1-D7. It will default to all the data on the sheet.

If you select Inline Table, QuarkXPress will allow you to style the table.

Regular tables

Once you've created an ordinary table, whether linked to external data or not, you can reshape it using the Selection tool, and edit using the Text tool, which allows you to select the boxes, enter and format text, and apply text colours and backgrounds. You can also hover with the text tool to move or change the grids, but this is tedious. Instead, using the Picture Box tool or the triangle tool from the Bézier tools flyout, you can move them around more easily, and also set the line qualities either using Ctrl-click/Right-click and the contextual menu, or from the Measurements panel's Frame tab.

If you paste a table inside a text frame (make sure it is narrower than the frame, or all your text will disappear), the frame will then flow with the text. To control how it does this, including header rows if you want them, use Table—Table Break, or do the same thing by Ctrl-click/right-click in the Contextual Menu for Tables. There you can also combine cells, split cells, add rows and columns or delete them.

Inline tables

If you find QuarkXPress tables fiddly, you would not be alone. The truth is, after you have used tables in a spreadsheet, neither QuarkXPress nor Word nor InDesign nor anything else is really quite as convenient. However, although table construction in Excel is easy, formatting tables so that they fit a conventional page is tedious.

QuarkXPress offers both importing of Excel tables and also Inline Excel tables. Inline tables can only be edited in Excel (or a compatible spreadsheet application), but they can be formatted with a very great degree of precision using Window—Table Styles.

You must choose Inline Table when you create your Linked to External Data table, but you can apply a different style

Tools

sheet retrospectively by selecting the entire table using the Text tool and applying the format in Window—Table Styles.

See **Table Styles** for more information.

To see which Excel based tables you have, and whether they are up to date, go to Utilities—Usage—Tables.

If you want to create a table in Excel but don't want to manage a file, just copy the rang in Excel and then paste it into QuarkXpress.

Shortcut—G

Zoom has a flyout menu of zoom and pan . Opt/Alt-click with Zoom reduces magnification, clicking with it increases magnification, and dragging zooms the selected area.

You can also enter exact magnifications at the bottom left of the screen, or T for thumbnail.

Except when editing text, Cmd/ctrl-plus increases magnification, and Cmd/ctrl-minus decreases it.

Cmd/ctrl-1 sets magnification to 100%, and Cmd/ctrl-0 fills the screen.

Shortcut—Z

is the **Pan** tool. It can be invoked by pressing down Opt/alt and dragging.

Shortcut—X

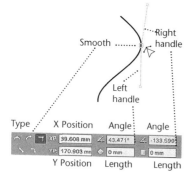

2 Measurements

If you are coming from earlier versions of QuarkXPress on a Mac, you may be wondering why Cmd-M doesn't open up a dialogue in which you can put specifications about a box, text, and so on— though it still operates on Windows. These functions are now in the Measurements panel. New to QuarkXPress 2016, you can now increase the size of this panel if it's too small. On the other hand, if you want to assign more space to the page—especially since modern monitors are wide but shallow, you can turn hiding on. Both options are accessed from the cog-wheel in the bottom left hand corner of the panel.

1 Home

The Home panel is contextual. Things on the left are the most stable: the X and Y coordinates and Width and Height are almost always there:

X,Y: The left and top coordinates of the working box

W,H: Box width and height, often linked. Click on their chain icon 8 (immediately right) to link or unlink them.

These controls are also in Tabs, Text Box, Picture Box and others, but we won't illustrate them again.

Almost all of the other modal measurements in the Home tab are taken from the other measurement tabs, so we will look at each in their proper tab.

There are three exceptions. Tables and Lines (see the Line tool, above, and the end of this chapter) change the Home tab with features not accessible in other tabs.

The ⚲ Select Point Tool changes the right-hand end of the Home palette—it's easy to miss this. It gives precise controls for changing point type, position, angles and length.

2 Character

Font selection. The up/down arrows on the left nudge the font to the preceding or following font in the list. This is useful if you have ordered sets. If you click in the box itself, you can start typing a name (from the beginning only) and the range of selection is narrowed down. If you click on the double arrow at the right, the entire list is displayed centred on the currently selected font. QuarkXPress will not 'see' newly added fonts unless you have a Quark compliant Xtension such as Extensis Suitcase or FontExplorer Pro.

Font Size. Left up/down arrows nudge harmonically, right double-arrow shows harmonic sequence. You can enter your own with any units.

P	Returns font to plain	cmd/ctrl-shift-P
B	Bolds font, possibly with faux-bold, indicated by a yellow triangle	cmd/ctrl-shift-B
I	Italic, same warning system as Bold	cmd/ctrl-shift-I
U	Underline	cmd/ctrl-shift-U
S	Single Strike through	
ABC	All caps	cmd/ctrl-shift-K
Abc	Small Caps	cmd-shift-H
A²	Superscript	cmd-shift-=
A₂	Subscript	cmd-shift-minus
fi	Ligature	cmd-shift-G
f	Additional functions: the above plus Outline, Shadow, Word Underline, Double Strikethrough and Superior	
O	Open Type features These depend on the installed features of your font. If in [square brackets] the feature is not present. Exactly what they mean depends a little on the font.	

Possible Open Type features:
(Examples where present:
Vollkorn)

Standard Ligatures	fifth
Discretionary Ligatures	fkfjfh
Small Caps	
All Small Caps	
Tabular Figures	123
Proportional Figures	123
Lining Figures	123
Oldstyle Figures	123
Fractions	½
Swashes	
Ordinals	I
Titling Alternates	
Contextual Alternates	
Localised Forms	
Position:	
Superscript	
Subscript	
Scientific Inferiors	
Numerator	1
Denominator	2
Stylistic Sets 1-20	JQa

In Gabriola:

SMALL CAPS

ALL SMALL CAPS

Swashes Q

Superscript:

Subscript₀₁₂₃

Scientific inferiors₀₁₂₃

Stylistic sets:

A a B b C c

A a B b C c

A a B b C c

A a B b C c

In the home tab, an additional icon appears alongside the character styles: ✔. This is the brush tool, and copies text formatting from one selection of text to another.

Chartwell, for example, uses Ligatures to engage its special features.

↕ Tracking. See the Typography section. For inter-word spacing, see Style—Remove Manual Kerning.

⌐A Shift baseline. This also applies to anchored boxes.

■ Colour, from the Window—Colours defined colours

▣ Opacity. You can create blurred text by setting the opacity to zero and creating a Drop Shadow with Inherit Opacity turned off.

English (International)
　Sets character language. It is generally better to set it in the Character Style. The entire document can be converted using Utilities—Convert Project Language. The language sets spell checking and hyphenation. To overlook a particular word, set the language to None.

Ā Set % adjustment to character width.

A⌐ Set % adjustment to character height.

100%—the percentage adjustment.

3 Paragraph

⊩ Left indent

⊐ Right indent

⊞ Space above

⊟ Space below

⊿ Leading—Baseline to baseline

⊞ First line indent

Measurements

- ⬌ Left justify
- ⬌ Centred
- ⬌ Right align
- ⬌ Fully justified (left and right)
- ⬌ Force justify (including final line)

H&Js Hyphenation and Justification—select from one of the presets. To edit or create presets, use Edit—H&Js.

▦ Hanging Punctuation. See Edit—Hanging Characters.

▣ Dropped Cap. The upper number sets the number of letters affected, usually one but often two if the first character is a quotation mark, and the lower box ≡ sets the depth of the drop, usually 2–4 lines.

▤ Keep with next (be careful with this one in a paragraph style, because if all the text is kept together, it will not be able to reflow and will disappear.

▣ Keep paragraph together. This can either be All Lines in ¶ Paragraph, or specified for the beginning and end of the paragraph. Again, be careful if used in conjunction with Keep with next.

A̲A̲ Locks text to grid, which is either the Page Grid or the Box Grid. You can also define Grid Styles in Window—Grid Styles. The locking is topline, bottomline, baseline or centre line.

•/123 Bullets, Numbering and Outlines. You can define these in Edit—Bullet, Numbering and Outline Styles.

▤ Minimum distance from text. You can refine the placement of the bullet or number with this.

¾₅ Restart the numbering here for this level. The new number goes in the accompanying box.

▣ Increase indent level. Cmd/ctrl-/

▣ Decrease indent level. Cmd-opt/ctrl-alt-/

Te Sets the vertical character alignment. Usually baseline, but a book spine might be centreline.

See Edit—Bullet, Numbering and Outline Styles for a full explanation of how you can make your own bullets and numbering systems.

Pro Tip—if your numbering unexpectedly resets, select all the text between the last good numbered section and the new, bad, one, and choose •/123: None in the Measurements Paragraph tab. This should clear any rogue formatting.

Book spine with baseline (l), top, centre, bottom (r), setting text in two sizes.

4 Rules

Call-outs can easily be created with above and below rules.

The rules will only appear if there is a paragraph above (for above rule) or below (for below rule) on the page, so if you want to have a page top title within rules, you must have a blank, possibly minimal leading, paragraph above it.

The Rules tab contains identical sections for above (left) and below (right).

For both:

⁋,⁋ Turns the rule on or off.

— The line control sets the type of line, either regular, dashed or striped. You can edit the presets or create new ones in Edit—Dashes & Stripes.

1pt The thickness, or weight, of the line. You can enter using any units, but it will be displayed in points.

■ The colour of the line, selected from colours defined in the Window—Colours Palette.

▣ The opacity of the line. You can create blurred lines by setting the opacity to zero and creating a Drop Shadow with Inherit Opacity turned off.

⊣ Line offset left.

⊢ Line offset right.

⟷ Length, either from the typographical indents, or the text, or the column, as modified by the offsets (above). The rule above applies to the top line of text if text width, and the rule below to the bottom line.

⇥ Horizontal Placement. This requires interparagraph spacing, ▣▣ from the Paragraph tab to have any effect.

How to make auto reversed text—above

You can create automatic reversed titles using the above rule or the below rule. First, create a rule which is thicker

Rule the world

Title rules may work better if text width only

Measurements

than the height of the text. Second, set the colour of the text to white. Third, raise the text baseline using the ⌐ᴬ character baseline control if using the Above rule, or lower it if using the Below rule. This is a trick, and won't always work. It creates a lot of space underneath if using the above line, or above if using the below line. Also, it is for one line only, per paragraph.

Auto reversed text—Below

If this is not going to work in your layout, consider using a single line table, pasted into the text (anchored).

Single line Table

The advantage of the auto-reversed title is that you can define it as a paragraph style, and quickly go through text formatting it. You can, of course, set the line to any colour you want and so have black on yellow, etc, but note the legibility implications (Part 2: Master Typography): the lower the luminance contrast, the less the legibility. You can also programme a dash to interrupt the letters. Best used judiciously.

Special Effects, of course, are possible.

5 Tabs

To edit tabs, first highlight your text by selecting it. The tab ruler will then appear at the top of the column.

Cmd/ctrl-shift-T invokes the Tabs panel—on Windows this opens as a separate dialogue. As well as opening the panel, it also places the tabs ruler at the top of the visible column. This remains editable even though—on Windows—a dialogue is open.

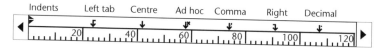

Left Tab—the old fashioned typewriter tab, appears as ↓ in the tab ruler

Centre Tab, appears as ↓ in the tab ruler

Right Tab, appears as ↴ in the tab ruler

Decimal tab, appears as ↓ in the tab ruler, aligns on the decimal point (UK & USA)

Comma tab, appears as ↓ in the tab ruler, aligns on the decimal comma (European)

Assignable tab, set using Align on at the right end of the Measurements panel. Appears as ↯.

Tabs works on the selection of text you have highlighted, or through the Paragraph styles.

To assign tabs, drag them from the Measurements panel to the ruler, or just click on the ruler, which will assign the last type of tab you used.

By default, QuarkXPress has courtesy tabs set across the column. The first time you set a tab in that selection, all of those courtesy tabs are removed, so if you've tabbed some text and then want to refine it, it will go funny initially.

6 Text Box

X: Y: W: H: set the box position and dimensions.

↗   Sets the rotation of the box

☐   Sets the skew of the box

Measurements

⌐▾ Sets the corner shape of the box. Click to choose rectangular (default), curved, concave or beveled. Choosing anything but rectangular sets a default radius.

0mm Sets the radius of the box corner. This defaults to curved if you don't specify concave or beveled.

⊘ Turns off output—shown as ⊘ when active. Suppressed boxes neither print nor export.

■ The colour of the box, selected from colours defined in the Window—Colours Palette. Shown as ⊠ when colour is 'none'. When the colour is white, a drop shadow creates a box shadow, not a text shadow.

▣ The opacity of the box. You can create blurred boxes by setting the opacity to zero and creating a Drop Shadow with Inherit Opacity turned off.

▥ Number of columns

▤ Gutter width (space between columns).

▤ Top alignment, the default

▢ Bottom alignment

▤ Centre alignment

▤ Vertical Justification, spaces the lines across the box. This invokes the maximum inter-paragraph control ▤, immediately below it. If you want all the lines equally spaced, leave this at zero. If you want to preserve some paragraph identity, enter a value.

▤ Turn on individual side insets. Otherwise, the next control, to the right, controls all of the insets. If you turn it on, the four boxes to the right become active, allowing you to set the top, bottom, left and right insets. This only applies to regular boxes with standard corners. For shaped corners and non-rectangular boxes, only an overall inset can be applied.

▦ Run text round all sides. Change this if you are not happy with the way text runs round a box.

⌐₄ Sets the rotation of the text within the box.

When working with text on a line, an additional part of the Text Box Measurement Panel appears on the right hand end.

This allows you to specify how the text follows the line, what part of the text is aligning, and, in the last icon, ⌐, lets you flip the text to the other side of the line.

ᴬᴮᶜ *Curved text*
ᴬᴮᶜ *Warped text*
ᴬᴮᶜ *3d ribbon text*
ᴬᴮᶜ *Stair text*
⌐ *Flip text to other side of line*

Vertical justification—how to make boxes that push all the text to the bottom or top, with a gap (as here).

Enter a very high value for inter-paragraph spacing. Ensure there is at least one paragraph break. All the text is pushed to the top and bottom. An additional break gives you a centre paragraph.

<table>
<tr><td>↗</td><td>Sets the skew of the text within the box.</td></tr>
</table>

⤢   Sets the skew of the text within the box.

⊞   Flips the text horizontally.

⊟   Flips the text vertically.

↥   First baseline minimum—sets how the distance from the top of the box to the first baseline is calculated, either Ascent, or Cap-height, or Cap-height plus Accent.

↥↥   First baseline offset. Shifts the first baseline up. This only works for regular boxes with rectangular corners.

7 Picture Box

When a picture is selected, this tab replaces the Text Box tab.

X: Y: W: H: set the box position and dimensions. When a box is anchored, this is replaced with controls to set the alignment of box to ascender ▣ or baseline ▣, with an offset if you choose baseline, which is the default.

⊿   Sets the rotation of the box.

▱   Sets the skew of the box.

⌐•   Sets the corner shape of the box. Click to choose rectangular (default), curved, concave or beveled. Choosing anything but rectangular sets a default radius.

0mm Sets the radius of the box corner. This defaults to curved if you don't specify concave or beveled.

⊘   Turns off box output—shown as ⊘ when active. Suppressed boxes neither print nor export.

Above, when a box is anchored in text, the X: and Y: controls change to alignment controls, above for ascent ▣ and below, with offset, for baseline ▣. This also changes the Home tab.

226   *Measurements*

■ The colour of the box, selected from colours defined in the Window—Colours Palette. Shown as ⊠ when colour is 'none'. When the colour is white, a drop shadow creates a box shadow, not a text shadow.

▣ The opacity of the box. You can create blurred boxes by setting the opacity to zero and creating a Drop Shadow with Inherit Opacity turned off.

X,Y% The scaling of the image in the box. Normally constrained, but you can click the chain link at the side to unconstrain.

X+,Y+ Sets the offset in the box. You would normally set this visually by dragging with the Picture Content Tool or using the arrow keys.

∠ Sets the rotation of the picture in the box (not the same as the rotation of the box).

▱ Sets the skew of the picture.

⊞ Flips the picture horizontally.

⊡ Flips the picture vertically.

◻ Sets the mask. If a layer mask is present, you can select either that or Composite. Otherwise defaults to Composite. See the Advanced Image Control palette.

▦ Shows the resolution at specified size and scale. You can't edit this directly.

For one-bit images only, you can also set the ■ foreground and background colours and ▣ opacity. This is, generally speaking, a legacy function from the days when one-bit hand scanners were common. If you want a retro look, this is where to achieve it.

⊘ Turns off image output—shown as ⊘ when active. You could use this to keep a box frame, but suppress comp images.

Below:
By default, frames and lines,
when dashed or striped, have
empty gaps, but these can be set
to any colour, shade or opacity if
required.

8 Frame

The frame controls are relatively straightforward. 'Frame' refers here to the printed edge of a box, not the frame which appears in blue on the layout to identify where the box is.

0pt   Sets the thickness or weight of the frame.

—   The style of line: solid, dashed or striped, in various options. You can change the presets or create new ones in Edit—Dashes & Stripes.

▪   The colour of the frame, selected from colours defined in the Window—Colours Palette. Shown as ☒ when colour is 'none'.

▣   The opacity of the frame. You can create blurred frames by setting the opacity to zero and creating a Drop Shadow with Inherit Opacity turned off.

☒   Gap colour. This only applies to dashed or striped lines. By default, the gap is colour: none, but you can set it to any colour defined in Window—Colour.

▣   Opacity of the gap.

On Windows, you can also access Runaround and Clipping as dialogue boxes from the Item menu.

9 Runaround and Clipping

The Runaround panel and Clipping panel work together and share many of the same controls. When the box is text, Runaround is either None or Item. When a picture box is used, and the file contains Alpha Channels, Clipping paths and/or white space, more options become available.

Remember that objects stack, so the objects 'on top' affect those below. If using Layers, you can turn this behaviour on or off. Item—Send&Bring will help you control the placement of boxes on top of each other.

1   Clipping

For a picture, the clipping control (left) can be:
- Item
- Embedded Path
- Alpha Channel
- Non-White Areas
- Picture Bounds

Item is the box itself. You can edit this using the Bézir tools by choosing Item—Edit—Clipping. For good control of text-runaround, in conjunction with the runaround tool, this is often the best choice. However, all clipping is 'hard' —you cannot have soft edges which interact with progressive transparency. For an EPS, AI or PDF file, as long as the box has not been assigned a background (often white, by default), only the actual vector items are 'present', so the clipping path is the outside lines of the file itself.

Embedded Path is a path in a TIFF or PSD file. To create this, you need to create a Working Path in Photoshop and then double-click it to give it a permanent name. This creates a hard line. When selected, the box below becomes active allowing you to choose which path.

Alpha Channel is a separate channel in a TIFF or PSD file. To create one, you would usually create a layer mask, but you must then duplicate that and give it a name. A layer mask on its own will not be counted as an alpha channel. When selected, the box below becomes active, allowing you to select which alpha channel. If you leave it on Composite, nothing happens.

If you have a soft mask, for example for flames, or a person's hair, set the Threshold to 100%. The default is 0%, which will produce a hard line.

Non-White Areas calculates where the image is, using the thresholds you specify on the right of the panel. It produces a hard mask.

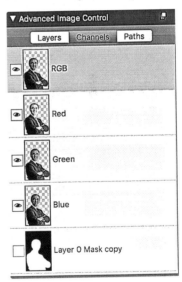

Martin Turner lives with his wife in rural Warwickshire. His background includes charities, the arts, automotive, the UK's National Health Service, and his own business as a brand consultant. He is a Chartered Public Relations Practitioner, qualified fencing coach and referee, and speaks English, Dutch and French.

*Above, the author, stepping out of the box: Alpha Channel mask applied, Restrict to Box off, so that the image can be outside the box background. The runaround path is set to Embedded Path. **Run text around all sides** is 'off' in the Text Box.*

Below, the mask seen in the Advanced Image Control palette.

▼ Advanced Image Control

Layers | Channels | Paths

RGB

Red

Green

Blue

Layer 0 Mask copy

Picture Bounds is the edges of the image, for example if the image only occupies part of the box. If you turn off Restrict to Box, you can have parts of the image which are cropped out. With Picture Bounds, you can set separate insets and outsets—for other types, only a general inset/outset can be specified.

Clipping does not affect the background of the box, so you can have an alpha channel which correctly composites someone onto a box background.

The **Outset** controls ▣ ▣ ▣ ▣ control how much additional margin is allowed beyond that specified, or cut into the image. In Picture Bounds only, you set these separately.

Outside edges only restricts these actions to the outside of an image. This is usually correct.

Restrict to Box, usually on, means that the edges of the box override the alpha channel, mask or non-white areas.

Invert clips invertedly.

Noise, **Threshold** and **Smoothness** are particularly important with Non-White Areas. For soft alpha channels, turn the threshold to 100% or near it.

To create a new box from a clipping path, use Item—New Box from Clipping.

Manual runaround for a Bézier line:

The dotted line shows where the original line was. With manual on, the line is changed, but the runaround stays as it was.

2 Runaround

The Runaround functions like the Clipping, except that it also includes the options **Non-white areas** and **Same as clipping**, and is available as **none** or **item** for boxes that do not contain graphics, including text boxes, graphics and lines. Lines offer the additional option **Manual**—see below. For manually editing the runaround otherwise, choose Item—Edit—Runaround.

Measurements

Essentially, the controls are exactly as the Clipping tab, except that the outsets ▣▣▣▣ control how much space is left around the item. This is by far the most important control in runaround. Multiple values for above, below, left and right can only be set for regular rectangles.

You *can* set negative values here. This is very useful if you have an anchored graphic which insists on allowing too much space either above or below.

When used in conjunction with Callouts, Item—Callout Anchor, runaround can create a situation where the runaround moves the callout, causing it to recalculate the runaround, moving the callout. At this point, QuarkXPress will get itself into an endless loop.

Generally, avoid callouts that cause runaround in the text which anchors them.

For lines, **Manual** works like this. Draw your Bézier curve as you want the runaround to be. Then turn on Manual and edit the line. The line changes, but the runaround stays the same.

You can edit the runaround as beziers by choosing Item—Edit—Runaround, and the clipping with Item—Edit—Clipping Path. In combination with Item—New Box From Clipping, you can autotrace the outlines of images.

Above, Item—New Box From Clipping creates a silhouette. Below, Item—Edit Runaround.

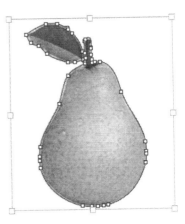

10 Space/Align

Space/Align allows you to line up or space objects based on their sides or centres.

You would normally apply Space/Align to two or more boxes, though you can apply it to a single box if you select the Page or Spread options.

X,Y,W,H control the position of the left-most, top-most box in a selection of boxes.

Alignments: the first box you se-lect is the key item, and the others will align or space accordingly.

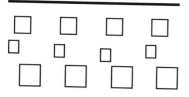

Above, spaced tops ᗱ, centres ᗱ bottoms ᗱ edges ᗱ.

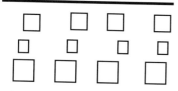

Above, spaced lefts ᗱ centres ᗱ rights ᗱ edges ᗱ.

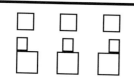

Above, aligned left ᗱ centres ᗱ right ᗱ.

Above, aligned tops ᗱ centres ᗱ bottoms ᗱ.

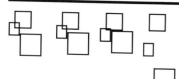

Above, 3mm spaced tops, centres, bottoms and spaced vertically.

Above *Space: Evenly* are a row of icons which space objects Vertically by top, middle, bottom or edges.

If you change the word Evenly to a number, it will add the relevant space between the items.

The default is that items are spaced or aligned relative to each other, but the three icons on the top left allow you to choose between item relative, page relative and spread relative. These last two allow you to position a box centrally, for example, on a page or spread.

When aligning pictures, first use Style—Fit Box to Picture.

11 Drop Shadow

Clicking on Apply Drop Shadow applies a shadow to the contents of a box if it has no fill, or the box itself if it has a fill. The defaults are fine for most purposes. However, you can broaden the range of effects by adjusting the controls.

Multiply drop shadow means that shadows darken backgrounds. Leave on for black shadows, turn off for light shadows. **Inherit opacity** causes shadows of transparent objects to behave as they would in the real world. However, if you turn this off, and turn the opacity of the object to zero, you will get just the shadow of the object, or, rather, a blurred version of it, coloured as the shadow is coloured.

If you set the objects's opacity to about 50% with inherit opacity off, and make the object (or its frame) and the shadow the same colour, it will appear to glow, especially if you set the distance to zero.

The other controls are colour of shadow ■ and opacity of shadow ▣, as with other tabs, angle of shadow ⊙, gap be-

Measurements

tween shadow and object ⬛, angle of skew of shadow ⬛, proportions of shadow ⬛ and spread (or blur) ⬛. If you set Synchronize Angle, all the shadows in the document with this on will have the same shadow angle. You can set the item to knock out the drop shadow rather than overprint it (for items darker than their shadows), and you can set the object to incorporate the shadow dimensions in its runaround.

On Windows, you can also access Drop Shadow from the Item menu.

If you just want a dropped shadow, use the defaults and change the angle, gap and blur. For the rest, experiment!

12 Table

The Table tab appears when a table is selected with the Text tool. X: Y: W: H: as usual set the Height and Width of the table, and its position. However, when a particular cell is selected, the left end of the Home tab changes to allow setting width, height and auto-resizing of the selection—see margin illustration.

Below, when a table cell is selected, the left of the Home tab changes to specifying width and height of the cell, whether the cells are auto resizing, and their maximum width and height if they are. Auto-sizing is overridden, and greyed out, if Maintain Geometry is clicked in the Table tab, which applies to the entire table. Auto width/height can be set per cell.

Back in the Table tab (as above):

⊿   Sets the rotation of the entire table (use Text Box text rotation for rotated elements within particular cells).

⊚   Turns off table output—shown as ⊚ when active. Suppressed tables neither print nor export.

⬛   The colour of hairline grids—these may not print or export well, but can be helpful while editing in Guides-off mode.

⬛   The opacity of the hairlines.

Table   233

⊞ Turns Maintain Geometry on and off. This cancels and greys out all settings you have made in the Home tab regarding auto width or height. It applies to the entire table. If you want particular cells to be auto-width or height, but not the others, set them in the Home tab for each group of cells.

▣ Opacity of the entire table and its contents.

⊞ Select all gridlines.

⊞ Select all vertical gridlines.

⊞ Select all horizontal gridlines.

0.25pt Thickness for selected gridlines.

— Style of selected gridlines.

◪ Colour of gridlines.

▣ Opacity of gridlines.

Gap ◪ Colour of gaps in dashed or striped lines.

▣ Opacity of gaps in dashed or striped lines.

ʒ Link order: order of text when linked

ʒ Tab order: Order in which tabs moves from cell to cell.

13 Line (Home)

When a line is selected, the Home tab changes.

X1, X2, Y1, Y2 control start and endpoints. This changes to a reference point and an angle when anything other than Endpoints is selected.

The other options are the same as for frames, except that there is an option for arrowheads at either or both ends.

Measurements

3 Palettes

All the palettes are available from the Window menu. Palettes differ from dialogue boxes in that they can stay open all the time. You can organise your palette sets in Window—Palette Sets.

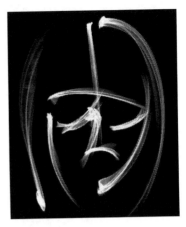

1 Advanced Image Control

The Advanced Image Control Palette is mainly for use with Photoshop PSD files. It gives access to Photoshop Layers, Channels and Paths. Note that the files need to be free of Photoshop layer effects—QuarkXPress will just look at the Composite file if these are present.

Layers should show you all the document layers. They will already have their relevant blend controls and opacity applied to them. Whenever Quark cannot render a layer—for example because of layer effects—it reverts to the composite image, so that the initial imported image is always identical to the overall Photoshop result.

Channels allows you to switch on or off the relevant colour channels and Alpha masks. For channels not required by the Composite, you can Ctrl-click/right-click to bring up the Channel Options. These allow you to specify the ink, shade and solidity—in other words, exactly the options you are after if you want to specify a spot UV varnish, and you want to set these in Photoshop rather than creating them in QuarkXPress.

Paths allows you to see the paths. The first icon, which has no tool tip, selects the path as text runaround, and the second selects it as the clipping path. However, the controls in the Measurements Panel offer more refinement here.

Above, below, layers for the cover illustration for a book, created in Flamepainter, based on the Sutton Hoo helmet, British Museum.

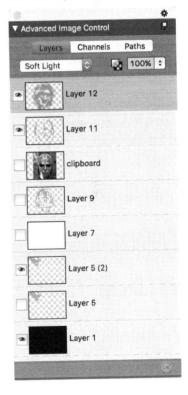

Above, the App Studio dialogue connects with AppStudio.net.

2 App Studio Publishing

The App Studio Publishing palette provides a login to App Studio—a separately hosted and payable service for creating native apps for smart devices. A trial account is available for App Studio. Any digital document created for HTML5 can later be republished via App Studio, and vice versa. See Part 3 for a full explanation of the differences between this and HTML5 publishing.

3 Books

Above, books connects, organises, renumbers, reorders, prints and exports collections of layouts in one or more Quark projects.

The M refers to the Master project from which other chapter style sheets etc are synchronised.

Status can be Open, Available, Modified or Missing.

Lists and Indexes work across the whole of a book, but automatic paragraph numbering does not.

The button icon functions are reproduced in the menu, top-right, underneath the cog icon.

The Books palette connects, organises, renumbers, reorders, prints and PDFs a set of layouts in the same project or different projects. It ensures that page numbering remains consistent and synchronised. If you synchronise chapters, it will also synchronise style sheets, colours and hyphenation. (If you want to synchronise style sheets across a non-book project, use a Job Jacket JDF—see Part 4.)

Usage is fairly simple. Create or open a book file by clicking on the selector in the top left. Then, using the + button, add chapters. You can reorder them with the arrow icons, synchronise them with the circle icon, delete with the trash can, and print or PDF with the print and PDF icons. Once you have started printing or PDFing, you will be taken to the same screens as ordinary documents, and the process from there is transparent. You do not need to have the documents open to work with a book.

Lists, index and page numbering all work across books.

4 Callout Styles

Callouts are a special way of anchoring boxes to moving text, which allow them to be outside the main column. You create Callouts anchors in the text in Item—Callout Anchor, and then assign them to boxes from the same menu item. These boxes are the 'Callouts'.

The Callout Styles palette itself is just a list of the styles you have defined. Use the ✚ to add a style, and the pencil ✐ to edit one.

This calls up the Edit Callout Style box.

Align horizontally relative to: allows you to choose Page, Anchor, Paragraph, Box or Spread. This depends on what you are doing. For this book, the top boxes—if we had chosen to do it this way—would have been page relative, aligning the callout's Outside Edge with the Outside Margin, while the vertical alignment would have been Page, Align callout's Top Edge with Top Margin.

The reason we didn't is that the grid specifies three positions for the marginal text, but, as the boxes reflow, they might need to end up occupying different positions.

There is a trade-off here. Callout styles might be most useful in a long book, but they will also require the most recalculations. For a highly complex document, it is worth making use of the Books function (previous section) so that callouts are not having to endlessly recalculate.

Callouts lend themselves particularly well to laying out a long document of essentially finished text. If the client comes back half way through and wants a different font, page size or whatever, all you need to do is make the changes to the Master Page and the styles, and then make a cup of coffee while everything reflows.

On the other hand, if you are editing as you layout, or looking for a strongly designed look, there will be at least a momentary pause while things rearrange themselves: it may be better to finalise the text and then use callout anchors.

Above, to access Edit Callout Styles, click the + or edit-pencil in the Callout Styles palette.

To create a Callout Anchor, place the cursor on the text which will act as the anchor and go to Item—Callout Anchor—Insert Callout Anchor. This places a marker in the text as here:

This calls up the Edit Callout Style box.

You can now click on the box which is to become a Callout Box and Item—Callout Anchor—Associate with Callout Anchor.

You can edit the Callout Settings directly per box, or you can create a style as in the Callout Styles panel (top) and apply it to the callout box using the same menu.

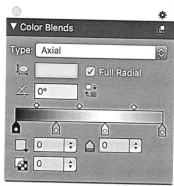

Above, the color blends palette. You can save as an item style.

With Axial Type selected and a transparent white placed left, a 50% black placed next (selected) at 27.3% of the way across, followed by opaque white and 50% grey.

The result is below: a classic steely blend.

Below, a simple radial blend, proportions 90%, 45° from black to white.

Above, combining various opacities of white in a box layered over text produces a glassy effect.

5 Color Blends

Colour blends were part of the Colors palette in previous versions of QuarkXPress. They have now gone through a significant makeover and have their own palette.

From top to bottom:

Type is None, Axial, Radial, Rectangular or Diamond.

The next box, proportions ⬚ only appears for radial, where it sets as a percentage how the radial appears. Full Radial changes how this is calculated.

Angle ⦜ is the angle of the blend. It is often worth setting this to 45° if the blend is subtle and not intended to be too obvious.

The button next ⬚ to it reverses the blend.

The wide bar is where you define the blend, clicking once to establish a point, which appear as a marker ⬚ below.

Once you have set the points, you can move them, and also adjust their midpoints with the diamonds ◇ above the line.

Underneath you have the colour ■ and shade of the selected point, and its opacity ⬚, as elsewhere in QuarkXpress.

On the right you have ⬚ for the exact position of the marker as a percentage. This will show where you have put the marker, and you can edit it numerically if you require an exact percentage.

Gradients across text is sadly all too reminiscent of the Word Art of a famous word processing application. If you are desperate to do this, convert text to box with Item—Convert Text to Boxes and then apply the gradient.

Layering a mixed opacity graphic box over text, however, can produce much more refined effects.

You can save a particular blend as part of an Item Style, which is useful if you are going for a consistent look.

6 Colors

The Colors palette is at the heart of Quark's approach to premium design. Paragraph styles, Item Styles and Character Styles are very convenient, but you *could* do all the formatting on an ad hoc basis and then spot the errors while proofing. This is traditionally exactly how those errors were spotted. Even with Matchprints and other colour proofing, it is nonetheless extraordinarily hard to spot a yellow which is just the wrong yellow, a shade of green which is just too bright—at least, while proofing it is. When you put the miscoloured object next to a whole window of correctly coloured work, the difference is all too obvious. Other applications allow you to create swatches and work from them, but Quark requires you to. In the business of life, it is all too easy to pick sort-of the right colour, with the intention of fixing it later. It gets left, until it is too late.

So, every colour you are going to use in QuarkXPress must be defined here, or be a shade of one you define here.

The top row offers ✤, for new colour, the pencil ✐ to edit a colour, and selections for frame ▣, text Ⓐ or background colour ☐. When a picture is selected, ☒ is picture colour

Below these, both at 100% in the example palette, are shade and opacity.

The third row, which is greyed out except for when a spot colour is selected, are knockout controls. These are either default ◔, or knockout ▰, or overprint ▰. Trapping is normally handled by the RIP immediately prior to the production of film or plate, so choke controls are not available.

The search pane is for searching in the palette only. If you type in Pantone, it will filter out everything which does not have the word Pantone in its name.

Below, you have the colours you have defined, with Black, None, White and Cyan, Magenta, Yellow as defaults. There is a CMYK icon at the side for CMYK colours. A target icon, representing the registration mark, denotes spot colours.

At the bottom, you have the eye-dropper ✐ panel.

A personal note:
If I were to pick just one feature which would be the pre-eminent reason why every communications department, every brand manager and every graphics bureau should specify QuarkXPress rather than its competitors, it would be the way it handles colours.

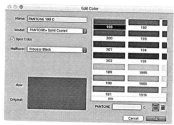

Above, Pantone colour edit. Below, Cmd/ctrl-clicking on an existing colour opens the colour list, where you can edit, duplicate and delete colours, and also import them from other projects.

Clicking on ✚, to create a new colour, or the pencil ✏ to edit a colour, opens up the Edit Colour box. You cannot edit the default colours.

The edit colour panel opens to CMYK by default, but you can also choose RGB, HSB, LAB, Multi-ink, DIC, Focoltone, the many kinds of Pantone specifications, TOYO, Trumatch, and web-named and safe colours.

If you are working to a brand specification enter the colours as given, with Pantone as your first choice, CMYK if Pantone is not given, LAB if CMYK is not given (unlikely), and only RGB or HSB as a last resort. If you have only been offered web-named colours, chances are that what you have been sent is not the full visual identity, but a reduced one for web-designers.

The colour editing panels are fairly self-explanatory, but do not be misled into picking colours from the colour wheels or swatches—these are there for confirmation purposes only. Unless your monitor has recently been calibrated to a very high precision, they are no more than approximations to the exact tones.

Note that you can choose Pantone colours and convert them to CMYK as you Export for PDF—although you can convert them in this box, there is no need to. You cannot convert CMYK back to Pantone if you later change your mind, or need to produce a two-colour job.

You can give a colour any name you like—it does not have to be the Pantone number.

If you click OK, you will return to the main colour palette.

Cmd/ctrl-clicking on any colour in the main palette opens the colour list window. Here you can create new colours or edit them, as above. You can also duplicate, delete, and append from another Quark project. Changes made here must be saved to have an effect. If you delete a colour, and it is in use in the layout, you will be asked what colour you want to replace it. Note that you can only select 100% colours, not shades, which is annoying if an imported file has created dozens of shades of grey.

1   Colour picker

New to QuarkXPress 2016, though picking up the functionality of an earlier Xtension, is the colour picker.

This is at the bottom of the colour palette. Its operation is very simple: choose the eye-dropper ✐, and click on anything which is in the QuarkXPress layout. This includes pictures, colour blends, even the colour of the guidelines. However, palettes and other interface elements which are not part of the layout cannot be used. Each colour appears in a candidate palette with fourteen slots. You can carry on clicking and the oldest ones will eventually disappear. To transfer a colour to the main palette, click the multi-coloured plus ⊞ at the right hand side. This opens up the Add Color dialogue, allowing you to specify the colour more exactly. Opt/alt-click adds the colour without this dialogue, and Opt/alt-shift-click adds all the colours.

If doing a one-off, photo-led job, or needing an organically harmonious palette, creating from a photograph has the advantage that, whatever the vagaries of your colour management process, your colours will harmonise with the photograph as it appears in the finished publication.

2   Proofing

Here is something important. If you turn View—Proof Output to anything other than 'None', the colours in your palette will change to represent what your Profiles think will happen when the colours are reproduced under that process. Actually knowing that your laser printer is going to make all the reds orange may not be very encouraging, but it can save a lot of headaches later. What's more, this applies in the colour edit and creation window, so, if desperate, you can choose new colours which better match what the results are supposed to be.

This does not apply to colours in the temporary eye-dropper area.

Above, the Conditional Styles palette, and, below, the Edit Conditional Styles panel.

7 Conditional Styles

Conditional Styles allow paragraph and character styles to be applied automatically and selectively to text based on conditions. They are very powerful, enable some extremely advanced formatting and automation, and are also the first place to look if your text is doing something strange and you don't know why.

The palette itself is simple enough—as with others, ✚ means new style, pencil ✐means edit style, and ⊚ means duplicate. Delete 🗑 is at the end, and all four of these are reproduced via the menu icon ▯ in the top right hand corner, under the cog ✱.(The cog is Mac-only.)

The main interest is in the create/Edit box:

The options are discussed on the facing page. Pressing + copies the selected line and places the new condition on the next line.

The conditional style sheet can be set to repeat at particular text, at a particular character, at a conditional style marker, or at every paragraph, or not at all.

Note that if you apply a conditional style and then turn the style off by clicking 'No Conditional Style', all the formatting remains as styled, but will not respond to changes in the text or the style sheet.

Using a Conditional Style as a Macro

Styles which are applied remain applied even if you then turn of the conditional style—provided that they are not over-ridden by a new conditional style. This means that if you can apply some general formatting to an entire document, and then turn off the conditional style and do more local formatting.

242   *Palettes*

Action	Style	Motion	#	Position	Marker	add del
Apply	Any style defined	Up to	1,2 etc	Cursor Position		-
				Conditional Style Marker		
				Character	A,7,*, etc	
		Through		Number	Any digit	
				Text	Any text	
				Number of Characters		
				Number of Sentences		
				Number of Words		
Go	[does nothing]	Backwards to		Beginning of the Sentence		+
				End of the Sentence	[Not used]	
				Beginning of the Paragraph		
		Backwards through		End of the Paragraph		
				Beginning of the Story		
				End of the Story		

Action—Apply or Go. This either applies a style sheet, or merely moves the point of activity somewhere else.

Style—Any character or paragraph style already defined.

Motion—Up to takes you up to but not including the Position Marker. Through takes you up to and including the Position Marker. Backwards to and Backwards through do the same, but in reverse.

#—the occurrence. This section has been formatted with a Body bold until em-dash Conditional Style. If the number were set to 2, it would look for the second em-dash to apply the style. Where the Position has no marker but a number, this number defines it.

Position—There are a number of options. A Conditional Style Marker only appears when View—Invisibles are turned on. Apply it with Opt-ctrl-| (Mac only) or Utilities—Insert Character—Special—Conditional Style Marker.

Marker—what marker is looked for. Character means any single character, Number means any string of digits, Text means any text string.

Right, combining Vertical Justification with Conditional Styles enables automation of this product box, where the lower part falls, correctly formatted, to the bottom of the box.

Product Name

Pompeii conubium santet Octavius. Cathedras negligenter corrumperet oratori, ut fiducias plane comiter miscere

Technobabble:

Tech 1	Text
Tech 2	Text
Tech 3	Text
Tech 4	Text

£The Price!

15   17   45   35

Hint, automate with conditional styles, turning the + to 0 opacity.

Above, the FF Chartwell fonts enable you to create graphs on the fly by typing in numbers, and these work well with conditional styles. But what if you also want to display the numbers and easily edit the chart? Shared text—see the next section, Content—with unsynchronised attributes, does just that—allowing you to have a Chartwell format and a numerical format automatically updating each other.

Content palette with text and layout files.

Shared item properties. This dialogue appears when you first create an item, or edit it. On editing, only the name can be changed—other options are fixed.

Above, the sharing box for a layout file or composition zone. Use the corner menu to add a composition zone (see Item—Composition Zones), and click Edit to bring up this window to make it shareable with others.

8 Content

The Content palette lets you share content between boxes, which could be images or text.

The icons across the top are unusual.

✚ is add. The next icon is import ⛫. I means insert ⧉, the pencil means edit ⟋, and the x icon unsynchronises all ⊠.

Begin by creating a box, typing something into it, and pressing ✚.

The Shared Item Properties opens. You can name your item, and then choose whether the box attributes are synchronised, whether the content is synchronised, and, if so, whether this includes content attributes, such as text formatting, or only the content.

Pressing OK saves this, and your named item now appears in the palette. If you click on the arrow, it shows you what it contains.

You can now use the icons to work on this. Clicking on the contents—ie, underneath the main item—you can import content into the box. If you now create another box, you can press the I icon to insert your content into it. Alternatively, just drag the contents from the palette onto the box, or drag the container onto the layout, which will create a box containing the content.

Any changes you now make will be reflected in every instance, with attributes according to what you chose. If you try to edit with the pencil tool, you will see that you can change the name, but the attribute choices you made on creation are now fixed.

You can make all the content independent by choosing the Unsynchronise All box. Changes will no longer be reflected in the boxes you already created, but you can still use the shared item to create new, synchronised boxes. Deleting, by contrast, removes the object from the sharing palette, leaving all text in place, unsynchronised. You can, of course, reshare one of those boxes. External Resources specified in the Job Jacket (see Part 4) will appear in this palette.

9 Content Variables

Content Variables are automatically generated short sections of text (though they will line-wrap, new in QuarkXPress 2016). The palette is self-explanatory, ✛ to add, pencil ✐ to edit, double-circle-arrow ⟲ to duplicate, an option to convert to text in the document ▨, and trash 🗑 to delete.

All of them update automatically. If you delete one, it converts everything to static text.

In use, drag the content variable into the text, or use Utilities—Content Variable and choose the one you want. There are various presets, and any that you have defined yourself. The content variables take any format you give them when used. Unlike Content, which has to be in its own box, Content Variables can be inserted into any text.

Clicking ✛ or edit ✐ opens the Edit Content Variable dialogue, and this is where the fun begins. You can also use Utilities—Content Variable—New.

Don't name your variable yet—it will offer a consistent name based on the type. Instead, click on Type, which brings up thirteen options.

Creation Date
Creation date allows you to specify the format and the order the document was first created. This is mainly useful as an internal audit tool: very few readers will be interested in when you pressed 'New' in QuarkXPress, and it will not take account of when the first draft was written on someone's iPad on the train from Tangiers to Casablanca.

Current Page Number
This gives the page number of whatever page it appears on. The result is the same as Cmd/ctrl-3 or Utilities—Insert Character—Special—Current Box Page #. In a Book, the page numbers will be ordered throughout unless you have specified otherwise by using Sections.

Custom Variable
A custom variable lets you combine several other variables with any text you define, for example, a Page reference fol-

Above, the Content Variables palette, with defaults, the running headers (or footers) for this book, and a couple of page references.

Use a systematic naming approach, which will allow the Search to display just the items you are interested in.

Above, the Edit Content Variable dialogue, showing the different types available

lowed by the Modification Date in brackets, for managing complex revisions.

File Name

The name of the File. You can choose whether or not to include the extension. If the file name is the title of the document, you can use File Name with the extension turned off to self-refer in the text, for example, this book is called QuarkBook-part 5.

Flow Box Page Number

If you have boxes which flow across several pages, the Flow Box Page Number allows you to define the previous page, as in 'Continued from Page 245' or the following page, as in 'Continued on Page 247'.

Last Page Number

The final page number of the project or section. Note that this is the page number as it would appear on that page, not the page count—if you have front matter numbered i, ii, iii etc, this will not add in those additional pages, though choosing 'section' rather than 'document' would mean that the last page number shown while in that section would be xvii, etc, rather than the end of the document. If you want to do a word processor style 'Page 17 of 49', which is handy when things are being passed around for meetings, make sure that you only have one kind of page numbering. In a Book, the number is the last page number of the current project, not the entire book.

Modification Date

The date the file was modified. You can specify the format.

Next Page Number

This gives the number of the next page in the layout, or in the section. If you choose 'section', and the current page is the end of the section, it will show <#> instead of a number—ugly, but potentially highly useful in finding out what has gone wrong with some monstrously complicated numbering system.

Output Date

The date on which the file was printed or exported.

Palettes

Page Reference

This allows you to reference an anchor ⚓ which you have created with Style—Anchor—New. The anchor can be in another document in the same project—especially useful in books, or when referencing sister publications. You can specify text that goes in front of or after it, such as 'See page <number> in Reference Sheet IV'. It will also allow you to create a hyperlink, which will be embedded into a PDF on export.

Previous Page Number

This is the number of the previous page. It works the same as Next Page Number.

Running Header

Running Header is not just for running headers. It looks at the first or last use of a particular style sheet on a page or spread—you choose which—or the most recent previous one if there is no example on the current page/spread, and inserts that as unformatted text.

Used judiciously, this can do many more things than merely putting a header or footer, like the one at the bottom of this page. You can use it for character or paragraph styles.

A word of warning—if the text is very long, QuarkXPress may take a long time to find and place it. You will probably decide it has crashed, and quit and restart it. It will get there eventually, but it probably isn't worth the wait.

Static Text

Static Text is anything you want to type in. It isn't actually static, as every use in the document will change if you change it. Very useful for things such as the name of a venue, the date of an event, and so on.

Index? List? Content variable? Cross-reference? Which should I use?

QuarkXPress offers several different ways of making your content intelligent. Knowing which to use can save a few headaches.

*Lists and Content variables can both address information based on the **Style Sheet** associated with it—Content variables to find the most recent usage, Lists to find all usages.*

*The Index relies on you **tagging** each occurrence you want to index, and it intelligently organises entries with the same tag as being the same thing (a list will list everything it finds separately).*

*Content variables can also find individual **anchors**.*

*Cross references allow you to refer to text by its **structure**, either Outlining or Foot/endnoting, and can quote text and context, or give a page or structural reference.*

Edit Footnote Styles

To footnote or endnote?
Footnotes interrupt the flow of
reading, endnotes are impossible
to find while reading.
Which is least bad?

To my mind, footnotes, if cor-
rectly formatted, are infinitely
preferable to endnotes. They add
to the rhythm of the page, lend
authority (or at least attribution)
to quotations and evidence, and
generally make everything feel
more cohesive. The only exception
would be notes which are more
than a page long—but, in that
case, they may be better organised
in some other way.

Journal articles may well have
two layers of footnotes, with the
larger text being additional (use-
ful) discussion, and the smaller
for abbreviated references.

10 Footnote Styles

Footnotes were introduced in QuarkXPress 2015, and the styles have been upgraded to satisfy user requests.

To insert a footnote, use Style—Footnotes/Endnotes—Insert Footnote (or endnote). There is a ridiculously complicated keyboard shortcut for this. On a Mac, if you are using a lot of footnotes, go to Preferences—Key Shortcuts and create a more sensible one, such as Cmd-`, or anything you find convenient.

To apply a style, just select the marker—ie, the *, or [1], and click on the style you want from the palette.

The styles palette operates as you would expect*. It's when you press ✛ to add or pencil ⁄ to edit that it gets interesting. Read on:

In **Edit Footnote Style**, first give your new style a name. Each style is for either footnotes or endnotes.[1]

You can use any **numbering style** you have defined. QuarkXPress 2016 has new numbering styles, set in Edit—Bullet, Numbering and Outline Styles, to reflect typographic practice, such as using *, **, †,††.

The **Marker Style** defaults to Superscript, but you can also have Subscript, or inherit from the Numbering Style.

You can set the **start number**, and you can also set numbering to **restart** never, each page, or each section, though this is only for footnotes.[2] [3]

---

* Except for the * icon, which is for a custom footnote. Sorry, couldn't resist doing this as a footnote.

Note |1 See side bar. If working with multiple types of footnotes, for example for a journal, make sure the fonts are distinctive.

Note |2 A couple of further thoughts on footnotes and endnotes. People who love endnotes and footnotes are by nature pedantic. Academics love them, as do journal editors. Designers may not love them—though, to my mind, footnotes, if well designed, lend magnificent typographic charm, and go well with a historic typesetting aesthetic. The novel Jonathan Strange and Mister Norrell by Susanna Clarke makes extensive use of footnotes for its fictional history.

Note |3 Footnotes and endnotes are placed within the text box, rather than underneath it. This is correct typographic practice, but it will mean that the useable length of the page is shortened. Footnotes work equally well for single column or multi-column text,

Palettes

Set the **Paragraph Style**[4] with any style you've defined[5]. This specifies the body of the note itself, including any character style and spacing.

The **Character Format** sets the text of the note number before the note itself. It defaults to Inherit from Marker Style, but you can set it to any character style you like.

You can prefix the number, but trailing spaces are not supported here. The same goes for the suffix—leading or trailing spaces are ignored. However, you can set a space separator of various kinds, and you can even have more than one—but non-spaces are ignored, and if you try to include them the space resets to \s, which is a regular space.

Finally, you can force the Endnotes to begin on a new page.

Endnotes, by default, appear at the end of text they relate to.

Now, at this point you are probably thinking: 'this is all very well, but where do I define the separator style?'

Separator Style

For the separator style, go to Edit—Footnote Styles and either edit the Default Footnote Separator Style, or choose New and use the dropdown menu to pick New Footnote Separator Style.

Here, you can define the spacing of the ruling line, and separately define the line style, width, colour, shade opacity and indents for the initial footnotes and footnotes which are continued on subsequent pages.

The **Endnote Separator style** is set by the Default Footnote Separator Style, and is not separately editable.

New in QuarkXPress 2016, you can create cross-references to footnotes with Style—Cross Reference—Insert.

Above, the Separator Style edit panel is in Edit—Footnote Styles.

You can cross-reference footnotes using Style—Cross Reference. This allows you to reproduce the entire text of a footnote elsewhere, or give its page or number reference. If you select 'include above/below' in the cross-references dialogue, it will be automatically insert whichever is correct of 'above' or 'below', depending on where your footnote is when you come to synchronise the cross-references.

To search for Footnote or Endnote reference markers in Find/Change, type \o. You can't use this marker to trigger Conditional Styles, though.

---

where the note is placed underneath the column.

Note |4 When pasting text, for example that began as body text and was relegated to the footnotes, use Edit—Paste Without Formatting, otherwise it will retain its original formatting, which is unhelpful.

Note |5 And, while we're commenting, you will see that once the footnotes reach a particular length, they move onto continuation footnotes, using the footnotes separator style of the first footnote, not that of subsequent footnotes.

11 Glyphs

Above, the Glyphs palette showing Stone Serif.

Below, Pfeffer Mediaeval offers numerous Open Type sets, including Historical Forms, which are not currently offered directly by QuarkXPress Open Type features.

The Glyphs palette offers you the entire font (or fount) to select characters from. It would be incredibly tedious to set text this way, but you could try a line or so of dragging (or double-clicking) from the Glyphs palette into the layout, and imagine that you are Peter Quentell in Cologne, 1525 with William Tyndale looking over your shoulder as you set the first printed Bible in English. If you have to set a few letters of text in a script unfamiliar to you, dragging them from the glyphs palette may be the best option.

Essentially, you choose your working font in the top drop-down menu, and then select either the Entire Font, Alternates for your current selection (if there are any), Special Characters, or a variety of other things depending on what features the font supports.

This includes Open Type sets which are not supported by QuarkXPress—which could be almost anything, as the Open Type specification allows non-standard sets to be created, even if no software can display them.

As you look at the glyphs, you will see a small triangle at the bottom right of some glyphs. This shows that alternates are available for that glyph. Alternatively, if you select a character in your text, choosing Alternates for Selection will show the alternate versions of that glyph in the font.

You can double-click a glyph, it will be inserted at the text cursor.

You can drag a favourite glyph, such as something your keyboard does not support, onto the Favorite Glyphs section at the bottom.

The magnifying glass ⊕ increases the size of the glyph and its grid. Below it, the ⊡ slider changes the proportions of the glyph within the grid, to help examining tiny features.

12 Grid Styles

You normally set the text grid for the entire document—if you are locking the text to a grid—when in the Master Pages mode in Page Layout, and using Page—Master Guides and Grids. However, if your design has two or more font sizes which are consistently used in different places, for example, the body text and the margin text in this book, you might want to have two separate lock-down grids.

You achieve this with Grid Styles, applied to individual text boxes. The functionality is the same as Page—Master Guides & Grids, but you can save as many styles as you want. Note that updating 'Normal' in this palette does not change what you have set on Page—Master Guides & Grids.

From the palette, click + or ∥ to open the Edit Grid Styles dialogue.

The main tab is Text Settings; Display Settings just specifies how the grid is displayed.

In Text Settings tab, specify your font size, its vertical scaling (which should be 100% for normal work) and the line spacing. It will then calculate the total leading. QuarkXPress's default is 20% additional leading, but you can change that in Preferences—Print Layout—Paragraph. You would normally set alternate leading as part of the Paragraph styles.

The Baseline Position section is how the baseline is calculated. This defaults to 25% above the Bottomline (ie, the lowest descender), but if you have settled on your font, you can Read From Font, which will calculate more accurately.

This only affects where QuarkXPress thinks the baseline is, not the actual spacing of the grid, which is set by the leading, above.

You can specify a baseline offset.

Finally, you can opt to lock your custom grid to the Paragraph Style Sheet Normal. This is helpful if you are going to create several grids and want to duplicate from one grid which matches your Normal.

Grid Styles palette, with the usual controls

Edit Grid Style—text settings

Edit Grid Style—Display settings

Above, the Guides palette lists and sorts every guide in the document. Below, the Guides menu.

13 Guides

You can drag ad-hoc guides from the rulers at the top and left of the screen at any time, and QuarkXPress 2016's dynamic guides, which appear when you drag or resize boxes, will take away much of the strain of getting things consistent. However, the Guides palette offers a great deal for guide management that is worth knowing about.

Two things to remember about the Guides palette:

First, it works on individual guides, per page, unlike the various Style palettes. Normally you would expect to set guides on Master Pages. However, if you want to make adjustments on particular pages or spreads, the Guides palette can do that.

Second, the additional menu ⊡ in the top right hand corner, underneath the cog ✲ (Mac only) is much more important than in other palettes, giving access to five separate dialogue panels.

1   The palette

The ✚ button adds a guide, as you would expect. The other icons across the top mirror the guides ⊞ (for a spread), show horizontal ⊟, show vertical ⫼, and show the current page guides only ⊡. There is also trash ⬤, for delete.

The next row is a click-to-sort set of columns.

Spread—sorts by spread.

Page—sorts by page. Double-click to open the edit panel.

Location—the vertical or horizontal position. Double-click to edit directly.

Colour—the display colour. Click and hold to select or create a new colour, using the System's colour setting tool. Note that these colours are not linked with your colour palette. The default is green, but you can change this in QuarkXPress—Preferences—Print Layout—Tools—Guides & Grid. New colours will have their RGB numbers, not names, and are not subsequently editable.

Palettes

Scale—the minimum view scale at which the guide is visible. Double click to edit.

Eye—👁 turn visibility on or of.

Lock—🔒 lock guide, unlock.

Page/Spread—⊞ click to confine to page, or take across spread (horizontal guides only).

Horizontal/Vertical—⊞ click to swap (careful here).

Generally speaking, create your guides as much as posable on Master Pages and lock them.

2 Guide Attributes

From the menu, or by double-clicking on the page number, you get to the Guide Attributes dialogue. We will look at the basic attributes here and refer back to them for the other dialogues.

Location—the location, in your default units, from wherever you currently have the origin point. This is by default the top-left hand corner of the page, but if you grab the corner of the main screen where the rulers meet, you can drag it anywhere. Ctrl-click/right-click on that corner opens up a contextual menu to set units and ruler direction, and opt/alt-click resets it to the default.

Direction—Horizontal or Vertical.

Type—Page or Spread.

Color—from the list, as in the palette (see above).

View Scale—minimum magnification to see this.

Locked—like it says.

Preview—allows you to see it before you agree it.

Add, Cancel, OK—you can add a guide and remain in this dialogue by choosing Add. Otherwise cancel or OK.

Below, the five dialogues available from the Guides corner menu: Guide Attributes, Grid, Rows and Columns, Guides from Box, and Bleed and Safety.

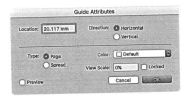

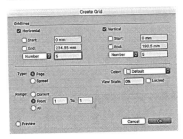

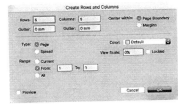

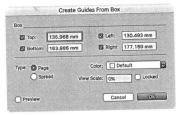

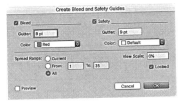

3 Create Grid

Create Grid opens an alternate dialogue which has the following extra features:

Horizontal and Vertical check boxes—switches on the controls for each.

Start—the position of the first guide.

End—the position of the last guide.

Number or Step—number of guides, QuarkXPress then calculates where they go, or step, and they are created up to the end point.

Range—you can specify on which pages they will appear.

Create Grid creates an evenly spaced graph-paper-like grid. If you want to create a page-design grid, unless you are a phenomenally hardcore member of the Swiss school of design, the Create Rows and Columns dialogue is likely to be better.

4 Create Rows and Columns

This is similar to Create Grid, but more useful for page design tasks.

Rows, Columns—set the number of rows and columns.

Gutter—set the gutters. You can, as in other dialogues, enter a mathematical expression, such as 6/85*210.

Centre within—Page Boundary or Margins. Margins would be the usual choice.

Other controls are the same as Create Grid or Attributes.

This would be the normal place to start if you wanted to create an underlying page grid.

5 Create Guides From Box

If you favour a more Dutch approach, where you create a page that looks aesthetically great and then make it the template for other pages (instead of calculating everything from mathematical aesthetics), then Create Guides From Box may be more what you are after.

In this case, first create a box where you want it to be, then open the Create Guides From Box dialogue from the corner menu. The measurements will be calculated automatically. You can turn the top, left, bottom or right lines off, but the simplest thing to do is to click OK, and your guidelines have been created.

6   Create Bleed and Safety Guides

The final type of Guides dialogue creates guidelines outside and inside the margins, and colours them appropriately. I have to say that I had been doing this for years by dragging the guidelines from the rulers, and only heard about this feature recently. A massive time saver.

Bleed—outside the page. This defaults to points, but 3mm is fairly standard.

Safety—inside the page. Again, 3mm is standard for trimmed paper, but for a book, which will be trimmed all at once, 6.35mm may be minimal.

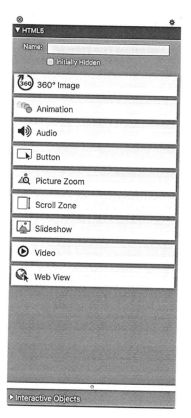

14 HTML5

For more on HTML5, see Part 3.

The palette is relatively straightforward. Name the object at the top, where you can also specify that it is initially hidden.

Even if you have no intention of using HTML5, you can still use this to name boxes, which will then appear in the Interactive Objects list at the bottom of the palette. In a complex document, this can help you quickly track down where crucial boxes are.

To preview, use the diagonal up arrow at the bottom left of the QuarkXPress screen. Note that previewing some of them from a print layout may cause unexpected results.

If you are familiar with web design, or even with creating animations in PowerPoint, most of the options will be self-explanatory.

360° image
If you have a correctly formatted set of images, this will allow you to load them, so that they automatically play a set number of times, and can then be navigated in a 360° fashion with the mouse or a finger.

Animation
The animation features should be familiar from PowerPoint animations.

Audio
Audio plays an audio file, either automatically or on-click, with or without a controller. It can play on loop or once through.

Button
A Button initiates one or more actions. Actions possible include navigation, playing or pausing an object, playing or pausing a sound file or animation, resting the page, taking a snapshot, opening a file, displaying or hiding a pop-up, and showing or hiding an object.

It's important to realise that a button does not have to look like a button to be an effective part of a layout. Putting a cube on screen, for example, encourages someone to click different sides of it.

Picture Zoom
Picture Zoom allows the user to pan or zoom an image, or to do so automatically using the 'Ken Burns' effect.

Scroll Zone
This makes the object the controller for scrolling to a new layout. You can either select a layout or create one.

Slideshow
This presents a standard slideshow with several options.

Video
This makes the object a video controller, either with embedded content, or URL content, or YouTube/Vimeo.

Web View
This offers a browser view of a file, web-page, or embedded image.

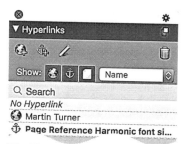

The Hyperlinks palette organises both hyperlinks and anchors. Where an anchor is used in a Content Variable, this is given in brackets after the name.

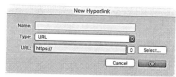

Choosing + opens the New Hyperlink dialogue. Give it a name. You can choose URL, Anchor or Page.

15 Hyperlinks

The Hyperlinks palette organises URLs and anchors.

URLs, of course, come from the web. QuarkXPress supports http:, https:, ftp: and mailto:. Naturally, you can use any additional parameters supported by the software that executes the URL. For example, mailto: can include instructions for the subject line.

The icons across the top are new URL ⊕, new anchor ⚓, edit ✐, and, delete 🗑.

On the next row, you can opt to display or hide URLs ⊕, Anchors ⚓ or Pages ▢.

Pressing the Globe+ button ⊕ opens the new hyperlink dialogue, which allows you to create hyperlinks, links to existing Anchors or Page links. Pressing the Anchor+ button ⚓ allows you to create an Anchor. You can equally create an Anchor in place with Style—Anchor—New.

Unlike Lists and Indexes, Anchors do not work across different projects in a Book.

16 Index

The Index is a powerful tool that replaces a job which might—in a long document—previously have taken someone weeks or months. Even so, the Index is not automatic: it does not produce a concordance of everything in the file. Each word to be indexed must be selected once, and it may need to be cross-connected to linked words.

Further, although the Index can be built across an entire book, each chapter must have the index words selected in it.

Hands on with indexes

To begin, select a word in the text. It automatically appears in the Text box in the Index palette.

Before you can do anything with it, you need to add it to the index, so, from the row of icons just above the word Entries, you can choose either ⬚ which adds that occurrence only, or ⬚ which adds all occurrences in the current project (though not in the rest of a book). ⬚ goes to the next occurrence. Adding all occurrences is usually the most convenient.

You can now mark the level at which the item occurs, and, optionally, specify that it should be sorted with a different term. You might do this if you wanted to sort typeface and fonts together.

Let's assume we pick the word 'font' to index, and add 'typeface'. For level, we choose First Level for 'font', and Second Level for 'typeface'. Additionally, we enter 'font' in the Sort As box for 'typeface'.

It's now time to go to the menu in the top right hand corner, underneath the cog, and choose 'Build Index'.

For now, we will choose Nested, the default, Replace Existing Index, and also select Add Letter Headings, for which we will give the *Paragraph title* style sheet, which is one we have been using in this book. We will assign B-Master B as the Master Page—often we would construct a special index page Master Page—and choose level styles of *Body text*, which is the text you are reading, and *Margin text*, which is the style we have used for the margins. Choose OK.

The following appears (if we only have those two index entries defined), on a new page after the final document page.

F
font 153, 154, 170, 180, 183, 184, 194, 195, 199
typeface 192

The F is the Letter Heading we added.

The 'font' entry has page numbers from this project only (we have not yet defined it in the other projects that make

Above, the Build Index command is in the top right corner menu.

Tidying the index
Although the text of the index will need to be analysed and improved manually, you can go a long way to tidying it using Conditional Styles. For example, if you want every headword to begin with a capital letter, you can create a character style with All Caps turned on, and use a Conditional Style to apply this only to the first letter of each entry. This can save hours of manual tidying.

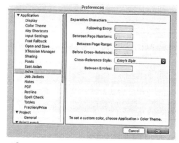

Why a computer-generated index is only the beginning
Computers are by their nature exhaustive. QuarkXPress can (and will) automatically search for every instance of a word. However, this produces data, not information. If you look at the index of a well-produced academic book from the 1940-70s, for example, FM Stenton's Anglo-Saxon England, you will see that the selection of indexed words is relatively streamlined, being almost entirely proper nouns. An example is:

Durham, 602; see of, 659, 660 n., 665, 666 n.; foundation of cathedral 435; monks introduced into, 678 [...] bps of: see Æthelwine; Ealdhun; Walcher; William.

However, this does not list every occurrence of the word 'Durham'. For minor figures, on the other hand, who are only mentioned in footnotes, all occurrences are given. The scope of the index changes with its content. While QuarkXPress will find all the occurrences and list them, it is for the editor to turn this into a true index.

up this book). It is in the *Body text* style; 'typeface' has been sorted in with 'font', in the second level *Margin text*. On its own, this is sufficient to build a complete index, if you go through and identify all your key words.

Every indexed entry is marked in the text with red markers ⌊-entry-⌋. You can change the marker colour in QuarkXPress—Preferences—Color Theme.

Going deeper
An **entry** can be one word or several. Each entry also has one or more **references**. It's important to keep this in mind, because otherwise the editing options make little sense.

The part of the palette marked 'Entry' refers to the overall keyword—or text, as it can be more than one word.

The part of the palette marked 'Reference' refers to a specific occurrence of that Entry.

If you go to your entry in the list, and click on the triangle so that it points down, a list of all the actual references will come up.

Click on one of these, and click edit ✎. You can now change the Reference's style, and also the Scope.

The default scope is the page number, but you can suppress the page number for that Reference, or you can extend it to any number of paragraphs, for example because you know that the index item introduces a twelve paragraph topic. You can even have it give a range to the end of the story or the layout. When you have finished, click pencil ✎ to apply it. The page number should change (or disappear). Click the pencil ✎ a couple more times if it doesn't.

Additionally, for a reference, you can point it to a different key word, using Cross-Reference.

Indexes can be nested or run-in. Nested indexes can go four levels deep, run-in just two levels, in the same paragraph. With nested, the paragraphs are separate.

If you Opt/alt-click on the ⊞ or ⊞, it creates a reversed entry with a comma, so that William Caxton becomes Caxton, William.

Palettes

17 Item Styles

Item styles take some or all of the attributes of the selected box and create a style from them. Like paragraph and character styles, you can change all of the boxes of a particular style in one go subsequently, though if you have adjusted them, for example by reshaping, the parameters you have adjusted will not be changed.

Unlike paragraph styles, when you create a style from a box, only certain parameters will be copied—but you can copy all of them by Cmd/ctrl-clicking on the style or pressing pencil ✏ for edit. This opens up a tabbed dialogue.

Essentially, each of those tabs mirrors the parameters set in the equivalent Measurements panel tab. You can turn any of them on or off—they begin by being mostly off except where you have specifically set an attribute, for example in the Measurements panel. If you turn one on, it will take whatever parameter it can deduce from the box you are making it from.

If this sounds complicated, it's actually very simple in use. Make your box, set it up the way you want, click ✚ in the palette, and name your new box. If you prefer, you can base it on another box (which will override what you've specified for this box) and the box will update with its inherited settings when you change the other box. In this way, you can have a structured set of boxes which self-update as required.

This is a good way of managing a lot of common settings, such as standard insets for text boxes, a standard corner radius, setting images to be at 100%, or setting a particular offset for the image. You can even set the position of the box, for example with Item Styles for column 1, column 2 or column 3 which automatically places boxes correctly.

Cmd/ctrl-clicking brings up the Item Styles Edit list (also Edit—Items), where Item Styles can additionally be exported and imported.

Note that some settings override each other. For example, you cannot specify corner shape and corner radius.

Above, the Item Styles palette. ↻ *resynchronises the styled items. Below, the Box parameters.*

Below, Item Styles edit list. You can import here, or, for one item, just paste a box from elsewhere.

18 Layers

By default, objects in QuarkXPress stack over each other like pieces of paper and photographs pasted onto each other on a sheet of paper. Just as you would with a paste-up, you can move things to the front or back, or shuffle them up and down, but moving a lot of stuck together pictures and scraps of text is tedious and gets confusing.

Layers goes beyond that idea by allowing you to put things on different layers. You can make layers visible or invisible, printing or non-printing, locked or unlocked, and you can move things between layers.

As usual, the ✚ icon creates a new layer.

The diagonal down arrow icon ⊟ moves the selected object to a different layer—once you press it, you then specify which layer it is.

The two-box icon ⊟ merges layers.

Double-click on a layer to edit it. As well as locking, visibility and output, you can control whether text on a lower layer runs around an object on a higher layer, and set the colour and name of the layer. Visible layers are shown in the dialogue with the eye 👁 and locked layers with the padlock 🔒.

Below: layers attribute box. The colour you set for the layer will then be used for the (non-printing) item outlines on that layer.

19 Lists

Lists are automatically generated tables of contents and other similar lists, based on what style sheets are in use. They can be formatted to provide just a plain list, or a list with page numbers before or after. The lists are also structured, so you can have different levels, and different formatting for each level, or even for items based on a different style sheet within a level.

Lists can apply to the current layout, or to an entire book.

To create a list, choose the ✛ icon. The Edit List dialogue then appears.

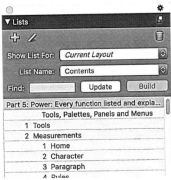

Above, a list used to generate a Table of Contents.

On the left of this dialogue you have a list of all your defined styles. On the right is a pane which is initially empty. Double click on a style to move it across, or use the arrow icons between the two panes.

Once inside the right hand pane, the style sheets will be listed in alphabetical order. However, this is not the order they will appear in the list. To set that, used the Level column, using the up/down arrow to increase or decrease the level, with 1 being the top level.

You can then number them text...Page#, Page#...text, or just text.

In the final column, you specify the style they are going to appear as. It's worth making a special Table of Contents (or ToC) style. When using page numbering, QuarkXPress inserts a single tab, which you can format using a paragraph style. Without formatting, the result will be haphazard.

Normally the items will appear in the order they are in the document, with whatever level styling you have set. Alternatively, you can have them appear in alphabetical order, giving a gazetteer of headings.

Press OK.

Back in the lists palette, Update synchronises the list with the document. Build inserts the list into whichever text

Tables of Contents

Like the Index, an automatic table of contents is only the beginning of the story, at least for a printed book. While Kindles and ePubs will be very happy to make use of your exhaustive and unaltered list, a book table of contents deserves rather more attention. Who is it for? What is it doing? It's not unusual to see the table of contents for a business book to go on for seven pages. But is this really useful? If at all possible, the main table of contents should show you the entire book at a glance. This will almost certainly require careful layout, using the automatically created list as a starting point. Needless to say, elaborate reworking of the table should only take place once the pages are more or less fixed—just as it always was in the pre-computer days of book production.

If a one page table does not do justice to the book, it may be worthwhile having an alphabetised gazetteer to supplement it, as well as additional back matter.

frame is currently selected. If none is selected, Build will be dimmed.

Lists are highly useful for a number of tasks.

As well as a table of contents, you can use a list of all headings to create the skeleton of a document summary.

You can also use lists to navigate round a document. Clicking on a list item in the palette will take you there.

If exporting for ePubs and Kindle, it is possible to set a list as the Table of Contents, rather than using the article names. This is useful if you have a book with chapters rather than separate articles.

You can list all the figures or illustrations as a separate list.

If you are checking a document, you can mark revisions with a character style, for example in red, bold, and then have a list of where they are created automatically.

Finally, lists can be layout-wide or book-wide, enabling you to keep a running list which encompasses separate chapters.

20 Page Layout

One of the oldest features in QuarkXPress—and among the most useful—is the Page Layout palette. Every page in the document is shown, and you can move the pages around, delete them or create new ones. Additionally, you access the Master Pages from here, and from them a number of options otherwise not available.

Clicking on the four icons at the top does nothing at all: you have to drag them. Normally you would drag them into the Master Pages area, but you can drag them onto the main, numbered page area if you prefer.

The flat sheet icon ⬜ creates a blank non-facing page. The folded corner icon ⌂ creates a facing page—it will automatically change its margins in the layout if put on the left or the right to match the page margins.

The double sheet icon ⬚ duplicates—but only in Master Pages. The down arrow icon ⬇ creates a new section.

1 Master Pages

The power of Page Layout is in the Master Pages.

In a new document, A-Master A is created automatically. You can add other masters by dragging the single sheet ⬜ or facing pages ⌂ icons into the Master Page area.

Double-click A-Master A to go to that page. If you have created a single side document, you are faced with just one page. If you have created a facing pages document, you will be looking at a double page spread. The margins will be whatever you set them to when creating the document.

After creating the document, it is only in Master Pages that you can change the document margins (with Page—Master Guides & Grid).

If Guides are not currently visible, press F7 to turn them on. You should now see your page margins.

Anything you put onto the Master Page will appear on every page you create using that Master Page. If you then edit that thing (box, guideline, etc), it becomes static and will not be updated, but if you leave it unedited, it will change with the Master Page. You can change this behaviour in QuarkXPress—Preferences—Print Layout—General.

You can use **Layers** on the Master Page, which is highly useful if you have a set of guidelines and boxes which you never want changed—for this, lock the layer—and others which are optional. If you are working on a shared project, you can also have an instructions layer, with output turned off, which the other users can switch on and off in the Layers palette as they work on the page.

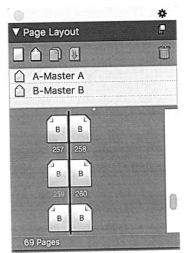

Above, the Page Layout Palette.

Below, the Left Master Page for this book, showing the margins (darker lines) and the page grid, as well as the running footer and the page number. The chain link in the top left is unbroken, meaning that the text automatically flows from page to page. The Right Master Page mirrors the left.

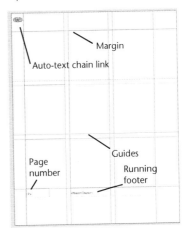

QuarkXPress—Preferences—Print Layout—General allows you to change the behaviour of Master Page edits.

Auto page insertion

On the Master Page, there is either a broken chain link or an unbroken one in the top left hand corner. This is on both pages of a spread. If the link is unbroken, it means that text that overflows from your main text box will automatically create a new page. If it is broken, this Auto page insertion is off. In a new document, this reflects the decision you made in the New Document Layout dialogue.

You can use the **Link** tool to link a broken chain to any empty text box on the page, and this will then cause reflowing text to create new pages. You can use the **Unlink** tool to break this.

You can have any links on the page you want. For example, you can have the automatic text chain flow through as many boxes as you like. Equally, you can link another set of boxes together, though you can't have these auto-create new pages.

Content variables

Content variables are especially suited for use on a master page. These include page numbers, running headers, last page numbers (for the '37 of 82' page numbering format), modification date for document control purposes, output date and file name. Typographically speaking, the less extraneous matter there is in the headers and footers, the better. However, for many corporate and technical documents, version control is more critical than aesthetics.

Shared content

Shared content can also appear on master pages. A company logo may need to be consistent throughout a document. You can also use Shared Content for the document title or a version number in a header or footer. This may be a better solution than a Content Variable because you can then change it from any page, and it will all update together.

Master Guides & Grid

At other times greyed out, Page—Master Guides & Grid is active when you are working in a Master Page. It combines two things: the margin and column guides, using the same method which you used in the New Layout or New Project command, and the grid controls, which are similar to Palette Grid Styles (see above). There are a couple of refinement here.

For Margin Guides, you can lock the top and bottom and the left and right (or inside and outside).

For Grids, there is an additional button for Adjust, and a button for Load Settings.

Adjust takes us to a new dialogue where you can nudge the settings and QuarkXPress will calculate the lines between the top and bottom margins that this produces, based on your Master Page size and margins, as set in the previous dialogue. If Preview is on (from the main dialogue), you can see these adjustments change as you nudge.

Load Settings allows you to load the settings from any other Master Page, any Paragraph Style, and any Grid Style.

Grid tricks
If you have set up a page grid for boxes, you might be relaxed enough to let running type fall where it may, but want to avoid major titles falling just off a major grid position. You can set up in **Grid Styles** a specific style which only allows a title to fall at particular places. You would leave most pages set to your Master Grid, but when a particular problem page arose, you would just click on the grid style to fix it.

21 Profile Information

The Profile Information palette offers some simple information about an image—bit depth and colour space, as well as allowing you to read its built-in profile, and reassign it (careful here), as well as to set the rendering intent. You can also specify whether the file will be colour managed by QuarkXPress, or simply pass-through its own colour profile.

For most images that have come from a camera, you will not want to change the settings unless somehow they have got lost or been incorrectly changed elsewhere. If the image

Above, the Master Guides & Grid dialogue is only available when working in Master Pages. The upper part is the same as in the New Layout command.

The lower part is essentially the same as the dialogue in Grid Styles, but with the addition of Lines within Margin... Adjust. This opens the dialogue shown below.

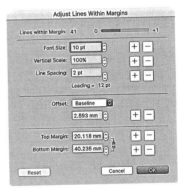

Adjusting Lines within Margins.

was generated by software, for example 3D rendering or a natural media paint application, perhaps on a smart device, it may have no profile attached to it at all. In that case, the final RIP will let the values pass through—which, chances are, will not represent what was on the screen when the image was created. For normal work, if there is no profile, assign sRGB, unless you have the calibration for the monitor in which it was created, in which case use that.

Rendering intent is usually best left on Perceptual, unless there is a good reason to change it.

22 Redline

Redline offers a simple set of controls for tracking and high-lighting changes, as you might find in a Tracked Changes Microsoft Word document.

To use it, you must turn Tracking on in Utilities—Redline, or by clicking the Track Changes button ▣ which is the left-most icon. Once on, you can turn Highlighting on ▣ (second icon) to see what changes there are. The next two icons move you backwards ▣ or forwards ▣ to the next change. You can then accept ▣ or reject ▣ changes, with a choice of all or current. The options ▣, at the end, allow you to specify what is highlighted.

23 Reflow Tagging

Reflow Tagging is used to prepare for Kindle or ePub publication, though you can use it in a Print layout if you are not intending to do a special ePub layout.

Kindle and ePub devices vary greatly in what formatting they support, mainly based on the age of the device or the app. At the simplest, to export for ePub or Kindle there must be at least one Article (even if it is actually a book length running text, it is still called an 'Article'). Reading will follow this article page by page, even on the simplest devices.

More advanced formatting is available for digital layouts using the HTML5 controls.

The palette has three functions.

First, you can assign one or more stories to be articles, and give them useful names (📑 icon and pencil ✏), as well as changing their order in the document, using the ↑ up and ↓ down arrows. You can also use Layout—Add Pages to Reflow to add pages.

Second, you can assign Components, such as a graphic or a text box to Articles, using the 🖼 button. You can also rename these with the pencil tool and move them with the arrows.

Third, you can map paragraph styles in your document to paragraph styles you are going to use in the ePub, using the ¶ icon.

The other icons highlight articles as you click on them, and rebuild the story.

Once you've added an article and perhaps a component, you are ready to export as an ePub, using the File—Export—Layout as ePub. What the result is will depend on what you are going to read it on. However, for a quick export of a narrative book, you can get an immediate idea. See the Digital section for more information on taking this further.

The Reflow tagging palette, above, is used to control reflow in ePubs and Kindles. For an explanation of how to use it, see Part 3.

24 Scale

The Scale palette, which replicates the Item—Scale dialogue, appears to be a simple tool to set scale, either as a percentage of the existing scale, or by typing absolute measurements. Underneath are calculations showing the original and scaled size, and a button which enables you to scale an entire layout (careful with this) rather than just a box. The measurements are normally connected by the chain icon 🔗, but if you click on this, you can rescale disproportionately.

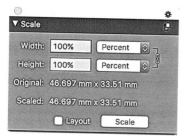

Above, the scale tool seems re-markably simple.
Below, accessed from the top-corner menu, under the cog, the settings are rich and powerful.

Below, the available settings:
Scale Text
  Allow Horiz./Vert. Scale
  Scale Paragraph Attributes
  Scale Entire Text Chain
  Scale Style Sheets
Scale Physical Text Box
Scale Runaround Outsets
Scale Text Box Insets
Scale Text Box Gutters
Scale Anchored Boxes
Scale Physical Picture Box
Scale Pictures
Scale Frame Width
Scale Line Length
Scale Line Width
Scale Contents of Empty Box
Try to Keep Relative Position
Scale to Item's Centre
Scale to Physical Table
Scale Table Grid

It's only when you click on the palette menu ⊡, that you see the scale settings.

Scale Text—specifies whether or not to scale the text with a box, and, if so, whether to allow distorted scaling if the overall box proportions change, whether to scale paragraph attributes such as indents, whether to scale an entire text chain, and whether to scale style sheets.

If scaling a layout, this means that you can effectively recreate a document in another format in the confidence that your typographic integrity remains.

The other options are self-explanatory, allowing you to scale all of the size-driven parameters of text and picture boxes.

If you have been using Item Styles in conjunction with your Paragraph and Character Styles, this means that you can rescale an entire document with just a few operations. The Try to Keep Relative Position will also ensure that less tidying up is required.

The Width/Height values are persistent if set to percentages, so that you can quickly apply the same scale to several items. If set to units, they will recalculate to give the same degree of scaling, rather than the same final size.

25 Style Sheets

Paragraph and Character style sheets are critical to consistent typography. The actual controls in them are explained under the Measurements panel, Character and Paragraph tabs. This section will look at how the style sheets work, aside from the formatting aspects.

The palette itself is straightforward: ¶+ or A+ creates, respectively, new paragraph and character styles, the pencil ⟋ edits, the ⊕ icon duplicates, ⟲ updates the style to match the selected text (can have unwelcome effects), and the trash ⊟ deletes.

Palettes

Option-clicking on a style marked with +, to indicate that the current text deviates from its style, restores the selection or paragraph to its styled state. Ctrl-click/right-click or using the corner menu offers a much broader range of choices for updating styles or text.

Cmd/ctrl-clicking opens up the Styles dialogue, which, in addition to the options here, allows styles to be imported with Append.

How styles work
When you create a paragraph style, a panel appears which contains:

Add shortcut

Based on:

Next Style:

Character Style:

Add shortcut allows you to create a shortcut key, such as F9 for Body text. This is useful when quickly formatting long text, and overrides defaults.

Based on is the style sheet that the new style sheet is going to follow. If based on 'Normal', then when you edit the Normal style, your new style will change as well, except for the things that you have altered from the normal style. If coming from digital, you will recognise this as the same concept as Cascading Style Sheets. This allows you to control all the typography of a document consistently.

Next Style specifies the style sheet that will automatically be applied when you press the return key while in that paragraph. For a title, for example, you might well want to have the next style Body Text rather than itself. Body Text, on the other hand, would want to be followed by more Body Text.

Character Style allows you to apply a previously defined character style sheet, make a new one, or, with 'default', just make some ad hoc changes that go with this paragraph style sheet. If you change your mind later and want a char-

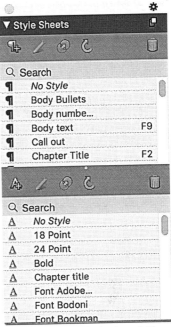

Above, Paragraph (top) and Character (bottom) style sheets are always connected in the same palette. Use the dot at the top of the Character icons section to show more or less of one or the other. The corner menu (top right, underneath cog) reveals a complete set of options for creating and applying paragraph and character styles, for returning text to a style, and for updating the style to match the text.

+ by a style name shows that the current text is of that style but has been altered. Opt/alt-click restores it to the styled format. Cmd/ctrl-click opens the Style Sheet dialogue, which also allows for importing style sheets with Append.

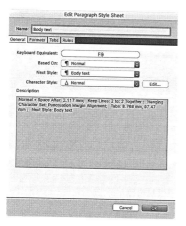

Above new paragraph style, below new character style.

acter style with that format, you can come back here and choose 'new'.

If you create a new Character Style, either here or directly from the menu, a panel opens up, and the first three lines are similar to what we just looked at: **Keyboard Equivalent** allows you to assign a key, and **Based on** allows you to follow another character style. Note that if you choose 'based on', any changes you had made to this dialogue will be replaced by what you are basing it on.

The rest of this dialogue offers you controls which are in the Measurements—Character panel. Note that the language is set here, rather than on a document-wide or paragraph-wide basis. You can set the entire document language, or change one language into another (for example, US to International English while keeping French the same) with Utilities—Convert Project Language.

Changing the format

Changing the actual formatting is relatively straightforward. In Character Style, all of the controls appear in a single dialogue.

In Paragraph Styles, you have four panes. The first one, where you establish the paragraph style, we have already looked at in part. As well as the decision controls about what it is based on, what the next style is and what the character sheet is, it will show you a summary of what the paragraph style contains. In an unstructured paragraph style, where it is based only on defaults or an example paragraph, there will be a long list. For a structured paragraph, based on another style, it will show something like "Normal+Left Indent: 3mm".

If you want to streamline your document and maximise consistency, it is best to use structured paragraph styles as much as possible.

The next three tabbed panels are Formats, Tabs and Rules.

It is generally fairly convenient to go through the Formats in the paragraph dialogue. They are the same as in Measurements: Paragraph.

It is often better to use the Measurements: Tabs and Rules to set those attributes, as you can see the effect as you work. Afterwards, update the style to suit with ℒ.

Space Before/Space After versus Lock to Grid

Setting before and after spacing is a fundamentally different design aesthetic from working to a text grid.

Traditionally, narrative text was set with indented first lines and no extra space between lines. This is not consistently Renaissance practice, but it was well established in 20th century printing. Typewriters, though, often used a space between lines, being an extra carriage return. Word Processors followed this practice, with the default style usually expecting two hard returns instead of providing a first line indent. Web-based design—and the user interfaces of most software—use an improved version of the typewriter style, with a spacing between paragraphs which is more than the inter-line, but less than an extra hard-return.

Aesthetically, provided you don't use both at once, you will not be incorrect (there are Renaissance and medieval examples of using both, though).

Locking to Grid is the complete version of the Swiss school of typography, which insists on identical frames on every page, and the text falling at exactly the same place on every page. This means that all baselines must fall in exact multiples, so there can be no smaller gaps between paragraphs. In other words, locking to Grid will override your space before and space below settings. However, if you have varying space before/space after settings for different types of typography, for example because bullet points want a little more room to breathe, or to give titles an appropriate spacing, and you then, retrospectively, decide to lock everything to the grid, the text will look okay for most of the way, and then suddenly hop, where a title is preceded by a bullet or some such at the end of the previous section.

What should you do? There is no doubting the beauty of a truly consistent grid layout. However, in the real world, you may be doing violence to your photographs (which are also the work of an artist) by forcing them into bad crops,

Above, the Paragraph formats tab. All the controls here are available in Measurements: Paragraph, but it is generally more convenient to work through them here as a set. Note that Drop Caps will create a dropped cap in the paragraph's character style sheet. For Renaissance dropped caps, create a separate character style and apply with Conditional Style sheets.

and making nonsense of your charts and technical diagrams. Also, to web-accustomed eyes, the inter-paragraph spacing looks more natural.

The bottom line is that you should let the work dictate the form. Just be aware that switching from one to the other mid-job can create inconsistencies that will only come up occasionally, and will be hard to track down.

Widows and Orphans, With Next

A single line at the top of a page looks bad. Called an orphan, this, and widows, which are the less bad single lines at the end of a page, can be controlled with the 'Keep Lines Together' settings. Likewise, titles need to be immediately above the text they refer to, not widowed at the bottom of the previous page. For this, the 'Keep with Next' setting is perfect. If you combine the two, though, especially if you set all text in paragraph to be kept together, you can get into situations where all text suddenly disappears, because there are no conditions in which it can reflow correctly.

You may be confident that you will never allow this to happen. However, if you are working on a draft document in which you insert all the titles with the intention of returning later to put in the text, then this is exactly what is likely to happen. The moral is, if your text disappears, check first your Keep Together and Keep with Next settings. If that fails, you may have pasted in a table or box which is too big for its container, and will thus never reflow.

26 Table Styles

For Inline Tables only—being tables which are edited in the source application, such as Excel, and then formatted by style in QuarkXPress—table styles offer a highly consistent and convenient solution to a vexing problem.

As mentioned earlier, although tables have been in word processors and DTP applications for years, they are never as convenient as working in a spreadsheet, where you can have an infinite number of new cells without having to think about making a new row and fitting the text in. Ta-

Above, below, the tabs (left) and rules (right) tabs are more easily set by changing a paragraph with Measurements: Tabs and Measurements: Rules and then updating the paragraph style.

Palettes

bles are most often supplied as Excel these days. Even if they are not, they can be rapidly imported into Excel.

When creating the table, you can set it to be linked with a style, as we saw in Tools: Table Tool. This is where you create and manage those styles.

The style palette itself is very simple: ⊞ creates a new style, pencil ✏ edits it, ✎ duplicates and trash 🗑 deletes.

It's when we create or edit a style that the complexity emerges. Below, we will try to format a simple table about potential holiday destinations in a well-known world.

	Population	Weather	Peoples	Government	Economy
Mordor	1.2 million	Dire	Orcs, trolls	Monarchy	Predatory
Gondor	.9 million	Variable	Humans	Stewardship	Agriculture
Shire	.05 million	Temperate	Hobbits	Elected	Cash-crops
Rohan	.7 million	Bracing	Humans	Monarchy	Horses
Lorien	Unknown	Autumnal	Elves	Unclear	Sylvan
Moria	.3 million	Subterranean	Orcs, Trolls	Anarchic	(was Mining)
Erebor	.1 million	Majestic	Dwarves	Monarchy	Crafts
Celebdil	0	Arctic	Wargs	None	None
Fangorn	.5 million	Sylvan	Ents, Trees	Entmoot	Tree-herding

The file is imported as Excel.

Opening the Edit Table Style, the first thing to do is to set the default style. This involves setting the indents (cell padding ▤ ▤ ▤ ▤ and the paragraph style—only paragraph styles are allowed, not character styles (these are contained within the paragraph styles). 2 pt cell padding all round, no lines, and Small Labels as the paragraph style.

Exiting, we take a quick look at what has been produced. The table now is reasonable in its space, but not especially clear.

We now go back to editing, and use +, underneath the light coloured pane, to create a new condition. This will be based on the Default. We choose 'Header Row' as the condition. We are now going to give this a background colour as

Table Styles palette

- ⊞ No Table Style
- ⊞ Default
- ⊞ Inline Table Style
- ⊞ New Table Style
- ⊞ Inline Table Style 2
- ⊞ Table of tables

Above, the Table Styles palette is simple enough.

Below, the Edit Table Style is not.

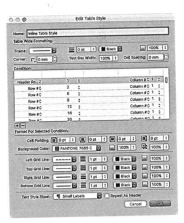

When setting tables styles, the controls are largely self-explanatory (see Measurements: Table), but the 'conditions' are somewhat hard to grasp.

*They are, from top to bottom, in the order best to work in (helpfully)—set the **Default** before you start on them.*

All Even#; All Odd#
—Choose row or column, and odds or evens are affected.

Every x Columns/Rows format y
—This is easier to grasp if you say it out loud: 'every three rows, format one row', or 'every two columns, format three columns'.

Row y, Column x
—This is confusing because it begins with 'Row', but you can choose 'any' or 'last' for either— these are at the top of the selection menus, above 1.
—This one is the most general: you can format any cell specifically, though you can only format a range if it is 'any' or 'last'.

Header Row y, Column x
—Format this one last, as you'll want to override any other formatting with the headers. You can choose 'any' both for row and column. For this to do anything, you have to have selected 'include header rows' and given a number when importing the Excel file. If you didn't, it is easy enough to import it again.

Black, at 39% opacity, and a Text Style Sheet of Margin Text. We'll also change the cell padding a little.

Next, we will create a Row# condition. This is slightly misleading, because it is the condition which gives complete control. In the second column, scroll up the numbers until you get to 'Any', and choose that. By Column, choose 1. We'll now assign that Small Labels Bold. By starting with the Header Row already highlighted, we've also copied over the 39% opacity. This now gives us the left hand side.

Finally, we'll create a new Row# condition, for which we'll take row 4, column 4, and set the opacity darker.

The result looks a bit cramped, so we'll go back and add in Cell spacing, at the top, for the entire table of .353 mm. We could also add a frame, though, to my mind, frames look cheap and word processor unless required by the layout.

With a table this size it isn't necessary to put in shaded columns (and anything unnecessary should be avoided), but we could do so by taking the Every… option.

However, if we try that, to see how it looks, we hit a problem. If we choose *Every 2 columns Format 1 column*, it overrides our *Row Any, Column 1* setting: the styles stack from the bottom, and the newest, those on top, override the lower ones. For this reason, do the most general formatting first, and go on to specifics last. Also—know when to stop: once a table is sufficiently clear, it becomes only more cluttered if more features are added to it.

27 Welcome Screen

The Welcome Screen, Mac only, is a visual display that gives you an easy route to App Studio, Designpad (for iPad), the public Facebook page, Twitter feed, and also takes you straight to where the documentation is hidden on your drive.

4 Menus

This section describes and comments on the Menus briefly. Where possible, it references explanations elsewhere.

The Menus are more or less the same in both Mac and Windows versions. If you can't find a menu element, go to Help—Search.

1 QuarkXPress (Mac)

With the exception of Preferences (below), these items are in the Help menu on Windows.

About QuarkXPress—opens the About Screen which gives Licence Code, version number and build number. Tech support may want to know this.

Edit License Code—allows you to change your licence code.

Check for Updates—forces checking for updates now.

Quark Update Settings—goes to the settings for Quark Update, an external application.

1 Preferences (for Windows: Edit—Preferences)

The Preferences are extensive. Some refer to the project currently open, some to the application as a whole. If you want to make project-specific settings the default, close all documents and then make the changes. This also applies to all other menu items which are not greyed out when no document is open.

Display—sets the Pasteboard width, allows you to add the Pasteboard colour in Trim view to the colour theme (below), allows you to make Text boxes opaque during editing, and sets the computer monitor colour profile.

Colour Theme—allows you to create new colour themes (Mac), redefining most of the interface. This does not affect your palette of print colours. On Windows you can select pre-defined colour themes.

Many of the Preferences reflect specific workflow needs that will be irrelevant to some designers, but enormously useful to others. If you are thinking 'if only QuarkXPress did this', or 'if only it would work like that', check the preferences: there may be exactly what you are seeking already there.

Pro-tip—to find the shortcut for an item on a Mac, use Help—Search, which will show you the item and also its shortcut key. This will be updated automatically to whatever you have defined.

Key Shortcuts (Mac)—allows you to define any menu command, measurements palette command, text formatting command and some others with a particular shortcut key. It's helpful to have a couple of keys which you keep reassigning based on the task at hand. For example, on a Mac, Cmd-~ is an easy control to assign for combining boxes in a table, assigning a particular size when formatting boxes, and so on.

You can save your choices as sets.

Input Settings—selects the type of smart quotes and turns them on or off, sets the Page Range separators for specifying sequential and non-sequential pages (by default, '-' and ','), sets keyboard controlled drag-to-zoom, allows or disallows drag-and-drop text, and turns maintaining picture attributes on and off while importing.

Font Fallback—sets whether or not to fallback to other fonts if characters are not present, how far to search for an active font in that case, and which fonts to use per language if no active font with that character is found. This only works for scripts that QuarkXPress knows about. If you enter the Runic character ᚠ (for Gandalf, or grand?) and the current font does not support it, even specifying a fallback font that does support it will not work, as Runes are marked in Unicode as language: none. Also sets the slug line (text outside the registration marks giving file name, output date, etc).

Open and Save—sets the all-important auto-save and auto-backup, and its location. If you have deleted preferences because you are having trouble, make sure you go back to turn this on immediately—these are things that get you out of trouble. Also sets the auto-library save and whether to maintain its position, and (somewhat oddly) the script language for non-unicode support.

Xtension Manager—sets the behaviour of the Xtension manager, either always opening when QuarkXPress starts, when something changes, or when there's a problem. You can open the Xtension manager at any time in Utilities: Xtension Manager. Unlike Photoshop Plugins, which only activate when invoked—and may cause an instant hang—Xtensions are checked when QuarkXPress opens. The default behaviour is that the Xtension manager will then open if there has been an error. Typical errors would come from Xtensions which have not been updated to match a change in the Operating System, Xtensions that only work with older versions of QuarkXPress, Xtensions which have been damaged—for example when a component has accidentally been deleted or moved elsewhere—or Xtensions which are in conflict with each other. Where there is a problem, Quark will switch off the Xtension.

QuarkXPress 2016 keeps the same Xtension interface as QuarkXPress 2015, so 2015 Xtensions should work.

Sharing—this sets the defaults for Content sharing. If you share content via the Content palette, you will get access to these whenever you create new shared content. If you use the Content Sharing Tool (in the flyout menu from the graphic rectangle) then these defaults will be applied directly.

Fonts—this allows you to turn off font previews in the font menu (which will speed performance), as well as setting the behaviour for if fonts are missing (normally the font replacement dialogue will open), and the default replacement font. Although QuarkXPress is quite intelligent with its font replacement, you may want to consider FontExplorer Pro, Suitcase Fusion or some other font management utility.

East Asian—this turns on the East Asian functionality. You will need to restart QuarkXPress for the changes to take effect.

Job Jackets—sets when Job Jackets are evaluated, and where they are stored by default.

Notes—sets the attributes including colour and font for the sticky notes. The default is yellow, Arial, but you can even change it to Comic Sans for a guilty indulgence. Use Item—Note—Insert to create a note.

PDF— sets the PDF workflow. If PDF creation is causing problems, you can increase the Virtual Memory. If that doesn't work, you can switch to exporting to a .PS file and distil later, either via Preview (Mac), Acrobat Professional, or another utility. You can also set the default project naming and the error logging.

Redline—sets the colour and style of redlining. Unusually, this will be set from the print colour palette.

Spell Check—sets preferences for the spell checker, especially German, and for ignoring URLs and numbers.

Tables—allows anchored tables to break automatically. I would strongly recommend leaving this on. You can always turn it off for an individual table, but switching this off globally could cause substantial reflow problems.

Fractions/Price—sets how QuarkXPress constructs faux-fractions and prices. This does not affect the behaviour of true font-based fractions in Open Type.

Project
General—turns auto-picture import on or off, allows single layout mode to be turned on globally as the default, allows Open Type kerning to be turned off, and allows Multi-coloured Open Type Transformations to be turned on. Auto-picture import reimports all modified files when the project is opened. This slows down opening, but speeds up exporting. Open Type kerning should normally be on. If you are using the Chartwell fonts, Open Type Transformations need to be on.

Print Layout
General—allows you 'Greek' text below a certain size and/or pictures. This may marginally speed up performance, but will degrade the look of the layouts on screen. It does not affect print or export. You can also recolour hyperlink display, set the behaviour of Master Pages, allowing overriding of page changes, set where automatic pages are inserted (or not), specify whether frames are inside or outside a box, turn auto-constrain on or off, and auto-justify for Chinese, Japanese and Korean (CJK) characters. Frames by default are inside a box, so reduce the imaged area of the box or the space available for text. Putting them outside means that boxes grow larger as the frames grow. If

Timeo Danaos et dona ferentes.
Aeneid II: 49.
Greeking was a necessary activity for desk top publishing during the 1980s and early 1990s, because waiting for an entire page of text to refresh could take more than a minute. What's more, the much vaunted 'WYSIWYG' (what you see is what you get) was more a WYSISLWYG (what you see is somewhat like what you get). Greeking is not really necessary now, though some still prefer it.

you find that new pages are not being automatically created when text overflows, it may be that this preference has been reset at some point.

Auto constrain is a neat little feature which is a real time saver if you need it. When you check Auto Constrain, every item you create and paste in the layout is constrained by the borders of a box stacked behind it, if those borders surround the borders of the new box. Every box you create automatically becomes capable of constraining another item.

If Auto constrain preference is checked and a box is active, items will be pasted in the center of the active box. For example, if a text box is active and you paste a picture box, the picture box will be pasted within the text and constrained to the centre of the text box.

Measurements—sets the units of measurement for the document, though many units will default to points, especially for text sizes, sets how many points per inch and the size of a cicero, and sets whether coordinates are page or spread relative. The reason for allowing the size of a point or cicero to be set is because historically, these have had different sizes in different countries.

Paragraph—this sets the auto-leading, normally at 20% but better at 30% for novels, allows maintained leading to be turned off, sets the way in which grid-locking takes place, if in use, and sets the hyphenation algorithm for all supported languages. Usually, the most advanced algorithm is the best one, but in case of problems, you can return to an earlier type.

Character—sets the defaults for superscript, subscript, superior and Small Caps when generated by QuarkXPress instead of being a true OpenType version, along with options for ligatures, minimum kerning size, flex space width, cap accents and standard em space.

Tools
   Item—sets the nudge increment. Opt/alt-nudging (ie, moving with the arrow keys) nudges by $\frac{1}{10}$.

Zoom— sets the minimum zoom, maximum, and increment. The increment is especially useful if exact 1:1 representation on your monitor is an odd amount, such as 155%.

Content tool—sets the behaviour of the Content tool to create or select boxes.

Table tool—sets the defaults for the Table tool and allows you to turn off the dialogue on creation. If you intended to create numerous identical tables, you could set the defaults here and turn off the dialogue. You cannot link to external data or create inline tables as part of these default settings.

Guides and Grid—sets the snap distance for guides, their colour, and whether they are in front of or behind content. You can also set the page grid visibility (ie, the size at which it appears and disappears), whether it is in front of or behind content, and, potentially, in front of or behind the Guides. Normally, the Guides are in front of content and the page grid is behind. If you find the snap to guides distance annoying, here is where to reduce or enlarge it.

Color Manager—defaults for low-level colour management decisions. You would not normally need to change these. The proofing options can be set directly from View—Proof Output. Colour management of EPS and Vector files is now on by default (this is different from previous versions).

Layers—sets the defaults for new layers. You can change any of these via the layouts panel.

2 File

1 New Project

New, or Cmd/ctrl-N, creates a **new project**, opening the New Project dialogue box. This is visually identical to the Layout—Layout Properties dialogue, but Margin Guides and Column Guides and Facing Pages on/off can be set here, whereas they can only be viewed in Layout Properties.

Layout Name—this will be incorporated in PDF export default naming (subject to Preferences—PDF, see above), and will appear on printer slugs.

Layout Type—print or digital. All previous digital versions are now wrapped up in a single digital layout type.

Single Layout Mode—this removes the layout tabs from the interface. Essentially Single Layout Mode saves around 7mm of screen space. You can still add another layout using Layout—New, which then switches multi-layout back on again.

Page
Size—offers the most common presets, and a New option which allows you to add your own. You can also create layout specifications in Job Jackets, which offer many more refinements.

Width, Height—the width and height.

Orientation—swaps between narrower than height (portrait) and wider than height (landscape).

Page Count— how many pages to create initially. Leave as 1 if using Automatic Text Box.

Facing pages, allow odd pages on left—sets the document as a facing or single page document. You can change the 'allow odd pages' setting in Layout Properties.

Margin Guides—Top, Bottom, Left, Right, or Inside, Outside for facing pages. To edit these later, you need to be in Master Pages and go to Page—Master Guides and Grid.

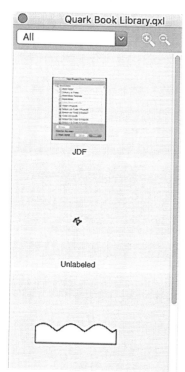

Library palette. QuarkXPress can have up to 25 files open at any one time, and this can be any combination of library and project files.

Column guides—sets the number of columns and gutter width. Also only adjustable later from Master Pages, Page—Master Guides and Grid.

2 New Project from Ticket

Project from Ticket opens the list of previously defined JDF Job Jackets tickets, and enables one to be selected to create the new project file. See Part 4—Job Jackets for information on how these are created and managed. A Job Jacket can contain a wide range of information including styles, rules for job evaluation, paper sizes and language resources.

3 New Library

A library file is a collection of graphics and text which can be used at any time. Libraries are independent of projects, so you can have the same library file for numerous projects. Equally, you can open two or more libraries drag items between them.

To put an item in the library, drag it there. To use it, drag it from the library onto the layout. To delete it, Cmd-back-space/ctrl-delete. If you double-click a library item, you can give it a label. Any label you give it will join a list of labels that appears when you do this. You can therefore use a label to uniquely name or describe a library item, or to label a whole category of library items.

Libraries store links to files, just as QuarkXPress does, except where the file does not have a separate existence—for example because you pasted it onto the layout—in which case it will be stored in the library in addition to being stored in QuarkXPress. Ordinary graphic files update in the same way that project graphics do.

Libraries save when you close them, unless you have turned Auto-Save on in the Preferences.

Menus

4 New Book

This creates a new book, which combines a group of projects into a consecutively page-numbered publication which can be indexed, listed, printed and exported as if it were a single document. See the Book palette section for more information.

5 Open

This opens a QuarkXPress project, book or library file. You can open project files from QuarkXPress version 7 or up. There is a free document converter available on the Quark.com website to convert versions 3-6 to current formats. This also does batch conversions.

QuarkXPress has a number of problem-solving routines which are automatically applied on open. It will come up with the dialogue 'This project requires minor repairs'. Normally you should let it go ahead and do them. The project will not open until the repairs are made.

If Quark quitted unexpectedly while last working on a document, it will offer to restore an auto-backup. This does not overwrite the saved version until you save it.

6 Open Recent

Shows a recent list of files, for convenience.

7 Close Window

This closes the currently open window, like clicking on the close window button. If the current window is the only window open for the project, QuarkXPress will offer to save it, if unsaved, and close the project.

8 Save

Saves the project. If you have backups turned on in the Preferences, saving first renames the existing version of the

Importing a graphic file offers options for PDF and Excel. PDF page numbers must be specified on import. Bringing in a chart from Excel by this route will import a low resolution image. Use Paste as Native or PDF import instead.

Below: Xpress Tags look like gobbledygook but are highly useful for importing database-driven text.

```
<v12.00><e8>
@Normal=<Ps100p100t0Y1h100z10k0b0c
Kf"NewBaskervilleStd-
Roman"n0o("Calt","liga","locl")L0G0>
@Normal=[Sp"","Normal","Normal"]<*L*
AL*h"Standard"*s"None"*m"None"*bn(7
.2)*kn0*kt0*ra0*rb0*d0*p(0,0,0,0,0,0,g(P,
S))>
@Title=[Sp"","Title"]<*L*AL*h"Standard"*
```

file as a backup, and then saves the current version. I strongly recommend having this turned on: if something goes wrong while saving—power outage, system hang, Quark error—you will still have a properly saved file.

9 Save As

Saves the file with a new name, and continues to work in the newly named copy of the file.

10 Revert to Saved

Reverts to the most recently saved version.

11 Import

Imports text or graphics, depending on the type of box selected. If no box is selected, it will create a new box depending on your imported file.

Graphics:

QuarkXPress will import JPEG, TIFF, PSD, and PNG images, and EPS, AI, PDF, vectors. Xtensions may be available to import other formats.

It will also import a chart which is in an XLSX Excel file—however, it will come across as an image file. To import Excel charts as vectors (much better), either copy them via the clipboard and Edit—Paste as Native Objects, or save as PDF in Excel and import the PDF, which can be converted to native objects if you want to work on the styling (which you usually would).

For PDF files, you can specify which page to import for a multi-page document. You can't change this later without reimporting. You can also specify whether to import using the bounding box, the media box, etc. For most files this will make no difference—experiment if the result isn't what you were expecting.

For all types of graphics, a summary of information is given underneath the file list. This includes size, resolution, for-

Menus

mat, colour depth and date. You can choose whether or not to maintain the attributes of the box you are importing into. The default for this is set in the Preferences—Input Settings.

Text:

QuarkXPress imports plain text, Word Docx (but not legacy Doc), HTML, RTF and Xpress Tags XTG, which is a special Quark format highly suitable for constructing with a database such as FileMaker Pro for automating publishing.

All text imports offer smart quote conversion, which, usually, is worth leaving on.

Xpress Tags offers to interpret Xpress Tags, which should usually be on unless you want to display the tags themselves for the purposes of writing a book like this one.

Word import brings in footnotes and formatting, but only graphics which are anchored in the text. To bring in other Word graphics, you can copy them then Paste as Native Objects, although Word often sends its graphics as images, which is unhelpful, or PDF the Word file, import the relevant pages, and then Style—Convert to Native Objects which will bring them in as vectors for editing.

Word also has an option to import styles. Be very careful before you choose this! A typical Word document may contain dozens or even hundreds of styles, as Word adds styles on the fly when tables are formatted.

If any of the styles you are importing have the same name as styles in your document, you will be shown the Style Conflict box, which allows you to Replace, Use New, Auto-Rename or Use Existing. Styles not in the project already will be added to the styles list. Even if they are the 'correct' styles, they will not be structured, so changing Normal will not then change all the styles that are similar to Normal.

The best workflow—in my opinion—if you know that a Word document has been carefully tagged with the right styles, and you want to follow the original structure, is to create a new document and import it into that. Then rename the styles in that document to match those you have

Above, the Style Conflict box, when importing text with styles from Word or Xpress Tags.

Rescuing Word users

If you work in the corporate world, you will occasionally have users who come with excessively long and complicated Word documents which have become so cumbersome it is impossible to work with them.

In this case, importing from Word with Styles turned on is a good choice. For the graphics, PDF the Word file and import, possibly converting to native, from that.

PDF Export options. You can save these as presets. The existing presets will usually be right, though.

already defined in your main project, File—Save Text as Xpress Tags and reimport. You will be shown the Style Sheet Conflict again, but this time choose 'Use Existing', and select 'Repeat for all conflicts'. In this way, all of the structure of the document will be imported, fully formatted, but it will be in clean QuarkXPress typography.

12 Save Text

You can save text in any of the supported formats—Docx, HTML, RTF, Xpress Tags and plain text. Only the text is saved, not the layout. If you want to create a Word version of the entire document—some clients want this—then export as PDF and convert in Acrobat Professional.

13 Append

Append allows you to add various styles, colours etc to your project from another project. It does not allow you to import text or graphics, though you can import a layout, which is highly useful. The dialogue will ask you which you wish to import. This may generate the Style Conflict dialogue if the items have the same names as ones in your current document.

14 Export

Export allows you to export the project as PDF, as another Quark project (including saving down to version 2015), as an HTML5 publication, as an Article, as ePub or as Kindle. It also allows you to export the current page as an EPS or image, or the current box as an image. This is especially useful if you have a lot of pasted images and want to slim down your QuarkXPress project while also making the images available in other documents.

PDF

PDF is now the principal means of sending a publication to a print house or pre-press service, as well as creating an email or downloadable version for more general use. Print houses do not need to own a current copy of QuarkXPress, nor do they need to have separate copies of your fonts or images.

When you export to PDF, you are offered a list of presets, an options button, and an option to open the job in your default PDF viewer once the export is complete.

The presets have been carefully constructed to industry specifications such as those of the Ghent group. Generally speaking, pick the Press option for sending to a print house. Slightly confusingly, the 'Print' option is for sending to someone to print on an office laser printer. PDF/X options are for verification to particular industry standards.

Although you generally don't need to work with them, we will now look at the Options.

Page—turns on spreads, allows you to send every page as a separate PDF, includes blank pages, and embeds a colour or mono thumbnail. All of these options are off by default and in the presets. Including blank pages is liable to prompt a telephone call from your print house—why are we printing a blank page? I personally detest 'this page intentionally left blank', but there should at least be a page number, otherwise, the chances are that it will go missing at some point and the spreads of your layout will suffer.

Metadata—allows you to enter Title, Subject, Author and Keywords. The title of the Layout is automatically loaded. The rest you have to specify yourself if you want it included, for example if you are going to upload the document. Slightly irritatingly (though in other ways usefully), the data is *not* copied over from Layout—eBook Metadata.

Hyperlinks—irrelevant to output for printers, but highly useful for document sharing, the hyperlinks panel sets which links are included in the PDF, and how they are presented. By default, links and indexes are exported as clickable links, and lists are exported as bookmarks (also becoming clickable links when they appear in a table of contents). If you have several lists, some of which were just to help you navigate round the document in draft, you might want to specify just one list. By default, hyperlinks

The PDF Export—hyperlinks panel

are invisible, which makes the PDF file represent the printed version best.

Note that this option only sets their visibility when clicked—they are otherwise invisible. If you want old-fashioned blue underlined hyperlinks, then set these as character styles in the document. In previous versions of QuarkXPress, these defaulted to being visible and underlined.

This option pane also sets the default zoom.

Compression—this sets the compression for colour, greyscale and black and white images, as well as compression for Text and Line art. **Important**: the compression controls do exactly what they say—compress. Therefore, 'Zip/JPEG low' means that low compression is used, and therefore high quality. This is the opposite of the Quality setting that many applications have for JPEGs, where 'high' means low compression.

This option also allows downsampling of images. Generally speaking, use the defaults for this which come with the presets. If you don't select a default, the images will not be downsampled, which may mean you have a file of several gigabytes: far too big to email, and occupying a large amount of disk real estate. The default for press is 300 dpi with bi-cubic sampling.

Colors—this sets how colours in your document are exported. Note that these are the colours used. Unused colours which are in your palette will not appear. Also, this is not synchronised with your View—Proof Output settings, although the same settings are on offer, including any that you have defined via Edit—Color Setups—Output.

As a general rule, the Composite workflow is now preferred, though a pre-press or print house may specify In-RIP separations. When you send Composite, the RIP settings will determine how the separations are made. The key is to set out clearly in your job specification what process you are expecting, eg, CMYK + 1 spot colour. If the print house can't separate what they need from your file, they will tell you.

The Press preset is for CMYK. You will need to change this to CMYK plus spot if you want additional spot plates.

For printing Pantone Extended Gamut (XGC) colours, which allow up to 95%[1] reproduction of Pantone PMS colours using CMYK + two of Orange, Green, Violet plates, consult your printer about how they should be output. Current estimates are that about 20% of printers in the USA now support XGC, but this is expected to rise to 50% by 2020.

Fonts—normally you should select all. Some fonts have copyright restrictions on them and will not embed in a PDF. QuarkXPress will warn you of that when you try to export, and the rogue fonts will be unchecked in this dialogue. You have a couple of choices here. If the text is example text, such as Lucida Casual earlier in this book, you can use Item—Convert Text to Boxes—Anchored, and then use Find/Change with Ignore Attributes switched off to track down any phantom text, such as spaces.

Alternatively, you can look for another version of the font which has embedding allowed—it will only usually be very old fonts with embedding turned off. Certainly any font you have actually paid for should allow you to make a PDF. You might go back to the font vendor and ask either for your money back, or for an unlocked version. It is somewhat possible that a font is in the public domain, with a Creative Commons free to edit license, but has embedding turned off—possibly due to user error earlier. If the font is genuinely public domain, you can go into FontLab or another font editor and re-export with embedding allowed. However, it is worth doing just a bit of research first. A number of so-called public domain fonts are in fact copyrighted fonts which some poorly advised individual has chosen to make public. Sometimes, people specify 'non-commercial use only' and disallow embedding because they have heard that this gets round copyright. It doesn't. If in doubt, set the text in a different font, or find the 'real' version of the font and pay for it.

---

1 According to Pantone. Esko estimates 80% for its Equinox product.

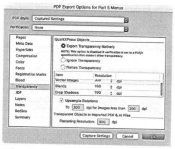

The Transparency dialogue

Registration Marks—these will be on by default in the Press preset. You can have them set centred or off-centre, if, for some reason, a layout element is going to get in the way. However, you would generally be better advised to not have any element protrude beyond the bleed area (or turn on 'clip at bleed' in the next box. You can additionally include Bleed Marks. This could be important if you have a nervous printer who wants to know if there is supposed to be bleed on something. On the other hand, having the registration marks, which include the crop marks, should tell them that you know what you're doing.

Bleed—bleed can either be symmetric, typically at 3.175mm, which is the press settings default, or asymmetric, for whatever complicated reason you've agreed with your printer, or 'page items' which is the same as 'off'. If you are using press preset but there is no bleed in your publication, it might be worth turning this off, though most imposition software is clever enough to work out what to do either way. Turning on 'clip at bleed edge' is a good idea, again, unless there is some complicated and agreed reason not to.

Transparency—this sets both the transparency and also the rendering of images in vectors, blends and drop shadows, as well as upsampling rotations. Normally, the presets will sort this out for you, but there can be problems.

First, QuarkXPress normally exports transparency natively in imported PDF and AI files. This is fine, unless there is a transparency problem with the file, in which case flattening transparency should preserve the look of the file, using the flattening resolution at the bottom of the screen. However, if that causes QuarkXPress to quit unexpectedly, or produces an error, then the file problem is one that even Quark can't solve. You could go back to the application that created the document, but that isn't always possible. The best bet would be to convert to native objects, but if the file is in a very poor state, that might not work either. The last resort is to turn transparency for imported PDFs off entirely. This will affect all the PDFs in the document, but it might not actually look much different—applications that are cavalier in how they handle transparency may have it on by accident, and without function.

Resolution of Vector Images and Blends should be fine at 300 dpi for the press preset. Because shadows (by definition) contain no sharp lines, 150 dpi is sufficient. However, some pre-flighters will flag up any file at 150dpi as an error, and your printer will tell you that you've prepared the file wrong. There is no point arguing. Change the drop shadow resolution to 300 dpi and resend the file.

Transparency will be off for PDF/X verified documents, as the standard doesn't support them.

By default, image rotations are upsampled to 300 dpi for images less than 225 dpi. You can only turn this off or change it when flattening transparency.

JDF—this allows you to include a Job Jacket JDF, and, optionally, the name of the contact. This streamlines the process if your print house has a JDF workflow, provided that you are yourself working to a Job Jacket. See Part 4—Job Jackets for more details.

Layers—this allows you to select which layers to print, and tells you what plates are needed for those layers. It reads from your Layers palette. If you make changes here and check 'Apply to layers' it will write those changes back to your layers palette. Otherwise, they will be retained when you export to PDF until changed.

Notes—Exports your Notes from Item—Note with the PDF. Useful for client approval, highly embarrassing if left on during final export for print, or if you've left unflattering internal comments about the client on them.

Redline—allows you to include changes marked up according to your Redline settings. Again, good for client approval, not good for final export.

Summary—this contains no settings, but is a useful sanity check that your file is as intended.

As well as using the presets, you can make your own. This is highly useful for organising your own internal and client-facing workflows, as well as for providing files just the way your print house wants them.

Layouts as Project

With this option, you can save your layouts as QuarkXPress projects, including to QuarkXPress 2015 format. Naturally, you will lose 2016 specific features, especially in regard to Open Type settings. You can specify which layouts in the file to save. Also, you can save as Project Template, which creates a special file that replicates itself every time you use it. If you already have a template-based workflow, or your requirements are simple, this may be a good way to operate. However, it will not synchronise styles across projects. For that, use Job Jacket JDFs (See Part 4). Templates include all project features, such as Master Pages and content variables, as they were at the time you saved the template. If you want to exactly replicate a project in that way, but also keep styles synchronised, use Templates *and* JDFs.

Layout as HTML5 Publication

This creates a new folder with your complete HTML5 publication. To function, you need to upload it to a web server. However, if you just want to quickly create an HTML5 page, for example to work on further in another application, go into the html5output folder and look for Landscape.html or Portrait.html. Here you will find a web-ready HTML page, provided that it is uploaded with the contents of the html5output folder.

In addition to its app building capabilities, this makes QuarkXPress a powerful tool for prototyping websites. You can create a typographically perfect page using Quark's interface, and then convert it with, for example, PineGrow, to a WordPress site.

As a general rule, the more powerful an HTML file tool is, the harder it is to actually make sites that look good. Traditionally, designers have prototyped in Photoshop, but Photoshop as an image editing tool is not necessarily a good place to start. If you wanted to create, for example, a circle filled with text, you would have to exert considerable ingenuity to accomplish in Photoshop what you can accomplish in QuarkXPress in less than 20 seconds, from start to finished export.

This option is only available from digital layouts.

Layout as Article
This publishes the selected story as a Quark Copy Desk QCD article. These files are for use with Quark Copy Desk, an external editor for QuarkXPress articles.

Layout as ePub, Layout as Kindle
These two output formats share a similar set of options. See the Digital section for a full explanation. To export for Kindle, you must download Amazon's free Kindle Gen application. However, our experience is that you may have more success, especially with using a list as the Table of Contents, if you export as ePub and then convert to Kindle using an ePub editor such as Calibre (free, Mac and Windows).

You set the Metadata for eBooks and Kindles in Layout—eBook Metadata.

The options are:

Pictures—Override Default Settings to render images at a higher or lower resolution, in a different format or quality.

Text—Export Dropped cap as native (default) or ignore. QuarkXpress now supports native dropped caps, but it is possible that some ePub or Kindle readers do not. Experiment to see what works.

Table of Contents—Enables you to use a List as the Table of Contents, to change the name of the cover in the Table of Contents, and to change the name of the Table of Contents. If you are publishing a novel, there may be only one article, which is the main text. By default, Kindles and ePubs would include solely that article as the only item in the Table of Contents. If you have a List of the chapters, this would be much better. You can select any one list as the table of contents. QuarkXPress is dependent on Amazon's Kindle Gen to create Kindle Mobi files directly. I have to say that I have never had much success getting the Table of Contents option to work. However, if I export to ePub, and then go from ePub to Kindle mobi via Calibre, everything works as it should. It may be that by the time you read this, Amazon has updated the Kindle Gen application. As with all things eBook, experiment until happy.

East Asian—options for setting East Asian text.

Page Layout—sets how footnotes are exported and whether page layout is automatic, portrait or landscape for fixed layout, with spread options.

Miscellaneous—for the ePub option only, allows you to target Windows readers or iBooks, Kindle and universal readers.

15 Collect for Output

Traditionally, the way to send files to print houses from QuarkXPress was by collecting for output. This meant that all the files arrived at the printer's, and any problems could be fixed there.

Collect for Output is still an option, but it is more suited to creating off-site backups, for example on DropBox, than communicating with a print house.

Essentially, Collect for Output saves a selection or all of the files necessary to work with your Quark project on a different computer, provided that it has a copy of QuarkXPress 2016. This includes not only the Quark file, but also colour profiles, fonts, pictures, and a report saying what should be included. The report is in Xpress Tags format, and can be imported into a Quark document for reading—this in itself is a useful tool if you want to see what all your style sheets are doing.

In my workflow, if I'm working with a key client on an important document—potentially an official submission with hard deadlines and enormous ramifications if they are not met—I will Collect for Output to Dropbox prior to leaving the house, with or without my MacBook Pro. I then send the client a link to the Dropbox folder, with instructions to download the 3-day trial version of QuarkXPress should I get knocked over by a bus. (I'm not being morbid—this is actually a standard expression in organisational resilience). If my laptop gets stolen, the house goes up in smoke, or I lose my memory and am found wandering in Scotland with no knowledge of my own name, the client can still open the document and finalise it.

However, I haven't sent a client a QuarkXPress collect for output since 2001. Print houses no longer all keep the same versions of the software (QuarkXPress 3.32 was the only version people used for years), and they no longer expect to make final changes on behalf of the client.

This reflects the dramatic change in technology. We used to take files to printers on Syquest Drives and Zip Drives, or send them over ISDN. It might take hours or days to get a new version of a file to the print house if an error was detected. PDF was nowhere near ready for print workflows, and most printers would not accept them. During the 1990s, I frequently used to drive from Belgium to Holland with a laptop and a .ps Postscript output file, and drag the document through the imagesetter myself (I worked for charity and the printer was sympathetic enough to allow me to image and develop the films after hours, at reduced cost). My first use of QuarkXPress was when I found an error on the films and quickly had to open Quark for the first time on their Macs (we were Windows Ventura-based) and output a tiny box of text to the Agfa imagesetter, and subsequently stick it onto the film with blue tape, having first removed the offending original text with a scalpel— those were the days. But I digress.

These days, a composite PDF for an entire book can be emailed and on the RIP within twenty minutes. Corrections made by the design team are likely to be more reliable than those made by the printer's assistant anyway. There is less work at the other end, which cuts down cost, and leaves less chance of error. File sizes can be a few megabytes, because the PDFs are fully optimised for press. Things can still go wrong, but it is less likely, and easier to fix.

The other side is that it is technically a breach of copyright to send the font files, even if the print house deletes them afterwards (and, seriously, did print houses ever do that?) In an increasingly litigious society, it isn't worth the risk.

16 Job Jackets

See the Job Jackets section in Part 4 for a discussion on what they are and why they are important.

Link Project—this links a job ticket to a project. A list appears of available tickets to attach, or you can browse files.

Modify Job Ticket—this allows you to make certain modifications to the current job tickets.

Evaluate Layout—this allows you to set rules and run a pre-flight to check that your publication is compliant. You can set Preferences—Job Jackets to force evaluation of the document at particular times. The available rules go substantially beyond pre-flight verification, enabling you to impose minimum text sizes, reject indexed colours, GIFs, or pictures enlarged above 100%, unprintable shades or colours, and many other formal issues with files which would not prevent them from printing, but would produce unacceptable results. See Part 4—Job Jackets section for more information.

The Print dialogue looks complex, but almost all of the settings are identical to those of PDF Export. It is best to create a basic output style for each printer that you use, with alternates for other stock.

17 Print

The Print dialogue is by far the most complex thing in QuarkXPress. However, it is relatively easy to manage and, with a couple of exceptions we will look at here, the settings are identical to the PDF Export options above.

Main Dialogue
The main print dialogue has four panels. Only the centre bottom panel changes as different panes are selected.

At the top is the physical printing machine which you installed through your Mac or Windows system. You can use this setting to switch between installed printers.

Underneath is the Print Style setting. By default, this is 'Captured Settings', which means any edits you've made. If you press Print, these are stored with the document. If you've made changes but aren't yet ready to print, you capture them with Capture Settings at the bottom.

However, once you have made the basic settings, you would do well to use this box to save as an Output Style. This will also appear (and be editable in) Edit—Output Styles. You can make a separate setting for each printer.

The rest of this area is self-explanatory: number of copies, which pages—you can specify a range using a hyphen and non-sequential pages using commas, and combine these as much as you want. Sequence sets all, evens or odds, scale sets the scale, you can set collation on (if your printer doesn't do this automatically) which will then print as many complete, ordered sets as you have set copies. You can print to spreads, print back to front, meaning last page first, for printers that do not manage this, and fit to print area, which will override scale.

All these changes (and any other visible changes you make later) will appear in the preview on the right, which will also allow you to look at previous and later pages. The ? reveals the colour code used. In our example, dark border is the clipped area which is not part of the final trimmed sheet.

The left hand lower pane has the options for what will appear in the centre pane next to it. By default it is set to Device when you open the dialogue.

Device pane

The first item in this pane is the PPD. This should be installed on your system by the printer's own software. Often the manufacturer will have bundled all of its printers into the same installation, so you will need to scroll down the list until you find your model. If it isn't there, and you have no time to hunt for it, pick Generic Colour, Generic B&W or Generic Imagesetter. For colour and B&W, you will have to go into printer and page settings, bottom left hand

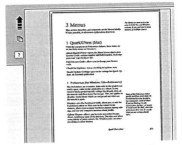

Above, the top pane of the print dialogue, below, the lower left and centre panes.

The page preview pane. On the left, icons show direction of print, cut sheet or roll media, and ? to show the colour key dialogue.

Important:
Files for distilling in Acrobat
See the margin note in the File—Export—PDF section, above. If you need to create .PS files for Acrobat to distil, don't do it through the Print dialogue, which will include extraneous printer instructions and may work poorly or not at all. You can set Preferences—PDF to produce clean .PS files, which you create via Export—PDF.

corner, to set paper size. With the correct PPD, QuarkXPress will handle those settings itself.

If you have the correct PPD installed, Paper Size will offer you the range of available paper. At the bottom of the list 'Custom' will allow you to define your own.

By default the position is top left, but you can centre it horizontally, vertically or both. This becomes important when using crop marks, as these will otherwise be off the page.

Resolution nominally changes the printer resolution. With my LaserJet CP5225n, it does nothing of the kind, as the printer's own built-in RIP captures and discards uninformed instructions by computer users of that nature.

You can print negatively—useful for some imagesetter/ platemaker combinations. Oddly, the other command of that vintage, Flip Page, is in the next pane, Pages.

The Postscript error handler should normally be off. It prints a page if there is a Postscript error. This is mercifully rare these days, and will not mean much to you unless you understand the Postscript language.

Above, the Pages pane.

Pages

Orientation—also slightly oddly—is in this pane, along with 'Include Blank Pages'—a waster of paper but necessary for soft imposition (see the comments on this under PDF Export).

You can also print page thumbnails—very useful for analysing the shape of an entire document.

Page Flip mirrors the page vertically or horizontally. Page Tiling allows you to print oversize pages. Before the roll-printer era, in-house PR teams across the world used this function as they busily cobbled together displays for projects with aspirations larger than their budgets.

Colours

This pane is the most important for colour proofing. Assuming that you have set up the correct colour profile for your printer in Edit—Color Setups—Output, you choose it here. If you have profiled your printer and your monitor, you should be seeing a reasonably consistent colour workflow from camera to monitor to printer, subject to the capabilities of the devices.

You can also (bravely) try to set the frequency, angle and function of the line screen here. As noted in Section 2, this would mean that you could print with a line, ellipse, diamond or tri-point screen, and also lower the frequency to the point that your laser printer gives good photo rendition. In practice, I haven't found a printer since the 1990s that actually allowed you to do this, as resolution enhancement technology takes over. The result will be better than the straight 600 dpi of our old LaserJet III, but less flexible.

Below, the Colours pane is where you choose the colour setup which you created in Edit—Color Setups—Output.

Pictures
This pane allows you to output in low resolution or rough, or to send TIFFs at full resolution. There is very little point in doing either using today's technology. You can also send pictures in different formats. Again, unless you are trying to solve a technical problem, these settings should not be changed. The same goes for overprinting EPS black.

Fonts
Like the PDF Export dialogue, this allows you to turn fonts on and off, and also to send them in a slightly different format. This is really only for tracking down problems.

Registration Marks
This is identical to the PDF Export panel of the same name.

Bleed
This is identical to the PDF Export panel.

Transparency
This is identical, but with slightly fewer functions, to the Transparency panel in PDF Export.

JDF
As with the PDF Export, this outputs a JDF in addition to the other pages.

Layers
As with the PDF Export, this allows you to choose which layers to print.

Notes
This prints your notes, from Item—Note.

Redline
This prints out redlining, defined in the Redline panel.

Advanced
Subject to your printer's PPD, you can pick which Post-script level to use. You should not normally need to do this.

Summary
This is a summary of your settings.

3 Edit

The Edit menu begins with familiar functions such as Undo and Redo, and becomes progressively less familiar as it resembles increasingly the job of an Editor, as opposed to the metaphor 'Edit' adopted by computers.

1 Undo and Redo, Cut, Copy, Paste, Select All

These all function as they do in most other applications.

2 Paste without formatting, Paste in Place

Pastes without any attributes. Paste in Place pastes an item in the same position as on the page it was copied from.

3 Paste as native objects

The stand-out new feature of QuarkXPress 2016 (along with Style—Convert to Native Objects), Paste as Native Objects does something very simply which every other application has so far failed to do: it pastes from pretty much anywhere, and inserts as native, editable Quark Objects.

This applies not only to well-behaved files, such as those from Adobe Illustrator and InDesign, but also to the notoriously badly behaved graphics from Excel.

The order of this section is the Edit menu order on a Mac. The same items are present on Windows, with the addition of Preferences (see under QuarkXPress menu, above), but the order is slightly different: Grid Styles, Hyperlinks, Item Styles and Underline Styles are all at the bottom of the menu on Windows.
Kerning Table Edit is under Utilities on Windows.

A few types of graphics will not paste well—the more lurid Excel charts, for example, are sent across as images. For those, export as PDF and then Style—Convert to Native Objects.

For an Excel chart, which is a challenge that, up to now, Illustrator has not been able to manage without turning the text into gobbledegook, simply copy from Excel and then Paste as Native Objects in QuarkXPress. As much as possible, Excel sends across the outlines as vectors, though its gradient backgrounds will come across as images clipped by those vectors.

On paste, a dialogue comes up. You can ignore the settings unless you aren't getting what you want.

What arrives is a grouped file, in colour. If you have View—Proof Output—Greyscale on, these colours may not be visible, so turn off proofing for the moment.

Ungroup the file. For any Excel file, even the Cones, which are sent across as an image, the text should have come across correctly in editable format. This is absolutely essential, because, imported as a straight PDF, the text of an Excel chart is usually in the wrong font and typically illegibly small. If you want to edit a whole host of tiny text boxes that have come across, use Utilities—Linkster to make them all one story, to which you can then apply character or paragraph styles as a block.

The backgrounds are still in their lurid, Excel state. You can keep them as they are, but they will not usually gel well with a properly designed layout. To remove the backgrounds, click on them with the picture tool and press Delete. You can now recolour them as you like—recolouring them before this will have no effect, as the background will be hidden by the image file. Remember to recolour any keys in the same way. You can explode the pie, or part of it, if you like. Once you've done this a few times, the whole process takes about 30 seconds.

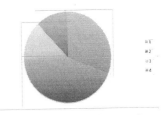

Above, the Excel pie-chart as it arrives pasted into QuarkXPress—fussily overstyled, with fonts too small to read, and almost certainly not brand-compliant for colours or typeface.

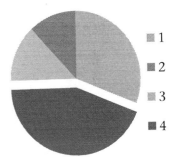

Above, after 30 seconds reworking in QuarkXPress

QuarkXPress is still at the mercy of how applications—especially Office applications—send their files to the clipboard. When pasting as native objects doesn't produce the right result, PDF the document, import that, and use Style—Convert to Native Objects. Occasionally this will still be an image file: if an application insists on sending the file in that way, and it can't be made brand compliant, you will have to go back to the redrawing board.

Above, Find/Change when it is first opened is similar to Search/Replace in a word processor, thought it offers additional refinements of searching in story or layout, locked content and footnotes. Below, with Ignore Attributes off, it presents a full selection of features, in an easy left-to-right flow.

4 Find/Change

Find/Change, and its sister, Item Find/Change offer a uniquely powerful way to typographically rework text and items.

It's also a user experience triumph, working, unlike most advanced search/replace functions in other applications, in human-understandable left-to-right format, rather than vertically.

Essentially it has two modes. On first open, Ignore Attributes is on, giving you the simplified view. Everything you enter on either side is remembered, and you can retrieve it by clicking the double arrows. This is exceedingly helpful when working with a client who insists on adding double spaces after full stops, doing two carriage returns for a new paragraph, or using '...' (with dots) instead of '…' (ellipsis).

There are various special codes you can enter for special features. You can also paste any text, including invisibles such as tabs, returns and special characters, and they will appear with their correct special codes. For example, if you've imported a document from Word with Styles turned off (highly recommended) all of the bullet points will come across as bullet-tab: "•   text".

If you copy that and paste it into the Text frame of Find What, it will appear as •\t, because \t is the code for tab. Most glyphs will come across natively, though specialist glyphs may come across with their standard version, and you will need to specify the font as well.

You can combine attributes in any way you like. For example, if you have the mistyped 'fair' consistently in French passages instead of 'faire', you can find *Text: fair, Language: French*, and replace with *faire*, without upsetting correctly spelled English 'fair', meaning 'juste' or 'égale', or possibly 'foire'.

New in QuarkXPress 2016, you can now distinguish between breaking and non-breaking characters, and also find and change Open Type features. So, for example, if you have an old document which used a TrueType font that did not support true Small Caps, you can find *Type Style: κ* and change to *OpenType: Small Caps*, if your new OpenType version supports them.

If you have a very complex set of changes, for example if you were changing a document in Dutch old spelling to new spelling, there is a QuarkXPress script (Mac only) that supports replacing long lists of things in batch mode. In operation, Find Next finds the next item, Change, then Find changes that one and finds the next, Change just changes what you found, and Change All (the dangerous option, though you can unchange it all with a single Edit—Undo) finds and changes everything. Your choices on story (the default) or whole layout, whether locked text is affected, and whether footnotes are searched, apply.

5 Item Find/Change

Item Find/Change uses the same left—find, right—change format. However, as there are so many more attributes, it is tabbed into Box, Box Color, Frame, Line, Picture, Text and Drop Shadow, with a highly useful Summary at the end, so you can check what you are really finding and changing. Underneath, across all the tabs, you can specify what kind of items you are searching for—Text Boxes, Picture Boxes, None Boxes (ie boxes defined to have Content:None), Lines and/or Text Paths.

The level of changes goes down to every settable attribute of a box or line. If it's too complicated, you can use the corner menu (top right) to acquire all the attributes from a selected item, or just those that relate to the currently open panel.

If you want to use this to check, for example, for accidentally rotated boxes, you can't: it will only find an angle of rotation, not a >0°. However, you can accomplish that with File—Job Jackets—Evaluate Layout, where you can set a rule to forbid, or to flag, rotated boxes, and, indeed, many other potential problems.

Above: Item Find/Change uses a tabbed dialogue, with a summary in the final tab.

6 Colors

This brings up the Colours edit list. Please see the Colours Palette section for a discussion of this list.

7 Style Sheets

This brings up the Style Sheets edit list. Please see the Style Sheets Palette section.

8 Item Styles

This calls up the Item Styles Edit list. See the Item Styles Palette for more information.

9 Callout Styles

This calls up the Callout Styles Edit list. See the Callout Styles Palette for more information.

10 Conditional Styles

This calls up the Conditional Styles Edit list. See the Conditional Styles Palette for more information.

11 Bullet, Numbering and Outline Styles

Edit—Bullet, Numbering and Outline Styles calls up the Bullet edit list, which allows the creation and management of three kinds of styles.

Edit Bullet Style

The dialogue allows you to name the Bullet, set its character style, which defaults to Inherit from Paragraph, but can be any defined character style—for example, because you want to use a dingbat character—enter the bullet character, or paste it, set the outset, either as an absolute or a proportion of one em, set the bullet size as a percentage of the character size, if inherited from the paragraph, and set it to align (in its own area, which is always to the left of the

Edit Bullet Style allows you to set the Character Style, the Bullet Character, Outset, Size and Alignment.

line) left, centre or right. Essentially, this allows you to put a character of your own choice and styling in the margin.

This means that you can create side-stripes, of the kind seen in many popular manuals of a particular type. Achieve this by creating a character style-sheet that stretches a dingbat vertically 400% and adjusts its offset. You need a new paragraph every couple of lines, but the effect is fairly convincing and easy to achieve.

Edit Numbering Style

Edit Numbering Style works in the same way as bullets, except that sequential series are generated. These are Arabic, Roman, alphabetic, East Asian, and typographic symbol sets. The typographic sets, *, **, †,††,‡,‡‡, etc were introduced into QuarkXPress 2016 to enhance footnote typography. For automatic numbering, prefixes and suffixes can be added.

Edit Outline Style

An outline style organises previously defined bullet and or numbering styles, with the ability to include lower (or higher) levels and a separator, as required. Indents are set per level. Combining Numbering Styles with prefixes and bullet styles, we could have:

§1 Preamble

   §1·¶1 Introduction

      §1·¶1·1 Wherein that the people…

         ❀ upon the first of the month

            ∗ and subsequently each Thursday

               i) shall first make good…

Lists continue from where they left off, unless you restart them. If you want to include numbered points in the text, but also have section numbers, simply create two separate Outline Styles. These will then not interfere with each other.

You can create cross-references for numbered sections with Style—Cross Reference.

Edit Numbering Style is similar to Edit Bullet Style, except that it offers number sets in Arabic and Roman numerals, alphabetic, East Asian characters, and typographic symbols, with prefixes and suffixes.

Edit Outline Styles combines sets of numbering, bullets or both into an indented, structured list, controlled from Measurements Panel—Paragraphs Tab •/123 and $^3 4_5$.

Sadly, no automatic numbering can produce the following:

Firstly	*Partridge in pear tree*
Secondly	*Turtle Doves*
Thirdly	*French Hens*
Fourthly	*Calling Birds*
Fifthly	*Gold Rings*
Sixthly	*Geese, laying*
Seventhly	*Swans, swimming*
Eighthly	*Maids, milking*
Ninethly	*Ladies dancing*
Tenthly	*Lords, leaping*
Eleventhly	*Pipers, piping*
Twelfthly	*Drummers who drum*

12 Footnote Styles

This opens the Footnote Styles Edit List. For an explanation, see the Footnote Palette, above.

13 Hyperlinks

This opens the Hyperlinks Edit List. See the Hyperlinks Palette, above.

14 Underline Styles

This opens the Underline Styles Edit List, which allows you to create new Underline Settings. You can apply these using Style—Type Style—Underline Styles. Although you can't currently integrate these into character or paragraph styles, you can set up a set of consistent underlining options which will generally be superior to the default Underline. This includes setting the colour, shade, width and offset. Underline is not a 'proper' typographic feature—it is a hangover from the days of manual typewriters where typists went back and created underlining with the _ character. This was used to denote italics in typeset text. However, with the rise of underlined URLs, you may (on rare occasions) wish to choose to underline one. My opinion is that people now know what URLs are, and it is sufficient just to write out www.etc. Word processors insist on underlining URLs, whether you want them to or not, which makes the text look amateurish.

Above, underline settings in Underline Styles.

15 Hanging Characters

Hanging Characters allow significant typographical refinement, provided that you are willing to invest a little time in specifying which characters should hang and by what amount. They can be applied in the Measurements: Paragraph tab, or as a paragraph style.

The Edit list contains two types of items: Classes and Sets. The classes have narrow icons, the sets have wide icons.

Classes

Use New—Class to create a class. You are offered the choice of Leading (pronounced 'lee-ding', not 'led-ding', as in the inter-line spacing), Trailing, or Dropped Cap. You can set the hang to any percentage between -50% and 200%, but the default list of options offers useful increments, which you can refine afterwards.

What we are doing here is moving characters into or away from the margin so that they line up to the eye. While Open Type kerning should enforce good spacing between the letters, it does not currently take account of the beginning and end of lines, although this could be programmed in as a contextual alternate. This means that, especially in fully justified or right justified text, punctuation appears overly indented at the end of a line, and leading punctuation, mainly as inverted commas, appears to push the text inwards.

Dropped caps create their own problems (see example). Leading inverted commas create an enormous gap, without adding anything to the visual interest of the page. One solution is to set them at ordinary size, followed by the dropped capital, using a conditional style sheet. This can be further improved by creating a dropped cap class.

Defaults are in place for Hanging and Leading Punctuation, which can be switched on for all text. If you want to refine the way the page appears, you can also set a 5% or less leading hang of 5% (which pushes them into the margin by 5%) for W, Y, and possibly V. Examine your extended text carefully to see if these create a problem: this is not only font dependent, but also related to the leading, column width, and other page interactions.

Above, Hanging Characters Edit list, truncated.

Below, edit hanging character.

Below, the Edit Hanging Character Set list. Hanging Characters must be combined into sets before they can be used.

Although an alternative solution is to begin with an ordinary sized pair of inverted commas, QuarkXPress allows you to create a Dropped Cap hanging character class which will automatically push leading punctuation (or any character you wish) into the margin. Either solution is significantly better than a three line punctuation mark followed by an ordinary sized letter. We also superscripted the inverted commas, with a Conditional Style. Note also the trailing punctuation for the comma in the attribution, allowing the words to line up.

It is also worth noting, here, the way the text creates its own visual rhythm, which is further developed by the incantatory quality of the names, which Lewis made up entirely for their sound and effect. It is important in children's literature to let the typography carry some of the magic of the text being read aloud.

Above, Gap between standard and optical margin alignment.

Adobe Illustrator offers 'Optical Margin Alignment' though, at the time of writing, InDesign does not. This means that if you want to cheat slightly, you can put your alphabet into Illustrator, check the difference between optically aligned and unaligned, and use that as a guide. For Stone Serif Medium, Illustrator suggests substantial realignment of A, V, W, X and Y, with a minimal adjustment to M, S, T and U, and a virtually invisible adjustment to D,K, R and Z. The results are given above. Although the offsets look quite different, measuring the letters suggests that 7.5% will do for all of them, W being a wider letter and 7.5% therefore having more effect. The more invisible adjustment to T could be 2%, and to the others 1%. It is certainly worth improving the quality of the margins for A, V, W, X and Y. There will be an inevitable slowing down for long text if you do the others as well, and the results will probably not be visible even in extended copy.

Once you have set up your classes, you can assemble them into sets. This is a relatively simple matter: create a new set, and select the classes that you want included. QuarkXPress will not allow you to include contradictory classes. For example, you can have the letter W in three different classes for leading, trailing and dropped cap, but you cannot have W set to, say, 7.5% and 5% in two different classes which are included in the same set.

If you just want to try all this out, do it on a short document. The more text you have, the longer it will take for document-wide changes to be applied. Once in place, you shouldn't notice much difference in speed. However, if you are just experimenting, waiting while a 400 page novel re-formats is perhaps not the best use of time.

Typographer's ragged text

If your client objects to hyphenation (see below) then you will find that your Flush left, Ragged right text, which gently curving right margin like a torn piece of paper, resembles a hedgehog, with lines sticking out all over the place.

Rather than going through and reworking every line, you can set the entire alphabet to a Trailing class at 200%. If you now turn on justification and set the hyphenation to Very Narrow Measure, you will be treated to the much desired gently torn right margin. Justification controls are working for you to keep the lines a more or less constant length, but the 200% trailing adjustment allows some but not all into the margin. You will find that your text now overflows the margins, ruining your beautiful design grid, so introduce a couple of millimetres of paragraph right indent to compensate. Despite the availability of hyphenation (which you can turn off in a custom H&J if the client really objects to it), almost all of the management is done by justification, so hyphenation does not occur.

16 Lists

Opens the Lists Edit List. See the Lists Palette for details about how to use lists.

17 H&Js

Edit H&Js brings up the Hyphenation & Justification styles list. Create New or double-click to open the Edit dialogue.

Auto Hyphenation

Auto Hyphenation turns automatic hyphenation on and off. You can still put in manual hyphenation with Cmd/Ctrl-hyphen, and you can ask for suggested hyphenation with Utilities—Suggested Hyphenation. When auto hyphenation is on, you can prevent a particular word from hyphenating by putting a Cmd/Ctrl-hyphen at the beginning of the word, and you can insert a manual hyphen at

Typographer's ragged

Out of love for the truth and from desire to elucidate it, the Reverend Father Martin Luther, Master of Arts and Sacred Theology, and ordinary lecturer therein at Wittenberg, intends to defend the following statements and to dispute on them in that place.

Left justified

Out of love for the truth and from desire to elucidate it, the Reverend Father Martin Luther, Master of Arts and Sacred Theology, and ordinary lecturer therein at Wittenberg, intends to defend the following statements and to dispute on them in that place.

Top, typographer's ragged text, below, left justified text. Typographer's ragged uses a hanging margin of 200% for the whole alphabet, in conjunction with Very Narrow Measure H&Js. Because of the way the two interact, hyphenation is relatively infrequent, but the justification function creates a gently ragged right margin.

(Text—Ninety-five theses, Martin Luther.)

Bottom, the Hyphenation and Justification Panel. H&Js are relatively complicated and the differences are subtle. However, the presets provided will be suitable for most uses without the need for additional tinkering.

Below, setting justified text in narrow columns is not recommended. With Very Narrow hyphenation, the result is dramatically better. It also allows more words per line. Careful attention is still needed (and perhaps a writing style with shorter words).

None:

"Extraordinary Professor Potterton", I

remarked unwittingly as he reproachfully discerned my

Wide:

"Extraordinary Professor Potterton", I remarked

unwittingly as he reproachfully discerned my observation of Ms Fitzgerald.

Standard:

"Extraordinary Professor Potterton", I remarked

unwittingly as he reproachfully discerned my observation of Ms Fitzgerald.

Narrow:

"Extraordinary Professor Potterton", I remarked unwit-

tingly as he reproachfully discerned my observation of Ms Fitzgerald. "Bremen is so

Very narrow:

"Extraordinary Professor Potterton", I remarked unwit-

tingly as he reproachfully discerned my observation of Ms Fitzgerald. "Bremen is so

any point in the word, which overrides automatic hyphenation, but is itself overridden by prevent hyphenation.

Auto Hyphenation has the following options:

Smallest Word—the smallest word that will hyphenate.

Minimum Before—the number of letters that must be before hyphenation to allow it to hyphenate.

Minimum After—the same, but for the end of the word.

Break Capitalized Words—allows or prevents words starting with capitals to break. This affects both the start of sentences and proper nouns.

Hyphens in a Row—you can specify the maximum number of hyphens in a row, but not the maximum number in a paragraph. Automatically hyphenated text requires inspection to ensure that the paragraph has not become 'spikey'.

Hyphenation Zone—the distance from the right hand margin where hyphenation is allowed. A word that does not fall into this space will not hyphenate.

Justification Method
This only applies to Justified text.

Space—sets minimum, optimal and maximum width of a standard space.

Char—sets the minimum, optimal and maximum tracking of a character.

Flush Zone—the zone in which the last word on the line must fall for it to justify if it is the last line of a paragraph. A very large setting for this is equivalent to Forced Justify.

Single Word Justify—allows a single word to justify, preserving the column appearance at the expense of the word.

My experience is that clients tend to overlook hyphenations in text they read, but are hyper-critical of it in their own documents. Try Typographer's Ragged, above, if stuck.

18 Grid Styles

Opens the Grid Styles List. See the Grid Styles palette, above, for more information.

19 Dashes & Stripes

Opens the Dashes and Stripes editor. Clicking New offers you a choice of a dash style or a stripe style.

Dashes

To specify dashes, click on the ruler and drag a little way. Arrow markers will appear pointing to the begin and end of a dash, and the dash will appear in high, short preview, and the long, low preview. You can then move the arrows, or drag them off the ruler to delete. Up to five dash components are allowed. You can change the proportions of the preview using the slider to see a longer, thinner line, or a shorter, fatter one.

Dash Attributes—you can specify how often the dash repeats in points or as a multiple of width. You can set the Mitre to angular, rounded or bevelled, which determines the shape of corners. By default the dash maintains its shape at corners, but you can set it to stretch. You can also set the endcaps to flush square, rounded, projecting square or projecting rounded.

Segments—you can type in a position as a percentage if you prefer that to clicking with the mouse.

If you are returning to QuarkXPress after a long absence—perhaps lured by the glitz and glamour and early price breaks of other applications—you may be wondering where the exciting borders are. These were bitmaps, and don't really stand up to today's publishing needs. You can achieve the same—and many more—results with Utilities—Shapemaker and Item—Super Step and Repeat, or by pasting vector art from elsewhere.

Stripes

Stripes work in the same way as dashes, but without the Endcap or Stretch options.

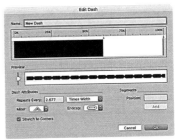

Above, the Edit Dash box allows you to place your dashes with the mouse, and see immediately what the result will be. Below, Edit Stripes works in the same way.

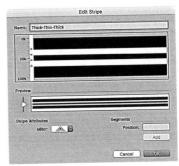

Edit Stripes works the same way as dashes. Use the Mitre option to create soft corners.

Soft cornered boxes. The usual way to create round cornered boxes is with Box Corner Style in Measurements. However, that won't allow multiple insets or vertical alignment. You can create a round mitred stripe and apply it to a regular box, and it will behave just like one.

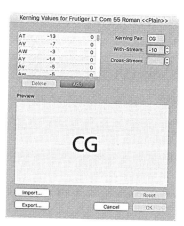

Above, the font list for Kerning Pair Edit. Below, editing the kerning values of a pair. You can edit horizontally (with-stream), vertically (cross-stream), or both.

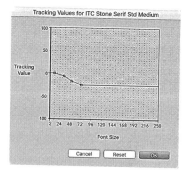

Below, editing the font tracking tables. This may be fiddly.

20 Kerning Pairs

With the Kerning Pairs dialogue, you can individually edit troublesome kerning pairs which are either not kerned in the font definition, or where the kerning does not meet your needs. There are 516 common kerning pairs, and these must be applied to each weight of a font. If you want to comprehensively re-kern a font, QuarkXPress is not the tool to do it with[2]. However, if you have an abbreviation, such as CCG, which does not fit well in, say, Frutiger, you may find that there is no previous kerning, 'CG' not being a common component in English. To change it, go to the font you want (typing a couple of letters will take you there more quickly) and double-click to edit. The dialogue will come up, with already kerned pairs in the top left, along with their adjustment.

Kerning Pair—type in the pair you are interested in. If already defined, the list will move to show you, and the values will be loaded into the boxes.

With-Stream—horizontal kerning. Changing it is immediately updated in the preview.

Cross-Stream—vertical kerning.

You can export and import kerning for entire typeface weights. Any kerning you apply will affect every use of the font in document.

21 Font Tracking Tables

As fonts get larger, their tracking should usually decrease. Equally, at small sizes the tracking should be slightly wider to improve legibility. You can create a tracking curve graphically for particular fonts. This is not directly exportable, but you can copy your QuarkXPress preferences round the office to share the values. As with kerning, this has to be done on a weight-by-weight basis.

---

2 But see Robert Bringhurst, The Elements of Typographic Style, section: Grooming the font. Bringhurst argues that every font should be edited, because many of the spacings are just wrong. This is almost certainly a breach of your font licence if you do it in a Font Editor, but you can refine your kerning using this dialogue and stay legal.

22 Set Tool Preferences From Selected

For tools with settable preferences, such as the Starburst tool, you can set the current preferences for the tool for this document, or for new print layouts.

23 Restore Tool Preferences to Defaults

This allows you to return the tools to their default settings.

24 Color Setups

Color Setups allows you to control how QuarkXPress treats incoming colours and how it controls them for output. Normally speaking, you will need to create a profile for output devices you control, such as printers. Your monitor's profile should be set automatically, or you can change this in Preferences—Display. For incoming colour, and for standard devices such as Standard Web Offset Printing, you should not need to change any settings, though you can if there is a particular problem. Use an X-Rite or Spyder tool to calibrate your monitor and local printing device. You should then be able to see the calibration in Utilities—Profile Manager. You can also browse an auxiliary folder if, for some reason, your profile is not in the default location.

Above, the Edit Source Setup options aren't usually required—your images should already come with profiles, and the Quark defaults will work with them.

If you need to edit the Source Setup, duplicate the Quark 7 defaults and work from there.

Output

If you have a proofing device, it will be necessary to enter its profile. This is relatively painless. From Edit—Colour Setups—Output, click New and the dialogue appears. Give it a reasonable name, and then choose your profile from the drop-down list. Leave the defaults as they are, unless you know they should be something different. Save the profile, and then apply it in Output Styles.

Below, creating an output setup.

25 Output Styles

See the Print and Export options for settings. You can also save output styles in Print and Export.

4 Style

1 Font

Sets the font. If the font menu takes too long to come up, you can turn off previewing in Preferences—Fonts. However, this is probably a sign that you have too many fonts loaded. A Quark-compliant font manager such as FontExplorer Pro or Extensis Suitcase should help.

2 Size

Sets the size from harmonic presets. It is more flexible to use the Measurements panel or Character styles.

3 Type Style

This generally replicates the functions of Measurements: Character, but with three exceptions.

Make Fraction
This combines 2/3, 1/16, etc, on selection, into $\frac{2}{3}$, $\frac{1}{16}$. Although highly convenient, these are 'faux' fractions, inferior to true Open Type fractions. The method is controlled from Preferences—Application—Fractions/Price.

Make Price
This turns £5.00 into £5^{00}, €2.50 into €2^{50} and $3.20 into $3^{20}. The method is controlled from Preferences—Application—Fractions/Price. Both this and Make Fraction are done by offsetting and changing sizes. If you change the preferences later, the prices and fractions will not update automatically.

Underline Styles
This is the only place you can apply styles created in Edit—Underline Styles. You can also create ad-hoc styles.

4 Color, Shade, Opacity

Sets colour, shade and opacity. Context dependent.

5 Alignment (text)

Sets alignment to left, right, justify or forced. See Measurements—Paragraph for more information.

6 Centre Picture, Stretch Picture, Scale Picture to Box, Fit Box to Picture

These controls only appear when a picture is selected, and are self-explanatory.

7 Convert to Native Objects

New to QuarkXPress 2016. See Edit—Paste as Native Objects.

8 Character Alignment

Sets the alignment to Top, Centreline, Baseline or Bottom.

9 Paragraph Style Sheet

Chooses any paragraph style sheet. See the Styles palette.

10 Character Style Sheet

Chooses any character style sheet. See the Styles palette.

11 Footnotes/Endnotes

Inserts a footnote or an endnote, or moves to the relevant footnotes, or back to the text. See the Footnotes palette.

12 Footnote Separator Style

Applies or creates a footnote separator style. See the Footnotes palette section for details.

13 Update Style Sheet

Updates the current paragraph character stylesheet to match the selected text, if different. See the Styles palette.

14 Item Styles

Applies an item style. See the Item Styles palette.

15 Change Case

Changes the case of the text to UPPER CASE, lower case or Title Case. This permanently changes the case. If you want to apply upper case as a style, use the Type Style ALL CAPS, available in the Measurements panel, Character, or Style—Type Style. Note that Title Case sets the first letter of every word in upper case, including 'of', 'and', 'the' and so on. This is therefore not true title case, and will need manual adjusting.

16 Flip Horizontal, Vertical

Flips the content of a picture or text box.

17 Cross Reference

New to QuarkXPress 2016, the cross-reference pane is persistent, so you can have it open like a palette while you add in references.

You can reference Numbered items, footnotes or endnotes, and show the Page number, the full text, the number either with or without context (paragraphs) or formatting (notes), along with automatic 'above/below'. You can synchronise cross-references either from the dialogue or the menu. Use View—Highlight Cross References to see them in grey.

The cross-reference dialogue. Cross-references are highlighted from the View menu.

18 Hyperlink

Creates, edits, removes hyperlinks. See Hyperlink palette.

Menus

19 Anchor

Creates, edits, and removes anchors. See Hyperlink palette.

20 Remove Manual Kerning

Removes manual Word Space Tracking, as opposed to regular tracking which is available in the Measurements Panel. You can only apply Word Space Tracking from the keyboard.

Mac:

Increase space by 05 em	Command+Control+Shift+]
Increase space by .005 em	Command+Control+Option+Shift+]
Decrease space by .05 em	Command+Control+Shift+[
Decrease space by .005 em	Command+Control+Option+Shift+[

Windows:

Increase space by .05 em	Control+Shift+@
Increase space by .005 em	Control+Alt+Shift+@
Decrease space by .05 em	Control+Shift+!
Decrease space by .005 em	Control+Alt+Shift+!

5 Item

1 Duplicate

Makes a copy of the selected item, with the same offsets as the last time an item was dragged or drag-copied.

2 Super Step and Repeat

Super Step and Repeat allows you to repeat an object while changing its position, angle, size, frame width, shade, skew and contents size. It can act relative to an object's centre,

The order followed here is for Mac. The Windows order is slightly different. Most importantly, Super Step and Repeat is near the bottom, with a regular Step and Repeat at the top. On Windows, you can also access Runaround and Clipping modal dialogue boxes, which reproduce the functions discussed under Measurements (above), and further down, Drop Shadow.

Super Step and Repeat, above, can be used to create spirals, glows, and intricate geometric patterns, as well as simple multi-item grids and arrays.

Below: some examples of super step results.

corners, or a selected point. The best thing to do is to open it up and play with it.

Repeat Count—how many times to repeat.

Horizontal, vertical offset—how far to move it.

Angle—how much to turn it by.

Scale contents—scales text and pictures.

Rotate & Scale Relative to—pick the reference point.

End frame/line width, box shade, item scale, skew—sets parameters for the final item. Everything in between will be a gradation of that with the original.

Nota bene: on **Windows**, Super Step and Repeat is near the bottom of the menu, with regular Step and Repeat at the top of the menu.

3   Delete

Deletes an object.

4   Lock

Locks either the position of an item, or the text of a story, or the picture in a box.

5   Fit Box to Text

New in QuarkXPress 2016, fits the box to the size of the text. This is very useful if you want to align boxes of text. Likewise, when you convert imported vector graphics to native objects, or paste as native objects, the boxes will be their original size, but if the text is not in the same font, it will overflow. Fit box to text will sort this out.

6   Send & Bring

Moves objects to the back, to the front, or shuffles them up and down. See the Layers palette for an explanation of how QuarkXPress stacks things.

7 Group/Ungroup All

Usually shortcutted to Cmd/ctrl-G and Cmd/ctrl-U, Group and Ungroup clump the selected boxes or unclump them, so that they become (for many operations, but not all) equivalent to a single item. You can still access the content from the Text and Picture content tools. As well as being more convenient, Grouped items respond more quickly, which is important when dragging a set of reflowing items across long text, causing it to reflow.

8 Insert inline table

Inserts an inline table to fit the existing text box. See Measurements—Tables tab and the Table styles palette for more information.

9 Space/Align

Spaces or aligns boxes. See Measurements: Space/Align tab for details.

10 Unconstrain

If Constrain is turned on in preferences, removes it.

11 Content

Sets the current box to be a picture box, a text box, or a box with no content. This means that if you create a box with the wrong tool, you can switch it. Content—none is useful because the box won't have an X across it, as with an empty picture box, nor will it keep insisting on you putting text in when you double-click it by accident.

Want to quickly convert a group of lines into a shape? You will see that the Shape item is greyed out when a group is selected. Rather than ungrouping, you can simply use Union in Item—Merge or Split Paths (next section).

12 Shape

Converts different kinds of shapes. You can convert a regular shape into an editable curve (go to the shape that looks a bit like an artist's palette), convert a box into a line, or a

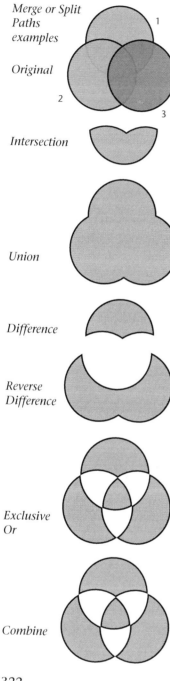

Merge or Split Paths examples

Original

Intersection

Union

Difference

Reverse Difference

Exclusive Or

Combine

line into a box, make a curved or angled line into an orthogonal line, and also quickly apply a couple of different kinds of corners. When converting a line, Opt/alt-clicking joins the ends of the line to make the box. Regular clicking makes a shape with a very narrow content area.

13 Merge or Split Paths

Merge or Split Paths provides a powerful toolbox for combining objects and paths. This is calculated from the item at the back forwards to those at the front.

Intersection—the area where the back shape intersects with one or more of the others.

Union—the total outline of all the shapes together.

Difference—the back minus the front shapes.

Reverse Difference—the front shapes minus the back.

Exclusive Or—only areas with an odd number of overlaps, ie, one item only, shape; two items, shape removed; three items, shape.

Combine—the same as Exclusive Or, except the points are constructed in a different way.

Join Endpoints—joins two lines if the points are close together.

Split Outside Paths—makes the outside path a separate shape you can work on with the Bézier tools.

Split All Paths—makes every shape a separate shape.

With a little creativity, these tools can create a vast array of shapes which can be text boxes, picture boxes, lines, or curves for text on a curve.

14 Point/Segment type

With the ⟨K⟩ Point Tool selected, you can convert corner, smooth or symmetrical points and turn a straight segment into a curve or vice versa.

Menus

15 Convert text to boxes

Converts text to boxes. This is sometimes the only option if a font will not export or print. You can also use it to turn dingbats into editable shapes, to create text with a photographic background, or to insert a rotated character. This can anchor the new box where it was in the text, make it unanchored, or convert an entire box.

16 Edit Runaround/Clipping Path

Edits runaround or clipping path of an appropriate object.

17 Flip Shape

This flips the shape horizontally or vertically (rather than the content). It doesn't work on groups.

18 Share, Unsynchronise size/item/content, Copy to Other Layout

These commands relate to sharing content. See the Content Palette for details.

19 Callout Anchor

Inserts a callout anchor, along with other options. See the Callout Styles palette for details.

20 Composition Zones

Composition zones create a new layout from an area of the page. This layout can then be edited independently. You can add the layout to the Content palette by using the corner menu on that palette and then choosing add.

There are two main uses for this.

First, if it is inconvenient to work on a part of the layout in the main document, creating a composition zone will let you work on it separately. This could be because it is highly

Above, text on a path made by combining shapes. Text on a shape is very easy. Make sure that the Content of the object is 'none' in Item—Content, then double-click on the frame. You can start typing. The options for text on a line now appear in the Measurements palette. See the Text tool, above, and Measurements—Text Box for more details.

Above, after adding a composition zone to the Content palette by clicking 'add' in the corner menu, you can edit it to make it available across all projects, and to make it an external file which others can work on.

complex and everything is going too slowly, or because it is layered underneath something else and you don't want to keep having to switch layers on and off, or because it is rotated, for example by 180˚ as part of a document that is going to be folded, but does not merit separate imposition. Once created, you can rotate the composition zone in the main layout so that it is the right way up for print, but work on it in a separate layout the right way up for editing. All changes you make on the composition zone layout immediately update in the main layout. If you want that composition zone layout to appear in the layout tabs, you can select this in the edit box from the Content palette.

The second use is if you designate an area of a document to be worked on by someone else. This could be a cover, an advertisement, a highly technical table, or because you are splitting up the spreads of a magazine across a department.

To do this, create a composition zone using the Composition Zone tool, or by clicking on an item and choosing Item—Composition Zones—Create. If you then choose Item—Composition Zones—Edit, you can see the layout you just created, and create anything in it that you want to be seen by your co-worker. Returning to the main layout, with the Composition Zone selected, go to the Content palette and Ctrl-click/right-click or click on the corner menu and choose Add. You can now double-click or choose the pencil to edit, brining up the shared item properties dialogue for layouts and composition zones. You can now make the zone available to all projects, and make it external, so that someone else can work on it. To tidy things up, you can make it internal again once it is ready.

You can also share entire layouts by the same method, making them shareable from Layout—Advanced Layout Properties or by Ctrl-clicking/right-clicking on the Layout tab at the top of the screen to give access to the same menu item.

Menus

21 Digital Publishing: Add to Reflow/Add Pages to Reflow

This allows you to add the selected item or a set of pages to the Reflow for an eBook or Kindle, while remaining in the Print layout. If adding an item, you can add it as a new article or to an existing article. See the Reflow Tagging palette and the Digital Publishing section for more details.

22 New Box from Clipping

Creates a new box from a clipping path. See Measurements: Runaround and Clipping for details and examples.

23 Note

Adds a sticky type note, deletes one, allows you to navigate between notes, open notes and close notes.

Notes are essentially the electronic equivalent of putting Post-It™ notes on your screen, or, more annoyingly, on someone else's screen. You can export the notes with the PDF and you can print them, though you have to explicitly select those options. Like something stuck to your screen, they are always the same size, irrespective of page zoom.

Before you build them into your workflow, take a moment to reflect that the less formal the method of communication, the more likely it is that you or someone else will assume too much. Whether this be assuming that someone else shares your sense of humour, or that they are using the same units as you, the results can be equally disastrous. If you are going to share notes, take the same care over them that you would with an email to a client.

Above, notes are always the same size, no matter what page zoom you have. You set their font and size in Preferences—Notes. Knowing as you do that Comic Sans was created for this kind of communication, you can ironically use that font, though for no other purpose, ever.

24 Scale

This has the same function as the Scale palette. See that for more details.

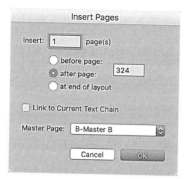

Above, the Insert Pages dialogue.

Above, the Delete Pages dialogue. Below, the Move Pages dialogue.

This one is actually far more dangerous. Save first!

Section dialogue.

Section dialogue.

6 Page

1 Insert

This opens the Insert Pages dialogue, which allows you to insert any number of pages before a page, after a page, or at the end of the layout, optionally link them to the current text chain, and set which Master Page will apply to them. You can do the same thing visually in the Page Layout palette, but for a lot of pages, this is quicker, simpler, and more powerful.

2 Delete

Delete allows you to delete a specific range of page numbers. You cannot delete all the pages. If you want to do this, first create a blank page at the beginning of the document and then delete from 2 to the end.

3 Move

Move allows you to move a range of pages to before a particular page, after a page, or to the end of the document. Save first, and check that you have got everything where you want it before doing any more work. Check especially carefully that things are not linking round each other. This is easy to miss, because going down with the cursor will take you to the correct page even if there are a hundred pages in between.

4 Master Guides & Grid

This is only available when working in Master Pages. See the Page Layout palette for details.

5 Section

This enables you to create a new section. A section is essentially a new numbering sequence. You can prefix it, you can specify the start number, and you can specify Arabic or

Menus

Roman numerals, or alphabeticals. You would often have the front-matter of a book done in this way. This reflects print house practice of the last two hundred years.

6 Previous, Next, First, Last, Go to...

Controls to navigate to other pages.

7 Display

Displays the Master Pages. See Page Layout palette.

7 Layout

The Layout tabs are at the top of the layout window, just below the window controls. Ctrl-clicking/right-clicking gives access to New, Duplicate, Delete, New Layout Specification, Layout Properties and Advanced Layout Properties in the same way that this menu does.

1 New

This creates a new layout, opening the same dialogue as for a new file. See File—New Project for details.

2 Duplicate

This duplicates the current layout and all its contents.

3 Delete

This deletes the current layout and all its contents. It cannot be undone, though you can File—Revert to Saved. You cannot delete the only layout, and it will also be greyed out in some other circumstances.

eBook Metadata is set here, not in File—Export options.

4 New Layout Specification

This creates a new JDF Job Jacket layout specification. See the Job Jackets section for full details.

5 Layout Properties

This opens the Layout Properties dialogue. See File—New for a discussion of this.

6 Advanced Layout Properties

This is where you make a layout shareable. See Item—Share for a discussion of this.

7 Add Pages to Reflow

This opens up the Add Pages to Reflow dialogue. See the Reflow Tagging palette for more details, and the section on digital publishing.

8 eBook Metadata

This is where you set the metadata for eBooks. Default (and unhelpful) metadata is set if you don't put anything here, so if you are publishing anything, set at least the Title and Author. You can also set Publisher, Copyright, ISBN, Language, description and keywords, separated by commas.

9 Previous, Next, First, Last, Go to

These navigate you to other Layout panes.

8 Table

Tables are created with the Table tool and mainly managed from the Measurements Panel, or, for Inline Tables, from the Tables Styles palette. The controls here are replicated in the Contextual Menu, which is usually a more convenient place to locate them. For most of these options to work, you have to have a table open and be at a cell or selection with the Text Content Tool. Generally, these commands do not apply to Inline Tables, which are managed from the Table Styles palette and are not directly editable for content in QuarkXPress.

Insert—opens a dialogue to insert a row or a column, offering above, below, number of rows, and the option to retain attributes.

Select—offers a wide range of choices for selecting rows, columns, headers, odds, evens, horizontal grids, vertical grids and the borders.

With ordinary tables, It is not possible to set the frames for individual cells, only for an entire vertical or horizontal grid, though combining cells will interrupt these, which may produce the desired effect. If you need to manage frames of individual cells, then either format until you are satisfied and then Convert Table—to Group, which will enable you to work with every cell individually as they will now be frames, or else create your chart in Excel and import as an Inline Table.

Generally speaking, information placed in complex tables is ignored by readers of a narrative document, but is often the first information people examine when looking for specific data. Tables need to be constructed to make it easy to access information, rather than to make a particular point. For this reason, simplicity and clarity should always be at the top of the table maker's list.

Tables are often used by web designers and word processor users as the easiest way to lay out information in columns. Tables provided like this should usually be laid out in a more appropriate way.

Table   329

Above, table break properties are key in properly managing tables that go across more than one page.

A table about tables				
Purpose	Often arrive as	Action to take	Design	Identify by
Put text in columns	Word or HTML	Convert to text	Columns	Internal formatting, eg bullets
Match up items	Word or Excel	Convert to Group	Use boxes	Subtitles
Financial information	Excel	Inline table	Table styles	Financial content
Scientific tables	Backs of envelopes	Create in Excel, Inline tables	Table styles	Science stuff
Gantt charts	Excel	Remake as Gantt	Chartwell fonts	Time divisions

Delete—Delete an entire row or entire column.

Combine Cells—combine two or more cells, retaining only the content of the leftmost, topmost cell in the selection. It is worth setting a hot-key for combine/uncombine cells, because this is by far the most useful tool for creating distinctive tables which do not fit easily into one of the categories.

Table Break—this sets a number of key properties for managing tables, especially anchored tables, that run over more than one page or are likely to. You can set header and footer rows, and determine which are continued, and also control the maximum width (which should be just less than the column width, to prevent irresolvable reflow) and height.

Make separate tables—when you have tables that have broken across more than one page, you can use this to make them separate tables, which may be more manageable.

Above, Gantt chart recreated from a Gantt made in Excel. It's possible to do it, but it takes twenty minutes and doesn't look great when it's finished. Although the origin is Excel, it can't accept numerical data.

Repeat as Header—only for a row selection including the top row, sets it to repeat as the header on each new page.

Repeat as Footer—same as for header, but at the bottom.

Convert text to table—turns a properly tabbed set of text into a table. Copy and Paste from Word or import from Word will often bring across these kinds of tables, as well as importing tab delimited files. However, think carefully before you do this: many tables would be much happier simply set up as tabulated data. Generally speaking, if you can get all the information on one line, tabs will look better and be far easier to manage. On the other hand, if gridlines or shading are crucial, or if text is going to wrap frequently, a table is more likely to do the job.

Convert Table—to text, or group of boxes. If you copy and paste a table from Excel into QuarkXPress, it will come across as a table. It may be better to convert it to text, as discussed above, or to convert it to boxes. A table is also a convenient way of making a grid, which can then be converted to boxes. A table converted to text can be converted back. You cannot convert boxes back to a table, though Utilities—Linkster can make it much easier to manage a group of boxes.

Link text cells—if you did not choose that option when you created the table, you can change it here.

Maintain geometry—if your table is set to autofit rows or colums, Maintain Geometry switches that off and keeps the table the same shape. It isn't a bad workflow to start with Autofit, and, once you are happy, switch on Maintain Geometry to fine-tune.

Below: making this Gantt chart using Chartwell Bars takes about five minutes, and data can be typed in directly or loaded from Excel. This chart is running text: it doesn't need to be anchored as a separate box.

Table   331

9 View

1 Fit in Window, 50%, 75%, Actual Size, 200%, Thumbnails

This sets the magnification. You can also type this in at the very bottom left hand corner of the layout screen. Typing T or selecting Thumbnails here goes to thumbnail mode. When two documents are in thumbnail mode, pages can be dragged from one to another. This is often a good way of rescuing a document which is showing signs of corruption.

2 Enter Full Screen

Enters full screen mode (Mac only)

3 Dynamic Guides

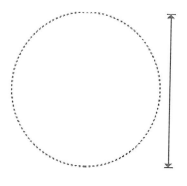

Above, Dynamic Guides appear vertically or horizontally whenever an element you are dragging matches that dimension of any other element on the layout. While you drag, a tooltip appears at the bottom right hand corner to tell you exact width and height in your preferred measurements.

Dynamic guides are largely new in QuarkXPress 2016. By default all are on, which means that red guide measurements with double arrows or transitory guides appear whenever one of the following happens:
Centres are aligned
Edges are aligned
Item is aligned to centre of page
Equal dimensions in at least one direction with another box on the spread
Equal spacing between other items.

Additionally, a measurement tooltip appears as you drag. You can turn any or all of them off here.

4 Guides

F7 turns the guides on or off, including page margins, box outlines and guides you have assigned. It's usually best to keep this assigned to a hot-key, as this is one of the most frequently used functions. On the one hand, the guides are necessary to ensure everything is in the right place, on the other they can create a false sense of bustle and, conversely, of structure.

Menus

5 Hide Selection

When Guides are off, the boundaries of the current box are still displayed. You can turn this off (but not for the rest of the text chain) with this function. However, it also hides drag- and shift-selected text highlighting, which makes it useful only for previewing, rather than for actual editing.

6 Page Grids, Text Box Grids

Shows the Page Grids and the Text Box Grids

7 Snap to Guides, Snap to Page Grids

Snaps to Guides or Page Grids. You can set the degree of snap in Preferences—Print Layout—Guides and Grid.

8 Rulers, Ruler Direction

Turns the rulers on and off, and swaps the direction of measurement.

9 Invisibles, Visual Indicators

Shows the Invisibles: spaces, tabs, returns, and so on, and the Visual Indicators, which are non-typographic invisibles, such as the icons that go with HTML5 attributes.

10 Highlight Content Variables

Turns highlighting on and off for Content Variables.

11 Highlight Cross References

This turns highlighting on and off for Cross References.

12 Trim View

Turns on the Trim View, which hides everything which is off the printed page. This is essential for visualising full-bleed documents, where the bleed can give a false sense of page proportions.

13 Hide Suppressed

Hides items which are suppressed and will therefore not print or export. This is useful if you are using a non-printing template, such as for packaging or a book cover. It also hides other non-printing items, such as Index markers and notes.

14 Proof Output

This offers options for all of the Colour Output Setups you have set up in Edit—Color Setups. Assuming that your workflow is properly colour managed, you can see a good rendering of output in greyscale, 100K black, CMYK, Spot, and so on. 100K black is 'true' printed black, as opposed to a black made from enriching black with other colours from the CMYK palette. When proofing on a laser printer, rich black, aka greyscale, will be blurrier, though the black itself will be very flattering. When printing to a true mono printing press, there will be no additional colours 'improving' the look of black, so greyscale 100K will give a truer proof.

When set to As is, soft proofing is off.

15 Story Editor

This opens the Story Editor, which is a simple text editor built into QuarkXPress for working on the underlying text. This is useful if you have all kinds of transformations going on which make it hard to see where the cursor is going, or what you are editing. The story editor retains numbering, and also shows you where anchored graphics fall.

16 Hide Notes

Hides all notes. You can close rather than hide the notes in Item—Notes—Close all notes.

17 View Sets

View sets are collections of decisions from the View menu, including Guides, Grids, Rulers, Ruler direction, Visual Indicators, Invisibles, Trim View and Hide Suppressed. Three presets are supplied: default, authoring view, which maximises the visual indicators, and output preview, which hides everything but the printed result. You can create your own from whatever settings you have when you create a new set. Use in conjunction with Window—Palette Sets.

10 Utilities

1 Insert Character

This allows you to insert a variety of breaking and non-breaking characters which are typographically important, especially different kinds of spaces. It is also where you can find Conditional Style Markers. Some shortcut keys are assigned, but you can also assign others for characters you use frequently.

2 Content Variable

This is an alternate method of working with Content Variables. See the Content Variables palette.

3 Check Spelling

This runs the spell checker. It works as most spell checkers do. However, if you want to build a glossary of proper nouns and other non-standard words, first create a new auxiliary spell check file before you run the spell checker. When you run it, add rather than skip words which are specific to the publication. When you have completed the spell check, you can open the Auxiliary Dictionary in a text-processor. It will be in XML format, but very little tidy-

The Windows and Mac versions of the Utilities menu are essentially the same, except that Windows includes IME Reconversion, and Kerning Table Edit is in this menu rather than Edit. IME Reconversion is for Far Eastern Text. When Far Eastern Text is enabled on the Mac, this has its own menu. Windows also contains a Component status information dialogue.
The order of the Windows and Mac versions differs slightly.

ing up is needed to produce a pristine list of words, which will become the basis for your glossary.

4   Word and Character Count

Counts the words and characters for the layout or the story. The dialogue gives word count, unique word count, character count and symbol count, as well as many East Asian counts. The count includes footnotes and endnotes.

5   Line Check

Line check allows you to search for loose justification, auto-hyphenation, manual hyphenation, widows, orphans, and text box overflow. Computer typesetting should always be seen as the beginning rather than the end. In many cases it is better to turn off automatic controls for widows and orphans (in Paragraph styles), let the text flow as it will, and then manually add in the controls afterwards. Hyphenation can also be technically correct, but visually wrong.

6   Suggested Hyphenation

Suggests options for the 'correct' hyphenation from QuarkXPress's own algorithms. Some languages have very strict rules of hyphenation. Others, such as English, have conflicting rules and numerous exceptions. It is often better to turn off automatic hyphenation and then hyphenate manually, which this tool assists.

The search criteria for Line Check.

7   Hyphenation Exceptions

Computers hyphenate 'doesn't' as 'does-n't' and 'didn't' as 'did-n't', which are clearly wrong. There are many other exceptions to computer algorithms, and even hyphenations considered correct a hundred years ago (and so still in dictionaries) but which are now clearly wrong, because of shifts in pronunciation. You can enter hyphenation exceptions in this menu item which will apply only to the specified language in the current document. QuarkXPress will query this every time the document is loaded. A better way is either to set the hyphenation in the job jacket, or close all documents and set the hyphenation exceptions for the application. This will then apply to all new documents.

8 Convert Project Language

This converts every instance of a particular language in the project, including in style sheets, to a different language, or to a variant of the same language, for example from US English to International English, or from Portuguese (Portugal) to Portuguese (Brazil).

9 Usage

Usage brings up a dialogue box with six panes which cover the usage and updating or replacement options for Fonts, Pictures, Profiles, Composition Zones, Digital Publishing and Tables. Note that this relates only to the current layout.

Fonts
This lists all the fonts in the current layout, and gives you an information panel with details including internal font name, file name and location, type and version. It allows you to find the first usage of the font, and to replace it. This is particularly useful when you have inadvertently mixed two versions of the same typeface—for example, Microsoft Office-supplied Baskerville with ITC Baskerville.

Pictures
This shows all of the pictures in the document, with their names, page numbers, type and status (ok, modified or missing). 'PB' with a page number refers to a picture on the pasteboard—ie, which is off the page and will therefore not be printed.

Pictures pasted from the clipboard show less information because no disk file exists. Where the disk file does exist, further information is shown below. You can choose to show an image in the document, and to update it if it is modified or missing.

The Usage dialogue has separate panes for Fonts, Pictures, Profiles, Composition Zones, Digital Publishing and Tables.

The Item Styles Usage shows every usage of each item style, giving its page number and whether it has been modified or not. Items can be updated (or rather, reconformed) to the original style.

Profiles

This shows the Source colour profiles, as defined in Edit—Colour Setups—Source or loaded in with picture files. If you open a profile which is used by a picture, the list of pictures using that profile is then shown. Technical profile information is given in the information panel. This is mainly useful if you discover that an image has come across with the wrong profile, or if you have an image which is printing differently from what you expect. The full path of the image is shown, and you can replace the profile with another if you wish to. Unless the image has a wrongly assigned profile, usually a result of user-error in another application, you should not need to do this.

Composition Zones

This shows any composition zones which have been made External, for example by adding them to the Content palette and then editing to make them external. It does not show composition zones which are only in the current project. The status is given (ok, modified, or missing) and you can update a modified composition zone file.

Digital Publishing

This does the same as the Pictures pane, but imported digital assets such as video files which are not pictures.

Tables

Works as the Pictures pane, but for linked Excel tables.

10 Item Styles Usage

The Item Styles Usage opens a dialogue box showing every usage of each item style, which page it appears on, and whether it has been modified. You can choose to show it, or to update it, though, in this case, 'update' means reverting a modified box back to the current version of the item style, even if that is older than the modification.

11 Job Jackets Manager

This opens the Job Jackets Management window. See Part 4—Job Jackets for a full discussion.

12 Insert Placeholder Text

This inserts an endless string of faux-Latin text, sufficient to fill the selected text box. It will not, however, cause the text to overflow to the next page. If you prefer to use your own text, you can achieve this by creating a shared content text frame and filling it with your preference, for example in another alphabet, or with a different frequency of word-length, if you want to get an idea of how text will work in narrow columns. With box and text attributes turned off, you can then apply it wherever you like.

13 Cloner

Below, the Cloner allows a selection or set of pages to be copied to the current layout, a new layout, an existing Quark file, a new project or to all open layouts. It also allows layouts to be split into single pages, and multi-layout projects to be split to single projects.

The Cloner lets you clone a selection, range of pages, or an entire layout or project, putting it in the same layout, a new layout, a new project file, an existing Quark file, many Quark projects each one page of the selected, or into separate projects, one per layout. You can specify where the clone is inserted, and how many times, and you can choose to put the pages in sections, either contiguously even if you have selected discontinuous pages (eg, 1-3,7,15), or preserving the source section structure.

If cloning to a new project, all the style sheets in use will be automatically carried over. Click 'Copy Style Sheets' if you want to copy unused styles as well.

There are numerous uses for this. If you were making a set of personalised invitations, you could create as many identical pages as you need, and then, with a Master Page, run a single linked text box on each page right the way through. If you then paste a text file of names, the file will automatically populate, fully personalised.

14 ImageGrid

The Image Grid creates a matrix of images across one or more pages to display a folder of picture files. The obvious use for this is to create a contact sheet of images, or else to create a display book. However, with a little thought, all kinds of results are possible, including laying out a long

document which has previously been created as a PDF, and just needs headers, footers and page numbers reworking.

There are three ways it can work:

Autosize—fits the right number of pictures on the page for a specified number of rows and columns, with the gap setting you specify.

Fixed size—every picture has the box size you specify, separated by the gap size.

Autofill—you set a size limit, and Image Grid attempts to fill each page using that limit.

There are a number of options:

Add picture info—puts the file name only or file name and type, size and colour information underneath the text.

Apply drop shadow—applies a default drop shadow with the offset you specify.

Box shape—allows you set the box shape to rectangular, rounded or round, optionally using your tool preferences.

Picture sizing—imports at a set percentage, fits proportionally to the box, or stretches to fit the box.

Fit box to picture—resizes the box to fit the picture.

Process subfolders—processes everything in the subfolders of the folder you specify.

Process Folder then activates it, once you have selected the folder to process.

OK does no more than save the settings. Cancel reverts to the previous settings.

As many pages as are necessary are created, but they do not use Master Pages. You can apply these afterwards, along with item styles.

It's worth playing around with ImageGrid, just to see what it can do, as it may be the solution to a problem you have not yet encountered.

Above, image grid with rounded corners and shadows can produce what looks like a collection of coffee-cup coasters. On the other hand, it can also be used to import and place into layout an entire book, as long as the PDF file has been converted into single pages. This is a task which comes up fairly frequently: pages have been deleted from a book and renumbering is required, but the original is no longer available.

15 Linkster

Linkster links and unlinks boxes. You can link selected boxes, or you can specify pages, in which case the main auto-linking box is selected.

Unlinking offers four options. The icons are a bit difficult to decode, but once you have identified them they are intuitive.

The first 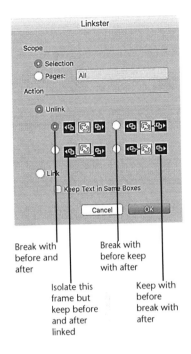 (top left) breaks the selected box from both the box before and after it, and breaks the chain. In other words, you will have three separate stories.

The second (bottom left) unlinks the current box from the chain, but keeps the chain intact. Your selected box and its text are now a stand-alone box, but the rest of the story flows as before.

The third (top right) breaks the chain between this box and the previous one.

The fourth (bottom right), breaks the chain between this box and the next one.

You can also link, and choose to keep text in the same boxes, or allow it to flow freely. Always save first.

16 ShapeMaker

ShapeMaker is a tool which creates mathematically defined shapes by changing their options and parameters. You don't need to understand the mathematics to make it work, though.

There are five tabs: Waves, Polygons, Spirals, Rectangles and Presets.

In each case you can create any kind of box, or just lines, and you can specify its width and height. If creating a text box, you can specify its columns and gutters. You can also alter the existing box.

The easiest way to get to grips with this is to open it up and play.

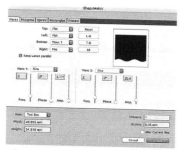

Above, ShapeMaker constructs shapes based on parameters. The best way to learn how to use it is to play with it.

Above, a spirogram from the Polygons tab, with Outer Swirl edges, as a rule box. Below, a square wave from the Waves tab.

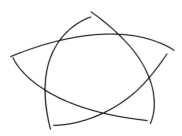

Strange as it may seem, this shape is actually made using the rectangles tab.

Waves—undulating lines on one or more sides of the box. These can also be square or triangular lines, depending on the wave type.

Polygons—all kinds of multi-sided shapes, not just the regular polygons they taught you in school. You can specify curves, twirls and other fancy options. Try the Spirogram type. This is also where you can make a golden rectangle or a double square.

Spirals—golden, Archimedean and custom spirals. These are very good as templates for the overall layout of the page, if you are one of those people who believe that the golden section is a key aesthetic principle.

Rectangles—if you want complete control over the shape of rectangles, such as turning them into speech bubbles, this is where to look.

Presets—when you have a shape you like, type in a name here and add it. All the parameters will go into your new preset, which will appear with a silhouette of its shape.

Because the shapes are mathematically derived, they respond very fast in a layout. You can Super-Step-and-Repeat them, merge or combine them with other shapes, and edit them with the Bézier tools.

17 Font Mapping

This menu normally comes up if you open a document for fonts not installed on your system, and allows you to map a font you don't have to a font you do have. You can set this behaviour in Preferences—Application—Fonts.

Normally, when a project opens up and fonts are missing, the font mapping dialogue will come up. It will tell you which fonts are missing, and allow you to specify what to replace them with. You can edit, delete, import and export these rules, though you can't actually create them in this menu.

The rules then apply to your copy of QuarkXPress—they don't affect the document itself, which will open with the

Menus

original fonts on other computers. So, for example, if you were working with a design agency that was setting a document in fonts you don't have, you could receive the project, edit it, and send it back, and it would be in the correct fonts when you did.

If you want to actually change the fonts—for example, because you have upgraded from True Type fonts to Open-Type, use the Usage—Fonts dialogue to identify where they occur, then update the style sheets (easy if you have used structured style sheets), and then, from Usage—Fonts, replace any ad hoc uses.

18 Convert Old Underlines

This is a one time utility which finds any legacy underlines from QuarkXPress 3.x and turns them into contemporary underlines.

19 PPD Manager

The PPD Manager lists all of the printer PPD files—which QuarkXPress needs to correctly control your printer—installed on your system. You can specify an auxiliary folder if you have downloaded a PPD but the system is not seeing it.

The PPD Manager lists all the Printer definitions installed on your system.

20 XTensions Manager

The XTensions Manager allows you to turn off XTensions, and also to see XTensions which have been turned off because of a problem. Clicking About will give you full details about an XTension, including contact details for support. You have to restart QuarkXPress for changes to take effect.

Normally, you shouldn't have to use this menu, but if there is a problem with an Xtension, for example one you have from a third party, you can use this to track it down.

QuarkXPress has had an extensible architecture through Xtensions since its early days. A number of specialist Xtensions exist, including for database publishing and right to left scripts, as well as more general ones such as font management and autocorrect.

21 Profile Manager

This is a simple list of installed colour profiles which allows you to switch them off, and also to use an auxiliary folder. Profiles are actually managed in Edit—Color Setups. You should not normally need this item, as there is generally no harm in having all of your profiles turned on, and ICC profiles which are embedded with imported documents should come across with them, and be visible in Utilities—Usage—Profiles.

22 Make QR Code

This allows you to make an image (left icon) or vector (right icon) Quick Response Code, either with text or with a VCard. Once the 'next big thing' in youth and business advertising, they have largely fallen out of use because iPhones and Android devices do not support them directly—you have to use an app, such as Scan. They are still a useful tool for providing a link.

23 Redline

See the Redline palette for more information.

Above, QR codes are either PNG images or native objects.

11 Window

1 New Window

You can open a new window of the current project. When you close the last open window of a project, QuarkXPress will prompt you to save it. If you try to open a project already open, QuarkXPress will tell you this, and offer you the option of opening a new window.

2 Split Window

Splits the window so that you can scroll to different parts of the document and compare them.

Menus

3 Bring All to Front

Brings all QuarkXPress windows to the front of the windows open on your computer.

Pro-tip: to maximise the document window on a Mac without going to fullscreen, Option-Click the green button.

4 Tile

Tiles the open windows on the screen. If you want to tile pages for print, this is in the File—Print—Pages pane.

Tile controls are also at the bottom of the screen

Below: at the bottom left of the layout window, the magnification box (100%), the page number (1), navigate by preview arrow ▲, page left ◀ and right ▶, view master page ▣, split horizontally ⊟, split vertically ⊞ export ↗ and HTML5 app preview ◑ (digital layout only) may easily be hidden by the Measurements panel.

5 Palette Sets

You can save the positions of all your open palettes and retrieve them with this item. This is convenient for different kinds of working, and also if you use a laptop which you connect to an external display, and want to preserve as much screen as possible on the laptop. You can also have all the palettes on an additional display if you want.

6 Turn Hiding On (Mac only)

With this you can hide palettes at the bottom, top, left or right, or all docked palettes. Docked palettes are ones which have become magnetically attached to one of the docking areas—you will see a grey background appear when you move a palette there. If palettes are hidden, they spring back into view when you hover the mouse over that area of the screen.

7 The palettes

See the Palettes section, above.

12 ⑤ Script (Mac Only)

This gives access to a number of useful Apple Scripts. You can also create your own scripts and place them there.

13 Help

This gives access to Help. Search allows you to find a feature in the menus. To open the Help file, choose Help Topics.

Most of the items in QuarkXPress menu (Mac) are in Help on Windows.

Index

Further reading

Smashing Ux Design
Allen, Jesmond; James Chudley
1 ed., John Wiley & Sons, 2012.
An excellent introduction to User Experience (UX) design which will be extremely helpful to print publishers venturing into HTML5 and Apps.

Packaging the Brand
Ambrose, Gavin, and Paul Harris
01 ed., AVA Publishing, 2011.
Useful introduction to packaging from a brand perspective.

Reading Letters
Beier, Sofie
01 ed., Bis Publishers, 2012.
Essential reading for typographers: critically summarises more than a century of research into legibility, debunking many myths and drawing reliable conclusions.

U&lc: Influencing Design and Typography
Berry, John D.
01 ed., Mark Batty Publisher, 2007.
Only available second-hand, this is a magnificent reminder of the influential U&lc magazine.

Color Psychology, Color Therapy
Birren, Faber
Martino Fine Books, 2013.
One of the foundational books on colour psychology. Almost every other book on the subject references this one.

Lateral Thinking
Bono, Edward de
Penguin, 2009.
A classic on creativity. Apply even one tenth of the methods in this book and you will find originality is no longer a problem.

Elements of Typographic Style
Bringhurst, Robert
4th -20th Anniversary ed. ed., Hartley & Marks Publishers, 2013.
The principal reference guide for correct typography, published to a standard to which other books can simply not aspire.

Designing Type
Cheng, Karen
Yale University Press, 2006.
Valuable reading even if you never intend to design a typeface: this book gives you insight into the type creation process.

Package Design Workbook
DuPuis, Steven, and John Silva
Reissue ed., Rockport, 2011.
Sturdy and useful guide.

Pantone Book of Color
Eiseman, Leatrice; Lawrence Herbert
Harry N. Abrams, Inc., 1990.
Highly useful for understanding the impact of colour.

Pantone Guide to Communicating With Color
Eiseman, Leatrice
Design Books International, 2001.
More on colour and its impact.

Color, Messages and Meanings
Eiseman, Leatrice
Hand Books Press, 2007.
Pantone's latest guide on colours and their meanings.

Pantone 20th Century in Color
Eiseman, Leatrice; Keith Recker
01 ed., Chronicle Books, 2011.
Essential guide if you are intending to use colour to reference a particular period in living (or TV-extended living) memory.

Composition for Photographers
Haile, Richard Neville, 1936.
This is by far the best book on photographic composition I have ever found. Out of print for more than sixty years, copies can be obtained online.

Fonts & Encodings
Haralambous, Yannis
1 ed., O'Reilly Media, 2007.
The definitive reference guide to programming and encoding fonts, including Open Type.

Symbol
Hyland, Angus; Steven Bateman
01 ed., Laurence King, 2011.
A beautiful, though non-definitive, collection of symbolic logos, organised thematically.

Why Fonts Matter
Hyndman, Sarah
Virgin Books, 2016.
Summary of Sarah Hyndman's empirical research into the impact fonts have on people. Makes every opinion-based book on font associations obsolete.

Thinking, Fast and Slow

Kahneman, Daniel

Penguin, 2012.

Nobel prize winner Daniel Kahneman presents his work on the two-speed brain in a way which is accessible for most readers and highly useful for designers and publishers.

Universal Principles of Design

Lidwell, William, Kritina Holden, and Jill Butler

Revised edition ed., Rockport, 2010.

A search for design universals throws up many cross-discipline principles which are not even referenced in most other texts.

Symbols

Liungman, Carl G.

1 ed., HME Publishing, 2004.

Definitive guide to the symbols used in Western Culture over the last thousand or so years. Always worth checking if you find an interesting symbol that you want to use graphically, if only to make sure it doesn't mean something you don't want it to.

The Oxford Handbook of Eye Movements

Liversedge, Simon, Iain Gilchrist, and Stefan Everling

1 ed., OUP Oxford, 2013.

Rich resarch-based handbook to eye movements, for those wishing to understand how the eye responds better.

Les Tres Riches Heures Du Duc De Berry

Thames & Hudson, 1969.

The 1969 edition is greatly preferable to the more recent reprint, this is a beautiful collection of pages from one of the finest medieval manuscripts extant.

Shaping Text

Middendorp, Jan

01 ed., Bis Publishers, 2012.

Eminently readable and excitingly illustrated, this is the Dutch school of design: historically aware but also iconoclastic, more interested in what works than in adhering to or opposing any one particular system.

Grid Systems in Graphic Design

Müller-Brockmann, Josef

Bilingual ed., Verlag Niggli, 1999.

Definitive text of the Swiss school of modernist, grid based design. You will feel that every design you ever did is inferior after reading this. It's probably worth reading Jan Middendorp's Shaping Text afterwards, if only to remind you that everything which worked was successful.

Viral Marketing

Nelson-Field, Karen

OUP Australia & New Zealand, 2013.

In a world of nonsense written about social media, this is a short entirely research-based book on what actually works.

Ogilvy on Advertising

Ogilvy, David

New edition ed., Prion Books Ltd, 1995.

David Ogilvy invented modern advertising, and almost everything he says in this book is worth learning by heart and applying.

On Brand

Olins, Wally

1st ed., Thames & Hudson, 2003.

Wolf Olins is to branding what David Ogilvy was to advertising. A lifetime of experience in this book.

The 22 Immutable Laws of Branding

Ries, Al, and Laura Ries

New Ed ed., Profile Books, 2000.

Combatative and controversial, this summarises a series of articles in Ad Age which set the agenda for modern branding. The content is more or less the same as all the other Ries books. Short and easily applied.

Out of Our Minds

Robinson, Ken

2nd Edition ed., Capstone, 2011.

Ken Robinson on learning and teaching creativity.

Store Wars

Thain, Greg, and John Bradley

2nd Edition ed., John Wiley & Sons, 2012.

Anyone involved in FMCGs (fast moving consumer goods) needs to read this.

Chartered Public Relations

Waddington, Stephen

1 ed., Kogan Page, 2015.

A collection of essays by Chartered PR Practitioners. Herein you can read the extended explanation of Outcomes—Audiences—Messages—Delivery in my essay "Micro-strategies for communications…" Dont' be put off by the title—it's a very easy read.

Fonts and Logos

Young, Doyald

1st ed., Delphi Press, 1999.

A beautiful book on typography and, to a lesser extent, logos. Well worth reading, though not directly practically applicable.

32127356R00199

Made in the USA
Middletown, DE
23 May 2016